19-

AMERICAN
POETS
IN
1976

AMERICAN
POETS
IN
1976

·

EDITED
BY
WILLIAM
HEYEN

Bobbs-Merrill Educational Publishing
Indianapolis

For Han, my wife,
and for Bill and Kristen,
our children.

Copyright © 1976 by The Bobbs-Merrill Company, Inc.
Printed in the United States of America

The Bobbs-Merrill Company, Inc.
4300 West 62nd Street
Indianapolis, Indiana 46268

Third Printing—1978

Designed by Joseph P. Ascherl

Library of Congress Cataloging in Publication Data
Main entry under title:

American poets in 1976.

Bibliography: p.
1. American poetry—20th century—History and criticism—Addresses, essays, lectures.   I. Heyen, William, 1940–
PS325.A8   811'.5'409   75–37522
ISBN 0-672-61349-2 (pbk)
ISBN 0-672-52174-1

ARCHIBALD MACLEISH

from
A Continuing Journey
1967

*Why do we teach poetry in this scientific age? To
present the great alternative, not to science but
to that knowledge by abstraction which science
has imposed. And what is this great alternative?
Not the "messages" of poems, their interpreted
"meanings," for these are abstractions also—
abstractions far inferior to those of science. Not
the explications of poetic texts, for the explication
of a poetic text which goes no farther ends only
in abstraction.*

*No, the great alternative is the poem as itself,
the poem as a poem, the poem as a work of art—
which is to say, the poem in the context in which
alone the work of art exists: the context of the
world, of the man and of the thing, of the infinite
relationship which is our lives. To present the great
alternative is to present the poem not as a message
in a bottle, and not as an object in an uninhabited
landscape, but as an action in the world, an action
in which we ourselves are actors and our lives are
known.*

CONTENTS

Robert Bly

4 *Wallace Stevens and Dr. Jekyll*

9 The Temple Bell Stops—Basho

10 The Sea Grows Dark—Basho

13 Mankind Owns Four Things—Machado

19 Already the Ripening Barberries—Rilke

John Malcolm Brinnin

22 *"Pray you undo this button:" The Sentimental Strategies*

34 My Father, My Son

Robert Creeley

46 *Was That a Real Poem or Did You Just Make It Up Yourself?*

54 For My Mother: Genevieve Jules Creeley

John Haines

60 *Poems and Places*

63 The Traveler

65 The Stone Harp (early version)

65 The Stone Harp

67 To a Man Going Blind

68 Listening in October

71 The Weaver

John Haislip

74 *Seal Rock*

75 Missing the Old Boy

83 For Robert Blanchard

87 *from* Storm Journal

89 Hunting for "Blues" in the Rain

William Heyen

92 *What Do the Trees Say?*

92 The Pigeons

94 Oak Autumn

96 Oak Spring

vii

99 Providence
103 The Numinous
104 The Return

Richard Hugo

108 *The Real West Marginal Way*
112 West Marginal Way
113 Between the Bridges
116 Duwamish No. 2
118 Hideout
121 Neighbor
122 No Bells To Believe
124 Duwamish

David Ignatow

130 *The Beginning*
134 Sometimes on the Subway . . .
135 Business
137 Paymaster
141 Communion

John Logan

146 *On My Early Poems*
147 *from* Homage to Rainer Maria Rilke
148 Lament for Misenus
151 The Preparation
155 Two Trees
157 *from* Epilogue, Songs of the Spouses, Complaint of Love
158 At Sundown a Slow Procession
159 *from* On the Death of the Artist's Mother Thirty-Three Years Later
160 New York Scene: May 1958
163 To a Young Poet Who Fled

William Matthews

168 *Moving Around*
169 Moving
172 Driving Alongside the Housatonic River Alone on a Rainy April Night
176 Moving Again

Jerome Mazzaro

180   *Returns*
181   Lorjou and My Mother
183   For Harold
185   Auto-Wreck
187   Changing the Windows
188   After Spring Storms
188   Flowers

William Meredith

192   *The Luck of It*
193   A View of the Brooklyn Bridge
197   Winter Verse for His Sister

Joyce Carol Oates

202   *Many Are Called . . .*
203   The Impasse
205   Flight
208   Promiscuity
209   Dreaming America
211   Many Are Called

Linda Pastan

214   *Roots*
214   Emily Dickinson
216   Notes from the Delivery Room
217   Penelope
217   You Are Odysseus
218   Hurricane Watch
219   Geneticist
220   Artificer
221   A Real Story
222   Rachel

Raymond R. Patterson

226   *Statement*
227   Sun and I
229   I've Got a Home in That Rock
234   When I Awoke

John Peck

238 *Strata Satura*
238 Early Thirst and the Carved Ring
239 Rick of Burning Wood
242 Refinding the Seam
244 Let Us Call This the Hill of Sotatsu
246 Lucien

Stanley Plumly

254 *The One Thing*
255 The Iron Lung
257 Now that My Father Lies Down Beside Me
258 Out-of-the-Body Travel
260 Horse in the Cage

Ishmael Reed

264 *Flight to Canada*
267 Sputin
270 The Reactionary Poet
272 Flight to Canada

Adrienne Rich

278 *When We Dead Awaken: Writing as Re-Vision*
283 Aunt Jennifer's Tigers
284 The Loser
288 *from* Snapshots of a Daughter-in-Law
288 Orion
290 Planetarium

M. L. Rosenthal

296 *We Begin These Sequences Lightly*
296 We Begin These Things Lightly
296 Riddle of the Swan
297 Suddenly, at the edge . . .
298 Bequest
303 *from* She

Anne Sexton

306 *From 1928 to Whenever: A Conversation with Anne Sexton*
307 With Mercy for the Greedy

313 Unknown Girl in the Maternity Ward
320 The Little Peasant
328 The Fury of Cocks

Louis Simpson
332 *Rolling Up*
336 The Foggy Lane
336 Dinner at the Sea-View Inn
338 Baruch

Dave Smith
344 *Sailing the Back River*
345 Among the Oyster Boats at Plum Tree Cove
347 Hard Times, But Carrying On
348 March Storm
350 The Shark in the Rafters
352 The Spinning Wheel in the Attic
354 The Wives at Old Point Comfort
355 Mending Crab Pots
357 Near the Docks
358 Cumberland Station
361 Night Fishing for Blues

William Stafford
366 *Making a Poem/Starting a Car on Ice*
368 Whispered into the Ground
371 My Mother Looked Out in the Morning
371 One of the Stories
372 Saying a Name
373 Run Sheep Run
373 Kinds of Winter
374 Stereopticon

Primus St. John
378 *The Way the World Has Entered*
382 Biological Light
386 Violence of Pronoun
388 A Splendid Thing Growing

Lucien Stryk

392 *Making Poems*

394 Zen: The Rocks of Sesshu

397 South

399 Burning Oneself to Death—Shinkichi Takahashi

400 Letter to Jean-Paul Baudot, at Christmas

402 Étude

403 The Fountain of Ammannati

404 Awakening

Lewis Turco

410 *Sympathetic Magic*

414 A Dedication

415 Tick

419 The Dream

421 The Moon of Melancholy

423 Fetch

James Wright

426 *Letters from Europe, Two Notes from Venice,*
    Remarks on Two Poems, and Other Occasional Prose

426 Letters from Europe

433 Two Notes from Venice

435 On the Occasion of a Poem

436   On Minding One's Own Business

440 On the Occasion of a Poem: Bill Knott

448   Willy Lyons

452 The Infidel

456 Italian Moments

456   1. (Untitled)

456   2. (Untitled)

457   3. (Untitled)

457   4. Poetry of the Present Moment

457   5. A Small Grove

Paul Zimmer

460 *The Importance of Being Zimmer*

461 Father Mendel at Brünn

462 Lord Fluting Dreams of America on the Eve of His
    Departure from Liverpool

463 Imbellis Strolls Out Among the Trees and Imagines
the World To Be as Peaceful as Their Seasons
464 Zimmer's Head Thudding Against the Blackboard
465 The Sweet Night Bleeds from Zimmer

Selected Bibliography **467**

ACKNOWLEDGMENTS

Robert Bly Selections from "Thirteen Ways of Looking at a Blackbird" and "Six Significant Landscapes," copyright 1923 and renewed 1951 by Wallace Stevens, and "On the Road Home," copyright 1942, renewed 1970, by Holly Stevens, are taken from *The Collected Poems of Wallace Stevens* and appear in Robert Bly's essay by permission of Alfred A. Knopf, Inc. Translations, "The Temple Bell Stops" and "The Sea Grows Dark," by Basho; "Mankind Owns Four Things," by Machado, and "Already the Ripening Barberries," by Rilke which appear in the essay are copyright by Robert Bly.

John Malcolm Brinnin "My Father, My Son," copyright © 1967 by The New Yorker Magazine, Inc., is taken from *Skin Diving in the Virgins* by John Malcolm Brinnin, a Seymour Lawrence Book/Delacourt Press, and is reprinted by permission of the publisher. "The World as Meditation" by Wallace Stevens, from *The Collected Poems of Wallace Stevens*, appears in Brinnin's essay by permission of Alfred A. Knopf, Inc.

Robert Creeley "For My Mother: Genevieve Jules Creeley" appeared in *Sparrow* magazine and is reprinted by permission of Robert Creeley.

John Haines "The Weaver" is from *Leaves and Ashes*, copyright © 1974 by John Haines, and is reprinted by permission of Kayak Books. "The Traveler" and "Listening in October" are from *Winter News*, copyright © 1966 by John Haines; "The Stone Harp" and "To a Man Going Blind" are from *The Stone Harp*, copyright © 1971 by John Haines. All four poems are reprinted by permission of Wesleyan University Press and "The Stone Harp" is reprinted by permission also of Rapp & Whiting, London.

John Haislip "Missing the Old Boy," "For Robert Blanchard," the passage from "Storm Journal," and "Hunting for 'Blues' in the Rain" are copyright © 1975 by John Haislip and used with his permission. "For Robert Blanchard" first appeared in *Northwest Review*, "Missing the Old Boy" in *The Back Door*, and "Hunting for 'Blues' in the Rain" in *New Letters*.

William Heyen "The Pigeons," "Oak Autumn," "Oak Spring," "Providence," and "The Return" are from *Noise in the Trees*, copyright © 1974 by William Heyen, and reprinted by permission of Vanguard Press. "The Numinous" first appeared in *The Southern Review*.

Richard Hugo "West Marginal Way," "Neighbor," "No Bells to Believe," and "Duwamish" are from *A Run of Jacks*, copyright © 1961 by Richard Hugo, and published by the University of Minnesota Press. "Hideout," "Neighbor," and "Duwamish No. 2" appeared in *Death of the Kapowsin Tavern*, copyright © 1965 by Richard Hugo, and published by Harcourt, Brace & World. All poems reprinted by permission of the author.

David Ignatow "Sometimes on the Subway," "Business," "Paymaster," and "Communion," copyright © 1965, 1970 by David Ignatow, are from *Poems 1934–1969* by David Ignatow and are reprinted by permission of Wesleyan University Press.

John Logan "Lament for Misenus" is from *A Cycle for Mother Cabrini* (1955) Grove Press; selections from "On the Death of the Poet's Mother Thirty-Three Years Later," "New York Scene: May 1958," and selections from "Epilogue, Songs of the Spouses, Complaint of Love" are from *Ghosts of the Heart* (1960) University of Chicago Press; "To a Young Poet Who Fled" is from *Spring of the Thief: Poems 1960–1962*, copyright © 1963 by John Logan, published by Alfred A. Knopf, Inc. The selection from "Homage to Rainer Maria Rilke" is from *The Zigzag Walk: Poems 1963–1968*, copyright © 1969 by John Logan, and reprinted by permission of the publishers, E. P. Dutton & Co., Inc. "Two Trees" appeared in the *Beloit Poetry Journal* and "The Preparation" in *Saturday Review*. Both appear here by permission of the author. Lines from "In My Craft or Sullen Art," by Dylan Thomas, appearing in Mr. Logan's essay are from *The Poems of Dylan Thomas*, copyright © 1976 by New Directions Publishing Company and are reprinted by permission of New Directions and J. M. Dent & Sons, Publishers.

William Matthews "Moving," from *Ruining the New Road*, copyright © 1970 by William Matthews, and "Driving Alongside the Housatonic River . . . ," from *Sleek for the Long Flight*, copyright © 1971, 1972 by William Matthews are reprinted by permission of Random House. "Moving Again" first appeared in *The Atlantic*, copyright © 1975 by William Matthews.

Jerome Mazzaro "For Harold" and "Changing the Windows," from *Changing the Windows,* copyright © 1966 by Jerome Mazzaro, are reprinted by permission of Ohio University Press.

William Meredith "A View of the Brooklyn Bridge," copyright © 1950 by William Meredith, and "Winter Verse for His Sister," copyright © 1967 by William Meredith, are from *Earth Walk: New and Selected Poems,* by William Meredith and are reprinted by permission of Alfred A. Knopf, Inc.

Joyce Carol Oates "The Impasse" appeared in *Prairie Schooner;* "Flight," "Many Are Called," and "Dreaming America" appeared in the *Hudson Review;* "Promiscuity" appeared in *Prism International,* and all poems are reprinted by permission of Joyce Carol Oates.

Linda Pastan "Emily Dickinson," "Notes from the Delivery Room," and "Penelope," from *A Perfect Circle of Sun,* copyright © 1971 by Linda Pastan, are reprinted by permission of the Swallow Press. "Hurricane Watch" appeared in *Esquire;* "Rachel" in *Poetry Now,* and "A Real Story" was a broadside from Cold Mountain Press. All are reprinted by permission of Linda Pastan.

Raymond Patterson "Sun and I," "I've Got a Home in that Rock," and "When I Awoke" are from *26 Ways of Looking at a Black Man,* copyright © 1969 by Raymond R. Patterson and used here with his permission.

John Peck "Early Thirst and the Carved Ring" and "Lucien" appeared in *Salmagundi;* "Refinding the Seam" in *Plowshares,* and all are reprinted by permission of John Peck.

Stanley Plumly "The Iron Lung" appeared in *The New Yorker* magazine, copyright © 1974 by The New Yorker Magazine, Inc. "Out-of-the-Body Travel" appeared in the *Ohio Review.* Reprinted by permission of Stanley Plumly. "Now that my Father Lies Down Beside Me" is from *In the Outer Dark* copyright © 1970 by Stanley Plumly and is reprinted by permission of Louisiana State University Press. "Horse in the Cage" is copyright © 1975 by Stanley Plumly and used with his permission.

Ishmael Reed "Flight to Canada" appeared in *Aftermath of Invisibility;* "Sputin" in *Dark Waters,* and "The Reactionary Poet" in *Hambone.* All are reprinted by permission of Ishmael Reed.

Adrienne Rich "Aunt Jennifer's Tigers," from *A Change of World* (1951) Yale University Press, is reprinted by permission of Adrienne Rich. "The Loser" and "Snapshots of a Daughter-in-Law" are from *Snapshots of a Daughter-in-Law: Poems 1954–1962*, copyright © 1969 by Adrienne Rich; "Orion" is from *Leaflets: Poems 1965–1968*, copyright © 1969 by Adrienne Rich, and "Planetarium" is from *The Will to Change*, copyright © 1971 by Adrienne Rich. All are reprinted by permission of the publisher W. W. Norton and Adrienne Rich.

M. L. Rosenthal "We Begin These Things Lightly," "Riddle of the Swan," "Suddenly, at the Edge . . . ," "Bequest," and the lines from "She" are copyright © by M. L. Rosenthal and used with his permission. "We Begin These Things Lightly" first appeared in *The Ontario Review*.

Anne Sexton "With Mercy for the Greedy," from *All My Pretty Ones*, copyright © 1961, 1962 by Anne Sexton; "Unknown Girl in the Maternity Ward," from *To Bedlam and Part Way Back*, copyright © 1960 by Anne Sexton, "The Little Peasant," from *Transformations*, copyright © 1971 by Anne Sexton and "The Fury of Cocks," from *The Death Notebooks*, copyright © 1974 by Anne Sexton, are all reprinted by permission of the publisher Houghton Mifflin Company.

Louis Simpson "The Foggy Lane," reprinted from *Adventures of the Letter I* (1971) Harper & Row, and "Baruch," formerly appearing in *The Southern Review* are reprinted by permission of Louis Simpson. "Dinner at the Sea-View Inn" is copyright © 1975 by Louis Simpson and used here with his permission.

Dave Smith "Among the Oyster Boats at Plum Tree Cove," "Hard Times, But Carrying On," "March Storm," "The Shark in the Rafters," "The Spinning Wheel in the Attic," "The Wives at Old Point Comfort," "Mending Crab Pots" and "Near the Docks" are all from *The Fisherman's Whore*, copyright © 1974 by Dave Smith, and reprinted by permission of Ohio University Press. "Cumberland Station" appeared in *The New Yorker*, copyright © 1975 by The New Yorker Magazine, Inc.

William Stafford "Whispered into the Ground," appeared in *The Atlantic* (August 1974) and is reprinted by permission of the author. Mr. Stafford's other six poems appear here for the first time.

Primus St. John   "Biological Light" is reprinted from *The Poetry of the Modern American West*, Brigham Young University Press; "Violence of Pronoun" is from *Skins on the Earth*, Copper Canyon Press; "A Splendid Thing Growing" appeared in *Northwest Review* and *The Poetry of the Modern American West*. All are reprinted by permission of Primus St. John.

Lucien Stryk   "Zen: the Rocks of Sesshu" and "Étude" are reprinted from *The Pit and Other Poems;* copyright © 1969 by Lucien Stryk; "South" and "Letter to Jean-Paul Baudot, at Christmas" and "Awakening" are from *Awakening*, copyright © 1973 by Lucien Stryk; "The Fountain of Ammannati" is from *Notes for a Guidebook*, copyright © 1965 by Lucien Stryk. "Burning Oneself to Death," by Shinkichi Takahashi, is translated by Lucien Stryk and Takashi Ikemoto and appears in *Afterimages*, © 1971 by Lucien Stryk. All poems reprinted by permission of Swallow Press, Inc.

Lewis Turco   "A Dedication" is reprinted from *Awaken, Bells Falling* by permission of the University of Missouri Press, copyright © 1968 by Lewis Turco. "Tick" and "The Dream" are from *The Weed Garden* (1973) Peaceweed Press; "Fetch" appeared in the *Michigan Quarterly Review*. All are reprinted by permission of Lewis Turco.

James Wright   "On Minding One's Own Business" and "Willy Lyons," copyright © 1958 and 1962 by James Wright, are reprinted from *Collected Poems* by James Wright and appear here by permission of Wesleyan University Press. "Willy Lyons" is reprinted by permission also of Rapp & Whiting, London.

Paul Zimmer   "Father Mendel at Brünn" and "Lord Fluting Dreams of America on the Eve of His Departure from Liverpool" are from *The Ribs of Death*, October House, Inc., copyright © 1967 by Paul Zimmer. "Imbellis Strolls Out Among the Trees and Imagines the World To Be as Peaceful as Their Seasons," and "Zimmer's Head Thudding Against the Blackboard" are from *The Republic of Many Voices*, October House, Inc., copyright © 1969 by Paul Zimmer. "The Sweet Night Bleeds from Zimmer" appeared in *Poetry Now*. All poems reprinted by permission of Paul Zimmer.

PREFACE

American Poets in 1976 represents twenty-nine contemporaries writing on their own lives and work, on their art and on the people and landscapes that have entered their poems. Adrienne Rich's "When We Dead Awaken: Writing as Re-Vision" has been substantially revised from a previous publication; the other essays, during the course of which the poets quote what amounts to a good-sized anthology of their own poems, appear here for the first time. Essays/poems—an unusual book and, I believe, an important one.

I became acquainted with John Ciardi's *Mid-Century American Poets* (New York, 1950) about ten years ago, and since then have had a book like the present one in mind. Ciardi's book impressed me, and still does, as being very interesting, very important, and very helpful. The essays that the poets wrote about themselves provide what one critic has referred to as "inside information," and I have since paid close attention to books for which editors managed to get poets to write about their own work, the work of others they admire, their senses of the tradition, their sources and directions, their senses of themselves. Anthony Ostroff's *The Contemporary Poet as Artist and Critic* (Boston, 1964) and Howard Nemerov's *Poets on Poetry* (New York, 1965), are other notable collections. Briefer prose contributions by contemporary poets are included in Paul Engle's and Joseph Langland's *Poet's Choice* (New York, 1962), William J. Martz's *The Distinctive Voice* (Glenview, 1966), and Stephen Berg's and Robert Mezey's *Naked Poetry* (Indianapolis, 1969), and *The New Naked Poetry* (Indianapolis, 1976), to name just four. *American Poets in 1976*, thanks to the talent and generosity of its contributors, is the most substantial book of its kind, and one from which I will continue to learn over the years. It is not the kind of book that can become stale or dated. It can speak to us, if we will listen, for as long as we live.

I suppose that there are dangers when a poet writes an essay about his or her own work, or even about someone else's work. For one thing, prose may feed the appetites of those who, though they themselves may not even know this, would rather talk about and read about poetry than read the poetry itself. It may also be that prose statements by poets, as John Ashbery wrote me when he declined to contribute to this book, "are used forever after as a kind of can-opener to get into a poet's work." Abuses are certainly possible. At the same time, I think, a collection of primary prose materials such as this one can help create an audience for the poem, can help us appreciate the long and hard, thoughtful and inspired way to the crafted utterance which is the poem. I am thankful that John Ciardi got Theodore Roethke to write "Open Letter," that Howard Nemerov got John Berryman to write "Changes." My reading of these essays, for example, does not freeze my understanding of the poets' poems, and anything that sheds light, that widens, ought to be encouraged. These essays have become a valuable part of the great tradition, and the present book hopes to lodge some words, to paraphrase Robert Frost, where they are hard to get rid of. It has not been easy putting *American Poets in 1976* together. I have often regretted that I ever had the notion, and I will never undertake a project like this again; but I do take satisfaction in the belief that there are many germinal essays in this book that would not have been written except for my nagging and persistence, my belief in such a book.

I wish this volume could have included essays and poems by a hundred poets, but it could not, and it was difficult and even distasteful for me to limit my invitations. Although not all of the poets whose contributions I hoped for are included—some just refused, some didn't answer letters, three poets agreed and then did not manage to write essays—the list of contributors remains very much a personal choice. I range in my feelings from respect to deep admiration and love for the work of each of the poets here, and very much appreciate their outpouring of energy on behalf of this book. I had the feeling, during the spring, summer, and fall of 1974 when so many of these essays were being written, that I was making life miserable for a score of American poets. I only hope that they are now pleased to be a part of this gathering.

I have once or twice tried to write something about my own poems, and have found it excruciating. For this reason I did not insist, though I did urge, that each poet write about his or her own work. Nor did I attempt to organize the collection by asking certain questions, as did Mr. Nemerov (e.g.: "Do you see your work as having essentially changed in character or style since you began?" "Does the question whether the world has changed during this century preoccupy you in poetry?"), or by assigning specific topics. I realized that my invitation to the poets to write about whatever they wished for such an occasion might result in a hodge-podge, a ragtag collection with no center at all, and for this reason (and because it just made good sense) I did ask that all poets, whatever their subjects, quote some of their own poems during the course of their essays. (I am happy that about one hundred and fifty poems made their way into this book.) In this way, though the subjects might range far and wide, the poets would be showing us directly, even if doing this were incidental to their main thrusts, how their poems grew out of their lives, their lives out of their poems. At the same time, although I believe that this worked just enough, although it seems to me that self and place and poetry are the abiding concerns here, I am happy that these twenty-nine essays, as a *whole*, manifest our current range, our diversity of interest, our understanding of ourselves and our worlds as we enter the last quarter of this twentieth century and begin America's third.

WILLIAM HEYEN
Brockport, New York
December 1974

AMERICAN
POETS
IN
1976

ROBERT BLY

ROBERT BLY (*b. Dec. 23, 1926 in Madison, Minn.) was
graduated from Harvard in 1950. After living for several
years in New York and one in Norway, he moved back to
Minnesota where he lives on a farm with his wife and three
children, and from where his Fifties, Sixties, and
Seventies Presses have sent out influential books and
magazines. In 1966 he founded, with David Ray,
American Writers Against the Vietnam War. A prolific
poet/translator/critic, Bly reads widely at schools in this
country and abroad. He won the National Book Award for*
The Light Around the Body *(1967).*

(Photo by Gerard Malanga)

Wallace Stevens and Dr. Jekyll

I

The literature of the American earth is many thousands of years old, and its rhythms are still rising from the serpents buried in Ohio, from the shells the Yakuts ate of and threw to the side. The literature of the American nation is only two hundred years old. How much of the darkness from under the earth has risen into poems and stories in that time?

All literature, both of the primitive and the modern peoples, can be thought of as creations by the "dark side" to enable it to rise up from earth and join the sunlit consciousness again. Many ancient religions, especially those of the matriarchies, evidently moved so as to bring the dark side up into the personality slowly and steadily. The movement started early in the person's life and, in the Mysteries at least, lasted for twenty to thirty years. Christianity, as many observers have noticed, has acted historically to polarize the "dark personality" and the "light personality." Christian ethics usually involves the suppression of the dark one. As the consequences of this suppression become more severe, century after century, we reach at last the state in which the psyche is split, and the two sides cannot find each other. We have "The Strange Story of Dr. Jekyll and Mr. Hyde." The dominant personality in the West tends to be idealistic, compassionate, civilized, orderly, as Dr. Jekyll's, who is so caring with his patients; the shadow side is deformed, it moves fast, "like a monkey," is younger than the major personality, has vast sources of energy near it, and no morality at all. It "feels" rage from centuries of suppression.

How did the two persons get separated? Evidently we spend the first twenty or twenty-five years of life deciding what should be pushed down into the shadow self, and the next forty years trying to get in touch with that material again. Cultures vary a lot in what they urge their members to exile. In general we can say that "the shadow" represents all that is instinctive in us. Whatever has a tail and lots of hair is in the shadow. People in secular and Puritanical cultures tend to push sexual desire into the shape under our feet, and also fear of death; usually much ecstasy goes with them. Old cave impulses go there, longings to eat the whole world—if we put enough down there, the part left on top of the earth looks quite respectable.

Conrad is a great master of shadow literature; *The Secret Sharer* de-

4

scribes the healing of the same split that Stevenson could not heal. Conrad suspects that at times the shadow will not rejoin the consciousness unless the person has a serious task, which he accepts, such as captaining a ship. *Heart of Darkness* describes a failure in the same effort. Conrad noticed that the European solved his shadow problem less often after the invasion of Africa. The European now has a financial interest in the suppression of the shadow. Kurtz's history suggests that for a white man to recover his shadow at the same time he is exploiting blacks is a task beyond the power of the human being.

This speculation sends reverberations through American fiction also, both North and South. Mark Twain makes a similar point in *Huckleberry Finn*, brilliantly, joyously. Sometimes in the U.S. the "decent man" is hidden in the shadow, along with a lot of other stuff, and, as Huckleberry Finn finds out, the "decent man" will rejoin you only if you refuse to sell Jim.

Most of our literature describes efforts the shadow makes to rise, and efforts that fail. Ahab fails; it isn't clear why; he has a strong connection with the "old ethic" through the rhetoric of the Hebrew prophets. Dimmesdale's shadow fails. Apparently his fear of women blocks his own shadow from rising. I prefer to use the term "shadow," rather than "evil," in talking of literature, because "evil" permanently places the energy out there, as a part of some powerful being other than ourselves. "Shadow" is clumsy, but it makes it clear that these energies are inside of us.

Alexandra David-Neel tells a disturbing story. When she was studying with some Tibetan teachers early in this century, they suggested she try to get a clearer experience of her life-energy or libido. They suggested that she put it outside herself, where she could see it more clearly, and not into objects, but into a thought-form, a figure she herself would visualize and which would not exist outside of her head. She decided not to choose a typical Tibetan visualization—some energetic dancing figure, with necklaces of skulls, and flames coming out of the hairs on his chest —on the grounds that she herself might consider it to be a simple transfer from a Tibetan unconscious. She decided instead to visualize an English monk of the Middle Ages. After a few weeks of visualization, which she did among some other duties, she noticed one day, while walking outside the monastery on the road, an English monk dressed in gray who approached and passed her. After several such meetings, he began to greet her when they met, and she could see his eyes. He would disappear if she "unthought" him. Soon, however, she noticed that he was growing bolder; he appeared to be drawing energy from her without her will, and to be taking on a life of his own. She became frightened then. Eventually she went to her Tibetan teacher, who taught her how to perform a rather long ritual to get rid of the monk. A man or woman who talks of evil in *Moby Dick* is the kind of person who would believe that monk was real.

II

The group of American poets born from 1875 to 1890, namely Wallace Stevens, Frost, Eliot, Williams, Marianne Moore, Pound, and Jeffers, are all shadow poets. They are not only shadow poets, but they did much shadow work. Most shadow work appeared in novel form in the last century; in this century it has tended to appear in poetry. Wallace Stevens is usually not thought of as a shadow writer, so we can take him; and his work will have to stand for the others in that marvelous group.

It is interesting to compare Wallace Stevens's background with Kenneth Rexroth's, as it appears in Rexroth's autobiography. The Rexroths tended to live out their shadow. Stevens's family, upper middle-class German Americans, appear to be successful repressors of the dark side. How the shadow returns in a complicated man like Wallace Stevens I don't know; I don't understand the return of the shadow at all well, and everything I say here is speculation. But it seems the shadow energies need special channels in order to return. Eliot's sharp griefs, coming first in his marriage, and followed then by his wife's insanity, are linked with the rising of much shadow energy in him, but none of that violent anguish appears in Stevens. In Stevens the shadow material rises in perfect serenity, associated with the awakening of the senses, especially of hearing and smell. The senses do form a natural bridge to our animal past, and so to the shadow. The senses of smell, shades of light and dark, the awareness of color and sound, so alive in the primitive man, for whom they can mean life or death, are still alive in us, but numbed. They are numbed by safety, and by years inside schoolrooms. Wallace Stevens, it seems, when he was working in insurance early on, would try to end the day at some New England town that had a museum. He would then spend a couple of hours looking at pictures. This is a practical way of reawakening the senses, as walks are. Both reawaken more of the senses than reading does.

> Among twenty snowy mountains,
> The only moving thing
> Was the eye of the blackbird.

It is said that eyes in the West receive a disproportionate amount of psychic energy; all the other senses have become weakened to the degree that reading has laid emphasis on sight. The old harmony between the five senses has been destroyed. Stevens is careful of hearing:

> I do not know which to prefer,
> The beauty of inflections
> Or the beauty of innuendoes,
> The blackbird whistling
> Or just after.

> . . .

> It was evening all afternoon.
> It was snowing
> And it was going to snow.
> The blackbird sat
> In the cedar-limbs.

The last poem has the most marvelous and alert sense for changes of light, the deepening darkness, sensed with the body, as snow is about to fall. He pays more attention than most men to uniting the senses of color and smell:

> The night is of the color
> Of a woman's arm:
> Night, the female,
> Obscure,
> Fragrant and supple,
> Conceals herself.
> A pool shines,
> Like a bracelet
> Shaken in a dance.

He works to join the eyes to the sense of touch:

> The light is like a spider. . . .

> The webs of your eyes
> Are fastened
> To the flesh and bones of you
> As to rafters or grass.
>
> There are filaments of your eyes
> On the surface of the water
> And in the edges of the snow.

He works to become aware of weather, and its mergings with emotion:

> Passions of rain, or moods in falling snow;
> Grievings in loneliness, or unsubdued
> Elations when the forest blooms; gusty
> Emotions on wet roads on autumn nights;

He begins to see how, if the senses are sharpened by labor, you begin to merge with the creatures and objects around you:

> I am what is around me.
>
> Women understand this.
> One is not duchess
> A hundred yards from a carriage.

Curious and mysterious substances rise in the poems when he starts to glide out on the rays of his senses:

> He rode over Connecticut
> In a glass coach.
> Once, a fear pierced him,
> In that he mistook
> The shadow of his equipage
> For blackbirds.

That describes a pure shadow instant, in which shadow material shoots up into the conscious mind. Often, when the shadow shoots up into consciousness for a split second, it brings with it the knowledge that we will die. Oddly, concentration on ants sometimes carries that information to the consciousness:

I measure myself
Against a tall tree.
I find that I am much taller,
For I reach right up to the sun,
With my eye;
And I reach to the shore of the sea
With my ear.
Nevertheless, I dislike
The way the ants crawl
In and out of my shadow.

I would guess it would be difficult for readers who read Stevens in translation to understand the shadow energy moving so elegantly through the senses, because the extraordinary richness of his sensual intelligence appears as delicate auras surrounding the words in English, as a perfume surrounds each sort of metal and each tree. Readers brought up in English whose sense of language has been coarsened by too much newspaper reading probably don't feel the complicated aura around Stevens's words either.

By this light the salty fishes
Arch in the sea like tree-branches,
Going in many directions
Up and down.

Senses intersect in those phrases. It is the opposite of academic poetry or philosophic diction. Stevens notices that:

It is better that, as scholars,
They should think hard in the dark cuffs
Of voluminous cloaks . . .

Basho said, listening in his garden to a temple bell:

The temple bell stops—
but the sound keeps coming
out of the flowers.

Basho worked both as a Buddhist meditator and as a haiku poet in awakening the senses:

The sea grows dark.
The voices of the wild ducks
turn white.

American haiku poets don't grasp the idea that the shadow has to have
risen up and invaded the haiku poem, otherwise it is not a haiku. The
least important thing about it is its seventeen syllables or the nature
scene.

The "Harmonium" that Stevens talks of, and wanted, in vain, to use
as a title for his *Collected Poems*, refers to this union of all the five
senses, and perhaps of eight or nine more that only Australian hunters
or Basho could identify. The serenity that gives music to Stevens's lines
is a mark of the presence of that ancient union of the senses.

It was amazing to me recently to find out that one of his main helpers
in this effort was William James. We ordinarily think of the senses and
thought as opposites, so we assume that if one wants to reawaken the
senses, one must stop thinking. When I first read *Harmonium* I was
surprised to see that the thinking is expressed through odor and sound
images, and the sense images become more intense through the thinking
going on. What I didn't know is that the thinking is of the sort recommended by William James. Margaret Peterson set all that out in a
spirited essay printed in *Southern Review*'s Stevens issue, Summer 1971.
It turns out that some of the most enigmatic and vivid poems in *Harmonium* are rephrasings of paragraphs by James. How unpredictable it
all is!

William James warned his students that a certain kind of mind-set was
approaching the West—it could hardly be called a way of thought—in
which no physical details are noticed. Fingernails are not noticed, trees
in the plural are mentioned, but no particular tree is ever loved, nor
where it stands; the hair in the ear is not noticed. We now see this mind-
set spread all over freshman English papers, which American students
can now write quickly, on utterly generalized subjects; the nouns are
usually plurals, and the feelings are all ones it would be nice to have. The
same mind-set turns up on the Watergate tapes, and working now with
more elaborate generalizations, in graduate seminars in English, in which
all the details in Yeats's poems turn out to be archetypes or Irish
Renaissance themes. It is the *lingua franca*, replacing Latin. The mind-set
could be described as the ability to talk of Africa without visualizing the
hair in a baboon's ear, or even a baboon. Instead the mind-set reports
"wild animals." Since the immense range of color belongs to physical
detail—the thatness—of the universe, it is the inability to see color.

People with this mind-set have minds that resemble white night-gowns. For people with this mind-set, there's not much difference between 3 and 742; the count of something is a detail. In fact the number they are most interested in, as James noted, is one. That's a number without physical detail. As I read Peterson's essay, I was amazed to see "Metaphors of a Magnifico" which I had always loved as a zany poem of high spirits, become a serious process poem. The poem describes how to begin to free yourself from this mind-set; how to avoid being murdered by it. (So Ph.D's on *Harmonium* are especially funny.) He begins:

> Twenty men crossing a bridge,
> Into a village,
> Are twenty men crossing twenty bridges,
> Into twenty villages,
> Or one man
> Crossing a single bridge into a village.

He knows he is beginning by singing the sad little song hummed by Ph.D. candidates and politicians and experts in government planning: "One thing equals another thing."

> This is old song
> That will not declare itself . . .

Then he says what to do. Stop juggling ideas. Go to this place with your body, bring the senses forward, sound first, then sight, then smell if possible. Ask your imagination to bring you the sound:

> The boots of the men clump
> On the boards of the bridge.
> The first white wall of the village
> Rises through fruit-trees.
> Of what was it I was thinking?
> So the meaning escapes.
>
> The first white wall of the village . . .
> The fruit-trees . . .

How strange! It is a Purgatory poem, laying out a road, a sort of guru poem. How beautiful!

   William James observed the approaching mind-set and associated out from it sideways. He noticed the mind-set resembled the upper class of Boston. They too disliked the sordid details—the hair in the ear of religion, the smells of the Irish entry-way—and preferred the religion of the One. Naturally, they became Unitarians. If the "cultured people" move into this mind-set, a curious thing happens: the upper (spiritual) half of life and the lower (sensual) half of life begin to part company. One part ascends; the other part, no longer connected to the high, sinks. The gaps between grow wider and wider. The educated class has the Pure One, the working class people are left with nothing but the crude physical details of their lives—the husband's old pipe and the spit knocked out of it, the washing tub, the water and slush from the children's boots on the entry floor, the corns on the feet, the mess of dishes in the sink, the secular love-making in the cold room. These physical details are now, in the twentieth century, not only unpenetrated by religion, but they somehow prove to the unconscious that "religion is a nullity." James emphasized that perception, and Stevens grieved over the insight all his life. For the working class there's nothing left but the Emperor of Ice Cream. The middle class is now the working class, and so the majority of people in the West are worse off than they were in the Middle Ages.

James also noticed that the presence of this mind-set in India explains why certain Vedanta philosophies are so boring. An Indian meditation teacher, working with Ananda Marga, told me recently that before he did any meditation at all himself, and while he was working as an engineer in a compressor factory in India, he would at night visit the meeting of whatever holy man was in town. After the talk, he would ask the man, from the audience: What is the relation of your path to the poor in India? Usually—I think he said invariably—ten or twelve times in a row—two husky-looking men would come back and escort him out of the hall. Stevens would have understood that. For most holy men in India, the poor are the hair in the ear of India. They prefer the One, who has no hair.

James made sure his students understood a third sideways association, namely, the link of the mind-set to the German idealists. They were represented in England by Bradley and in the U.S. by Josiah Royce and the Anglo-Hegelians—horrible types, specialists in the One, builders of middle-class castles, and upper-class Usher houses, writers of boring Commencement speeches, creepy otherworldly types, worse than Pope Paul, academics who resembled gray jars, and who would ruin a whole state like Tennessee if put into it; people totally unable to merge into the place where they live—they could live in a valley for years and never become the valley. Antonio Machado, who did all his academic work in philosophy, describes them also:

> Everywhere I've gone I've seen
> excursions of sadness,
> angry and melancholy
> drunkards with black shadows,
>
> and academics in offstage clothes
> who watch, say nothing, and think
> they know, because they do not drink wine
> in the ordinary bars.
>
> Evil men who walk around
> polluting the earth . . .

Machado also remarked:

> Mankind owns four things
> that are no good at sea:
> rudder, anchor, oars,
> and the fear of going down.

If we think of the idealists in terms of Jung's speculations about the shadow, it's clear the idealist is a man or woman who does not want to go down. They plan to go to the grave with the shadow still repressed. The idealists are shadow-haters. They all end as does Dr. Jekyll, with a monkey-like Mr. Hyde scurrying among back buildings elsewhere in the city.

By exclusive interest in "the truth," they exile the shadow, or keep it exiled. . . . When Stevens takes his stand against all that, he takes a stand against perfect Paradises, against abstract churches, against the statistical mentality, against too easy transcendentalizing, too easy ignoring of the tragic:

> The imperfect is our paradise.
> Note that, in this bitterness, delight,
> Since the imperfect is so hot in us,
> Lies in flawed words and stubborn sounds.

Stevens did not make Dimmesdale's mistake. He invited the feminine in; Florida, the moon, convolvulus and coral, glade-boats, sombreros, the soles of feet and grape leaves, cabins in Carolina, and so much sound!

Only the shadow understands the ecstasy of sound. You know the shadow has found a way for part of it to return when you hear the joyful and primitive music of Vincentine, as energetic as Mozart, as insistent as Australian drums:

> Yes: you came walking,
> Vincentine.
> Yes: you came talking.
>
> And what I knew you felt
> Came then.
> Monotonous earth I saw become
> Illimitable spheres of you,
> And that white animal, so lean,
> Turned Vincentine,
> Turned heavenly Vincentine,
> And that white animal, so lean,
> Turned heavenly, heavenly Vincentine.

So Stevens learned how to go home. He learned that the idealist-Christian-Hebraic insistence that there is one truth is all that is needed to block the shadow from rising forever, for a human being, with his frail psychic processes, so easily altered or ground to a stop. He wrote the clear and sweet poem, "On The Way Home":

> It was when I said,
> "There is no such thing as the truth,"
> That the grapes seemed fatter.
> The fox ran out of his hole.
>
> You . . . You said,
> "There are many truths,
> But they are not parts of a truth."
> Then the tree, at night, began to change,
>
> Smoking through green and smoking blue.
> We were two figures in a wood.
> We said we stood alone.

It was when I said,
"Words are not forms of a single word.
In the sum of the parts, there are only the parts.
The world must be measured by eye";

It was when you said,
"The idols have seen lots of poverty,
Snakes and gold and lice,
But not the truth";

It was at that time, that the silence was largest
And longest, the night was roundest,
The fragrance of the autumn warmest,
Closest and strongest.

III

After writing such a masterpiece as *Harmonium*, guided by the secret knowledge James offered him in his books, and walking the path—he knew he was walking it—why then is there no more to the story?

Sometimes we look to the end of the tale
where there should be marriage feasts,
and find only, as it were,
black marigolds and a silence.

Critics usually accept the world the poet creates. If he says east is north, they say: Why didn't I think of that before! So Stevens's critics on the whole see constant development in his work, in a chosen direction. But it's not so. The late poems are as weak as is possible for a genius to write; what is worse, most of them have the white night-gown mentality.

There are some good poems, but somehow there are no further marriages in his work. Yeats's work picked up more and more detail as it went on, the sensual shadow began to rise, the instinctual energy throws off its own clown clothes and fills more and more of the consciousness.

Why that did not happen to Stevens I don't know for sure, but I think we have to look to his life for an explanation. Boehme has a note before one of his books, in which he asks the reader not to go farther and read the book unless he is willing to make practical changes as a result of the reading. Otherwise, Boehme says, reading the book will be bad for him, dangerous. We have the sense that Wallace Stevens's relation to the shadow followed a pattern that has since become familiar among American artists: he brings the shadow into his art, but makes no changes in the way he lives. The European artists—at least Yeats, Tolstoy, Gauguin, Van Gogh, Rilke—seem to understand better that the shadow has to be lived too, as well as accepted in the work of art. The implication of all their art is that each time a man or woman succeeds in making a line so rich and alive with the senses, as full of darkness as:

quail/Whistle about us their spontaneous cries

he must from then on live differently. A change in his life has to come as a response to the change in his language. Rilke's work moves on, shifting to deeper and deeper marriages, over wider and wider arcs, and we notice that he was always ready to change his way of living at a moment's notice if the art told him to. He looked one day at a statue for a long time, an old statue centered around ecstatic Apollonianism, and saw that the shape was alive not only in the head parts, but in every square inch of the body, throughout the chest and stomach, all of which dived down toward the genitals: every inch is looking at you, he said. Out of that he drew the conclusion that by tomorrow morning he would have to make some changes in the way he lived. I recall teachers at college laughing at Yeats for a remark he made in his journal during his twenties, something like: It seems to me my rhythms are becoming slack; I think I had better sleep on a board for a while. But that says the same thing as Rilke's poem.

Wallace Stevens was not willing to change his way of life, despite all the gifts he received, and all the advice he read in his own poems. He kept the house fanatically neat, evidently slept in a separate bedroom for thirty or forty years, made his living through the statistical mentality, and kept his business life and poetry life separate—all of which amounted to keeping his dominant personality and his shadow personality separate in his daily life. That was so much true that when he took a literary visitor to his club to eat, it seems Stevens entered and conversed there as a businessman, and warned visitors against eccentric behavior. In 1935, during Mussolini's attack on Ethiopia, when Stevens was 56, he wrote in a letter to Ronald Latimer:

The Italians have as much right to take Ethiopia from the coons as the coons had to take it from the boa-constrictors.

This sentence was intended to be playful, in part at least, and it does not represent a crime that has to be laid to him. And yet it is a sentence that

everyone who loves Stevens's poems has to face sooner or later. It seems
to indicate that he was not living his shadow very intensely. He had
urged the shadow energies to enter *Harmonium,* but at the point where
they might have disturbed the even tenor of his life, or the opinions
appropriate to it, he shut the door.

I realize that making serious comment on a group of poems by mentioning details of the author's life violates every canon of New Criticism,
canons still very much alive. But surely we must see now that this
critical insistence on examining only the work is another example of
shadow-hatred and shadow-ignoring. It is an idealist position. William
James's and Stevens's warning on the mind-set were rejected, and by the
1940s the idealist position in literature was established, and all of us
who began to write in the '40s and '50s felt that fact keenly. The critic's
assumption was that the author's life had no bearing whatever on the
poem. Eliot helped to bring that attitude about, yet I heard him com-
plain in a hockey stadium in St. Paul around 1957 that one of his poems
had recently appeared in an anthology holding eight long poems, and
that nothing whatever was said about the authors of the poems—their
nationality was not given, nor the century in which they had lived.
"They were all dead except me, and opening the book made me feel
dead too." The mentality of the anthologist was exactly what Stevens
called the mentality of the white night-gown. In any case, by 1950 the
idealist position had found a good home in literary criticism, and none
of us writing then got much help from it on how to bring our own
shadows—or the national shadow—into our poems.

Wallace Stevens's statement at the club—don't talk too much about
poetry, or too wildly—is somehow the opposite of Tolstoy, who, when
he got ready in his old age to free his serfs, found to his amazement that
his wife and two of his daughters were ready for no such thing, but
considered them part of the property and dowry, and that was an end of
it. He left the house in a blizzard with his youngest daughter, Alexandra,
and died in a railway station shortly after. He was willing to change his
way of life that late!

That story is probably a bad example, because it implies that changing
your way of life involves sensational events, catastrophes, turmoil,
leaving wife and children, leaving husband and children, slamming the
door in the Ibsen manner. The contrary seems to be true. Enormous
changes—divorce, throwing away children, abandoning responsibilities,
look to be clear ways to join your shadow again, but oddly that doesn't
happen most of the time. When a person divorces, he or she usually

sets up a similar life with a different person. All the verbal storms of confessional poetry that the poets and readers have gone through in the last years did not achieve anything for the poet—the poet's shadow is still miles away after the confessional book is written. As Plath's and Sexton's and Berryman's lives made clear, nothing has happened at all, and the death energy is still waiting to pounce on the unintegrated soul.

What is meant by Rilke's "You must change your life" is evidently something more subtle. I don't understand it at all myself, so I can only speculate. Conrad evidently made use of the information the shadow gave him by ceasing to be a ship's captain on the Congo, and so a low level exploiter of Africa. Rilke, when he realized what his work was telling him, interrupted his writing of poetry, and spent months watching animals in the zoo, and blind men on the streets, and years alone. He began to ask less from the world, not more. The Taoists would probably say that changing your way of life means giving up having an effect upon the world. It involves "wu-wei," not playing any role. Wu-wei is also translated as doing nothing. Wang Wei said once:

> In the old days the serious man was not an important person.
> He thought making decisions was too complicated for him.
> He took whatever small job came along.
> Essentially, he did nothing, like these walnut trees.

His friend P'ei Ti answered this way:

> I soon found doing nothing was a great joy to me.
> You see, here I am, keeping my ancient promise!
> Let's spend today just strolling around these walnut trees.
> The two of us will nourish the ecstasies Chuang Tzu loved.

A man has an effect on "the world" mainly through institutions. So we could say that in the second half of life a man should sever his link with institutions. I think the problem is more complicated for women, but I don't understand it. Conceivably for women the change might involve accepting more responsibility for affecting the world.

In any case severing ties with institutions is not a habit in the U.S., where a man ordinarily becomes more deeply embedded in the institution, whether it be an insurance company or a university, during his forties and fifties than he ever was earlier. John Barth is a contemporary example of the American artist who tries to bring the shadow into his work, but refuses to live it. His work cannot help but follow the same path as Stevens's—it is an ascent into vacuity, intellectualist complexity, a criticism of dry reason from inside the palace of dry reason.

If the shadow's gifts are not acted upon, it evidently retreats and returns to the earth. It gives the writer or person ten or fifteen years to change his life, in response to the amazing visions the shadow has brought him—that change may involve only a deepening of the interior marriage of male and female within the man or woman—but if that does not happen, the shadow goes back down, abandoning him, and the last state of that man is evidently worse than the first. Rilke talks of the shadow retreating in this poem.

> Already the ripening barberries are red,
> and the old asters hardly breathe in their beds.
> The man who is not rich now as summer goes
> will wait and wait and never be himself.
>
> The man who cannot quietly close his eyes
> certain that there is vision after vision
> inside, simply waiting until nighttime
> to rise all around him in the darkness—
> he is an old man, it's all over for him.
>
> Nothing else will come; no more days will open;
> and everything that does happen will cheat him—
> even you, my God. And you are like a stone
> that draws him daily deeper into the depths.

JOHN MALCOLM BRINNIN

JOHN MALCOLM BRINNIN (b. Sept. 13, 1916 in Halifax, Nova
Scotia, of American parents) was educated at the
University of Michigan and at Harvard. He taught at
Vassar for five years, the University of Connecticut for ten.
From 1949 to 1956 he directed the Poetry Center at the
YMHA in New York, organizing readings by many British
and American poets. Since 1961, traveling widely between
terms, he has taught at Boston University.

(Photo by Thomas Victor)

"Pray you undo this button:"
The Sentimental Strategies

My title is one of the famous moments in the drama of *King Lear,* a part of the old monarch's dying speech. By the time it occurs we have been witness to the story of a king, foully betrayed and pitifully reduced, whose simple human grandeur has somehow not been touched by the ravages of other men's cunning or his own gullibility. We have seen this king sorrily abused by his children and his minions. We have watched him wince at flashes of lightning and ingratitude. We have seen how a sovereign in his majority can become the most wretched of outcasts. High art and something close to profane philosophy have been joined to acquaint us with an archetype of man's fate. We might, at this conclusion of the drama, expect to be sent home consoled by some neatly turned iambic homily, to be eased into our overcoats by some promise of justice still to come. These expectations are denied us; but not entirely. For one instant Shakespeare forces us to stand aside from a sequence of actions that has threatened to overwhelm us. Lear on his windswept heath has loomed as tall as the pillars of Baalbek. But he is not a pillar; he is a man who, like all men, "smells of mortality" and must accede to its conditions. And this he does by a request, a most ordinary little request for physical comfort. As you or I might ask: "Toss me that pillow, would you, please?" or "Is that draught too much for you?" the eloquent old man shows for a moment that he also depends on kindness and the smallest of courtesies. His comprehension of his fate has been taxed to its limits. His heart extended almost beyond endurance; and now, as his one faithful daughter lies dead in his arms, the final blow of his life has been struck. It is then he says:

> No, no, no life!
> Why should a dog, a horse, a rat, have life,
> And thou no breath at all? Thou'lt come no more,
> Never, never, never, never, never!
> Pray you undo this button. Thank you, sir.
> Do you see this? Look on her! look! her lips!
> Look there, look there!

"Pray you undo this button"—the first of my "sentimental strategies." It is sentimental because it overtakes us wholly in the realm of feeling;

it is strategical because the emotional reaction it provokes seems to happen quite naturally when, in fact, there is nothing natural about it. The poignant request of King Lear may be consonant with his character, but the important thing about the request is that it is a quietly calculated device of William Shakespeare's.

Enlisting this moment as a model and, implicitly, as a premise, I would like to offer a few instances of literature that first made me aware of my own personal taste, then began to shape it and perhaps finally helped me to understand what an apocalyptic millimetre it is that separates art from life. In so doing, I mean to pay only passing attention to precept and to put my emphasis on example—somewhat in the manner of Marianne Moore's mosaic association of apparently disparate materials. Hers was an unusual and somewhat cranky way of composing an article, a review or a lecture, and to some people it was incomprehensible. When Marianne Moore's audiences leaned forward to hear her opinions, they were instead presented with a sort of literary button box of appositions, hints, and exotic irrelevancies. This would often lead to dissatisfaction, even to sharp disappointment. But most of us came eventually to see that what she was doing was not only idiosyncratic but surreptitiously illuminating. Marianne Moore never let her readers or listeners lose sight of the fact that literature was hers not only to use but to serve. And in serving literature—the ephemeral pamphlet as respectfully as the Great Book—she *made* literature. Who can forget how very much she had to offer and how very little she had to say?

To further my explorations in sentimental strategy, I would like to make use of a playwright's term, a term denoting quick changes in action, swift reversals of what has been accepted or assumed, piercing awareness of what has previously been hidden, suppressed, or masqued. For the playwright, it is that point of surprised engagement known as "the recognition scene"—a dramatic strategy with a history at least as old as Sophocles. Sometimes the sudden awareness involves a lover who disappears only to turn up as a congenial transvestite; sometimes it involves a princeling who wanders incognito among the peasantry in suspiciously handsome rags and tatters; sometimes a prodigal son too far gone in debauchery or too shy to come home. When this figure is suddenly revealed for what he or she really is, the recognition comes as a shock devised to quicken attention or resolve a dilemma or, in some cases, to reverse the whole course of action. But in all cases, quite beyond the dramatic maneuvers by which the playwright toys with expectations, there is one thing that makes all recognition scenes alike. This is the fact that *what* is being recognized is but incidentally a lover, a princeling, or a wayward son. The deeper thing offered for recognition is the broad underlying seam of human innocence, human vulnerability, human-*ness*. The deeper thing that is being recognized is the truth that, somewhere in the lower depths of the psyche and soma, we are all alike—culpable, dependent, and of the mortal fabric. No matter how ingeniously it may disguise itself in the costume of a time, a place, or a social convention, a quotient of mortality is the thing ready at any moment to be revealed and, being revealed, to modify circumstance by humanizing it. When this happens—when, in a flash of insight, all the veils, masques, disguises, and impostures are removed—it is as though the particular were instantly to become the universal. And this is the point, the point of recognition, that can take one's breath away.

To propose a crucial significance in this matter of sentiment is to venture onto thin ice. It involves a look into that part of experience that occurs as honest and ordinary feeling, yet finds its uses in all the forms of exaggeration that make for sentimentality and, sooner or later, must take into account all the dreadful and delicious stuff of the soap opera, the lending library romance, the melodrama, the Indian Love Call, and the lyrics of rock and pop. For safety, one might refer to—or defer to— the cultural anthropologist, the psychologist or any one of that new breed of disaffected gurus who have made bonfires of their sheepskins in the groves of totem and taboo. They would very likely tell us that there are, after all, only a very few human dilemmas, only a very few human responses, and that these have long ago been counted, charted and graphed. But none of us is quite willing to give over our own hard-bought perceptions to those who would run them off on some morbidly neutral computer and give us back statistics, threshold responses, or tabulations of coincidence in comparative religion. We really don't want to hear that the prodigal son is a figure who inevitably turns up in moribund societies and that he represents the flight from reality. We don't want to hear that the frog prince is suffering a regression fantasy . . . or that the grandmother in a nightcap who looks an awful lot like the big bad wolf is just one more victim of an identity crisis.

My own sense of the "sentimental strategies" represents a less dramatically obvious version of the recognition scene. The sense of them I would emphasize has less to do with the encounter of character with character and more to do with the encounter of authors with themselves, with what they mean or think they mean. Again, the drama of King Lear provides a distinction: only a few moments before Lear makes his

dying speech, the Earl of Kent who—banished by the king himself, has
nevertheless disguised himself as a servant in order to attend and care
for the old man—is at last revealed to Lear's sight and to his comprehension.

"Who are you?" Lear says to this stranger beside him. "Mine eyes
are not o'th'best." Kent replies: "If fortune brag of two she loved and
hated, / One of them we behold." "This is a dull sight," says Lear. "Are
you not Kent?" And when Kent says, "The same—Your servant Kent,"
Lear says: "He's a good fellow, I can tell you that. He'll strike, and
quickly too. He's dead and rotten." "No, my good lord, I am the very
man. . . . That from your first of difference and decay / Have followed
your sad steps." And when it is all too late, when there is no place for
welcome, no corner of the world that might take him in, Lear at last says,
"You are welcome hither."

The recognition is brief and pathetic, yet it remains an essential part
of the machinery of the plot and part of Shakespeare's way of playing with the kinds of blindness and sight that make up the moral thesis
of the play. The conventions of the recognition scene are nicely accom-
modated: the blind man sees, so to speak, the sacrificial hero is rewarded
on the spot, the design of the drama is symmetrically filled out. But
when, a few minutes later, fumbling with his buttons, Lear asks for
help, that recognition and the "recognition scene" are put into quite
another kind of focus. What happens there is something different: we,
as spectators, recognize what Lear, the actor, does not; and what we
recognize is neither a person nor a condition but a state of being beyond
good and evil where wisdom perhaps ends but where, surely, it begins.

If literature can be said to have "uses," one of these is to give voice
to the large part of life that transpires wordlessly, to find words for that
part of life that shows itself in impulse, mood, temper; to give expression, even eloquence, to feeling, and thereby to honor its sources. We
are, all of us, familiar with the inarticulate, simply because to be tongue-
tied is to share one of the most common of failings. If you have ever
heard a tape recording of your own conversation made when you were
not aware of it, you were perhaps ever so slightly amused and, secretly,
outraged and appalled. Think of what we say as we stumble and stutter
through farewell scenes in railroad stations and at airport gates, as we
try to comfort one another in funeral homes and as we do our little star-
turns at weddings and baptisms and graduation ceremonies. When we
hear, actually *hear*, what we say on these occasions, even the most sober
of them, we have to laugh. But what we laugh at is, after all, only the

words: the occasions remain. And we even forgive the words because, knowing what they have tried to express, we are reminded of their pitiful inadequacy and become resigned to that fact. The disparity between what we feel and what we say is a lapse that most of us simply have to accept with resignation. But for the writer, this gap between feeling and its expression is opportunity; it affords him the place where he works best. This is the place where strategy—the disposition of sentiment for effect —can make even a deliberately inchoate stuttering ring with the resonance of scripture. Listen to Gertrude Stein.

[My example is the last scene of *The Mother of Us All* where, speaking in the *persona* of her heroine Susan B. Anthony, Gertrude Stein undoubtedly speaks for herself as well. Both women followed a conviction through many long difficult years with little sign of reward and even less hope of it. Each in her own way used the language as a means toward a noble end; each was a crusader—one for the political rights of women, the other for the transformation of discursive literature. Now, joined in the distance of time, they stand as one: a statue that speaks. The struggle is over, the end approaches; and here Gertrude Stein, the author-heroine, sums up the meanings; not in so many words that might rehearse issue and event, but in a little incantation that returns all of the meanings to the final pathos of the public self engaged with the private self.]

> *Chorus.* To vote the vote, the vote we vote, can vote do vote will vote,
>   could vote, vote the vote.
> *Jo the Loiterer.* I am the only one who cannot vote, no loiterer
>   can vote.
> *Indiana Elliott.* I am a loiterer Indiana Loiterer and I can vote.
> *Jo the Loiterer.* You only have the name, you have not got the game.
> *Chorus.* The vote the vote we will have the vote.
> *Lillian Russell.* It is so beautiful to meet you all here so beautiful.
> *Ulysses S. Grant.* Vote the vote, the army does not vote, the general
>   generals, there is no vote, bah vote.

> *They all bow and smile to the statue.*
> *Suddenly Susan B.'s voice is heard.*

> *Susan B.'s Voice.* We cannot retrace our steps, going forward may
>   be the same as going backwards. We cannot retrace our steps, retrace
>   our steps. All my long life, all my life, we do not retrace our steps,
>   all my long life, but.

A silence a long silence.

But—we do not retrace our steps, all my long life, and here, here we are here, in marble and gold, did I say gold, yes I said gold, in marble and gold and where—

A silence.

Where is where. In my long life of effort and strife, dear life, life is strife, in my long life, it will not come and go, I tell you so, it will stay it will pay but

A long silence.

But I do want what we have got, has it not gone, what made it live, has it not gone because now it is had, in my long life my long life in my long life.

Silence.

Life is strife. I was a martyr all my life not to what I won but to what was done.

Silence.

Do you know because I tell you so, or do you know, do you know.

Silence.

My long life, my long life.

Curtain.

Even the metaphysics of cubism remain in the realm of feeling. The woman who, more adventurously than anyone else, tried to do the impossible—literally, to bring the fourth dimension into poetry—is revealed as self-doubting yet resigned, celebrated yet uneasy. Once more, the buttons are tender.

Perhaps an even more intimate example of an author recognizing his mortal state and, by inference, yours and mine, comes from that other metaphysician of the modern James Joyce. Though they are still "Joyce and Stein"—curiously paired in the popular report—Gertrude and James are actually as far apart in their techniques and intentions as it is possible to be. Gertrude Stein was, and for the most part remains, hermetic —a literary sport that helps to define the norm; while Joyce is—as Pablo Picasso one day said to Gertrude—"ah, James Joyce—an obscure writer whom all the world can understand." The differences between them are properly the concern of the investigators of language and of consciousness. I am concerned with the similarities in their effects, that common juncture of feeling which puts them first in that small society of writers who dared everything and forgot nothing as they pressed language to the very limits of its power to communicate.

From Joyce my example is the nominal ending of *Finnegans Wake*—nominal in that the book as an entity of lines on pages ends with these words while the "ending" is also the beginning—"a commodious vicus of recirculation"—that allows the last word, the article "the," to be the springboard to the first word on the "first" page. This is the meandering speech of Anna Livia Plurabelle, the river meeting the ocean, life flowing into death and eternity, the particular into the universal. All the detritus of her existence, Joyce's existence, yours and mine, is being carried along in a kind of slow, funerary procession. Yet what she remembers, what remains most vivid to her as her individual consciousness is about to join the mind of God is not what she has come to, but where she began. As she speaks, she dwells on the events of her own childhood and, if you like, the childhood of the race. This is Eden, this is Paradise; but it is also that house on an ordinary sidestreet where you and I grew up. The breadth of Joyce, it's conventional to say, is cosmic. Yet here is one of a thousand instances where the cosmic is located in the familial. The riverine force of history and human consciousness called Anna Livia is about to quit the land for the sea; at the same time, speaking like the little girl she always was, a child named Anna Livia is trying to find her way back into her father's arms.

"Ho hang! Hang ho! And the clash of our cries till we spring to be free. Auravoles, they says, never heed of your name! But I'm loothing them that's here and all I lothe. Loonely in me loneness. For all their faults. I am passing out. O bitter ending! I'll slip away before they're up. They'll never see. Nor know. Nor miss me. And it's old and old it's sad and old it's sad and weary I go back to you, my cold father, my cold mad father, my cold mad feary father, till the near sight of the mere size of him, the moyles and moyles of it, moananoaning, makes me seasilt saltsick and I rush, my only, into your arms. I see them rising! Save me from those therrble prongs! Two more. Onetwo morements more. So. Avelaval. My leaves have drifted from me. All. But one clings still. I'll bear it on me. To remind me of. Lff! So soft this morning ours. Yes. Carry me along, taddy, like you done through

the toy fair. If I seen him bearing down on me now under whitespread
wings like he'd come from Arkangels, I sink I'd die down over his feet,
humbly dumbly, only to washup. Yes, tid. There's where. First.
We pass through grass behush the bush to. Whish! A gull. Gulls.
Far calls. Coming, far! End here. Us then. Finn, again! Take.
Bussoftlhee, mememormee! Till thousendsthee. Lps. The keys to.
Given! A way a lone a last a loved a long the . . ."

Attempts like this to open seams of filial and familial sentiment occur
in the most diverse kinds of writing. Essential as they are, the impact
they make has tended to embarrass critics in almost the same degree
that it has moved readers. As a consequence, they have never received
the kind of attention that critics have quite willingly given to a writer's
ideas, his sense of composition and to the pretty ripples of meaning made
by his symbols. This neglect of sentiment as an object of critical inquiry
is perhaps due to the fact that sentiment does not easily lend itself to
established forms of analysis; perhaps because it necessarily evokes the
messiness of life with all of its sniffles and tears and stifled sobs; perhaps
because it is in the nature of the literary scholar to be entertained and
challenged more happily by intellectual things. This has been especially
true in recent history when we have been asked to think of poems and
novels not as living documents or *cris de coeurs* but as "nice structures,"
"symbolic choreographies," "models of confusion," and so on. Although
we knew that men and women wrote them, we were urged to think of
the works themselves as immaculately conceived. When anyone dared
to point out that some author's nose was running or that another's slip
was showing, this was considered nothing but bad behavior—rude, dis-
ruptive and irrelevant. The poem *qua* poem and the novel *qua* novel, we
were told, should ideally exhibit an "internal structure" and a "reticulum
of ideas" that would obviate such unseemly exposures of ignorance.

This was the kind of thinking that led to that interregnum of the
literary mechanic we call The New Criticism. As a critical affection this
movement had its classroom uses in that it gave rein to a whole generation of instructors whose performances were awesome. These were
the linguistic technicians who could, in a mere thirty minutes, dismantle
an epic and, in the next twenty minutes, put it together again with not
even one pathetic fallacy left over to clean up. These were the academic
prodigies who could take some little old Model T of a poem, clean its
spark plugs, drain its crankcase, pack its wheelbases, and have it back
on the road twenty seconds before the eleven o'clock bell.

For them, the excellence of a poem or of a novel was located not so much in its sufficiency as in its *efficiency*. How did it work? How did stress, strut, balance, counter-balance, cantilever, and flying buttress hold the thing together? Something crucial was missing in all of this; and that thing was any kind of gauge, any kind of instrument that might register the fibrillation of the human heart or that might calibrate the force and density of human emotion. Almost any lending library customer at the corner drug store knew that a novel was not the sum of its parts; and any buyer of rhymes on a greeting card knew that a poem was not. Yet, against all the weight of vulgar good sense and common acceptance, the zealots among the New Critics continued to deal in abstractions and to keep their own kind of heresy lively and persuasive.

History has changed that picture. After they had dominated a generation or two, the masters of the nice distinction began to lose ground to the barbarians; and they have been losing ground ever since. To some extent, their retreat has been regrettable; to a larger extent, it has been liberating. Some of the disciplines and insights of the New Critics were salutary. Under their tutelage, many students and teachers for the first time understood the ways in which a creative imagination works. The New Criticism showed us that novels and poems were constructions, not visitations; that novelists and poets were as much craftsmen as they were dreamers or lay saints or prophets. But when its disciples became over-zealous, when an obsession with the writers' means replaced or corroded concern for the writers' meanings, the movement became decadent and vulnerable to assault. When the attack came, it was two-pronged. First, poets and novelists cut the supply of those acrostical constructions without which the literary mechanic was left with nothing to go by but abandoned shibboleths like "taste" and "fitness," followed by a clamorous demand for "relevance." Then readers, especially among the very young, began to respond to certain new writers, first with relief, then with a parochial sort of passion, then with Like Wow! Like Out of Sight! *Their* chosen writers were not judged by craft or intellectual detachment, but only by the degree in which these writers were involved in what goes on in the huge heartbreak house of adolescence. Writers were judged, above all, by manifestations of what their young readers termed "sincerity." The taste of these readers was awful and their tendency to take sincerity as Delphic dogma allowed no quarter to anything like wit or verbal play and simply closed off that happy hunting ground of the New Critic known as Ironic Distance. Altogether, these young buyers of paperbacks responded with enthusiasm to the most deplorable reductions of literature. Yet a good part of their response was not only inevitable, it was "right." The young hungered for something and their hunger had led them to discovery. Impatient with writers who saw literature as a spiritual and cerebral discipline, they turned to writers who saw it as impulsive expression. Unwilling to enter the company of artists who respected only intellectual probity and aesthetic restraint, they turned to writers to whom art—literature or anything else—was as free and "uncontrived" as finger painting. Writers of this dispensation were blowzy, simple, sophomoric, deliberately infantile, self-deceptive—yet *sincerely* self-deceptive—and they filled the bill. Sentiment was exploited, sentiment was abused, sentiment was beatified. No matter: sentiment had come back to the forefront of a scene from which it should never have been excluded.

To characterize the temper of any run of years is a chancy undertaking and it would be foolish to suggest that all of the young people who, one year, were happily deciphering Dylan Thomas's "Altarwise by Owl Light" were, the next year, swooning over the cookie-box lyrics of Richard Brautigan. Yet there was a change. Works of literature had been forced to confess their parentage, their sleazy childhoods, and all the accidents, lucky breaks, and good turns that had brought them into being. The poem, long separated from the poet, had rejoined its author. Even the unmarried novelist had to acknowledge her real baby. As poets began to leave the doors of the confessional box open, then to wire it for sound and finally to start broadcasting from it in stereo, unemployment among the New Critics became rampant. In the general panic and confusion, the deathbed admission of T. S. Eliot was probably the last straw. For some forty years, "a symbolic representation of the alienated sensibility" who bore the name of J. Alfred Prufrock had gone walking on the beach, his trousers rolled, his ears attuned to what the mermaids sang. Then, in one well-calculated slip of the tongue, Mr. Eliot gave up the ghost and left his astonished disciples in the lurch. "Shucks, fellers," he told them, "*that* wasn't J. Alfred anyone. That was Old Possum hisself."

Sentiment may at times be too hot to handle, too sloppy and unwieldy to carry, too much charged with appetite to be appeased. Yet there is a demand for it in our make-up which any writer must both answer to and transcend. When that demand is met by a writer in whose imagination fancy plays but a minor role, the very nature of imagination asserts itself as perception of the mundane. For an example, let me cite a poem by Wallace Stevens which suggests that feeling, when it is in harmony with necessity, is the central reality. The poem is "The World as Meditation." When Stevens gave it that title, I don't think that he meant to suggest that our lives in this world are not real, but merely that the events of our existence arrange themselves in patterns beyond our comprehension and that we are sustained, ultimately, by a kind of wisdom we sense and, without "knowing," count upon. In this poem we meet an old and familiar *dramatis personae*. Penelope waits for Ulysses to come back from Troy; we assume the details of the famous story—how she politely entertains her suitors yet holds them off, how she weaves her tapestry then secretly unravels it, just as Homer tells us she did. The plot, the suspense, the play, the deception, the very business of it all is part of the zest of Homer, the zest of the tribal bard. Yet what Homer saw and felt and what, in fact, Homer *meant* is exactly that which, four thousand years after the telling, Wallace Stevens means and makes explicit. In Stevens's "reconstruction," we have another instance of that kind of recognition that ignores people and events in favor of a perception of the fact that, whether we know it or not, the world as "meditation," the world as a mystery beyond the range of our questions or the consolations of our answers, is half of our understanding. Every day, these poets indicate, we exist in the event, yet we live, as all men live, in the cause.

THE WORLD AS MEDITATION

*J'ai passé trop de temps à travailler mon violon,
à voyager. Mais l'exercice essentiel du compositeur—
la méditation—rien ne l'a jamais suspendu en
moi . . . Je vis un rêve permanent, qui ne
s'arrête ni nuit ni jour.*

Georges Enesco

Is it Ulysses that approaches from the east,
The interminable adventurer? The trees are mended.
That winter is washed away. Someone is moving

On the horizon and lifting himself up above it.
A form of fire approaches the cretonnes of Penelope,
Whose mere savage presence awakens the world in which she dwells.

She has composed, so long, a self with which to welcome him,
Companion to his self for her, which she imagined,
Two in a deep-founded sheltering, friend and dear friend.

The trees had been mended, as an essential exercise
In an inhuman meditation, larger than her own.
No winds like dogs watched over her at night.

She wanted nothing he could not bring her by coming alone.
She wanted no fetchings. His arms would be her necklace
And her belt, the final fortune of their desire.

But was it Ulysses? Or was it only the warmth of the sun
On her pillow? The thought kept beating in her like her heart.
The two kept beating together. It was only day.

It was Ulysses and it was not. Yet they had met,
Friend and dear friend and a planet's encouragement.
The barbarous strength within her would never fail.

She would talk a little to herself as she combed her hair,
Repeating his name with its patient syllables,
Never forgetting him that kept coming constantly so near.

In a swiftly descending spiral of significance, I would like to name and use a few recognitions out of my own experience. "The business of the poet," someone has said, "is to move the reader's heart by showing his own." This is of course an ideal; and, before it can be realized, there are severe hazards to be faced and overcome. When the poet's heart visibly throbs, it calls to itself two kinds of attention: a glance of clinical curiosity or a muted snigger. Like most of my contemporaries, when I hear Shelley say "I fall upon the thorns of life! I bleed!" I have only one reaction: So what else is new? The heart on exhibition tends to stay in isolation from the concerns of its observers. Yet when a poet's heart beats in the ordinary rhythms that we all can hear and count; when it endures, fast and slow, what we all endure, it calls attention not to itself but to what it is nourished and regulated by. In having the bravado to include my own attempt to use the sentimental strategies, I hope I offer not a bleeding heart but one that keeps council with feelings everyone knows and situations of a kind almost everyone has experienced.

[Some of my allusions—at least for people under fifty—should probably be identified: a Hupmobile is a motor car; a Gladstone is a suitcase; a Morris Chair is a piece of living room furniture with an adjustable back; Maxfield Parrish was a painter who worked with a spray gun to paint dawns and sunsets in which there were always one or more naked people (men? women?) with the sexual parts brushed out; "A Message to Garcia" is an inspirational essay by the yokel philosopher Elbert Hubbard; *The Outline of History* is a book by H. G. Wells, a work of popular history that became an enormous best seller in the 1920s; Bebe Daniels and Ben Lyon were Hollywood actors married to each other; *Liberty* was a weekly magazine; the *S.S. Berengaria* was an ocean liner belonging to the White Star Line; Lucrezia Bori was a prima donna of the Metropolitan Opera Company; Tristran Tzara was the founder of the art movement Dada; Aschenbach is the hero of Thomas Mann's *Death in Venice;* Henri Barbusse was the Frenchman who wrote a famous book about World War I entitled *Under Fire* and who later became a leader in the international Communist movement; U.A.W. is the United Automobile Workers' union.]

If there is a story in the poem it is this: a son recalls the life and death of his father. His father is a scenic artist who leaves Halifax, Nova Scotia, where he has begun to raise a family, to go to the city of Detroit in the boom times of the early twenties. There he becomes a real estate agent until the Depression sends him back to his paint brushes and those catwalks in the flies of theaters on which scenic artists work.

The poem has one initial strategy, one basic presumption: it is supposedly written on the very day when its author has lived longer than his father, that watershed occasion when the father—the aged figure up there, Daddy, Papa, Sir, God—is suddenly dissolved by a trick of time. The son inherits the father, the child is father to the man, the relationship is overturned, the Oedipal antagonisms tamed and domesticated. This is its strategy and, of course, strategy is always a device of the intellect. Emotionally speaking, the poem is located in what we know as the generation gap. All those things that could not or would not be said when conversation was possible are finally said. But it is all too late. Words that might once have served no longer serve; except, in the irony of it, to add one more slightly inchoate analogue to the unfinished lessons of life and, by extension, to the unfinished lessons of art.

MY FATHER, MY SON

I

Father,
            one day longer on this earth than you,
I want you home—not
as a sage arthritic in red silks
to whom I proffer
                        birds of jade
& berries on a stick—not

as a totem with a spittled lip,
forked beard
                    blown sidewise & Assyrian—
not as a democrat of rhetoric,
                              calligraphy,
astride bowlegged Chippendale—but
just as the man you were
                          in dull Glen plaid,
high collar, homburg hat,
                          Kodak'd
beside our bathtub of a Hupmobile.
Your new estate is mine;
                          & if, at first,
I treat you like a well-scrubbed foreigner
to whom one gives a suit of clothes,
                              five dollars
& a map of the city,
accept the circumstance: I need
help in the yard,
                    a hand with heavy things,
someone to keep the books.

II

Flames I've not eaten
                    I have quashed
with a small cap of silver—yet
what was it like when,
                        clacking west,
you heard the waters hiss & part,
                              & saw
the sun rise cold as cash?
                          Your eyes
like plums in fifty watts
                          of washroom light,
you shaved, halfway across Ontario,
with a straight razor & your braces down.
Bandbox fresh,
                    whisked to your high-topped shoes,
when you stepped from a Grand Trunk sleeping car,

what was it like to be,
                         emblazoned in your tracks,
one man alive,
                    Gladstone in hand?
Those boom-town dollar bills—were they
not barbarous as they were absurd?
When, Sunday afternoons,
                              they showered
out of canvas biplanes onto
                                lots for sale,
& craven girls, knee-deep
in goldenrod & Queen Anne's lace,
picked them like lettuce,
                            was not history,
finally, a subdivision of brown bungalows,
                                             a small
down payment on the Middle West,
& good clean fun?
                      On the Tashmoo boat,
its splashy paddle wheels
                            walking the water,
did I not watch
                  the snake dance
                                    deck to deck
of realtor and typist,
                          branch manager and clerk?
Your hands outstretched,
                            your fingertips upon
a boozy woman's pin-striped back,
                                     two other
hands on yours,
                  et cetera—Yes! you sang,
your flint face mesmerized,
                              Yes!
we have no bananas,
we have no bananas today!

III

Set down in our raw suburb
                            Mother wept,
her old life now a province in a mist

where military bands,
     caged in an iron wedding cake,
played Humperdinck & Grieg
      to the King's swans;
& years of calling cards,
     laid in a silver dish, ·
tallied the last turns in the vestibule
of waltzing osprey & high-stepping fox.
       You must
have understood,
    though you would not,
the vast leer of our Morris chair,
the desolations of Caruso on the console,
       the ache
of Maxfield Parrish's blue dawn
above a five-foot shelf of books,
     glassed in.
Why was she crying?
Where did she hurt?
    Shrunk in the threat
of something still more awful
     than the oven eyes
of grizzlies,
   chained,
    snarling, to a pole,
that wanted to get at me,
     I lay, eyes shut, awake.
"He's not asleep."
    Her sob
broke like a bubble on a pink geranium.
"He's a good actor. Jack, see what you can do."
Shoshonis gobbling at the sight of him,
      Buffalo Bill,
that worn-out hero of your one-man repertoire,
skirmished across my bed.
     What a brute!
I think you thought so too.

IV

Father,
   what do I do with years

still hovering like a castle quarried to its floors,
wrapped,
   piece by piece in burlap,
        stacked away
in some red warehouse just outside of town?
To whom can I show off?
      Where now can I talk big?
Blood on my hockey stick,
      I limped home
pitifully.
    Marbles in my mouth,
I got my message through to Garcia,
       & stalked
the dining room for liberty or death.
Erasmus redivivus,
I fell asleep in the encyclopedia.
      When you
told your one joke
     (Irate Diner: Waitress—what is
this fly doing in my soup?
      Waitress: Why—it does look like
the breaststroke, sir.)
     I laughed
louder than anyone. I said
your Friday haircut was the cat's pajamas.
I said
  So's your old man!
     & bit my tongue.
You pondered *The Outline of History,*
      you took up golf.
I sulked & fasted,
    told my beads,
     slammed
out to Mass at dawn.
    The simplest form
of tyranny, I learned,
    is holiness.
Remember our most delicate of interviews?
I had to know what it was all about;
      you had to say.

My eyes outstaring yours—
                       yours fixed,
first on my saints, all smiles in their blue lights,
then on my 2-for-25 cent photographs
                             of Bebe Daniels & Ben Lyon,
then on the water-falling tails
                     of birds of paradise
you'd painted on my walls—
                   you began
at the beginning, you told it all.
                      Hushed
by great news, I sat stock-still as,
                       surfacing
from 20,000 leagues,
                  you lit a Camel
& then studied it. "Do you think you understand?"
I nodded,
             completely in the dark.
                       That's where I stayed
until,
         one morning in a field,
                     instructed
by a playmate grown up fast,
I thought my head, like a boiled egg,
was sliced off at the top.

V

You couldn't bear it,
                  yet every June
you'd pack us off, dolls in a box,
to summer in the Maritimes.
                 "Hon,"
you wrote from the East Side Y.M.C.A.,
"I don't think I can stand it.
                 I eat
at some dog wagon near the office,
read *Liberty*, take in a show."

Stalled like a whale,
              her hawsers loose,

the *S.S. Berengaria*
lay sidling at the Ocean Terminal.

>   At noon,
her deck rails lined with duchesses,
she churned the harbor skidding in her bells,
then dropped her tugs

>   & slid
basso profundo out to sea.

>   I still
had graves to dig:

>   a cricket skewered on a pin,
a grasshopper dismantled to its knees.
I put them

>   side by side,

>   a few
limp dandelions for one,
purple clover for the other,

>   a matchstick
cross for each. I had no sympathy.

VI

Up in the smoke of 1929 went your big deal.
Grass withered in the cleats

>   of your golf shoes.
You closed the office,

>   hocked your turnip watch,
replaced the lining in your overcoat.
Across a neighborhood of rotting mortgages
you saw your future out of sight.
They even tried to repossess the car!
Thank God,

>   you still had brushes & a union card.
You climbed a ladder,

>   you began to paint
a painted desert, streets in Trinidad,
a salmon-colored *auberge* in a forest where,
descending,

>   weightless,

>   from a tulip coach,

Lucrezia Bori,
   like a walking tent,
embraced the full measure of illicit joy.
       Back
in overalls, you made good money
        & you grew morose.
What could you do with a kid afraid of heights,
half-crocked on Proust,
      tooling a sonnet
on the very day the Tigers clinched the pennant?

VII

Father,
   riddle me this:
      If I'm not half
the man you were,
      what fortune makes you
all I am?

You gave me your car keys.
I put you on the shelf.
      What did you know
of Tzara, Aschenbach, Barbusse?
How could you stomach Hitler & Republic Steel?
Out all night,
     my fingers mimeo'd
with U.A.W. strike bulletins,
I made the breakfast nook my drumhead court.
Charged with murder,
      you sat still.
Hectored out of conscience, you,
with crypto-fascist nonchalance,
       ate two
fried eggs,
   a slice of ham,
      & dolloped
cream into your coffee. You had to see a man,
you said, about a dog,
      then wiped your lips
& handed me a week's allowance.

VIII

Cranking a winch one working day,
                              your hands went white.
A stippled garden shuddered to the stage.
So much to say,
                    I couldn't get there fast enough.

Time eats you in that box I bought
next morning in a sort of catacomb
on Jefferson near East Grand Boulevard.

Tailgating your black Packard to Mount Olivet,
lights on,
              we ran the lights,
                              stopped dead
in a charred grove &,
                    ill at ease,
                              stood witness
to your last embarrassment.
                              Traffic with insane
persistence scratched the hedges.
                              Overhead,
like pterodactyls sitting on the wind,
Ford Tri-Motors snored importantly
                              & side-slipped home.
Broken at the wrist,
                    the hand you never shook
hung at my side.
                    I can't remember—
did the rain hold off?

In your collar box I found
                    love poems—
Love poems! When had you written them? To whom?
Your heart, you said, it "burned,"
                              it "yearned."
You said, "You make the winter rains seem glad, my dear.
              The sky above me smiles when you are near."

They were so bad I cried.

With the exception of my own (which must stay in the realm of the Good Intention), the examples of sentimental strategy I have brought together here are moments in literature when authors have plumbed the water table, so to speak, broken through the surface to tap the reservoir of man's nature where the affections are benign. Their clear implication is that beyond good and evil there is a bedrock stratum of compassion in which, ignorant or aware, willing or not, we are in union. Once we have an intimation of that human underground, they seem to say, our sense of self and not-self is equally quickened, our will to action emboldened. When we "know" on the level of cause, they suggest, we are free to act in terms of event. It is a sense of connection—man in touch with the *human*—the kind of knowing, the kind of inter-relatedness that informs our will to stand against inhumanely motivated aggression and the cynicism by which unelected emotion is subverted to the meanest dimensions of the *realpolitik*. It is the kind of knowledge that allows us to see that our real adversaries are those who have lost or denied connection, who exist in the event, the plot, the polemics of circumstance, and nowhere else. It tells us that our adversaries are those who believe that solutions can be final, who regard life as a perpetual argument over rights, who prefer the ossified forms of society to the claims of the individual.

The buttons of King Lear! the cretonnes of Penelope! the long silences of Gertrude Stein, the estuarial sighings of James Joyce. I have deferred to them, "placed" them, "evoked" them and I am not sure that the whole roster of them says anything more than that they are the individual touchstones of a personal disposition. Yet, pressed to make a final brief for them, I think I would say that each, in his way or hers, tells us what we know by reminding us who we are.

ROBERT CREELEY

ROBERT CREELEY *(b. May 21, 1926 in Arlington, Mass.) left Harvard in 1944 to join the American Field Service in India and Burma. He returned to Harvard a year later, but dropped out again. In 1954, after other travels, he joined Charles Olson at Black Mountain College where he founded the* Black Mountain Review *and taught until 1956. In 1957 he married the artist Bobbie Hall. Two prolific decades of poetry and prose have followed. Creeley is now Professor of English at the State University of New York at Buffalo.*

(Photo by Thomas Victor)

Was That a Real Poem
or Did You Just Make It Up Yourself?

As I get older, I recognize that my thinking about poetry may or may not have anything actively to do with my actual work as a poet. This strikes me as no thing cynically awry, but rather seems again instance of that hapless or possibly happy fact, we do not as humans seem necessarily aware of what we are physically or psychically doing at all. One thing, therefore, that does stay put in my head, as something said in youth, is "we live as we can, each day another—there is no use in counting. Nor more, say, to live than what there is, to live. . . ." I did not feel that a pessimistically argued reality back then, nor do I now. It is very hard for me to live in any projection of reality, in a plan or arrangement of the present moment that uses it primarily as a "future" term. I have long experience of my own restlessness and impatience, and have managed quiet and a feeling of centeredness only when the *here and now* literally discovered it for me. Elsewise I have battered myself and the surroundings with seemingly useless energy, pleased only that something at least was "happening."

My writing seems to me no different. Of course I learned as much as I could about the *how* of its occasion. Like many of my contemporaries I felt myself obliged to be an explicit craftsman so as to have defense against the authoritative poetry of my youth—whose persons I'd like now not to recall, just that it's taken me so long to forget them. So, from that initial, crotchety purview, I've continued, finding and choosing as heroes men and women who must at this point be familiar to anyone who has read me at all: Williams, Pound, H.D., Stein, Zukofsky, Olson, Duncan, Levertov, Ginsberg, Dorn, Bunting, Wieners, McClure, Whalen, Snyder, Berrigan—and so on, being those I can almost see out the window if I look. Put more simply, there's been a way of doing things which found company with others, and in that company one has found a particular life of an insistent and sustaining kind.

That has been part of the situation of "what poetry means to me," but dear as it is, it has not been either the largest part nor the most significant. A few months ago I was sitting with friends in a lovely house on a lovely afternoon, and we began a collaborative poem, on impulse, using an electric typewriter that was on a nearby table. It took me real time to get to it because it intimidated me—I've never used one particularly—

46

and also intrigued me, and so my feelings and thoughts began to singularize me, isolate me in relation to the others. But I've always been able to do that, so to speak. But is it some necessity of my own working? In any case, my contribution to the poem stood painfully clear in its twisted, compressed statement—even the spacing of lines shrank to a small fist of words, defensive and altogether by itself.

No wonder that I've never forgotten Williams's contention that "the poet thinks with his poem, in that lies his thought, and that in itself is profundity. . . ." Poems have always had this nature of revelation for me, becoming apparently objective manifestation of feelings and thoughts otherwise inaccessible. Did I love Mary—a poem or story would quite usually make the answer clear, no matter it might take years to know it. A pleasant woman met this spring pointed out, for example, that "For love—I would/ split open your head and put/ a candle in/ behind the eyes . . ." was a literally violent proposal that was not demonstrably involved with usual senses of "loving" the recipient. Yet I had always felt that poem a true measure of an ability to love, and possibly it is.

As a young man, then, moved by poetry, feeling its possibilities as inclusive, bringing all the world to one instant of otherwise meaningless "time," I wanted, not unexpectedly, to participate in that wonder. We struggle with them a good deal, mutter, mistake, but *words* seem even so significantly common and in that respect accessible. My own commitment to them was not easily understood. Was it that nothing else was open to me? Did I turn to them simply that no other act or substance permitted me such occasion? I know that I felt in those years now past very often useless in other attempts to find place in the world. As so many of that time, I married primarily to reify what might be called my existence. The fact of wanting to be a social person, as well as a private one, seemingly demanded it. Again, there was nothing I otherwise "did" that argued my relevance to a general world.

In short, I was markedly self-preoccupied, lonely, inarticulate at crucial points in my relationships, and again, and again, restless. If they did nothing else, words gave instant reality to this insistent flux, which otherwise blurred, faded, was gone before another might in any sense witness it. The realization that poems, stories, fed on this experience of reality was of great use initially. Just as I had used reading as a place to be, a world of volatile and active nature yet also "unreal", not "flesh and blood"—and yet that surely, how else could it be—so now the possibilities that words might engender became a deep preoccupation.

At various times I've put emphasis on the fact that I was raised in New

England, in Massachusetts for the most part. So placing myself, I've argued that that fact clarifies my apparently laconic way of saying things, especially so in my early poems. But might that use of words not come also of feeling tentative with them, unsure of their appropriate significations—as though there were a *right* way that was being distorted, lost, by fact of one's ignorance? I sense an aspect of this dilemma in Williams's plaint, "many years of reading have not made you wise. . . ." I know that he did share with me a tacit fear of the well-trained, academically secure *good English* he felt the comfortable equipment of various of his contemporaries. We both depended, it would seem, on enthusiasms, rushes of insight or impulse, read only to a purpose if the appetite underlying would settle for nothing else. I was delighted, for example, to realize that Williams did not spend long hours researching *Paterson* in the library but rather, as Michael Weaver first told me, got his information from a lovely, old time *local* historian. To this day I am so intimidated by the *nature* of libraries, the feel of them, the authority of their ordering of books on shelves, etc., that I rarely if ever go into them. I feel toward them much as I feel toward telephones, that their function is disastrously limited by their form, no matter what efficiencies are also clearly the case.

But why worry about that? If one has spent close to thirty years writing books, in effect, why be so fearful of this one place they may come to rest? Why be afraid of *poems*, for that matter? Thinking of that world "out there," and recalling my own tentativeness in trying to find my own use in it, always the *general* measure of reality can hurt me, can say, in short, "of course *you* like it, you wrote it—but what about other people, don't you care what they think or feel or want?" More specifically, why not write poems the way they are supposed to be written— as simple acquaintance with poetry as a *subject* would easily define. Thus, if you seriously want to be a poet, you study the prevailing models of its activity and you set yourself to their imitation as diligently as you can. And slowly you acquire, or do not, the requisite ability.

I don't believe it. I *know* that attention to what has been written, what is being written, is a dearly rewarding experience. Nonetheless it is *not* the primary fact. Far closer would be having a horse, say, however nebulous or lumpy, and, seeing other people with horses, using their occasion with said horses as some instance of the possibility involved. In short, I would never buy a horse or write a poem simply because others had done so—although I would go swimming on those terms or eat snails. Stuck with the horse, or blessed with it, I have to work out that relationship as best I can.

Posit that music exists despite the possibility that no one might be consciously able to make it, that what we call *poems* are an intrinsic fact in the human world whether or no there be poets at this moment capable of their creation. That would characterize my belief—which gives me no rest, which, too often, causes a despairing sense of useless-ness and ineptitude. Why can't *I* write them, fall in love, reveal the actual world, and be the hero in it? Isn't it *mine?* No. Yours? No. Theirs? No. Ours? No.

Days, weeks, months, and sometimes years can pass in that sad place. Nothing gets done, nothing really gets even started. A vague, persistent echo of possibility seems all that is there to depend upon. Perhaps to-morrow, or later today—or even right now. To work. Useless paper, useless pen. Scribbles of habit and egocentric dependence. But you did it once, didn't you—they said so, you thought so too. Try again.

Sometime in the mid '60s I grew inexorably bored with the tidy con-tainment of clusters of words on single pieces of paper called "poems" —"this will really get them, wrap it up. . . ." I could see nothing in my life nor those of others adjacent that supported this single hits theory. Dishonest to say I hadn't myself liked it, haikus, for example, or such of my own poems that unwittingly opened like seeds. But my own life, I felt increasingly, was a *continuance,* from wherever it had started to wherever it might end—of course I felt it as linear in time—and here were these quite small *things* I was tossing out from time to time, in the hope that they might survive my own being hauled on toward terminus. Time to start over, afresh, began to be felt at first as increasingly limited, finally as nonexistent. The intensive, singularly made poems of my youth faded as, hopefully, the anguish that was used in the writing of so many of them also did. I was happier? Truly pointless to answer insofar as I lived now in another body and with an altered mind.

More, what specific use to continue the writing of such poems if the need therefore be only the maintenance of some ego state, the so-called *me*-ness of that imaginary person. Lost in some confusion of integrity, I had to tell the truth, however unreal, and persisted toward its realization, even though unthinkable. So writing, in this sense, began to lose its specific edges, its singleness of occurrence, and I worked to be open to the casual, the commonplace, that which collected itself. The world trans-formed to bits of paper, torn words, "it/it". Its continuity became again physical. I had no idea of its purpose, nor mine, more than a need to include all that might so come to mind and survive to be written.

My tidinesses, however, are insistent. Thus forms of things said moved through accumulated habits of order, and I felt neither ease nor possibility in the jumbled or blurred contexts of language. No doubt I will repeat the manners of small kid with mother, town nurse, and older sister most articulate in West Acton, Mass., 1930 to 1935 forevei. Only the town is changed, to protect the innocent.

If one were a musician, the delight might be in sounding again and again all that composite of articulation that had preceded one, the old songs truly. In poetry, the dilemma of the circumstance is simply that some*one* is supposed to write some*thing,* and it becomes a possessive and distracting point of view. It is interesting to remember that Archilochus and Sappho are known to us because literacy comes to "write them down," no necessary concern of theirs nor of lyric poetry more generally. Yet I am very much a person of my time in wanting to leave a record, a composite fact of the experience of living in time and space. It was Charles Olson's hope to make an *image of man,* in writing *The Maximus Poems*—not at all to write some autobiographical memoir. I use all poetry to write anything, and only wish I might know more of its vast body, which is seemingly as various as the earth itself.

What *is* poetry? In a dictionary I've hauled around for almost as long as I've been writing (*The Pocket Oxford Dictionary of Current English,* Fowler and Fowler, with a "New and Enlarged Edition Revised by George Van Santvoord," 1935) it says to my horror: "elevated expression of elevated thought or feeling, esp. in metrical form. . . ." If I turn to a more recent dictionary, *The American Heritage Dictionary of the English Language,* 1969, I'm told that poetry is "the art or work of a poet" which has got to be a cop-out. So all these years people have been screaming that one was not writing *real* poetry—and it turns out nobody, certainly no one in that crowd, knew what it was to begin with. No wonder they insisted on those *forms!* They wouldn't know it *was* a woman unless she was wearing a dress.

So now I will make up poetry, as I always have, one word after another, becoming something, as sounds, call them, as beats, *tum tum.* All very familiar. But each time I take the bus I do see something new, somehow. Eyes possibly? Certainly a turning world. Verse turns, and takes turns in turning—which are called *verses,* in my book, like changes—and not those *stanzas* or stops, standstills. *Onward then, multiple men, women too, will go with you*—boohoo. Which is a poem because I say so, it *rhymes.* That was a primary requisite for years and years. But so lovely when such rhyming, that congruence of sounds which occur in time with sufficient closeness, to resound, echo, and so recall, when *that* moves to delight and intensity, feeling the physical quality of the words' movement with a grace that distorts nothing. To *say* things—and to say them with such articulation can bring them physical character in the words which have become them—is *wonder*.

It is equal wonder when the rhythms which words can embody move to like echo and congruence. It is a *place*, in short, one has come to, where words dance truly in an information of one another, drawing in the attention, provoking feelings to participate.

Poems have involved an extraordinary range of human and non-human event, so to discuss that fact seems pointless. We will talk of everything sooner or later. Americans have had the especial virtue in the last hundred years of opening both content and form in an extra-ordinary manner, and the energy inherent continues without apparent end.

But again, one lives a life, and so, personally, one speaks of it, and of the people and places it was given to find. I cannot say that my children particularly respect or find other interest in my being a poet, and, at first, that bothered me because I wanted them moved by what moved me. False hope, I now think—although it might otherwise come to be the case. At times I hear the niggard comment that poets seem only to have other poets as an audience. It is certainly true that the dearest company I've had in reading has been so. But many people otherwise have heard too, through no intent of mine. I couldn't predicate that they would, in writing. As a young man I questioned that anyone would ever hear at all, although it did not occur to me that I might therefore stop writing.

The tacit lament in this way of speaking strikes me as pathetic. Getting a purchase on writing, so to speak, was for me a one way ticket to bliss. I've never really come back. In those long, lonely nights I've wailed the sweetest songs, possibly, certainly those most designed for my own pleasure. Years back, again, Williams said, why don't we make clear we write for our pleasure, that we *like* doing it? It's a fair question. Nobody wants their pleasures criticized, and that fact no doubt explains why nobody really wants to be explained, nor wants to explain either. And I suppose that's why one uses either a tendentiously "critical" vocabulary in speaking of "his work" or else pushes clear with a, gee whiz, fellers, it's really nothing.

At first I was intent upon getting *anything* to hold, so that the ex-perience in reading had the same qualities as the impulse in writing. But then I don't really know, nor have I ever, what's being said until it comes to some close, and it's now there to be read through, as one thing. Elsewise I trust the location implicit in feeling it's going well, opening, moving without a sense of hesitance or forced intention. I don't want to write what is only an idea, particularly my own. If the world can't come true in that place, flooding all terms of my thought and experience, then it's not enough, either for me or, equally, for anyone else. It must be somehow *revelation*, no matter how modest that transformation can sometimes be. Or vast, truly—"the world in a grain of sand."

The title for these divers thoughts comes from a lovely story told me about 1960 by John Frederick Nims in Chicago as he afforded us a charming lunch in his role of editor of *Poetry*. It concerned a friend of his, another poet, who had been on a tour of readings in the middle west. And, as was his wont, he invited questions from the audience at one particular college, on completion of his reading. And a guy puts up his hand and says, tell me, that next to last poem you read—was that a real poem or did you just make it up yourself? Terrific. That's stuck in my head so lucently so long! Much as the phenomenon of another friend and student at Black Mountain in the middle '50s who in truth could perceive no demonstrable difference between a cluster of words called *poem* and a cluster of words called *prose*. She felt the typographical form of the poem was all that apparently defined it—and that of course was a very arbitrary gimmick, to her mind. I tried everything, "Mary had a little lamb," tum te tum, clapped my hands with the beat, pulled out the vowels à la Yeats, probably even sang. Still it stayed flat and arbitrary. She felt the beat and texture of the sound was imposed by will of the reader and was not initial in the words themselves. All the usual critical terms were of course useless, far too abstract. Finally I truly despaired of gaining more than her sympathy and patience. Then one day, we were reading Edward Marshall's "Leave The World Alone," and for some immaculate and utterly unanticipated "reason" she *got* it, she heard all the play of rhythms and sounds bringing that extraordinary statement of primary humanness into such a density of feeling and song.

Would that all had such a happy ending—and "American poetry," like they say, soared on to the stars. Senses of progress, also familiar, really want that in the worst way. Meantime one's brothers and sisters are out there somewhere wailing on, to make the night a little lighter, the day a little brighter, like. Bringing that sun up and bringing it down again, every time. I don't know where it's supposed to "get to" in that sense, more than to persist in the clarity of human recognitions and wonder. Poetry, as Duncan says, comes "from a well deeper than time." It's "contemporary" in the way that fire, air, water or earth might be said to be, particularly involved in any apprehension of present existence.

Sadly it can, as these, go away, be lost to other appetites and acts. Talking to Michael McClure a few days ago, thinking of the primary *stances* in the arts, to the three most familiar (Classicism, Romanticism, and Surrealism) he felt a fourth might be added: the Beat, which, distinct from the other three, does not propose "the word" as a stable, physical *given* but, in ecological terms, realizes its fragility and thus the need for human attention and care.

As a poet, at this moment—half listening as I am to the House Judiciary Committee's deliberations—I am angered, contemptuous, impatient, and possibly even cynical concerning the situation of our lives in this "national" place. Language has, publicly, become such an instrument of coercion, persuasion, and deceit. The power thus collected is ugly beyond description—it is truly *evil*. And it will not go away.

Trust to good verses then.... Trust to the clarity instant in being human, that knows and wants no other place.

Bolinas, California
July 31, 1974*

---

* On this same day Robert Creeley wrote me: "Herewith the essay, like they say. I hope it's of use. The poem, 'For My Mother,' I'd simply like to have *follow* it (not precede)—as instance of what I'm now writing, etc." [w.h.]

FOR MY MOTHER:
GENEVIEVE JULES CREELEY

April 8, 1887—October 7, 1972

Tender, semi-
articulate flickers
of your

presence, all
those years
past

now, eighty-
five, impossible to
count them

one by one, like
addition, sub-
traction, missing

not one. The last
curled up, in
on yourself,

position you take
in the bed, hair
wisped up

on your head, a
top knot, body
skeletal, eyes

closed against,
it must be,
further disturbance—

breathing a skim
of time, lightly
kicks the intervals—

days, days and
years of it,
work, changes,

sweet flesh caught
at the edges,
dignity's faded

dilemma. It
is *your* life, oh
no one's

forgotten anything
ever. They want
to make you

happy when
they remember. Walk
a little, get

up, now, die
safely,
easily, into

singleness, too
tired with it
to keep

on and on.
Waves break at
the darkness

under the road, sounds
in the faint
night's softness. Look

at them, catching
the light, white
edge as they turn—

always again
and again. Dead
one, two,

three hours—
all these minutes
pass. Is it,

was it, ever
you alone
again, how

long you kept
at it, your
pride, your

lovely, confusing
discretion. Mother, I
love you—for

whatever that
means,
meant—more

than I know, body
gave me my
own, generous,

inexorable place
of you. I feel
the mouth's sluggish-

ness, slips on
turns of things
said, to you,

too soon, too late,
wants to
go back to beginning,

smells of the hospital
room, the doctor
she responds

to now, the
order—get me
there. "Death's

let you out—"
comes true,
this, that,

endlessly circular
life, and we
came back

to see you one
last
time, this

time? Your head
shuddered,
it seemed, your

eyes wanted,
I thought,
to see

who it was.
I am here,
and will follow.

October 15, 1972

JOHN HAINES

JOHN HAINES (b. 1924 in Norfolk, Va.) attended St. John's
in Washington, D. C., and the National Art School and
American University in that city. He studied from 1950–52
at the Hans Hoffman School of Fine Arts in New York.
From 1954–69 he was a homesteader in Alaska. The
recipient of Guggenheim and National Endowment for the
Arts Fellowships, Haines has taught in several colleges and
universities, most recently at the University of Washington
and the University of Montana.

(Photo by William Stafford)

Poems and Places

Asked to write something about my poems, or about poetry generally, I quickly discarded several possibilities. I knew I did not want to attempt at this time a sharp and stinging essay, saying what I thought was wrong with our poetry today. I had done this once or twice in the past, as well as I could, but was never to discover that I had affected the course of things appreciably. I had annoyed a few people, unnerved some others, and achieved for myself the satisfaction that perhaps I had said a few things of lasting truth about poetry. I could let that statement stand.

I thought of pursuing a suitable theme through contemporary poetry, something that might indicate in what direction I saw it moving, and attempt to use some of my own poems in support of this. But I soon began to feel uncomfortable with the idea of talking about my own work this way, assuming the poems themselves presented any such possibility, and I did not want to write about the work of others. So I left that idea for another day.

I discarded another possibility, that of taking two or three of my poems through various stages of composition, using notebooks, first drafts, worksheets and so forth. This has been done, and such things can be interesting. But there is a certain amount of egotism or arrogance in assuming that one's own markings on the page, an extended discussion of one's technique, or method of writing, is of abiding interest to readers. Every writer has his method, his routine of work. A page of manuscript from the hand of Keats or Wordsworth may be fascinating and useful to a scholar, but not to the general reader, I think. Besides, I no longer had the worksheets of the poems I should most like to talk about.

For a long time I have been looking for a way of talking about poems, their background in thought and feeling, the landscape, the climate that shaped them. Poems, after all, come out of a life and a person, what I have been and done at certain times in my life. Honestly told, this might be of real interest to the reader and, in the course of things, reveal something about the nature and origin of poetry. I had already done something like this in a short piece I wrote about one of my poems for an English Department newsletter at the University of Washington. That piece and the response to it seemed to open a way of talking about poems that would not only hold the reader's interest, but might add to, not take away from, the poem itself, or involve me, the author, in an unsuitable, classroom analysis of my own work.

Talking about the origin of poems involves certain risks of its own. I must admit right off to the possibility of deception, of distortion of events and motives. Describing as well as I can the circumstances that originated the poem, I know very well how far back the associations may reach, far beyond those more immediate ones I can tell of: conditions of temperament and training that established quite early in life what my response to any given event might be. But to pursue all the possibilities in a piece such as this would be impractical. I decided to tell as clearly as I could what I remembered of certain poems, and let the reverberations travel as far as they might.

In the late fall of 1962 I was away from home much of the time, looking after my trapline. I no longer had a dogteam, but went on foot the fifteen or so miles over hill and watershed to my camp on Cabin Creek; then back the next day, up Redmond Creek, down Banner Creek, and home. I set out small traps for marten, and an occasional larger one for lynx. Along the river within two or three miles from home I set a few snares for lynx, fox and coyote. It had been a pleasant fall so far; not much snow on the ground, and only a few days of minus-thirty-degree weather. We had no money, and that was why I was trapping. I had shot a moose, and we had plenty of potatoes and vegetables, and a good store of berries and fish. That ought to have been enough, and it was. But as I came footsore through the snow evening after evening, I felt a little abused by circumstances, and in a self-complaining mood. I was sure I wanted to be home at my desk, writing poems.

One evening I came up from the river to find a visitor sitting in our cabin, talking to my wife, Jo. He was a native, an Eskimo. He had been on a hunting trip south of Delta Junction, in the Alaska Range, and for some reason I never understood, the man he was with had gone off and left him, taking his sleeping bag and his parka. He had been forced to hitchhike back to Fairbanks. Walking on the road below the house, he had seen a light in the early dusk, and being lightly clothed, stopped in to get warm. At Jo's urging he agreed to stay for supper.

Supper was the usual moose roast and potatoes. Perhaps we had tea, and we might have had bread, but not butter or most of the other little comforts we sometimes thought so important. Never mind, we had enough. We sat around the small table in the light of the one kerosene lamp, and ate.

The native, whose name might have been Ed, did much of the talking.

He was perhaps in his late thirties, stocky and round-faced, and wore glasses. Unlike many of his race in the presence of white people, he was articulate in speaking of himself and his life. The conversation drifted among the three of us during and after supper, the lamplight striking our faces in that way I have so loved at times—not bright and without relief, as with a strong overhead light, but as a kind of lighted shadow in which it is possible to find depth and the darkness beyond it. And I thought briefly of a tent, my own pitched back on Cabin Creek where I was hunting one fall, and how the candlelight shone yellow through the white canvas.

We talked about trapping, hunting, and fishing, living in the woods; and much about his people, his family and their history. He came from a small village on the Yukon, named Holy Cross. As with so many native villages, the young people went away to work in the city during the summer, and the old people stayed home. In the fall and winter the family might get together again, but many of them were lost to the city, to alcohol, and trouble of one sort or another. And some, like Ed, stayed out of trouble, and pieced out wages by working a trapline during the winter, north or west of Fairbanks. We must have spoken of other things. He may have noticed the books on the shelves, and I may have mentioned that I wrote poetry in my spare time, something of that sort. There were, most likely, vast stretches of experience over which we would have found it difficult to speak to each other. But we had this much life in common, the art of living in the woods, the old and unchanged life of the food-gatherer. It seemed for that evening to be enough.

He left around nine o'clock in the evening, accepting the loan of a jacket, and perhaps even a pair of gloves. Standing outside in the cold, clear darkness, I could hear for a long time the sound of his shoepacs crunching the snow on the roadside as he walked west on the highway.

I thought for a long time of his visit, his presence in the room of the cabin, and the sound of his footsteps. There seemed to be so much resonance there, so much possibility in that figure of a man of his race walking on that road, the old route between Asia and America. I don't remember now how long after that I wrote my poem. As was common with me, I might have written down something that evening, but more likely it was at least the following spring before I finished the poem. Originally the first stanza contained a couple of lines that described his stopping to eat with us, but I discarded them. Several years later at a poetry reading in Michigan, someone I met objected to the phrase about

Holy Cross, claiming that it produced an unintended rhyme with "frost" in the line above. I at once began to hear this myself, and have ever since read the poem without it.

THE TRAVELER

I
Among the quiet people of the frost
I remember an Eskimo
from Holy Cross, walking one evening
on the road to Fairbanks.

II
A lamp full of shadows burned
on the table before us;
the light came as though from far off
through the yellow skin of a tent.

III
Thousands of years passed.
People were camped on the bank
of a river, drying fish
in the sun. Women bent over
stretched hides, scraping
in a kind of furry patience.

There were long hunts through
the wet autumn grass,
meat piled high in caches—
a red memory against whiteness.

IV
We were away for a long time.
The footsteps of a man walking alone
on the frozen road from Asia
crunched in the darkness
and were gone.

For a long time I kept a sound in my head, the sound made by telephone wires at dusk of a cold evening. Anyone who has lived in a cold climate and in the country has heard this sound, I'm sure. I never understood what caused the sound, a humming or thrumming in the wires, sometimes loud enough to be heard a long distance. It was common after a change in the weather from cloudiness to clearing, and with a steady drop in the temperature. One fall evening when the sound was particularly loud, I went to the pole below the house and put my hands to it. I felt the wood vibrating strongly under my hands, and the sound seemed to be coming up out of the earth.

I thought there might be something in that sound I could make a poem of. It seemed to be saying something to me, if I could only listen hard enough and long enough. But for a long time I had only a notation in one of my notebooks. I brooded on it, and slowly, autumn by autumn, a few images began to group themselves around my notes. I asked myself, what did I want in this poem? I wanted some suggestion of the sound itself, if I could have it, but without trying to describe it exactly. And there was the road below the house, a road that always seemed to me to be more than a state highway; a trail, a passage between Asia and America, flown over by birds, traveled by men and beasts long before the highway crews carved the hillsides and laid down their gravel and tar. I began to think of the earth as a harp, and the telephone wires as strings. That might be an obvious or trite image, but it seemed worth pursuing: the strings of an earth-harp touched by dry leaves blowing across them. And I wanted something of the light, coming across the hills and the river, a kind of dusk possible in mid or late fall, when leaves were on the ground and snow had not yet fallen deep.

What else? There were events in the world beyond Mile 68. The Vietnam war was spoken of more and more. Men were going west by ship and plane to fuel and fight that war. Could I have a figure for this? It was not in my nature then to speak directly of such things, but to find a way to suggest them. . . . A ship going down, and blood draining across the sea. There was the sun, after all, and sometimes little dark clouds like holes in the sky. And finally a figure, someone who might speak all these things in an adequate voice. A poet, perhaps, but some figure trying to speak.

Once, early in the progress of the poem, I described a hole dug in the hillside above the river, and the figure of a man buried there up to his head, the hole drifted in with leaves. It was a sort of tree figure trying to root itself, to flower the following summer. And I remembered when digging my root cellar some years before, how, deep in that hole, I had such a strange sensation of living in an other-world kind of light, seeing the flakes of mica in the soil, and bits of crumbled granite. I had uncovered the charred section of a tree buried there centuries before and preserved by the constant frost in the soil. That figure of a tree, long buried, might be made to stand up and sing.

Somewhat more than two years went by before I was able to finish the poem. At one time I was about to settle for a brief version of it, and actually published in *Chelsea,* the poem in this form:

> In Delta Junction
> the only poet is the wind,
> a drifter
> who walked in from the coast
> with empty pockets.
>
> He stands on the road at evening,
> making a sound
> like a stone harp,
> strummed by a handful of leaves.

Well, that was interesting, but there were more possibilities in it, I thought. I liked the figure on the road, and decided to keep that. This figure was partly myself, of course—years before I had walked from Delta to Fairbanks with empty pockets. But perhaps only the wind could really speak for the place and the continent, a figure of wind whose fingers were dry leaves blowing across the wires of a harp. And whatever that sound was, it should contain something of the future, not menacing perhaps, but mysterious and alert. I have never been certain what the poem says. Perhaps it *says* nothing; but it does seem to *do* something, to present a figure, a metamorphic figure, something trying to become another thing, and the ghost of a sound.

THE STONE HARP

> A road deepening in the north,
> strung with steel,
> resonant in the winter evening,
> as though the earth were a harp
> soon to be struck.
>
> As if a spade
> rang in a rock chamber:
>
> in the subterranean light,
> glittering with mica,

a figure like a tree turning to stone
stands on its charred roots
and tries to sing.

Now there is all this blood
flowing into the west,
ragged holes at the waterline of the sun—
that ship is sinking.

And the only poet is the wind,
a drifter
who walked in from the coast
with empty pockets.

He stands on the road
at evening, making a sound
like a stone harp,
strummed
by a handful of leaves . . .

One afternoon in late summer, while driving home from Delta Junction, I picked up a hitchhiker. He was a small, wiry looking man in his
thirties, dressed in a worn brown suit and a white shirt open at the
collar. He carried a small handbag, and wore a strange, bewildered look
on his face. He was headed for Fairbanks, and as we drove along he
began telling me pieces of his story.

He was going blind, slowly losing his eyesight because of a strange
accident. While working as a mechanic on one of the military bases in
the area, apparently around fuel storage tanks, a co-worker and friend
of his had somehow lost control of the hose he was handling and sprayed
jet fuel into this man's face. He washed his face almost immediately, but
the chemical had got into his eyes. Sometime later he began to have
trouble with his vision. An eye-specialist told him the chemical was
destroying the optic nerve; visits to other doctors confirmed this. Apparently it was too late, nothing could be done.

He told me all this in the baffled, hurt voice of someone who has not
quite understood what has happened to him. Nothing could be done. He
was faced with returning to his home town, somewhere in the Southwest, to sit in the dark and have someone read his mail and newspaper to
him. Already he could not see well enough to drive a car.

The man and his fate haunted me long after I let him out on the road.

He began to take form in my mind as a figure, a representative figure of the times—a victim. It was then toward the end of the 1960s, violence was in the air, and a strong feeling of some imminent catastrophe, as wayward and mysterious as the accident that had befallen this man.

I thought of some of the things I wanted in the poem that began to shape itself: the feeling of menace, impersonal and unstoppable, as in the coming on of a dreaded winter. Without trying to describe directly the accident, I wanted to suggest as much as possible of what I knew as fact. For a long time I found it difficult to make a stanza that would carry the idea of a gratuitous blow, the smell of gasoline and the sound of a jet plane. And finally the environment to which he was being condemned, and the man himself, waiting there, listening to a voice whose source he might never fully identify.

TO A MAN GOING BLIND

As you face the evenings
coming on steeper and snowier,
and someone you cannot see
reads in a strained voice
from the book of storms . . .

Dreamlike, a jet climbs
above neighboring houses;
the streets smell
of leaf smoke and gasoline.

Summer was more like a curse
or a scar, the accidental blow
from a man of fire
who carelessly turned toward you
and left his handprint glowing
whitely on your forehead.

All the lamps in your home town
will not light the darkness
growing across a landscape
within you; you wait
like a leaning flower, and hear
almost as if it were nothing,
the petrified rumble

from a world going blind.

Finally, I'd like to discuss two poems written several years apart and under quite different circumstances. In each there is a house, a room at dusk, and a human presence, implicit or directly stated.

The poem "Listening in October" was written on the homestead at Mile 68, Richardson Highway, during the early 1960s. It does not describe any particular evening, but is a composite of many such times. The time is mid-fall, before the snow flies. Almost every afternoon I stopped work outdoors around four o'clock, and went into the house. Jo would have coffee or tea ready, and perhaps a snack, some fresh bread, or a piece of cake, if we had the makings for that. It was a time of refreshment, to say a few words to each other. Sometimes we listened to the radio, or to music from the portable phonograph. Often we just sat and listened to sounds: the fire in the stove, the sound of the river below the house, or to some other sound of the year. The window above the table looked out on the southwest, toward the last light and the hills that came down to drink at the river. It was, in October, a time of waiting. Something was finished, accomplished as well as it might be. The garden and the greenhouse were picked clean; cranberries had been gathered, mushrooms dried, and salmon packed in the shed. If I was lucky, there was a moose hanging on the rack. The great drama of the year was sloping toward its close.

The poem speaks of death, and the promises there. And by that was meant death as a sleep and regeneration, but also as a realm beyond light, deep and mysterious. The poem does not speak directly of particular persons, only of a "we." I intended by that the two people who were actually there, but also another "we," the immemorial human witness to the slow coming on of darkness at the end of the year. During the time I wrote this poem I was reading certain poets in Spanish and German. One poem by a German poet, who may in fact have been Georg Trakl, held my attention for a while. In it, someone comes in from the winter dusk to a warm house, to a table on which there is bread and wine, and to an understood, though not stated, human presence.

LISTENING IN OCTOBER

In the quiet house
a lamp is burning
where the book of autumn
lies open on a table.

There is tea with milk
in heavy mugs,
brown raisin cake, and thoughts
that stir the heart
with the promises of death.

We sit without words,
gazing past the limit
of fire, into the towering
darkness . . .

There are silences so deep
you can hear
the journeys of the soul,
enormous footsteps
downward in a freezing earth.

"The Weaver" was written sometime during the spring of 1971. By that time I had left Alaska and was living in California. Life had changed in some decisive ways; I had remarried and was caught up in the tumult of family life with four step-children. The quiet and solitude of the wilderness seemed, and was, light years away.

The poem came of a happening with my oldest step-daughter, Blair, who was then fifteen. She had been taking a high school course that allowed her to develop her own study program in history, and she had chosen to do hers on American Indians. One project she set for herself was to build a primitive loom and weave a small rug or blanket on it. She asked me to help her build the loom; we talked about it and drew up a sketch. We then went into the local city park and found some rough lengths of tree limbs. In a couple of days' time, sawing and whittling, we put the loom together with a few nails and some strips of rawhide. She set it up in the living room, bought some yarn and cord, and began to weave her rug.

The weaving went on for several weeks. Whenever she had time to spare, after school or in the evenings, she sat on the floor before the loom and worked slowly and patiently. Sometimes she made a mistake and had to take a section of the rug apart and start over. She had the capacity, not unusual in a young person, to be completely absorbed in what she was doing. She sat there in her silence, on the floor by a window, passing her shuttle back and forth, pounding down the weave with a heavy batten. Even when I was out of the room and upstairs, I knew when she was working, for I could hear the thump of her batten.

Somehow the entire family became involved in that weaving. We all watched her as she worked, and watched the rug grow. In some unspoken way it was a project to which we all were devoted, and it became important to us that the work succeed. At times she became discouraged and thought of giving it up; but she always came back to it, and eventually finished it. The yarn was grey and black, the small rug a little sombre perhaps, but pleasing.

One late afternoon, just before sunset, Blair was working at the loom, while I and two or three others in the family sat in the room and watched. I was drinking a glass of wine. The sunlight came down through the window and shone, partly on her and on the floor, barred from the slats of a venetian blind. It lighted part of the wall behind me, and the face of her mother sitting next to me. There was even a little sunlight in my wine glass. The whole room was steeped in a warmth, a redness or ruddiness about to settle into dusk. And for a moment or two there was a complete silence, except for the sound of her weaving. It was one of those moments in which it is possible to feel that something deep and essential in existence, eternal and unchanging, is somehow contained, illuminated, held briefly; an insight not to be explained or deciphered; a moment of pure being. And I felt a great love for this girl with whom I had a sometimes difficult, thorny relationship, but whom I had always respected. I felt that her struggles at that loom were part of a great effort in which we were all counted. That she really *was* weaving the house, the dusk, and all of us into that cloth. This was, in a sense, only a projection of mine, but it was for all that an intensely felt thing, and for me it contained a real truth.

The moment passed, of course. Someone spoke, turned on a light, and that completely changed the room. We were back in *time*. I think it was soon after, perhaps later that evening, I began writing or sketching out the piece that became "The Weaver." I can't say how long it was before I was done with it, it may not have been long after. I recall coming downstairs late one evening with the poem and showing it to my wife. I later changed one or two details in the poem, and an unsatisfactory last stanza.

The poem has been important to me because it seemed to mark a turning, a turning outward if you like, though I am wary of simplifications. Most of my poems have concerned an "I"—me, or something designated as such; or another sort of being—a moose, an owl or a cabbage. But there are few poems in which another human presence is strongly felt; or to say it another way, poems in which the human presence has as much weight as the silence, the landscape, or the objects in view. I may be deceived about this, but if I compare this poem with "Listening in October," there seems to be this difference. I don't prefer one over the other, but in "The Weaver" there is possibly another dimension, a warmth or completeness. The poem is important to me for another reason. Dreaming along in my mid-forties, I had this strange, unsettling wish for something I had never had—a daughter. And there she was, sitting before me in that ruddy light, bent to her task.

THE WEAVER

By a window in the west
where the orange light falls,
a girl sits weaving in silence.

She picks up threads of sunlight,
thin strands from the blind shadows
fallen to the floor,
as her slim hands swiftly pass
through the cords of her loom.

Light from a wine glass
goes into the weave,
light passing from the faces
of those who watch her;
now the grey flash from a mirror
darkening against the wall.

And her batten comes down
softly beating the threads,
a sound that goes and comes again,
weaving this house and the dusk
into one seamless, deepening cloth.

JOHN HAISLIP

Jᴏʜɴ Hᴀɪsʟɪᴘ *(b. 1925 in Lancaster, Pa.) has lived on the West Coast since 1946. He received his Ph.D. from the University of Washington in 1965, and after teaching in various places, is a Professor of English at the University of Oregon in Eugene, where he lives with his wife and daughter. He is working on a volume of poems which will probably be called* Seal Rock.

(Photo by Toni B. Nasser)

Seal Rock

I

There was an old man I loved and respected who for years spent a lot of his time on the Oregon coast, up the Alsea river from my place at Seal Rock, in a cabin during the fall and winter, fishing the runs of chinook, silvers, steelhead migrating from the ocean seven miles downstream. He was the father of a friend of mine, and when I first got to know him he was seventy-five years old. For the greater part of his adult life in the '20s, '30s, and '40s he owned and managed bars and small restaurants in and around Portland, cooking and working long hours. After he retired, and only then, did he find the time to fish. His son, who knows more about certain coastal streams than anyone I have met, taught him, and especially he taught him how to fish the lower tidewater reaches of the Alsea. Harlan, his son, and I fished the Alsea too. Not very often, but often enough. Sometimes we wanted to get away from the pressure of our work, but we'd use the excuse that we needed to check on Curley. And it was true, he could use help. He had a bad heart, and besides he had been alone all week and needed supplies. Harlan and I would arrive late at night, often on a Friday, and there would be Curley at the door clamoring with news of the river: who caught what, how large, where, and with what lures. Before we got the car unloaded and had a chance to pour a drink and get warm by the fire, he would recite his entire week. "I got one in the fridge, a nice one, got him over by Taylor's on Wednesday. The hot spot now is Drift Creek. But Harry says there is plenty of big ones in front of his place too." Or: "What a lousy week, too much rain, the river's high, and nobody's doing a thing." And on and on it would go, while he fixed our meal just as he did all those years in the restaurant, shuffling in front of the stove, banging the pots and pans (why are pros noisy in the kitchen?), serving up the mush or what-ever straight to the plates which he slid along the kitchen counter with a here-you-go, come on, eat! After dinner, Harlan and I would plan the next day's fishing. And sip a little more whiskey by the fire. Curley seldom joined us. Sometimes he'd play solitaire at the table, or wash the dishes. More often than not, however, he'd climb into the lower bunk in the little alcove off the kitchen and nap. But every once in a while he would rouse himself, and leaning on one elbow, shout at us questions or instructions. "Did you remember we got to charge that extra battery in the morning? How about the leaders I wanted?" Or: "Stop drinking, you're talking too much." Then later, as it got close to midnight, he'd roar: "You blackschmits! You won't be fit to be on the river in the morning."

It was not much of an admonition. Curley was tolerant and easy-going. But on reflection I have come to believe that buried deep in the memory of his words is a basic truth about the American experience. The river was and is unspoiled. Tired or hungover, there was no telling, as far as Curley was concerned, what Harlan and I might do, or do wrong, and Curley was plainly against any defilement however small. His con-viction may have come from memories of his childhood and youth in Sweden. Or was it a reaction to the long years he spent behind the stoves in his restaurants? The latter is probably true. He arrived in Portland soon after WW I and buried himself for thirty years inside his kitchens in those restaurants and in those towns in a landscape as radically pristine as any in America. The Northwest. Emerging years later, he was determined to make up time. Lazarus? No . . . because I've heard him tell . . . but, his last twenty years on the river were nearly perfect.

MISSING THE OLD BOY

"You blackschmits!"

If you could have seen us
staggering out of the boat
with the thirty-pound chinook
swinging round on the gaff
you take it no I will
no you ok it's mine for now
and the damned dog barking
yipping whining snarling
snapping at the tail
going round and round
and to boat that beauty
god it was all morning
under the over-hanging brush
in and around the dead logs
first me then Harlan steering
and sucking on the bottle
on account of the cold
the rain the fear we'd lose him

under the slack tide
before he'd belly-up
and let us pull him
in and over the stern
and clobber him nice
on the back of the head
with the hard-wood billy
with the leather thong
and coming up river later
we didn't bother to troll
we drank laying up dry
under the old canopy
the leaves now raining
full on the current
but clearing out fast
as soon as they fell
but just the same that stuff
would have hit our lines
and popped the flashers
hooks everything straight
up and out of the water
it's too trashy Curley
used to say and besides
there's nothing doing
I'm cold I'm stiff
but after we docked
you're younger than me
bring that sucker here
I'll gut him now.

That's where I am. As always, working to write a good book of poems. Tentative title: *Seal Rock*.

Seal Rock is the name of a village on the Oregon coast, five miles north of Alsea Bay and the town of Waldport, and ten miles south of Yaquina Bay and the city of Newport. The main coast highway, U S 101, runs straight through our village, at mile-post 150, measuring south from Astoria on the Columbia River. The highway continues 200 miles further south into northern California. Because there is no way to travel the coast except on 101, it's crowded with log trucks and, during the tourist season, with campers, trailers, boats, bikes, hitchhikers. It's all there. A dangerous two-lane highway. And it's noisy.

Our house and cabin, two structures which I partially built with my own hands, are only 50 yards from the highway, but they are set deep in thick brush on a very high cliff over-looking the Pacific. When you turn into the lane, unload the car, lay and light the fire, and begin to unwind, it is impossible, even on summer evenings, to hear anything—anything except the ocean, the breakers, the surf. There is no way to direct your attention back to the east. And, of course, during the winter storms with the wind gusting in the 70's and the rain beating over the place in unheard-of amounts, maybe four inches a day for four days straight, you are riveted there.

One corner of the house is built on an old Indian shell-mound or refuse dump, called a kitchen-midden, a spot where the Indians got out of the weather to prepare the clams and mussels they gathered from the beach. I discovered it during the excavation, many layers of busted shells, and during one part of the operation the bull-dozer unearthed the bones of a horse. I have no idea why they were there, I could only guess then, and so did the red-neck carpenters who worked for me and were born and raised in the area. But they were quick to confirm that I had picked a good spot. The winter storms might rage, but they would not plague us.

There is another advantage: the relative isolation of our beach. To the south there is a natural barrier, a beautiful headland of seven-story-high basalt stacks that few people cross over from the state park beyond. To the north is Beaver Creek, emptying into the Pacific. West, perhaps a quarter of a mile out in the ocean, are the large formations that gave Seal Rock its name. One of them is flat and accessible enough to be the home of a pod of seals who appear regularly each year in early December and leave in spring about the time the whales pass our village on their annual migration north.

II

I go to Seal Rock to rest and to write and to work with my hands. But I do not go there for escape. On the contrary, I have found a home and acquired a sense of place I have not had since I was a young man in Pennsylvania. I hope I never have to leave.

It has been a long time coming. I have lived with that ocean and that particular stretch of beach, the village of Seal Rock, the coastal streams.

the people, and that weather for twelve years. But for a long time, as I worked on my first book, I spent weeks at our cabin writing about my childhood in Pennsylvania. Only gradually did I learn to see clearly and come to terms with the whole incredible experience called the Oregon coast. A subtle and fascinating transfer of allegiances took place, but slowly, as I spent more and more time there with my family, or alone, in every season, year after year. It's obvious to me that I must learn to know a place thoroughly before it gets into my work.

Other poets work differently, and live differently too. I think of Berryman, Schwartz, Jarrell, not because of the circumstances of their deaths, but because of the range and variety of American experience they covered in their careers. As for me, I know nothing about America, absolutely nothing, except tidewater Virginia and Maryland (where I spent a lot of time on my uncles' farms when I was a boy) and Lancaster County, Pennsylvania, western Oregon and Washington, especially Seattle. The east coast and the west. Three middle Atlantic states and two northwest states. I am not laying claim to a virtue that may be an accident of my provincialism, but the truth is that a lot of America is alien to me.

At one time, however, I did not feel that way. I was deeply involved in what I conceived to be my American cultural heritage. Only gradually have I come to realize that by temperament and because of my deepest experiences (many in adolescence and some within the last few years) that my attachment to the past was superficial and that I do not now need the security I got when I was young and was locked into that heritage.

And I was locked in. Let me recite some facts. My father's people were early settlers in southern Maryland, south and west of LaPlata, the county seat of Charles County. They were mainly farmers, with small general farms in and around Riverside on the Potomac. My father was confirmed in the Episcopal church at Ironsides. The church dates from before the revolution. I was confirmed there too. On the other hand, my mother's family was originally from Missouri. They had settled in Westmoreland County, Virginia, about 1914. Their past, if I may say this without offending the memory of grandfather Eaton, was acquired. Grandfather was a good but amateur historian who instilled in all of us a love and affection for the past. He was, before his retirement, a civil engineer, and a rather distinguished one at that: the chief surveyor (as we used to say) of the American party that re-surveyed the boundary between Alaska and Canada beginning sometime around the administration of McKinley. My mother recalls, however, that her father began the survey in 1904, and every summer for the next ten years, he was in Alaska, while his wife and seven children lived in Washington, D.C. It was after his retirement from government service, when he moved his family to Oak Grove, Virginia, that he began to research and write (and eventually publish with his own money) *An Historical Atlas of West-moreland County Virginia*. It is a minor, although important publication, not only because it is accurately done, but also because the county is the birthplace of George Washington, Robert E. Lee, and James Madison. Grandfather literally searched all of the old records of the original crown patents from the time of Charles I, and with a series of maps showed how the plantations and farms changed hands. The atlas begins with 1643 and ends in 1742. It was a complicated and difficult book to write. And it was history, his history of place—the land, the homes, the families.

I grew up with that history, and as a child I had the impression that my family was involved in it too. Of course, this was not true. But it was said that my cousins used the cradle that Washington used, and I believe it, since my aunt married into the Latane family, which was related to the Washingtons, and my aunt's farm, Haywood, was next to Wakefield where Washington was born. And besides, Aunt Frances had a ton of antiques at Haywood. I visited Wakefield often and would walk to the edge of Pope's Creek and think: This is where he threw that dollar, and on this ground is where he cut down his father's cherry. But of course none of this was true either: Washington moved to Mount Vernon when he was five.

My father left southern Maryland soon after he was married. And that was the beginning of the end of our family's romance with history, although my parents did not think of what they were doing in quite that way. For years we maintained close ties with our southern relatives, and a little of the romance, I think, is still with all of us. But my father's departure from Maryland was for very personal reasons. I have surmised that he was sick and tired of the farm's confinement. Orphaned at four, he had been raised by a stern uncle and aunt. Soon after he inherited the farm, he sold it, and with two suitcases, and my mother and brother, he arrived in Lancaster, the heart of the Amish German farming community in Pennsylvania.

He had heard there was work in several factories in the city: Hamilton Watch was it, or some power and light company? I don't really remember his saying, and it is not important. What is important is that about the time I was beginning to be aware, really aware, we were several years into the Depression and living in a village outside of Lancaster. And as Ted Roethke used to say, as god is my witness, the name of the village was Eden. (And as god is my witness again, I lived for the first five years of my life in Lancaster itself on a narrow miserable street of row houses called Ocean Avenue.) But Eden was the country, the small farms of the prosperous Mennonite and Amish crowding the village. Eden. That is what it was. Except for the fact that it was the Depression. Except for the people who seemed to me unbelievably different from my parents. I probably exaggerated. But at the time I felt like an alien in paradise. The whole tone of our neighbors' lives was different from ours. That goes for their language and their sensibilities. Many of them spoke Pennsylvania-Dutch, a corrupted form of Low German. My parents had slight southern accents. And many of the villagers were cold, stiff, and aloof. My parents and their relatives were relaxed, warm, easy-going.

I suspect that this account of my childhood, with some variations, could be written by countless American poets of every generation. No matter where we were born and raised, or where we live now, we have not ever been part of a cohesive community. There must be as many reasons for this as there are serious poets. I only know about my own life.

I used the past, my family, and nature as ballast through my childhood and adolescence. Interaction with anyone outside my family was painful. I can name names (but what's the use?) of boys and girls and men and women I struggled to get to know. Failure. So I made do alone. I withdrew, retreated into the woods and meadows around Eden, and I roamed the banks of the Conestoga. (Is that another symbolic name?) My world was constantly breaking apart from the inside, I guess, because of outside pressure. I became a terrible student. As a matter of fact, a pattern of defeat was so ingrained in me that I thought it was an ugly permanent condition of my personality and character. Even now I am prone to bouts of depression if . . . but what's the use . . . all such confessions are boring, boring. There are no exceptions.

Besides, my theme is not alienation, but a search for a real home and abiding friends. Not simply a place to live, to earn a living, to raise my children, and then retire from before I topple into my grave.

III

My wife and I sat together near the front of the congregation. Harlan was alone with himself in the last row. Blanchard's young widow and four children were isolated behind a veil of white drapes in a vestibule to the right. The church was plain, damned near ugly, the interior walls nothing but painted plywood, the large windows ordinary glass, the "pews" straight chairs. His coffin lay to the left of the center of the altar rail, beside the flimsy lectern.

A lot of people were gathered. Blanchard had a reputation. He had lived in Waldport almost all of his life. Born in Boston, he came to the west coast with his family when he was a kid. His father drank, and that was held against Bob. The old man was a carpenter of sorts and a house-mover, and he taught Bob his trade, I guess, under the houses he moved, sitting in the shade with a case of beer. But Blanchard, himself, was good at his work. He put in long hours and seldom drank, and yet the established builders on the coast considered him a marginal craftsman. It's also true that there isn't much of a living to be made moving houses on the thinly populated Oregon coast. So he specialized in new foundations for old houses whose rotted timbers were letting them down. He built one for us. A foundation. But most of his work it seemed to me was for widows who needed some jerry-built back room on their aging houses jacked up and set level; or for poor couples who bought a shack and wanted it shifted to a vacant lot they'd gotten for peanuts in the boon-docks. His reputation was good with the widows and the poor, but as Willie Loman said, not really good. The community generally ignored him.

But he was loved by a lot of people. My wife and I and Harlan and Harlan's wife for example. And the Finnigans, our other close friends here in the valley. He meant everything to us when we settled in on the coast. He built Harlan's new cabin on the Alsea river, and he helped me remodel my old one at Seal Rock. He taught me some carpentry and a little bit about mortar and bricks. And I learned to scrounge, not because I was broke, but because it was a way of life with Blanchard and he hated extravagance. Make do, he said. He watched over our places, Harlan's and mine, when we were not there. Once when the shingles on a corner of my cabin were ripped off in a winter storm, Blanchard covered the hole somehow, got in touch with me, and then later helped me shingle it right. He taught me many other things. Where and how to clam, how to rake crabs at low tide in the pools around the piers of the bridge spanning the bay, and what and what not to fear from the big storms. He knew that particular stretch of coast and the valleys and mountains inland better than anyone I've met. He had to. It was his survival and it had been since childhood.

But there were contradictions in his character. Hard as nails, yet I remember seeing in his ramshackle, thrown-together house a small abstraction he'd painted of a street scene in Paris. He'd gone there once when he was in the army. And he bought my first publication, "Elegy For Jake," which a lithographer and I did in a special edition that cost Bob twenty bucks. At the time, if he'd asked about the book I would have given him a copy out of friendship and appreciation, but instead he got it through Harlan in a roundabout way, later refusing to let me return the money. So even though he shared some of the qualities and interests of the other young men in Waldport, he went his own way.

He was a powerful man. About 6' 2", with shoulders and hips like a halfback. And he seemed indestructible, even though he took a lot of chances no matter what he was doing. Shortcuts, really, to save some dough. He gambled in other ways. He was a poacher, but this is not unusual on the coast. Half the men get to doing it to feed their families in the lean months when there's no work in the forest, the commercial fishing is *nyet*, or the mills in the coast range close down. Blanchard got his elk every year. When he clammed or crabbed he generally brought in some over the limit, being careful (as he taught me) to land at one of the old docks up river where the wardens never came. As for salmon: I guess he did some gillnetting now and then. I know he often got impatient and would cross the bar at Waldport when he knew for sure it was not really safe, but anything to get in the ocean for the big ones.

And that's what killed him. The bar at Waldport is unprotected. No jetty. A few large, but flat-hulled boats go over. And a few small ones dare it now and then. Bob's boat was a 14-footer, small for the ocean; in the swells, a mean ride, even if conditions are ideal. The tide must be running from low to high not more than a few feet or the surf at the mouth is rough. And beyond the bar, the sea should be flat for a 14-footer, like a pond, and the weather good, no wind to speak of.

Blanchard went over the bar on a beautiful Sunday in July. He had a friend with him, Old Red, a man he hired occasionally to do easy manual chores for him in town because nobody else would hire him. Bob's reputation extended to helping the stumblies, the half-educated, the really marginal guys. They hung out around his place or at the cafe where he had coffee occasionally. His sympathies were with the beats, and the outcasts.

What happened that afternoon and evening no one really knows. He was found the next morning six miles south of the mouth of our bay, drifting in his half-swamped boat, the motor gone, the gear gone, fairly close to shore, but alone. Old Red came ashore dead a few days later on a narrow gravel beach further to the south, near Yachats.

The talk in town was that the Coast Guard found Blanchard seated in the bottom of his boat, deep as his waist in water, his left arm locked firmly under a seat. Because the boat was empty, no motor or gear, it was assumed by some of us that the old 7-horse motor Harlan gave Bob quit, that night came on and the wind and swells picked up, that he capsized when Old Red jumped. But no one knew for sure.

So Waldport did a lot of guessing, and the mean little church was jammed and the preacher had his audience. My wife and I and Harlan drove over the mountains and down the Alsea for the service and the burial. But before they took him to the tiny cemetery in the backwoods on the hill above town, they opened the coffin and we reluctantly went by for a last look. I was stunned! The incongruity! Living, a tall, powerful man. Dead, I could not believe the rouged cheeks, the stiff hair, the awkward coat and tie. The incongruity: his head jammed into the satin; the same for his feet at the other end. I had the impression that if I stood his coffin on end and tilted it forward, he would *not* fall out. "Jesus, it's too small." Outside, I thought: no one bothered to take your dimensions dead, just as no one bothered when you were alive.

FOR ROBERT BLANCHARD
Who Died at Sea
Waldport, Oregon
July, 1966

1

Where to begin? The motor dead in the water?
Or that bright morning you cleared the bar,
Your hand steady, firm on the throttle,
Your small boat riding low, heavy
With gear? Or your crazy friend,
His back to the wind in the bow—
Red hair curling forward over his eyes—
Nagging and prodding for weeks
To change his luck?

2

Who said some months before,
Was it me or your wife
Or your friends, dead sober:

Robert drowned at sea?
Never, he knows too much.

But from a few—Jesus,
He ought to poach hisself

A new frigging motor,
Besides, he takes chances.

3

Under the bridge, now north, but still in the channel,
Then south and west, up to the bar, before
The slack's at its full, waiting, rocking, waiting,

Then brilliant in sunlight—winds moderate north and west—
You cross over, the stern riding high,
The bow dipping, climbing the up-hill swells.
To the north, a few breakers, the bar rising into dunes.

4

The motor, you, or the erratic tug of the current?
A moment only, a nothing, yet down along your arm:

Came later the full horror
Clamped to the low stern,
One dead motor, dead
In the water, wind
Rising, night
And your idiot friend.

5

Was there a moon? We can't remember.
Glacial-cold the night-black swells.
Sensuous by day, gleaming, alive,
But treacherous at night, moon or not.

6

You were found sprawling backwards,
Deep as your waist in water,
Your left arm crooked, locked, strong
As a vice under the bench.

And the heavy, cold sour brine
In the half-swamped boat, the small black boat,
Sloshing like so much pig-iron.

7

I can see it: how when Old Red was clambering
The low gunwale, thinking he'd swim ashore,

The boat went over so fast you half-screeched
At a man so cold, damn is he stoned with it?

And you in the water too must find the boat
And right it, but now Jesus where's the gear?

What's to be done, nothing, but ride it out.
No way to make her take this sea bow-first?

8

The surf, now can you hear the surf
At Yachats? But Jesus again, the cliffs,
Where would you land? I know, I know:

Any steep shingle of gravel would do,
Even if waiting meant waiting for hours.

9

Did you kneel in the water? Then kneel and bail.
Washing, the water against your thighs, working,
But steadily until your hands and arms are raw:

The strong tides of feeling
Pulling away, leave you quiet,
Aroused—your head, heart
Prone on the distant swells,
Your feet anchored lightly
Deep inside the cove—

Waiting,
Your hands heavy as bells,
Waiting.

10

And the dream?
Did you dream
The one dream?

Of the young gulls
High in the crowns
Of the great oaks
In the morning
In the silence
This storm done
That drove them
Into the marsh
And your meadow
Under the trees.

11
Not now
Say to yourself
Not now
Though the long swells lull you lull you
Though they break your will with rocking
And the wind
Coming round and down
At last over your back
Rubs its icicle
Yellow beak
On your
Burning
Neck.

IV

For several years I have kept a journal. It's not an ordinary journal, not one of those intellectual and philosophical bookkeeping systems employed by some writers. I never write down anything from my reading, never reflections that could be construed as profound, never any details about my work at the university, seldom a word about my family or friends. I've dubbed it: "Storm Journal," and although I carry it back and forth with me to the coast, I don't use it when I am at home. Perhaps it's because nothing seems to happen to me at home, or here in the valley, or at the university. At least nothing significant. Of course, that needs qualification: I am devoted to my family, serious about my teaching, involved with my friends. But Seal Rock is unique. Things happen to me there which seem not to happen here.

One evening last winter, January 25 to be exact, I was alone at the cabin. I had driven over the day before in order to finish a small writing project. It had been a difficult month, starting a new quarter at school, fighting the gasoline lines in Eugene, taking care of our daughter. My wife had been gone for part of the month, helping her father close his year-end accounts at his lumber yard in Nebraska. It was cold in the valley, and I hate the cold. So I went alone to Seal Rock, to isolation and rain, and completed the writing chore. That morning and the night before we'd had a storm, winds gusting in the 40's, tons of rain. But that evening, the cloud-cover broke, the wind died down, the tide was out, the beach deserted. I took a walk. A lot of things happened in the half-mile down to the cove and back. Later, I sat down and wrote them out, as I have done many times, in their exact sequence.

from STORM JOURNAL

On the beach late before sunset. Cold and 15 knots WSW. On the
ebb tide. Paced it off, 150 yards, from the cliff to the surf.
A few pipers here and there feeding and 4 large ducks down in the
water this side of the big rocks. Much bobbing in the criss-cross
waves. Occasionally out of the water, flapping their wings, as though
about to take off. But one gull to the south black against the grey
and red tinted sky down at the cove this side of the towering headland,
climbing, wheeling, plummeting in and around the chunks of
foam whirling up under it.

The rocky beach exposed. Great slabs and boulders dug out of the
sand from the winter storms, the high tides. Some of them as big as
rooms or locomotives. Not there in the summer, except their tops.
How many carloads of sand must the sea pull out from around
them and back into the waves? Climbing over them, the great
boulders, it's the eye that sees and not the ear that hears the surf.
Now walking between them, around them, in and out. What colors?
Grey, some red and iron colors in layers. Some browns too. BUT
it's the great sheen on everything! The luminous milk-mercury
burnish of the reality of it all. And I am in it to my waist, the rocks all
around me shining, shining. I back away.

A great storm last week, following the floods inland, so that our beach
is strewn with trash. Stumps, roots, branches. Most of it raw, not
yet worked over, smoothed by the long journeys in the swells, the
surf, the years of drifting in and out. And a lot of bark, too,

tiny bits, at the tide line, covered with gritty foam. Higher up on the beach, of course, the large logs, smoothed, rounded, curving and they, too, are gleaming wet.

Turned south and came on a few small rocks tossed or rolled from below the cliff onto the great slabs. Walking up to them from the north in the fading light, they are sitting there like bowling balls. They have to be rounded, pretty much, to roll in the surf of the storm the 100 yards from below the bank where they normally lie. They seem out of place. The wave action not lifting them, I think, but rolling them down the beach, and down the little gulleys between the flat rocks, then into the surf and then back up and into the hollows when the sea retreats. BUT they do not shine. Dull, rounded. A kind of lumpish, doughy dull-not-burnished counterpoint to the reality on which they rest.

SO into the cove, not deep, but into it wary, like moving out of the skin of it all and into the center of a dark sound, my pulse breathing with ease, and the whole shine gone.

A couple of acres of ankle-deep foam churned up in the cove. It's blowing and skidding on a thin layer of water, back and forth. I bend and pick up a handful the size of a baseball and hold it in my palm. There are grains of sand suspended in it. I pluck them out, rolling them between my fingers, freeing them between my fingers.

This walking into it. This seeing in a profound way. Seeing the light as the only reality and as though for the first time. But it was the light around the great boulders, the unexpected. AND it came on me back there, mixed up with the sound of colors. Reflect. It is often when I am going along in a dull way (where anxiety is a kind of force out there in the sea, out there in the surf, or further out in the swells, but out there) that it happens when I begin my little ritual of the naming of colors. That's grey, I say. That is not grey, I say. But more than grey, a white grey, green grey, blue grey, rose grey—my little ritual—and then, and then it overtakes me. Not rising around my ankles or descending like a breezy halo, but at or on my shoulder. Like a high, strong surf, urgent, and running on my shoulder. Walking along.

How is it that we come across a poem? That's a question I keep asking in the journal, over and over, but indirectly. Bound up with that, however, is a more basic question of how we come to see things clearly (or feel them strongly) in the first place. I believe rather firmly that I have always begun with an act of true attention. If I look hard enough, the things of this world look back. There is reciprocity. Yet the transformation of the primal stuff into poems is puzzling to me. Do poems just happen? Yes and no. If I am lucky, or blessed, or in some way ready for them, they happen. But I do not squat on my haunches at Seal Rock waiting passively for lightning to strike. I can never stop being a poet; so in some respects my Seal Rock experiences are deliberately sought and just as consciously shaped. But these journal entries are not poetry. Some of them might, however, just might become poems.

HUNTING FOR "BLUES" IN THE RAIN

So it's *not* all piss ants in the rain after all
when the great agates roll up out of the surf
in and around the flat round stones and up our
long beach coming down hard on me is a fat old
woman in her rain gear black comes right through
sheet after bruising sheet of water like a Crone
through tough Fifth Avenue plate except this is
has got to be that other end of the continent you
better believe we are shattering more than glass
out here busting up more than silence plowing
into finding more than little "blues" in the rain.

WILLIAM HEYEN

WILLIAM HEYEN *(b. Nov. 1, 1940 in Brooklyn) was raised
with three brothers by German immigrant parents on Long
Island. He received his Ph.D. (dissertation on Theodore
Roethke) from Ohio University in 1967, and since then,
except for a year as a Fulbright Lecturer in American
Literature to Germany, has taught at the State University
of New York College at Brockport, where he is now
Professor of English.*

(Photo by Michael Chikiris)

What Do the Trees Say?

Sunday. I've come downstairs this morning with every intention of managing to write. An essay for *American Poets in 1976* has been hanging over my head. I've made some starts, but my roads have ended. I'm thinking of not including an essay of my own—I wouldn't be missed, and my presence, in fact, is likely to be uncomfortably conspicuous. But it's true that I don't want to be just the compiler of this book, just the one who wrote hundreds of letters clearing permissions and urging poets to contribute essays. I have a feeling, though, that if I don't work something out today, I won't manage an essay at all. The deadline for this book is closing in, and there's so much to do. If this does not turn into anything, I'll just have to smile and say thanks when my friends compliment me on my humility.

But it should be possible to begin and to finish. Rattling around in my head are Robert Duncan's thoughts on the possibilities of entering a *process*, Richard Wilbur's feeling that what he does in a poem is exhaust his present knowledge of a subject (why shouldn't I right now be able to exhaust my present sense of where I am?), Joyce Carol Oates as a poet and novelist taking her lines and sentences right up to where she is as she writes them. It should be possible for me to write for a few hours or all day, today, and to finish something that, for now, will stand and seem to be true. If I've labored over most of my poems, I have also experienced the poem that wrote itself quickly, as this one did, in a few minutes, just after I'd read John James Audubon's description of those passenger pigeons, now extinct, that once clouded our skies.

THE PIGEONS

Audubon watched the flocks beat by for days,
and tried, but could not count them:
their dung fell "like melting flakes of snow,"
the air buzzed until he lost his senses.

He heard, he said, their *coo-coo*
and *kee-kee* when they courted, and saw trees
of hundreds of nests, each cradling two
"broadly elliptical pure white eggs."

Over mast, they swept in "rich deep purple
circles," then roosted so thick that high limbs

cracked, and the pigeons avalanched
down the boughs, and had not room to fly,

and died by thousands. Kentucky farmers
fed their hogs on birds
knocked out of the air with poles. No net, stone,
arrow, or bullet could miss one,

so horses drew wagons of them,
and schooners sailed cargoes of them,
and locomotives pulled freight cars of them
to the cities where they sold for one cent each.

When you touched one, its soft
feathers fell away as easily as a puff
of dandelion seeds, and its delicate breast-
bone seemed to return the pulse of your thumb.

The thing is that I've realized that I'm happiest when I manage to write. For years I've wanted to be able to write many more poems than I do. Just what *is* my problem, if it is one? Why can't I write more easily? Is it the nature of poetry, or the dilemma of my own personality, or some false aesthetic that's been drummed into me, or what? Why can't I write? What has stopped me the past few weeks? Where is the flow, its source? I know that I've been trying to loosen up for the past couple of years, in fact the past five years. The prose memoir in *Noise in the Trees* is evidence, was an attempt on my part to *write* down what was on my mind and wouldn't come out in poems, wouldn't, wouldn't, no matter how hard or long I tried. Why shouldn't it be a simple thing, right now, to surround a few of my own poems with words about them, as I've asked the other contributors to this book to do? More things rattle against my brain right now, and I want them out: W. S. Merwin once saying that part of the pain in being a poet is the agony between poems when the poet can't imagine writing another poem and can't remember how he managed the last one; Theodore Roethke saying a poet's bad poems are his own worst enemies; Diane Wakoski saying she's as much interested in a poet's bad poems as she is in his good ones; William Stafford saying that maybe one of the problems is that most poets are afraid to write their bad poems, while he isn't; W. H. Auden saying that patience is the great virtue, and also saying that one attribute of the "major" poet is that he writes a great deal; Ginsberg's suspicion that academic poets have spent too much time trying to perfect a surface, trying to write anthology pieces. What the hell, I could go on for twenty pages of such confusions. Maybe this is the problem. Too much going on in my head, ten contradictions rising to the surface for everything I could say. Impossible even to put forward a tentative truth. Turn it off. Get rid of all traces of literature in your poems, said Dr. Williams. In a recent rock song the singer yells something like "after all the crap I've learned in high school / It's a wonder I can think at all." I have all of these notions *about* poetry in my head. . . . I would like to turn off, and write, and not worry about what sixty-five other people have said or will say about what I'm writing. And why not? One life. Those things are in my head, and have been as helpful as they will be, and there were hundreds of literally sleepless nights years ago when I worried over *ars poetica*, and there is this other dimension, now, of a deadline and grass to mow and a friend coming home from the hospital tomorrow and letters to write and continuing nervousness over my son's slowly healing broken leg. But why shouldn't I write?

It is a clear and beautiful morning in Brockport. The sun shines autumn-gold through a window over my left shoulder onto this sheet of paper. . . . There, it happened, again: the oldest trick, or virtue, or habit of my mind, this switch thrown, when trapped or confused, to the sun and trees and grass and animals. Because the outer world is balanced for all contingencies, as Whitman said. When I've been stuck in a poem I've asked, so to speak, "What do the trees say?" It occurs to me that if I knew, for sure, I could write much more. Or could I? Yes, I think so, even though it would seem that in a mysterious world the possibilities for poems would be endless. But, yes, if I knew what the trees said, meant, were, I could write more, words based on a truth. No, I'm not sure, and don't want to go around lamenting my lost myths. In any case, something to explore, now, a place to begin past this old quicksand of writing about not being able to write. Whitman, the trees, a truth that recedes and mystifies. This essay beginning to take a kind of shape, happening like this. I feel fine. Here is a poem a year or two old.

OAK AUTUMN

Strict
as dry brush or
a steel engraving of
reeds, cattails, cracked
pods, it is pure
of limb, lifts blades

of lines, is limned
of cuts, this
oak of one windless
instant of late
autumn, only
sun in its branches, not
a gauze or shimmer or
web of sunlight but
sun that etches bark to black
shine, only
spare branches sharp
in the air, austere
trunk, no
sky, no
horizon to mention, an un-
remarkable brown
field over which
the rise of this
uncluttered
life.

I've just written "Oak Autumn" out, and still sort of like the way
its lines fall. Uncharacteristic, for me, short lines, ending in weak words
like "or" and "but." Thin. And written, no doubt, out of the anxieties
I have just described and the leap to the outer world, the "uncluttered
life." I made an attempt to image a spareness and sharpness that I enjoyed years ago doing india-ink scratchings of pods and cattails in an
art class, that I have enjoyed since in oriental drawings, and I have
tried to catch a bare black shining sunlight, the black shine meaning
much to me in many poems. I think, as the hard-line new critics roll over
in their graves, of a certain life of grace and earnestness when I think
of this poem. I think of Robert Bly's and Lucien Stryk's and William
Stafford's and Richard Wilbur's lives as I imagine their lives to be, of
John Ciardi's lines from "I Marry You": "Why should I bother / the
flies about me? Let them buzz and do," of Thoreau saying we are possessed by our possessions, of Emerson saying that the real man can keep
to himself even in the turmoil of a crowd, of this tree in one windless
instant being exactly what it is, perfect and easeful. The poem, to move
closer to it than I have as I've just indulged myself, speaks toward the
idea of a life that shucks off, sheds, cuts through entanglements, reaches

past the state of constantly becoming. A tree, rooted, reaching, but being still at the same time. The poem, of course, focuses on only one part of the tree's nature, only one side of the speaker's desire. And it *is* a poem about the speaker's desire. He admires the tree's purity, its aspect in air, even its solitariness; he connects, come to think of it, its solitariness with its "uncluttered life." But, whatever I could say now, . however I could at this moment read the poem, I'm outside of where I was when I wrote it. The poem catches the tree in its present, and is content to leave it there, if this is possible in any poem even suggesting a season. In any case, within a day or two of finishing this poem, I had written another.

OAK SPRING

Does not resist
its own leaves. These
appear, as easily as
snow, when winter snows,
or rain, when the sky rains,
or all the birds
it is always blind to.
But this blossoming, this
fulfillment, this
green explosion
every year of even its old age,
this different dimension
of miracle: snow, rain, birds,
yes, but imagine
all the sap of your own
wooden body beginning
to warm, your skin
breaking to bud and leaf;
imagine, coming
to everything you are,
without second, or third, or fourth,
or fifth thoughts
that each time you utter
this language of tongues,
you're living closer
to your last spring.

"Does not resist / its own leaves." (But just what *are* a particular human being's true leaves?) Another message made of oak, another of the mother's multitudinous natures, a kind of contradiction to "Oak Autumn" which insisted, at least on one level, on isolating an instant the speaker wished to emulate. "Does not resist / its own leaves." This, too. The speech of leaves without fifth thoughts—all the play is in the fifth one, as Frost wrote of Robinson. The poem says that the tree becomes what it is from within as easily as it is acted upon from without. Death appears here, at the end, a kind of monkey-wrench. I can think of several ways the poem engages it, its relevance to these two verbal constructs called poems. Thoreau once said that were he ever to meet a man who was truly alive, fully awake, he would not be able to look up into that man's flashing eyes. Death, the idea and knowledge of death, so often regulates our actions, internalizes us, but the oak goes on uttering the languages of tongues it does not even know it knows or, at least, that we do not understand, or have to understand. Two poems almost advocating, or at least imaging two different lives.

I want to mention that now, distant from the conception of the poem and, hopefully, objective about it, I think about it in ways that did not occur to me as I wrote it. There is so much going on at the end of "The Pigeons," for example—all sorts of reverberations that, I think, rise to me now, after the fact of the poem. I become a different reader every time I go through it. Robert Frost has zeroed in on what for me is the greatest pleasure in writing a poem and having it, for the rest of my life, to read: "Read it a hundred times: it will forever keep its freshness as a metal keeps its fragrance. It can never lose its sense of a meaning that once unfolded by surprise as it went." Egotism may be sneaking in here. This may be a selfish pleasure, but if it is, it is in part a defense against the essential loneliness of writing poems. I'll never have an audience of even fifty people who truly care about my poems. And since, surely, there is no one way to write, all I can hope to do is to write poems that please *me*, but in *truth* please me—sometimes I fool myself about this for years. Should you come, too, that would be gravy. But because of the relativity of excellence, I most want to write a poem I can myself take pleasure in, can feel and smell differently each time. And sometimes I have. I write to learn what I know, the act of writing being a learning process—one of my shortest poems goes: "A lizard can tongue its own eye, / wash it clean, and so can I" ("The tongue is an eye," said Stevens, and Williams once asked his nose, "must you taste everything? / Must you know everything?"). And I read what I have written to learn more of what I didn't know I knew and felt.

"Oak Autumn" and "Oak Spring" are not connected to a place, particularly, unless it is that place, not at all a field, in my mind where a white oak grew beside our garage in Nesconset on Long Island when I was a boy. I know that, as I wrote the poems, in the back of my own images and standing out clearly was Walt Whitman's oak in "I Saw in Louisiana a Live-Oak Growing." You know that poem's beauty and tenderness, and how Whitman's tree stood in his memory "uttering joyous leaves of dark green." He tells us that he broke off a twig from the oak and later placed it in sight in his room to remind him of his friends. It made him think of "manly love," as he says, and I will never be able to read my own two poems without thinking of him. "This language of tongues" flips back to him, I'm sure, but is he otherwise present in my two trees? I don't think so. But this is the way a beloved poet and poem give of themselves for so long—in this case I knew this poem from grade school—and so subtly, once we have made them a part of our lives. I have carried that pristine image of an oak "solitary in a wide flat space" with me for all these years. The "message" of Whitman's poem, his realization that he could never live as an *isolato*, without love, and be joyous, slants toward "Oak Spring," perhaps; at the same time, his vision of the divine human family never disavows completely the possibility that one man can stand by himself, possession-less and free, unencumbered. Whitman does not answer for me, nor should he, any of the questions implicit in "Oak Autumn" and "Oak Spring."

It seems to me that so many of my poems grow out of these same poles, these tensions. What kind of life can I, should I, must I lead? I sense a tentativeness about the mind of my poems as it moves from subject to subject. I've just noticed that I've talked about my two poems, in fact, in an order different from their order in *Noise in the Trees*, which provides a different sort of last word. If there is assertion in my poems, surety, the poems usually come to it carefully. This is a simple thing to say: I don't know what the world is, or means, if it means any-thing. But a poem creates a world, says the cliché. It does. It builds, from its first lines, on the assumptions of its own language. And, if it is a good poem, it convinces and satisfies, if not forever, then until our next reading of it. No danger here, unless we are readers with only one poem, writers who write poems of only one kind of knowledge. "Oak Autumn" and "Oak Spring" turn against one another. At the same time, of course, both poems are about the same oak, living its one life in time. "And everything comes to One," says Roethke, "As we dance on, dance on, dance on."

This is the way it will always be for me, I believe. I'll always lean eleven ways at once. It may be that my deepest self is convinced of a few things, but I'll always be enamored of the words "and" and "but" and "maybe." I think now of a poem called "Providence," in which I've tried to imagine what it would be like to hold a different kind of knowledge, an almost cellular emotional Truth about the world, the Truth that William Bradford knew and maybe had to know as the pilgrims survived their new world as best they could.

PROVIDENCE

Knowledge as sure to him as his name:
Bradford knows, as he looks back,
that God deflected the Indians' first arrows,
that God's "sweet and gentle showers"
spared the corn, that God's voice
echoed as though from a dream
to save the burning storehouse.
How could they otherwise have lived,
these, the chosen?—
eleven heads of households,
four wives, six young men, a handful
of children still alive at Governor William's
first of thirty elections.
These would descend to the land,
to fifty-pound pumpkins
to heft to their shoulders,
to whole trotlines of bullheads
pulled from the terrible swift rivers,
to turkeys with six-foot wingspreads,
to the myriad shellfish of the shores.

The cruel sailor who cursed them:
the first struck down
and pitched over the side.
Proof. How else could Samoset have risen
from the woods to speak to them in English?

> Evidence. Knowledge as certain
> as God's people, here, in His land,
> where they would *live*,
> and be useful with their backs,
> and look up to the Lord of the Air
> for sunlight when they needed sunlight
> to pray by. They all knew,
> and this knowledge never
> splintered off from a man,
> or cut him in half,
> or got lost angling to nowhere. The immediate
> odor of a rose, of Sharon's Rose:
> succor this sweet, knowledge this sure.
> O, Father, as he writes,
> the Governor's body blossoms only with Thee.

Bradford was among the chosen, he *knew*—elect, helping govern a chosen people as they marked time in God's service before entering the kingdom of heaven. What happened in the world was never accident, blind force, luck. It was as though God had stocked this wilderness for them, made for them a world of terror and beauty, flame and showers. All the doors of nature are opened with keys that have never slipped from Bradford's grasp. "And this knowledge never / splintered off from a man, / or cut him in half." The speaker of my poem, I think, is awed by the way the Governor orders the world. To Bradford, as it does so strictly for Jonathan Edwards, the world reveals the singular plan. The world is essentially allegorical sign, not symbol. He has made all the circle he needs to live his life. And Bradford's mind is true and beautiful in its own right. But the condition of our time is to enter, again and again, the outer world and to see what it yields. Sometimes frustration, or irony, as in Wallace Stevens's "Meditations of a Magnifico," whose speaker tries out several possible realities only to be thrust back to what he has and knows for sure: "The first white wall of the village . . . / The fruit-trees. . . ." Death for Stevens is "the the," the "vital, arrogant, fatal, dominant X," as he says in "The Motive for Metaphor." His very survival depends *ad infinitum* on the apprehension of objects, first, and then on an imaginative and ordered consideration of them. This birth and slippage and rebirth of possibilities is one of the miracles of poetry. Recall the sixth section of "Song of Myself":

A child said *What is the grass?* fetching it to me with full
      hands;
How could I answer the child? I do not know what it is
      any more than he.

I guess it must be the flag of my disposition, out of
      hopeful green stuff woven.

Or I guess it is the handkerchief of the Lord,
A scented gift and remembrancer designedly dropt,
Bearing the owner's name someway in the corners, that we
      may see and remark, and say *Whose?*

Or I guess the grass is itself a child, the produced
      babe of the vegetation.

Or I guess it is a uniform hieroglyphic,
And it means, Sprouting alike in broad zones and narrow
      zones,
Growing among black folks as among white,
Kanuck, Tuckahoe, Congressman, Cuff, I give them the same,
      I receive them the same.

And now it seems to me the beautiful uncut hair of graves.

Tenderly will I use you curling grass,
It may be you transpire from the breasts of young men,
It may be if I had known them I would have loved them,
It may be you are from old people, or from offspring
      taken soon out of their mothers' laps.

And here you are the mothers' laps.

This grass is very dark to be from the white heads of old
      mothers,
Darker than the colorless beards of old men,
Dark to come from under the faint red roofs of mouths.

O I perceive after all so many uttering tongues,
And I perceive they do not come from the roofs of mouths
      for nothing.

I wish I could translate the hints about the dead young men
      and women,
And the hints about old men and mothers, and the offspring
      taken soon out of their laps.

What do you think has become of the young and old men?
And what do you think has become of the women and
    children?

They are alive and well somewhere,
The smallest sprout shows there is really no death,
And if ever there was it led forward life, and does not
    wait at the end to arrest it,
And ceas'd the moment life appear'd.

All goes onward and outward, nothing collapses,
And to die is different from what any one supposed, and
    luckier.

All these things, all. "The flag of my disposition." A poetry of inclusion, rather than exclusion. A vision of inclusion, rather than exclusion. The filaments are thrown outward, tentative and testing, the world in its miraculous garb, its constant change, enough to stagger sextillions of infidels. And when no explanations, theories, quite suffice, or continue to suffice, back again to the image, the specific, the particular. In "Wales Visitation" Ginsberg enters a cosmos of meaning and concludes: "What did I notice? Particulars! The / vision of the great One is myriad." The last line of this beautiful poem is "upward in motion with wet wind." Not the poem that turns constantly in upon a knowledge held like a habit, but Stevens's "never resting mind" whose paradise is imperfection itself. This is one of the reasons Williams's red wheelbarrow is so important: as object, as thing to engage the mind, it is always there, it is matter. Perhaps the steps are sight, speech, awe, and silence. "Revision," speech again, wonder and silence again, looking up in perfect silence at the stars again, as Whitman said, the poet's art not to chart, but to voyage. Nature itself is the Zen master who sends us back day after day for as long as we live to study perhaps one inexhaustible leaf or sound or angle of sunlight.

And nature sends us back, in our time, not only to God, but to ourselves. "Our language has no term that can isolate distinctly and gather into one word the total numinous impression a thing may make on the mind," wrote Rudolf Otto. I have used his words to serve as a sort of ironic epigraph for this poem:

THE NUMINOUS

We are walking a sidewalk
in a German city.
We are watching gray smoke
gutter along the roofs
just as it must have
from other terrible chimneys.
We are walking our way
almost into a trance.

We are walking our way
almost into a dream
only those with blue
numbers along their wrists
can truly imagine.

Now, just in front of us, something
bursts into the air.
For a few moments,
our bodies echo fear.
Pigeons, we say,
only an explosion
of beautiful blue-gray pigeons.
Only pigeons that gather
over the buildings
and begin to circle.

We are walking again, counting
all the red poinsettias
between the windowpanes
and lace curtains.
It was only
a flock of pigeons:
we can still see them
circling over the block buildings,
a hundred hearts
beating in the air.
Beautiful blue-gray pigeons.
We will always remember.

This, too: one day a couple of years ago my wife and I drove to Bergen-Belsen, in northern Germany. Walking that camp was a frightening experience. We would never be the same. It may be that today, with our knowledge, none of us can enter totally or even partially for very long the transcendentalist's faith in the beneficence of man, God, the world that Whitman felt. Otto's sentence is from *Das Heilige*, the holy. The idea of the total numinous impression of a thing reaches toward the idea of the glory of God within all objects, bottomless, endless, mysterious. But as my wife and I walked the sidewalks of a German city, Hanover, one day a month or so after our experience at the camp, and those beautiful pigeons burst into the air in front of us, we stopped in our tracks, shocked and afraid. My own emotion was complex, had been building up. It was not just surprise. It was fear. Belsen entered the pigeons' wingbeats, as it entered for me the poinsettias and lace curtains. Whitman's war was fought for a great dream. Belsen is pure atrocity and nightmare. But the point is that the whole world is still there in Whitman's blade of grass, William Blake's worm and grain of sand. The total numinous impression of those beautiful pigeons. A hundred hearts beating in the air. Six million hearts beating in the air. Sight, emotion, speech, silence. What do the trees say?

In this next poem the world does not burst in upon the speaker. He waits, riding the boat of the unconscious, for a sign.

THE RETURN

"I will touch things and things and no more thoughts."
Robinson Jeffers

My boat slowed on the still water,
stopped in a thatch of lilies.
The moon leaned over the white lilies.

I waited for a sign, and stared
at the hooded water. On the far shore
brush broke, a deer broke cover.

I waited for a sign, and waited.
The moon lit the lilies to candles.
Their light reached down the water

to a dark flame, a fish: it hovered
under the pads, the pond held it
in its dim depths as though in amber.

Green, still, balanced in its own life,
breathing small breaths of light, this
was the world's oldest wonder, the arrow

of thought, the branch that all words
break against, the deep fire, the pure poise
of an object, the pond's presence, the pike.

"The world's oldest wonder" was "the world's single wonder" in draft, so strongly do I feel about the necessity of staring—it is harder, now that I am getting older, to *see*—, so much do I want to eschew talk and make a language that images and deepens the world as precisely as language can, so convinced am I that the best poems from "Sir Patric Spens" to Ginsberg's "Sunflower Sutra" to Archibald MacLeish's "Companions" begin with the gold combs and battered crowns and evening grasses our senses must always know. Jeffers once told an aspirer that the young man had enough soul in his poems and needed *body*. "The Return" does not freeze that fish by naming it, does not for long explain the world, does not end the waiting and searching for signs any more than one of my oak poems does. But I am glad that the pike rose to me as I fished that poem. . . . A title for all this to be imposed, maybe tomorrow. . . . For now, again, with thanks, silence.

Sept. 15, 1974

RICHARD HUGO

RICHARD HUGO *(b. 1923 in Seattle, Wash.) received his B.A. and M.A. degrees from the University of Washington. He worked for the Boeing Company in Seattle for thirteen years before beginning his teaching career. He has recently directed the creative writing programs at the University of Montana and the University of Colorado. "The Real West Marginal Way" is part of an autobiography in progress.*

(Photo by William Stafford)

The Real West Marginal Way

My grandparents raised five children and had known little other than a life of hard work. They must have been worn when my teen-age mother left me with them. They were well into their fifties by then and I was less than two. I was to grow up with far more freedom than most boys, but with little guidance or attention.

Ours was the only house on the west side of 15th Avenue S.W. in Seattle, and by the time I was five I was spending long parts of the day wandering alone in the woods on either side of our yard. I played for hours in the willow and alder trees, or sailed sticks on rain ponds until Grandmother called me to dinner. I fantasized the sticks into boats, battleships, and destroyers. One of my favorite games was trying to cross the woods north to Barton Street or south to Cambridge Street through the trees without touching the ground. When I had to step briefly on the stiff-stemmed salal bushes to reach the next tree, I didn't count that as touching ground on the technicality that my foot hadn't made contact with the earth itself.

My grandparents kept busy until the hours after dinner when they sat in hard straight-back chairs in the kitchen, often with heads bowed, staring silently at the floor. I would sit at the table with nothing to do and watch them. When Grandfather was not at his menial job at the Seattle Gas Company on Lake Union across town, he was often piling a load of slivery stove wood against the house or spading the vegetable garden. Grandmother spent long hours hoeing the garden, feeding the chickens, collecting the eggs, canning fruits and preserves.

I was left alone to play. As I grew older I was not asked to help, not even to bring an occasional armload of wood to the woodbox on the back porch. We used the kitchen stove both for cooking and to heat the house. I roamed farther as I grew older, first to Longfellow Creek, a mile away, and later to Salmon Creek, two miles away. I caught small trout in those tiny creeks. Sometimes I went with other boys in the neighborhood, and often I went alone.

Bored with play, I would climb onto the roof. It was a great view and I loved the windy days when I could watch the gray-white clouds pour north, and the dramatic Olympic range far to the west. On the Fourth of July I would sit alone up there in the night and watch roman candles and skyrockets flare and break into bouquets of stars.

Some days I would stare out the window of our front door. The front door was usually locked. We came and went through the back and when neighbors came to visit they came to the back door. When we heard a knock on the front door we knew it was a salesman or one of the religious fanatics come to sell us faith and salvation.

From the windows in front, I could see the dirt road we lived on, 15th Avenue S.W., the vacant lot across the street where we played neighborhood ball games, the Noraine home on 14th with Mrs. Noraine's beautiful flower garden. At 14th, the ground rose rapidly and 13th was on top of a hill. That was our eastern horizon, two blocks away. We called it First Hill. Four hills lay immediately east of us and we called them by number. Some days I explored east to Fourth Hill, about a mile away. From Fourth Hill, I could see the nation begin to extend, the wide green valley below, the dark green foothills of the Cascades beyond the valley and beyond them the blue-white Cascade mountains themselves. Perhaps due to my superstitious grandmother (red in the west, sailors like best), directions took on special meanings in my imagination. East meant knowledge and wisdom. How intelligent people must be in Chicago, Pittsburgh, New York. I've never gotten over that prejudice completely. To this day when I'm in New York, I have the notion that everyone I see is very intelligent.

My mother remarried when I was four and during the next few years when she and my stepfather came to visit, they often ended the evening playing cards with my grandparents. It was men versus women. Sometimes my mother would lose her temper as she became too involved in the game and my stepfather would try to calm her. Once Grandmother implied the men were cheating. Another time she started what turned out to be a long discussion of whether playing cards on Sunday was permissible.

I was pleased when my grandparents asked me to go to White Center for a pint of ice cream. I loved ice cream and I felt I was contributing something, being a part of the family. I ran out the back door, across the hard dirt walk between two plots of garden and through the woods on the dirt path to 16th, then the block and a half south to Bill Gagnon's drug store in the White Center business district. We had no refrigerator and to make sure the ice cream was solid when I handed it to Grandmother, I ran back fast as I could. She divided the ice cream into three equal pieces and we would sit in the kitchen and eat without speaking under the bare light bulb burning at the end of the cord hanging from the ceiling.

A zodiac calendar hung on the wall of Mr. Husted's barber shop at 16th and Henderson, a couple of blocks away. When Grandfather took me there for a haircut, I sat fascinated by one picture on the calendar, a color drawing of a desert with a crescent moon in a pale blue sky, a lone camel, one palm tree, one pyramid, no people. The hum of Mr. Husted's clipper seduced me into dreams of Egypt as I stared at that scene. Other lands were pictured but that one captivated me. The calendar remained on the wall for years, and Egypt stayed vivid in me as it faded year after year on the aging paper.

By the time I was nine or ten, I started fishing in the Duwamish Slough, sometimes alone, sometimes with chums from White Center. We walked east over to 9th, then a mile north to the top of Boeing Hill, then another near mile down the steep hill to where West Marginal Way intersected it at the base, and where the slough filled to the brim of the grassy banks on the intide backup from the bay and emptied to puddles and a trickle six hours later when the out-tide drained the murky water. What fishing. Porgies, shiners we called them, were so thick in that slough that we continued to catch them out of puddles in the mud flats following the out-tide drain. Sometimes we found a bloated dog in the mud, a gunnysack of rocks tied to its neck, and once I found a gunnysack filled with rocks and inflated staring kittens.

I remember we used to express regret we'd come, at the end of the day, when we faced that climb up Seattle's longest hill. But a few days later that was forgotten when with telescopic steel rods and worms, we went back, thinking about all those shiners.

A dilapidated shingle mill stood beside the slough where we fished. The metal screen on the teepee burner was rusted and when the mill was in operation the fresh odor of sawdust hung over the slough. I remember men stripped to the waist waving cheerfully, a huge whirring buzzsaw and the scream as the blade bit into a large log. A cat lived in the mill, a mascot of the mill crew I suppose, though I remember him still there when the mill was shut down. He was so tough, when he got hungry he would dive into the slough and catch a shiner. I felt lucky to know the only cat in the world who caught his own fish.

West Marginal Way bridged the slough just south of the foot of Boeing Hill, a few yards beyond the grassy bank where we fished near the sawmill. Someone, probably the mill crew, had built an outhouse under the bridge and sometimes we fished through the toilet down into the water several feet below. It made no difference. Shiners nibbled wherever we fished.

Back beyond the bridge was an abandoned brickmill, a large, low, red brick building. When we were bored with fishing, we went inside. The low arched doorways that a grown man had to hunch down to get through, let only a little light inside and it spent itself fast. It wasn't much fun knocking about the thick cold ovens in the dark and we soon got out.

Although West Marginal Way runs south for several miles, the West Marginal Way in my mind was the two miles of it that ran north from the slough to Riverside on Spokane Street, paralleling the Duwamish River down close to the mouth.

Around the time I started fishing the slough, my grandparents had a cement basement built. The house was propped on blocks, the basement dug and cemented, and the house set back down. That basement became another private playground. For hours at a time I rollerskated alone on the smooth floor. I kept my collection of bottlecaps there in a gunnysack. I had no interest in single rarities, only in volume. I collected hundreds of Nesbitt Orange caps and hundreds of Coca Colas. Others in lesser but substantial numbers: Royal Crown, Lemon Lime, Creme Soda, Strawberry Soda, Root Beer. Sometimes I imagined a contest on between Nesbitt Orange and Coca Cola and took a count to see who was ahead. The color picture of the Statue of Liberty that had hung upstairs had ended up in the basement. It was a vertically oblong oval frame, and using it as a model I would build a Statue of Liberty flat on the basement floor with my bottlecaps. Sometimes I'd use the Nesbitt Orange caps for the base and sometimes I'd use Coca Colas. Whichever I used for the base, I used the other for the clothed part of Miss Liberty's body. Then I arranged other colors and designs for the bare arms, hands and face, the Torch of Freedom, the crown. When I had the Statue of Liberty finished, I never showed it to anyone. I studied it for a few minutes, enjoying a sense of accomplishment. Then I destroyed it, swept the caps into a dustpan and poured them back into the gunnysack.

I first became aware of Riverside as a community when I was thirteen, starting high school. Getting to West Seattle High School from White Center involved a bus ride to Riverside at Spokane Street and a transfer there to a west bound street car. Sometimes a wait was necessary at Riverside, especially coming home. Bus service to White Center has always been wretched. Going home I would wait at the bus stop in the rundown grocery owned by two Greeks. Some of the merchandise had been there for years, dust-caked cellophane packs of peanuts and candy, canned food from firms no longer in business. But there was a soda fountain and with so much traffic coming and going, I suppose the Greeks did pretty well.

West Marginal Way started south from there, first down a slight hill. A cinder walk paralleled it down to the Riverside community at the bottom of the hill. Although the village was made up of drab frame homes, in layout it was more European than any other community in Seattle. The houses seemed jammed together giving the total village some definition. Some houses were flush against West Marginal Way with no yard separating them from the cars that passed a few feet away. Homes huddled and climbed the east side of Pigeon Hill up into alders and ivy, some of the higher houses on stilts with long steep wooden stairways leading up to the porches. Many immigrants lived there and the names were exotic: Vokov, Zuvela, Zitkovitch. The place always seemed beautiful to me. A big field covered by sawdust lay east between West Marginal Way and the Duwamish River where Riverside boys fished for cod.

Following is the first of several Duwamish River poems I wrote years later. I remember the idea of the drunk man walking down the cinder path from Spokane Street to Riverside was the first image that occurred to me when I started the poem, though he doesn't appear until the third stanza. It is one of the first poems I published, and was written eleven or twelve years before my first book was accepted for publication.

WEST MARGINAL WAY

One tug pounds to haul an afternoon
of logs up river. The shade
of Pigeon Hill across the bulges
in the concrete crawls on reeds
in a short field, cools a pier
and the violence of young men
after cod. The crackpot chapel
with a sign erased by rain, returned
before to calm and a mossed roof.

A dim wind blows the roses
growing where they please. Lawns
are wild and lots are undefined
as if the payment made in cash
were counted then and there.

These names on boxes will return
with salmon money in the fall,
come drunk down the cinder arrow
of a trail, past the store of Popich,
sawdust piles and the saw mill
bombing air with optimistic sparks,
blinding gravel pits and the brickyard
baking, to wives who taught themselves
the casual thirst of many summers
wet in heat and taken by the sea.

Some places are forever afternoon.
Across the road and a short field
there is the river, split and yellow
and this far down affected by the tide.

I tend to believe whatever anyone tells me, and as I got to know some of the boys from Riverside I didn't for a moment doubt the stories they told me about the people there. The Greeks who distrusted banks and kept huge amounts of cash in their houses. The Slavs who bought cheap bourbon in the liquor store, then mixed it with pieces of raw fruit in mason jars which they put on their roofs all summer for the sun to work on. The results were said to be staggering. Succulent dishes the immigrant women prepared with eels, cod, and sole the river provided. John Honyori, the Greek fisherman recluse with legend strength, who singlehandedly lifted the rear end of a Model A Ford and pulled the car from a ditch. He killed a bear in Alaska with his hands. When two robbers jumped him under the Spokane Street Bridge and split his head with a lead pipe, he beat them so savagely that the police put him, as well as them, in jail. When his cell was left unguarded, he spread the bars apart with his hands and walked out. I hoarded these stories and many years later they were available for poems.

BETWEEN THE BRIDGES

These shacks are tricks. A simple smoke
from wood stoves, hanging half-afraid
to rise, makes poverty in winter real.
Behind unpainted doors, old Greeks
are counting money with their arms.
Different birds collect for crumbs

each winter. The loners don't
but ought to wear red shawls.

Here, a cracked brown hump
of knuckle caved a robber's skull.
That cut fruit is for Slavic booze.
Jars of fruit-spiked bourbon bake
on roofs throughout July; festive tubs
of vegetables get wiser in the sun.
All men are strong. Each woman knows
how river cod can be preserved.

Money is for life. Let the money
pile up thirty years and more.
Not in banks, but here, in shacks
where green is real: the stacks of tens
and twenties and the moss on broken piles
big ships tied to when the river
and the birds ran painted to the sea.

On the other side of Pigeon Hill, the west side, was Youngstown
where many of the Riverside residents worked in the Bethlehem Steel
Mill, and where the children went to grammar school. In White Center,
those of us who lived inside Seattle city limits attended Highland Park
Grammar School.

The boys of Youngstown-Riverside and the boys of White Center
shared at least one concern. Many of us felt socially inferior to the people
of West Seattle. There, directly west of Youngstown, sat the castle, the
hill, West Seattle where we would go to high school. What a middle class
paradise. The streets were paved, the homes elegant, the girls well
groomed and simply by virtue of living in West Seattle, far more beautiful and desirable than the girls in our home districts. Gentility and
confidence reigned on that hill. West Seattle was not a district. It was an
ideal. To be accepted there meant one had become a better person. West
Seattle was too far to be seen from White Center, but for the children of
Youngstown and Riverside, it towered over the sources of felt debase-
ment: the filthy, loud belching steel mill, the oily slow river, the immigrants hanging on to their odd ways, Indians drunk in the unswept
taverns, the commercial fishermen, tugboat workers and mill workers
with their coarse manners.

In many minds, White Center was no better. When people from White Center applied for work in the '20s and '30s, they seldom mentioned White Center, either in the interview or on the application form. The smart ones said they lived in West Seattle. White Center had the reputation of being just outside the boundary of the civilized world.

The reputation was not without reason. White Center was tough. Roxbury Street, the south city limit of Seattle, splits White Center and following repeal of prohibition drinking laws were more lenient outside the city. Just south of Roxbury the taverns flourished and people from miles around came to White Center for a good time, and a good time often involved a good brawl. The reputation went back far before the repeal of prohibition I know, but it was compounded by the unusual numbers of joints that sprang up in White Center in the early '30s.

When I was fourteen, I went often at night to the roller rink, not to skate but to wait for a fight to start. Fights started in the rink, usually on the pretext of an imagined insult or a slight affront, and they ended outside with someone bloody and senseless in the gravel. I had my heroes, Bill Gavin, Tommy Silverthorn. I was too frightened to fight but I idolized those tough guys.

The first time I saw Bill Gavin was at Youngstown where he lived. I was thirteen at the time, playing end on a neighborhood football team from Highland Park. Since many of the players were older, some of them sixteen and seventeen, I was mostly getting out of the way, though I was a good place kicker and kicked off and tried the extra points. After the game a fight started. One of our players, Willard Purvis, started punching one of their players, Bill Gavin, in the face. Purvis threw his best shots, roundhouse lefts and rights. He must have hit Gavin six times as hard as he could right in the chops and all Gavin did was stand there and glower. Purvis might as well have been slugging ingots in the steel mill nearby. When he realized the futility of his fists he started to turn white and retreat. Gavin had ended the fight simply by glowering. What a man, I thought. Within a year he was spending his evenings in White Center, one of the toughs I admired. I thought him super masculine, and in high school, where he was in an English class with me, three or four years older than the rest of us and soon to flunk out for good, his weakness as a student didn't mar the heroic image I'd made of him. Not one bit.

Twenty years later, when I imagined myself along the river, I found I wrote in direct, hard language. I believe now that unconsciously I felt that for the duration of the poem, I was as tough as I'd wanted to be in real life.

DUWAMISH NO. 2

Mudhens, cormorants and teals take
legal sanctuary in the reeds,
birds and reeds one grey. The river
when the backed-up tide lets go
flows the only north the birds believe.
North is easy. North is never love.

On the west hill, rich with a million
alders and five hundred modern homes,
birds, deep in black, insist the wind
will find the sea. The river points
the wrong way on the in-tide
and the alders lean to the arid south.

Take away all water. Men are oiling
guns beside ripped cows. Wrens have claws
and clouds cascade with poison down
a cliff mapped badly by an Indian.
Tumbleweeds are plotting to stampede.
Where there is no river, pregnant
twice a day with tide, and twice each day
released by a stroking moon,
animals are dangerous as men.

When the world hurts, I come back alone
along the river, certain the salt
of vague eyes makes me ready for the sea.
And the river says: you're not unique—
learn now there is one direction only—
north, and, though terror to believe,
quickly found by river and never love.

At least the last stanza demonstrates a tough way of addressing myself.
Those "vague eyes" I wanted to escape were the eyes of nineteenth-
century sentimentality I'd inherited from my grandparents. In the third
stanza, the river seems a kind of protection against a brutal world I felt
I could not live in and survive.

I know what north means. In Seattle the usual flow is north. Winds
are usually from the south. Clouds go north. Trees and grass bend north.
Big ships leaving port sail north to exit from Puget Sound through the

Straits of Juan de Fuca. The Duwamish river flows north. Longfellow Creek, the first creek I ever saw or fished, flows north. As a child, I believed life was a northern journey and at some unknown point in the north, all things end. The river found acceptance in the sea. Clouds died and were laid to rest with some dignity peculiar to clouds.

Don and Ray Crouse lived on West Marginal Way, a half mile or so upstream from Riverside. Youngstown had no Park League baseball team, and Don and Ray used to come to Highland Park to play on ours. They even came for practice despite the long trip, which they often covered on foot. Ray played first, Don shortstop, and both were good ballplayers. When they appeared, I felt our team had filled out to ultimate strength. Later Don and I played American Legion and High School ball together.

Don owned a boat, and a motor which he'd won in a salmon derby, and in the fall he invited me salmon fishing. Morning, around 4, I caught the first bus from White Center to Riverside, then walked through the hard dark autumn morning down the hill and along West Marginal Way to Don's house. From there we crossed the road and a field to where Don's boat was tied in the reeds. I'd never been salmon fishing before but Don had plenty of tackle and we putted downriver to the bay. The river was steaming fog that morning and dawn lit the fog until it was blinding pink. The river was alive with salmon. They rolled and splashed everywhere. I could hear them through the pink diffused glare and some I could see, huge shadows that rolled the air and slipped back into the water so close I could have touched them with one of the rods. It seemed impossible that we could fail to catch a fish, but we caught nothing. We trolled the bay for hours and gave up. The salmon surfaced close around us and everywhere I looked after the fog burned away, but none took our plugs. The motor gave up too and the out-tide was pouring down the river. I tried rowing but made no headway. Don took over and with patient relentless strokes took us home. Years later when he had become a commercial fisherman, we chanced to meet and I noticed his arms were now enormous. I thought of the day he'd made that long tortuous row.

Another day I visited Don, he took me to a bird refuge. At high tide it was an island, but not after the out-tide drained the water from the channels next to the mainland. Don brought his shotgun and we walked through the reeds and tall grasses where grebes, teals, ducks, pigeons, doves and other fowl were nesting or catching a nap. Don shot a few birds and carried them in plain sight home along West Marginal Way.

He seemed unconcerned about getting caught, and that day I got the idea that no one cared what you did along the river. West Marginal Way was a world outside the mainstream of city life, isolated and ignored. Once you left the heavily industrialized area at the Spokane Street Bridge and started upstream from Riverside toward Boeing Hill, West Marginal Way was, in those days, a curious combination of the industrial and rural. A brickyard, a saw mill, or a sand-and-gravel company operated here and there. More often they were idle, abandoned beside the slow river. The street itself was an old worn concrete road with cracks and hunchings. Homes were mostly scattered, like remote farms, with wild thick lawns and roofs heavily mossed. I can't recall a mowed lawn or a kept yard, or even a defined one. It was as if the people had no concept of property. The natural took over, blackberry bushes, snakeweed, scotch broom. Houses were allowed to weather year after year. Two decades later, the impressions remained.

HIDEOUT

In the reeds, the search for food by grebes
is brief. Each day, inside the shack
the wind paints white, a man keeps warm
by listening to ships go by, keeps sane
by counting European faces
passing north in clouds. Tugs deposit
miles of logs outside. A tax collector
couldn't find this place with holy maps.

When salmon crowd each other
in the river, and the river boils
with re-creation's anger, what tall man
re-creates too clearly domes of mills
downstream, and the gradual opening
as if the river loved the city
or was crying loudly "take me" to the sea?
What odd games children play.
One shouts himself into a president.
Another pins the villain salmon
to the air with spears. A rowboat
knocks all night against a pile.

Morning brings a new wind and a new
white coat of weather for the shack.

The salmon moved upstream last night
and no bird cuts the river, looking
for a smelt. Ships sail off to Naples
and the bent face bobbing in the wake
was counted in another cloud gone north.

After high school, I felt I should move out of my grandparent's place. One of my closest high school friends, John Mitchell, invited me to move into his house, a huge frame home in West Seattle. John was next to youngest in a family of ten children, and only four of his sisters remained at home with him. The older children had married and moved out so there was plenty of room.

I'd never paid my Grandparents rent money, and though Mrs. Mitchell asked for little, just the paying of it seemed important. I felt I was growing up and beginning to live normally. But I had been the only child for most of my life and had little sense of responsibility to others. My habits were selfish and thoughtless. I wish I could recall this better but my memory here blurs. By the end of the first month I had alienated John's sisters and I suspect that they complained to their mother. I remember I had some argument with one sister and she humiliated me by pointing to my slovenly habits and the meagre rent I was paying. Though I was fluid during the argument and good naturedly admitted I was guilty as charged, her overt disdain hurt. It was an old familiar feeling. I didn't belong and it was my fault.

When I went to pay Mrs. Mitchell the rent for the second month, I could tell by the way she looked at the floor and not at me that I was no longer welcome. She made an awkward speech of regret never once looking at me, her eyes darting to the corners of the kitchen. It must have been hard for her. She was naturally affectionate, and she knew she was hurting me. I remember the hurt but my feelings were complicated because I sensed that getting rid of me was right and necessary. I made one more try. I moved in with a friend named Bill Ransom and his widowed mother. My stay there was even shorter. Mrs. Ransom asked me to leave within two weeks. She was less concerned with my feelings than Mrs. Mitchell had been.

I didn't know where else to go. I was ashamed of my inability to get along in the world. I went back to my grandparents and they took me in without question. They didn't ask me what had happened in West Seattle and I didn't tell them. Our bond wasn't verbal, just habitual, the result of living together seventeen years.

Pearl Harbor happened six months after I'd graduated from high school, and young men my age were just marking time in 1942 when my two attempts to live away from my grandparents ended in failure. In November of '42, I volunteered for the Army Air Corps. It was inevitable that my generation was going to war and Congress was preparing to pass laws making eighteen-year-olds eligible for the draft. I can see that the service was temporarily good for me. It tore me away from home and forced me to live with others, to become conscious of my personal habits and to control myself in ways that respected the rights of others.

Good for me up to a point. I came home in the spring of '45 from thirty-five heavy bomber missions out of Italy, drinking heavily to ward off vivid anxiety dreams that came any night I went to bed sober. I had never had a woman, not even the plump voluptuous girl in Rome forced into prostitution by war and deprivation who took me to an apartment filled with members of her family who paid us no attention as we passed them and went into the bedroom. I had gone at the urging of other soldiers, ashamed not to, and after a couple of hours of futile trying, I left. Though I was alone I went to a G.I. prophylactic station for treatment and since I had no companions I was trying to impress, I assume that I was either naive enough to think V.D. was possible despite my timid performance or I was trying to impress myself because I'd finally been to bed with a woman. A man in all ways except the important one.

Two things seemed clear. The war convinced me that the world was brutal and dangerous and I didn't belong in it. I had almost been killed several times and the fear that piled up in me over the months in Italy didn't go away just because I was no longer in combat. Then, a normal life, marriage, children, seemed beyond reach. Growing up and accepting responsibility was anything but pressing. I moved back in with my grandparents. Drab and dull as their house was, it was familiar and it was safe. I went to the University of Washington on the G.I. Bill and majored in creative writing.

Some didn't come back. Bill Ransom went on a B-26 mission one day forever. Friends in West Seattle urged me to visit his mother but I couldn't bring myself to though I held nothing against her for evicting me three years before. Once in a while it nagged at me, but time passed and the emotional statute of limitations ran out.

The neighborhood had changed plenty in the thirty months I'd been gone. Our street was still a dirt road but our house was no longer the only one on the west side of the block. New houses stood on either side where the woods had been. The vacant lot across the street was no longer vacant. A small house had been moved there and was sitting on blocks. A cheerful alcoholic lived there alone. He was often passed-out in the salal beside the path leading from 16th to our backyard and to 15th and I used to help him home and put him to bed. Some ten or twelve years later, he became a poem.

NEIGHBOR

The drunk who lives across the street from us
fell in our garden, on the beet patch
yesterday. So polite. Pardon me,
he said. He had to be helped up and held,
steered home and put to bed, declaring
we got to have another drink and smile.

I admit my envy. I've found him in salal
and flat on his face in lettuce, and bent
and snoring by that thick stump full of rain
we used to sail destroyers on.
And I've carried him home so often
stone to the rain and me, and cheerful.

I try to guess what's in that dim warm mind.
Does he think about horizoned firs
black against the light, thirty years
ago, and the good girl—what's her name—
believing, or think about the dog
he beat to death that day in Carbonado?

I hear he's dead, and wait now on my porch.
He must be in his shack. The wagon's
due to come and take him where they take
late alcoholics, probably called Farm's End.
I plan my frown, certain he'll be carried out
bleeding from the corners of his grin.

I took few early poems from White Center and those I did, like "Neighbor," involved an individual but, unlike the river poems, were not concerned with totality of scene. After years of drunkenness, sexual maladjustment, and amateurish social behavior calculated to convince others I was normal and therefore acceptable, I sought help in psychiatric treatment and came to realize that "Neighbor" had been no idle curiosity, no chance subject for a poem. I felt I might very well end up that way and to this day the idea isn't unattractive.

Within ten years after the war when I was writing obsessively, I turned again and again in my imagination to West Marginal Way and the river for poems even though my experiences there were limited to those early trips to the slough on one end, waiting for the bus at Riverside on the other, and only the two or three trips to Don Crouse's between. Sometimes in my imagination, I saw people who never were in a place I'd never seen, though it all happened there at the river.

NO BELLS TO BELIEVE

When bells ring, wild rain pelts the river.
Who rings bells in the abandoned chapel,
once a school, once a shed where hide
was stored? The painter painting reeds
a private color, poppy farmer,
and the seiner folding autumn's nets—
they hear the bells and don't look up.

Mad Sam, the nutty preacher rings the bells.
He remained despite that mess, twelve
years back—the squaw—the poisoned wine.
Not Sam. He drowned beneath a boom.

No bells. Even when Mad Sam went mad
with God each Sunday and the women wept
to hear their imperfections yelled across
the river while a drum knocked Jesus
senseless and the tugboats tooted home.
No bells then. None now. What rings here
is something in the air unnamed.

The wild rain rings. The painter's reeds
run down the canvas in a colorful
defeat, the seiner's nets gain weight
and poppies wash away. The women told
Mad Sam before he ran out on the logs,
you must accept the ringing like the day.

Where did that come from? I may have been thinking of that "crackpot chapel" from the poem "West Marginal Way" when I dreamed

Mad Sam. But I'd dreamed that chapel too. I don't know if nutty religious groups operated along West Marginal Way. They certainly operated around White Center. I must have been transplanting.

I know where I got the way Mad Sam died. When I was in the first grade, an Indian boy, a classmate, drowned in the Duwamish. He had been playing on a log boom and fell into the river, got trapped under the logs and died trying to find an opening. His mother flipped and for years called him to dinner every evening in prolonged fits of scream. They lived close to Highland Park School, and her afternoon screeching gave neighbors the creeps.

I see myself in the poem, "the painter painting reeds a private color." I thought of myself as a private poet in those days, almost to a point of arrogance. If someone didn't understand my poems, I was pleased. Could I have been the poppy farmer? Did I have some ego-maniacal Coleridgian notion that my poems might offer the euphoric glory of opium? I hope not but it's possible. The seiner folding autumn's nets must have been me and my sexual timidity, the fishing season over and the nets empty, able to gain weight not from a vital catch of thrashing salmon but only from the rain they soaked up lying useless on the ground. Certainly I was Mad Sam, ringing bells no one responded to, remaining on the scene of a shameful past hoping in time to be accepted, prejudiced against women, feeling the only salvation possible was through self-acceptance and equally convinced that only women, with whom I could not communicate, could tell me the truth about self acceptance. I and my poems were doomed. The paint would not hold on the canvas. Any chance for happiness would be cut off at the source as the poppies and their promise of euphoria washed away.

In the fall of '47 and winter of '48, I studied under Theodore Roethke who had just come to Washington. I was still living with my grandparents, and I took the hour-long bus and trolley ride across town to school, returning at night except when I got drunk in the University District and someone put me up for the night. One morning on the way to school, I was sitting alone, as usual in the right rear corner of the bus. The bus stopped at 16th S.W. and Holden Streets for a passenger, and I fixed on the neighborhood grocery on the far corner but I was thinking about Roethke and about the four hills east of home and the way the nation opened forever from the top of Fourth Hill. Those hills seemed not like four geographical sites, I decided, but like four stages in a journey. At that moment I was certain as I've been of anything that I'd be writing poems all my life. I had been writing off and on since I was nine. It was the one thing I'd always done and it was clear to me that I could not stop. I never said to myself: I want to be a poet, or, I'm going to be a poet. But at that one moment on that bus that morning, I knew with quietude there was no need for resolve. And I vaguely knew that it had something to do with those four hills east of White Center and with journeying away from home. I didn't know if I'd ever be good enough to publish. I think I believed I wouldn't be, but I was going to spend my life writing anyway. "Getting published isn't the point," Roethke told me one day, and I came to know the wisdom of those words years later.

Writing was very hard in those days. I wrestled with every word, rewrote poems out of existence, stayed up all night now and then and went to work with little or no sleep. Sometimes I had my notebook beside the bed as the poem I was working on kept returning inside me, keeping me awake or waking me after I'd dozed off. Then in a brief writing session I wrote a poem that seemed to come without effort, and for me at least it illuminated the need and reason to go to the river for poems.

DUWAMISH

Midwestern in the heat, this river's
curves are slow and sick. Water knocks
at mills and concrete plants, and crud
compounds the gray. On the out-tide,
water, half salt water from the sea,
rambles by a barrel of molded nails,
gray lumber piles, moss on ovens
in the brickyard no one owns.
Boys are snapping tom cod spines
and jeering at the Greek who bribes
the river with his sailing coins.

Because the name is Indian, Indians
ignore the river as it cruises
past the tavern. Gulls are diving crazy
where boys nail porgies to the pile.
No Indian would interrupt his beer
to tell the story of the snipe
who dove to steal the nailed girl
late one autumn, with the final salmon in.

This river colors day. On bright days
here, the sun is always setting or obscured

by one cloud. Or the shade extended
to the far bank just before you came.
And what should flare, the Chinese red
of a searun's fin, the futile roses,
unkept cherry trees in spring, is muted.
For the river, there is late November
only, and the color of a slow winter.

On the short days, looking for a word,
knowing the smoke from the small homes
turns me colder than wind from
the cold river, knowing this poverty
is not a lack of money but of friends,
I come here to be cold. Not silver cold
like ice, for ice has glitter. Gray
cold like the river. Cold like 4 P.M.
on Sunday. Cold like decaying porgy.

But cold is a word. There is no word along
this river I can understand or say.
Not Greek threats to a fishless moon
nor Slavic chants. All words are Indian.
Love is Indian for water, and madness
means, to Redmen, I am going home.

Even after I had overcome my sexual problems, I still had the need to
relive over and over my early personal sense of defeat to some sort of
poetic fulfillment. The solitude I felt in my youth later became license to
write a poem. Out of my past sense of personal futility I could create
something in language hard enough to avoid wallowing in the self pity
I'd felt for years. And it must have occurred to me, at least unconsciously,
that to have remained with my grandparents in that austere house long
years after I'd reached the age when I should have left was a kind of
passive madness. For all practical purposes, we had stopped speaking to
each other long before Grandmother died and I moved away. Years
later, imagining myself there along the river, I could convert myself into
a Greek long enough to survive my self disdain, and into an Indian long
enough to whisper myself the truth. For the duration of the poem, I was
honest and warranted my own approval.

If I once subjected girls to cruelty in fantasies of vengeance for the
pain and rejection I'd suffered from women, I could also create a snipe

who would dive heroically out of the sky to rescue them, even though the real heroes, men who accepted their lives without complaint or question, would not be interested. I would be better than I felt I was, better than a boy, who, desperate for masculinity, identified with the tough boys of Riverside snapping tom cod spines. Or desperate for acceptance, jeered at the foreign and the strange with whom secretly he felt allied. Did I really want to be a part of West Seattle? Or did my poems keep me honest to my isolated self, away from the smooth pavements and smooth girls of the respectable well-kept hill to the west?

I suppose our landscapes choose us and writing a poem is a momentary burst of self acceptance in alien country. If mine chose me, they don't let go easily. Whenever I get back to Seattle, I take a nostalgic drive in my new Buick convertible through West Seattle, swing south and around to White Center, then over to 9th and north, down the long hill I hated to climb carrying all those shiners, left at the bottom, then north downriver along West Marginal Way to Spokane Street.

West Seattle has become a bit tacky in spots. The streets in White Center have been paved for years. The Duwamish slough was filled in long ago in the name of progress. West Marginal Way is four lanes of smooth pavement. A few homes still remain in that stretch I barely knew between the slough and Riverside, but more and more industry has moved in. The bird refuge where Don Crouse illegally shot those birds has been filled and layered over and a large industrial building of some kind sits there. Youngstown is now called Delridge. Youngstown school is called *Frank B. Cooper*. Boeing Hill is Highland Park Way. White Center is still White Center though bursting with progress. Ten years back or so, a movement started but failed to change the name to Delridge Heights or something equally offensive in its sorry try for respectability. In some minds, White Center still means degradation.

I'm aware of the dangers of locating poems too close to home. Too much memory remains to interfere with the imagination. The West Marginal Way I created was a place where I could melodramatically extend and exploit certain feelings I had about myself and ignore others that, had I tried to root the poems in White Center, would have gotten in the way. Did a lone tug struggling to haul acres of logs against the out-tide pour of the river represent some melodramatic picture I had of myself? Was the lonely gray wind bending the marsh grass a force within me, persistent in its daily replay of futility?

Maybe every poet has his West Marginal Way somewhere. For some it may not even be a place, but some frame of mind, some region of the blood where he can accept those parts of self that elsewhere would be unwelcome handicaps. Rereading those early poems, and remembering how I once was, I can see that along the river my defeats and fears turned into raw ore, my loneliness became a dramatic toy, the desolation I felt made me a citizen of that ignored and unique world. Even one with the fish in the brackish water backed up on the in-tide from a bay to the north that, on our clear bright days, glittered blue and clean.

DAVID IGNATOW

David Ignatow (*b. Feb. 7, 1914 in Brooklyn*) *has not only taught in various capacities at the New School, Vassar, the University of Kentucky, City University of New York, and Columbia University, but has worked as a civil service clerk, shipyard worker, hospital clerk, and book bindery manager, as he tells us in "The Beginning." His* Notebooks *(1973) is a brilliant self-study of the ongoing life of an American poet.*

(Photo by Gerard Malanga)

The Beginning

At dinner, during the week, a dialogue on the family pamphlet bindery business would take place between my parents in the kitchen. On Saturday and Sunday evenings their dialogue would be carried on in the living room, there joined by guests, usually my uncle, my father's brother, and his wife. Clouds of smoke would roll from the cigars of the two men as they sat and talked before a radio playing music. I sat perched on the edge of the sofa and would alternately try to listen to the music and to the conversation. The year was 1927, I was a child attending elementary school, too young to be allowed out nights alone and so I made their interests mine. On weekends, the conversations were mild and studied in tone, partly in deference to the Sabbath but mainly out of a wish to keep up a confident and calm appearance in front of company. It was during the week when my father had only my mother to talk to that the tensions of business were brought home, and late at night at that, after a long, hard day's work by my father. At the kitchen table, under the prodding of my mother's anxiety, he would start on his topic, a first grudgingly and slow. To him, it seemed impossible that anyone else could enter into his worries with the same emotional intensity. He had been wrapped in problems alone for so many hours. My mother would sit hunched over the white porcelain tabletop across from him, her lips parted, waiting for the worst, as he chewed his food. He would be crouched over his plate as he chewed rapidly. Lifting his head for the moment, he would burst out with the news. It might be given angrily, depending upon the events that flooded back on him from the day. There seemed much to talk about, with something new to say each evening. To me, as a child, this outpouring was both terrifying and revealing. Nothing in the mechanics of arithmetic or spelling could compare to these nightly adventures with my parents. As I did my homework on the dining room table opposite the kitchen entrance, I would keep turning from my books to watch and listen, fascinated. They themselves would have for-

David Ignatow has written me that "The Beginning" was first drafted during the '50s, probably before 1955, and only recently completed: "The summary of my early thinking, which this essay represents, has become the basis for my continued thinking on the subject as a whole. I see this in retrospect and in my later poetry, so I hope you find the piece as relevant for your book as I do." Ignatow, at my urging, listed for me several poems he thought would fit into the essay. I am responsible for the choice of the four included and for their placement. [w.h.]

130

gotten everything else in their excited discourse, my father ignoring the taste of his food as it was chased down his throat in the rush to get out his words. My mother would be letting the soiled dishes in the sink wait to listen to him and join in with exclamations of anger or joy. Even as I sat alone in my room, studying with the door closed at a distance from the kitchen a whole room beyond the dining room, their voices would penetrate feverishly. During the day I found myself anticipating my father's return home at night. My whole existence seemed to have become absorbed in following the fortunes of the family business.

There was school where I was being taught the principles of Americanism, among them being the right of each person to the pursuit of happiness. The teacher, a grown person like my parents, would stand before the class and lecture us on the importance to us of the pursuit of happiness. It was not simply to be equated with money, clothing, and food. One could have them all in abundance and still not be happy. In the freedom of one's spirit one found happiness. On Friday mornings in the Assembly Hall the school principal would stand on his raised podium before the uplifted faces of his students to quote Text: What did it avail a man to gain the whole world only thereby to lose his soul? I would go home, my head drumming enthusiastically with this new revelation, so opposite from what I had absorbed listening to my parents talk together. I would proclaim the difference to them as their salvation. Each night as they searched for happiness in the toils of business they only found themselves even more passionately enmeshed. Once I arrived home from school, however, I thought better of my project, nor did I venture to discuss it with them. Just to recall their feverish nights was to realize how entangled they were in their affairs. To remind them of better would only plunge them deeper into their despair and perhaps direct their anger at me. I decided to live silently, free of their cares and obsessions, as an example that they could follow, if they wished.

In this swing from the real to the ideal, from home to school, from my silent thoughts to the spoken thoughts of my parents, I graduated from elementary school and entered high school. Stimulated by an especially interesting course in history or English, I brought home text books issued at the beginning of the term, as well as books borrowed from the public library. I did not fully understand these books, nor hope to soon, but their impact on me set me even further apart from my parents. The nightly talks between them still went on, now low and intense, now piercing and filled with angers. Subdued on weekends, it proved how sharp was their agony during the week. In time I began to write, in reaction to these ordeals, since to talk to my parents was out of the question. It would be unreal to them in their circumstances. To write was my only outlet. Eventually they would read my writing. The poetry of Walt Whitman prompted me, he who swung so freely through the universe, who was so typically American in spirit, as I understood it from my school lessons and books. He had set behind him the narrow worldly cares to stride down the open road of the freedom of oneself. Like no one else, he stood for the autonomy of the spirit. Body and soul together were celebrated in his poems. The spirit was of the flesh. One had only to turn to oneself for the reality. After graduation from high school, when my parents asked me to enter the family business, I refused.

I did not act on Whitman's proposition immediately. There still was the matter of getting a job. That was the alternative to refusing to enter the family business. Or else I had to leave home. My parents had neither the time nor the inclination to discuss the issues with me. I was shocked by their unilateral decision, particularly that of my father, but it went to prove the utter falseness in which my family found itself, bound to business, divorced or isolated from the reality of one's true self. But I was not yet prepared to go out into the world, which conceivably could prove to be an even worse experience, when I considered that my father was part of it. I thought of the strangers out there who had never heard of me and could care even less. The only real choice left to me, finally, was to enter the family business.

There I was confirmed in my thoughts about it. Freedom of oneself was not to be found in business. Of that I was now certain. Not in the roar of machinery, nor in the harsh commands and flareups. These were unreal and sordid. They dragged one down. As a person I expected consideration under any circumstance. My father's harsh, hysterical methods had not advanced him far in business either. Those nightly anxiety-ridden talks between my parents never ceased, and now they included me, my intransigence in the shop. For one, I refused to work longer hours than the ordinary worker in the shop and left promptly with the others at the end of day. But it was apparent to anyone there that my father's methods were failing with them, too. The shop was small and voices rising in anger and resentment could be heard constantly above the roar of the machinery. Wherever one looked was confusion and discord. Nothing could be worse than that in the outside world, I felt, my spirit was so depressed and bitter here. I had not expected anything quite like this, but given all that I had been taught and all that I had read, it was inconceivable to me that this and this alone was America. I would find a job to my liking and be free. I decided to leave home too, since that was where my unhappiness began.

My search for a better life never quite succeeded. My demands were exacting. There were no jobs precisely like the one I expected to fill my requirements. I wanted a job where I could also sit back and think and feel the freedom within. It seemed a perfectly normal thing to do, according to my thinking, yet each job would have a way of negating that belief. It would create a conflict in me and between my superior and me that invariably would be resolved by my search for a new job. In time, it became a discouraging process, each job at first offering the possibility of ease and freedom, only to make itself felt as a burden and a threat to me. I began to realize that I was being confronted by an order of reality different from mine, that there were others who, like myself, also were in search of their personal freedom and happiness and were going about it in a manner entirely opposite from mine and from an entirely different set of premises. They were the men to whom I was responsible on the job, the supervisors and often the actual owners of the plant or office. I could not deny them the right that I gave myself, to form their lives according to their innermost wishes. It was a confusing insight to come upon, after my years of search for my own personal freedom. It somehow did not accord with the principles of Walt Whitman. Manhattan was where my search took place, and Brooklyn was my residence, where I was born and where my parents still resided in their two-family, red brick house that conformed with all the others on the block.

As I tried to compromise and hedge as a last resort, to get over the rough spots, so to speak, it became obvious to me that I was bargaining away my freedom. One compromise would lead to another, as I acceded to that principle and saw it become a way of life. It was an unhappy development, but by now the search for freedom had become an actual dilemma to me, for by exercising my right to freedom I also was undermining my basis for it by depriving myself of the money and the leisure it afforded. I was filled with despair. Contrary to what I had been led to believe in school and in my favorite books, I could find no grounds anywhere in which to root myself as a free man, and yet in the city I saw the huge crowds coming and going in streets, shops, and offices with the air of a people utterly unhampered in their lives. They looked and acted content and free and energetic, while I was without freedom, weighted down with gloom.

Sometimes on the subway you see a face.
It transports you. The train moves
as if rattling to heaven, that face,
composed, a sign to be at peace.

Standing on your station platform,
the train moving off,
you firmly believe that someday
you will go with it all the way.

But there was refuge for me in my family. On each of my home visits
I would receive a warm welcome, good food and a relaxed hour or two.
There was a tacit agreement between us to avoid the bristly issue of
ideals. I was not yet prepared to acknowledge my defeat, not without
arriving at some arrangement between us in which I could be comfortable
with myself. We sought for it in casual random conversation about
living expenses and such prosaic problems for the single man on the
outside world. My mother, however, could not long restrain herself and
her shy, brusque manner would get to the thorny issue between us
through a stratagem. It would be triggered by a polite inquiry by me on
business conditions at the shop. She would promptly reply that business
was good and that there was nothing any longer for anyone to worry
about and get angry over. There was evidence enough of that in the
house, the plump new sofa and chairs and plush rugs everywhere and a
brand new expensive Oldsmobile parked in front of the house. My own
failure was clearly evident in my silences and glum look, and shyly she
would point out to me how everything in the shop now allowed for more
ease and freedom for everyone, even the workers. She was deliberately
oblique, as if to save me the embarrassment of having to assert my
dignity again by rejecting an overt invitation to return. Her stratagem
permitted me to think about her offer calmly as a solution indeed to my
problem. She was the restless one between my parents. My father was
satisfied with things as they stood. Success had come to him at last in
nice measure and he could afford to sit back of a weekend, truly relaxed. She was not so easily compensated for the past, not until she
could see me too share in the success. Usually these discussions between
us would take place on a weekend, the tone calm and measured, more
truthfully so than I could remember from those visits by my father's
brother in the early days. There no longer was the undercurrent of
anxiety, and so I felt there was a point to what she was hinting at. But by

this time it no longer was a question for me whether I could get along with others on my basis. I had no illusions about that basis now and in any case it had to be subordinated to the overriding need to hold a job. I could see now, too, that being son of the boss was valuable. It would be difficult, if not impossible, to fire me, but this time I would not leave in search of the impossible. To return, then, meant more than to further compromise myself. It was to give up my conception of personal freedom entirely. Several calm discussion-filled evenings subsequently helped me to make up my mind. Occasionally my father sat in on these talks, nodding approval of my mother's words. Nothing was left to make me hestitate. My poetry writing had begun to vanish amid the complications brought about by my endless search for personal freedom. In my writing I had tried to follow this commitment faithfully, only to find the words grow thin. They were becoming generalities, fading in the harsh rub of events, while those events had begun to lead me into other thoughts, decidedly unpleasant. I had begun turning to protest and satire in my poetry. It was, as I recognized, my way of stating that personal freedom was non-existent. From there it was a simple step to enter the family business.

But with it went no hope. There was nothing to take the place of what I had given up. For a while I had been living happily on a false assumption. The joy and bravery of it had been the whole of my life and now there was no happiness either in giving it up. There was nothing but an admission that happiness did not exist. I felt no motive for living. One simply waited, slackened off, waited and despaired and found oneself not writing at all.

In the meanwhile I did have to make a living.

BUSINESS

There is no money in breathing.
What a shame I can't peddle my breath
for something else—like what?
I wish I knew but surely
besides keeping me alive
breathing doesn't give enough
of a return.

Returned to my father's shop, I worked seriously and hard, forgetting myself in it. Eventually, under his guidance, I was given a position of authority. The bindery now was more than twice the size it had been when I left ten years before, and had more than twice the number of machines and workers. I was made production manager, in charge of scheduling and job specifications. It was gruelling work. Among other problems, customers had to be appeased for our failures to meet delivery on schedule. In the shop, workers and their foreman had to be appealed to or, as it happened, threatened every step of the way if we were to live up to commitments. They would resent me and I would be embarrassed at having to prod them all through the day. Often enough as these commitments turned out to be impossible to fulfill I would have to get on the phone and talk the customer into a new schedule or sit at the phone and take the abuse and anger of a man at the other end of the line frustrated in his own plans. It would enrage me to have to remain silent through his furious, humiliating harangue. The little that was left of me, now that I had returned defeated to the shop, was crushed altogether, and after hanging up I would stalk back into the factory and hysterically, like my father in the past, demand to know why our promises could not be kept and why it always had to be me who took abuse for broken promises for which other persons were responsible. The foreman and the workers would shrug their shoulders and look at each other, with disdain for me. It was the production man's job to take the blame, didn't I know? And if I became angry with them in earnest they would turn on me, with everyone else in the factory arrayed against me. My father would have to step out of the office and onto the factory floor where the argument was taking place and quiet the lot of us in his calm, authoritative voice and order us back to work again. I would be relieved but sullen, glad the heated words had been stopped before the workers and the foreman quit in a rising rage, and yet I would feel oppressed by a failure over which I had no control yet which had the power to give me this unwanted grief. I had felt no private commitment to my job and so had expected no personal blame or identity with it. Nevertheless, there remained the responsibility I had taken on with the job, of my own free will. I was caught.

During lunch, while chewing on a sandwich, I would be huddled over the accounting books with my father, figuring out the profit and the loss. A day's work had to show a profit and there were days of long run jobs when no profit was visible. These were the days hardest to bear. My father would be constantly on top of me, demanding facts and figures, and if he happened to be taking a hand in the production, soon tiring (he was growing old and feeble), he would be especially irritable and sharp.

That was when I really had to hold my temper; that was the test of my attitude towards my job. After a few restrained words of clarification to placate him, through which I felt the tension mounting between us, I would walk away, ostensibly to overlook another part of the operation but really to keep myself from blowing up and leaving. It was during these days that the tension would mount among the workers too. Their production would be under constant scrutiny by my father or myself, and a word of correction or advice would make the worker explode in anger and protest. I would have to stand there beside him silently, for fear of disrupting the schedule further by arguing back. Realizing how little all this meant to me in the way of happiness, this was a nightmare existence, and yet I had to go on with it with the passion and energy of a dedicated man. It was a bitterly ironic comment on my literary past to which I had given that same passion and energy.

After work, at home, the sullen faces of the workers kept entering my mind. Was it for this that I had searched for freedom and inner peace, to become a punishment to others?

PAYMASTER

The pay could have been more.
I felt I was giving myself
into his hands for judgment.
Thank you, he said, taking his check.
Thank me for what, I replied
silently. I am sending you home,
belittled in your own eyes.

I did not want to be alone in these thoughts; they made me feel so lost and abandoned in myself. I wanted to share my misery and self hatred with others, to confess, to unburden myself, to be able to live with myself, if only on the marginal basis of confession. And so I began to spend the days in a kind of subterfuge for conversation with the workers. I would approach one with an order to do this or that and end by talking to him confidentially. How did he like this job, I would ask, with a wry twist to my voice which was meant to let him understand that I shared with him his distaste for it and his distaste for me who had to give him his orders. At first, he would look me over suspiciously, with a hurried side-glance as he worked, perhaps wondering whether I was looking for a pretext, out of his own mouth, to fire him. I would persist in my questioning, satirizing the whole place to him as an assurance that

I was on his side. Out loud, as if addressing the questions to myself, I would wonder what caused any of us to work here? Were there no other shops where it might be easier or at least more congenial, closer to how one liked to live, in self respect? The money was not enough to keep one here. Other shops offered money too. As I would continue in this vein he would begin to grin slowly and look at me directly. It was a kind of comment on my words. I was being naive in his eyes, if not downright childish. The questions were not worth answering. Here I was a boss who should know better than to ask questions that obviously answered themselves. We were both in the same game, so to speak, for the same thing. Wiping his hands thoroughly of the grease and grime, he prepared his words. He liked his job, he would say finally. He was glad to be doing it. All shops were alike. What was wrong with that? As for the money, what was wrong in having it? That's what kept him here and if he could get more of it he'd be even happier. He was under pressure to produce and that always called for more money, didn't it? And he looked at me challengingly, with a brief smile. I would be unable to answer and would walk away. I wanted to think quietly, alone. His remarks would set me back. I would be stunned by the attitude behind them. He fully accepted his life, with its hardships and complications. He would have more of it, on a yet bigger scale, with more tension thrust on him, providing it assured him more money. In fact, it was as if he was notifying me that he meant to have it. My speaking to him on this confidential level had given him the opportunity which he may have been looking for all the while to hit me for a raise. I was confused.

During that same week, again under the subterfuge of checking on production schedules, I went from worker to worker, wanting to find out if each had this same attitude. All did, without exceptions. All were emphatic on the single point of more money, regardless that it meant increased work for them. They were making no distinction between themselves and the boss. He too was out for the money and so they demanded their share. The theory that they were being exploited had no basis in reality for them. The only purpose of having bosses was to gain money through them. My guilt and fears in my relationship to them was a myth, as far as they were concerned, and I began to sense my childishness towards them for having confronted them with such an issue as personal happiness and freedom. They had solved those problems by their immersion in money. During my questioning they had looked at me with surprise and suspicion as though suspecting my motives as perhaps seeking ways and means of getting more work out of them for less money, but they had made sure of squashing that thought by demanding more. I walked away from each conversation, always baffled and let down. Their attitude seemed incredible in the face of the hardships they had to put up with in this shop. What did they expect money would do for them? After a day's work, they were exhausted from the pounding noise of the machines and from the constant handling of materials that they placed on the machines and that emerged as finished products with the regularity of a clock. They had no respite from their work, except for the brief lunch time. The next morning they would return, sullen and grumbling, anticipating what was in store for them that day. I could hardly question anyone in the morning or hand him a schedule of required production for that day without getting in exchange a sullen look or rough answer. That was what their labor produced in them and so what more could they expect from it by an infusion of more money? They already had their refrigerators, cars, television sets, and washing machines and many among them owned their homes and cars. Yet they would come to work each morning just as determined to resist and be sullen as if they had none of these precious possessions. These were the pride and joy of their labors, judging from the way they spoke about them during lunch time. Sullen and grunting in the morning, they would sound off against the job with the free manner of a person of independent means and yet they were all bound to this shop, and would be to any shop for that matter, by household debts, mortgages, weekly bills, time payments, and ultimately by this overall belief that there was nothing else worthwhile to take the place of making money.

How then could they reconcile their passion for money with the agonies it put them through? If life was meant to be lived in the comforts with which they surrounded themselves at home, if it was possible, according to their beliefs, to call that happiness, then was not this factory, its tension and pressure to produce, its irritations and physical exhaustion, the very opposite of what they believed in and lived for? How were they able to tolerate it? I went around again to talk to each, probing. Were they really that content with their jobs? Was it the kind of life they had planned for themselves? Was there nothing else they had dreamed, better than this angry, tiring work? I could not put these questions directly, in my position as production manager. It was during lunchtime as they all sat around a big work table and ate their homemade sandwiches and talked that I was able to bring up the subject, but only obliquely, by referring to an item in the newspaper as basis for comment, or perhaps to some incident in the shop which had caught everyone's attention, personal and plain to see, as for example the not unusual incident of a worker suddenly expressing his disgust with the job and shutting down the machine to walk off to the toilet to smoke awhile and recover his composure before returning to the shop. It was all right, the others grinned at each other, but it was a bad habit and shouldn't be repeated too often. One could get fired. As unhappy as they were at their work, they were fixed in it. I tried to understand. They had grown up expecting nothing else out of life. They discussed their lives with the same detachment that they ran their machines. It had been given to them to live this way from the start. They had had no hand in shaping it. It was not that they were voicing their resentment or rebellion. They were simply stating the facts and the facts were a kind of symbol among them of what they shared in common with each other. It allowed them to go on to discuss other matters of more immediate concern about which they could talk more meaningfully, such as refrigerators, television sets, and washing machines. They talked with enthusiasm, quoting price and make by heart of nearly all models. They had their newspapers to refer to at once for corroboration and they would spread them out on the work table as they ate and point at items listed by the dozens, page after page. They would carry their newspapers underarm as they entered the factory and as they left each night. This was how they survived the day and got along. To me, it offered no explanation other than to see in it their confession of helplessness to do other than what they were doing and their readiness to do it, to exploit themselves like any boss.

It was harrowing to see them in that light and yet it was a life they accepted. They found good in it. When they did rebel, shutting down a machine to walk off to the toilet, they would come back, having temporarily modified their enslavement and affirmed themselves thereby, but to question their cars, houses, and refrigerators—these were the untouchables, the sacred, without which life itself did not exist for them. These were not to be questioned. Like themselves, they saw the boss too being driven, to make the business pay off his costs and earn him a still better car than theirs. He had his special problems to face, competition from other bosses, overhead, fixed expenses. They could sense that the world also was a vast, impersonal machine for which no one actually was responsible, not even the boss, whom they respected for his ability to make the machine work for him and give them work in return. He deserved his better car and larger, more elaborately furnished home, with perhaps a maid or two, but they could be angry with him when he lost out to a competitor on the price bid for a job. How often they would protest at a loss in their earnings during a slow week. He was there, they felt, to see that they earned a living as he did from their labors and he was not exempt from blame if he was losing out to the competition, just as they were not exempt from blame when they did not live up to their production schedules. It was a circle of mutual accommodation, they felt, in which all were joined and for which all were responsible in keeping it intact and healthy. To try to break this circle was like trying to destroy their own welfare and happiness. How often they would sit around the lunch table to compare notes on wages in different shops to note the advantage or disadvantage to themselves. And how angry they would become to learn that another shop was offering more work. They would make clear to me or to my father their anger and counter our defense with arguments of their own just as reasonable sounding as ours, such as their willingness to work longer hours, if necessary, to keep a job in the shop, a job that we might have lost temporarily or permanently because of a lack of time to produce it. And when we would hesitate to take on a job that showed a very slim margin of profit they would search out working methods that could produce more at less cost. These were methods that would make them work even harder, making it that much more difficult for them to break away from the machine for a smoke in the toilet. And so it went each day, with one side egging on the other to greater and greater exertions. It was a life lived in earnest.

COMMUNION

Let us be friends, said Walt,
and buildings sprang up
quick as corn and people
were born into them, stock
brokers, admen, lawyers and doctors
and they contended
            among themselves
that they might know
                each other.

Let us be friends, said Walt.
We are one and occasionally two
of which the one is made
and cemeteries were laid out
miles in all directions

to fill the plots with the old
and young, dead of murder, disease,
rape, hatred, heartbreak and insanity
to make way for the new
and the cemeteries spread over the land
their white scab monuments.

Let us be friends, said Walt, and the graves
were opened and coffins laid on top
of one another for lack of space.
It was then the gravediggers slit
their throats, being alone in the world,
not a friend to bury.

I, thinking about all this and feeling as helpless as the workers, saw it as an era like any other, with its central obsessive ikon dignified through suffering. It was our means to salvation. We could not do other than what we had been formed to do and so had raised that necessity to a faith.

I went home to write poetry again in this vision, tragic for its revelation of the kind of happiness it embraced. It was not what I had sought at the beginning. That had been foolhardy and even dangerous to life. One sought happiness through self surrender. And so there was poetry to be written, about this paradox of the perpetual search for personal happiness and freedom in things other than oneself.

JOHN LOGAN

JOHN LOGAN (b. 1923 in Red Oak, Iowa) has taught at
Notre Dame and San Francisco State and is currently
Professor of English at the State University of New York at
Buffalo. He has written criticism and fiction, has been
poetry editor of The Critic, Choice, and The Nation, and is
known to be one of the finest teachers of literature and
creative writing in the country.

(Photo by Gerard Malanga)

On My Early Poems

I'd like to tell the story of my early poetry and shall make references to my later work only where they fall naturally. When I was a senior pre-medical student (1943) at Coe College in Cedar Rapids, Iowa, I wrote two poems because I wanted to see my name in the student paper and because, honestly, I had some strong feelings I wanted to share—first, the sense of celebration and peace at having been accepted into the Navy and, second, rejection and solitude after having been sent home as a bad risk.[1] The poems were incredibly poor. I am punished for them by being condemned to remember how the first one began: "To travel out in winter time/When all is cleansed with white/While fade the brilliant hues of day/To solemn grays of night. . . ." The poem rhymed and metered.

A few years later (1947) when I was teaching at St. John's College in Annapolis, Md., I wrote a sonnet (the only one I ever worked on) which is blessedly lost, but of which I can remember that it took as epigraph some lines from the opening of the Third Book of *The Iliad* where the noise of the losing Trojans as they prepare for battle is compared to the clamour of cranes and contrasted with the quiet gathering together of the Achaians. The sense of the destructiveness of noise I have carried with me along with the necessity of solitude for creative endeavor and for love. I remember reading in Schopenhauer that the noise of the crack of a whip in the street can abort the birth of a great thought. I translated a poem of Rilke's that spoke of noise inhibiting love, and I took to heart and memorized Dylan Thomas's lines on art, love, and solitude:

> In my craft òr sullen art
> Exercised in the still night
> When only the moon rages
> And the lovers lie abed
> With all their griefs in their arms,
> I labor by singing light. . . .

[1] I had been accepted at the induction center in Des Moines where I had gone to enlist but was sent home from Great Lakes Naval Training Station because of a slight color-blindness and a heart murmur.

Here is the Rilke poem which I translated and published as part of my "Homage to Rainer Maria Rilke (in *Zigzag Walk*):

> If it were quiet once—
> if the casual and the probable
> for once would cease their noise—
> and the neighbors' laughter!
> If the clamor of my senses
> did not so much
> disturb my long watch:
> then in a thousandfold thought
> I could think through to the very brink of you,
> possess you for at least
> the season of a smile,
> and as one gives thanks
> give you back again.

The importance of Thomas came much later, but both Homer and Rilke were early very important to me, and I read them (haltingly) in their own languages—and more relevantly for my development as a poet I translated them into English. It was for my second book, *Ghosts of the Heart*, that I went to Homer and (with some cribbing from the Loeb classics edition) did a very free translation of the opening encounter between Agamemnon and Achilles, Book I, lines 1–351, for a poem I called "Achilles and the King: A Verse Re-telling."

Virgil was also important to me, both for theory of prosody and for subject matter. I was excited to discover in his poetry (through reading the research of W. F. Jackson Knight) that there was a functional counterpointing of the artificial rhythm set up by the verse ictus and the natural rhythm emanating from the flow of prose stress.[2] In my first book, *A Cycle for Mother Cabrini*, I published a poem called "Lament for Misenus" based on my translation (this time with some "help" from C. Day Lewis) of an incident from Book VI of the *Aeneid* which, as it

---

[2] I got very interested in the complexity of language achieved by such counterpointing, and I wrote to Ezra Pound (whom I had visited at St. Elizabeth's Hospital) for help in finding such technique in English poetry, but he did not reply. (He *had* written me earlier to condemn a poem I had sent him—"Protest after a Dream.") Later I discovered on my own two examples of counterpointing in English, one, the practice of Shakespeare of using four prose accents in an iambic pentameter line and, two, the practice of Auden (imitating the Anglo-Saxon) of using three alliterated words in a four-stress line.

happened, provided perfect imagery for the elegy I wanted to write: Fred Miller, son of the head of the Miller Brewing Corporation, was my student at Notre Dame, and we were studying the *Aeneid* at the time he went home for Christmas (1954) leaving a paper on my desk. A few hours later he and his father were both killed in the crash of a small plane which they had boarded to go hunting together. I was very fond of Fred and was very upset by the death. I wanted to write something. As it happened, the assignment Fred's class had been given for their return to school was the section of *Aeneid* Book VI relating the death of the gifted warrior (a trumpeter) Misenus. Young Fred was in the ROTC, and he was gifted at his studies, so I thought of him as a Misenus figure. Furthermore, the most anguishing things to me about his death—the fire in the plane and the burial beneath a snow-covered grave-stone— were given for me a beautiful transformation in the Misenus story, for Misenus is anointed by his friends and then laid tenderly upon a funeral bier set to flame by them, and he is buried at the foot of a snow-covered mountain.[3] Hence the poem:

LAMENT FOR MISENUS

> . . . *atque illi Misenum in litore sicco,*
> *ut venere, vident indigna morte peremptum.*
> *Misenum Aeoliden, quo non praestantior alter*
> *aere ciere viros Martemque accendere cantu.*
> P. Vergili Maronis *Aeneid VI*

By the cold shore we came on
Aeolus' son who lay
Young *ai* who lay
Ruined by his smashed
And slivering horn and spear.
He was Hector's friend and fought
By him; we loved him first
As one to move and fire us
On this bended horn.

It may be he was young
And mad and sounded gods
To combat over the sea;

---

[3] Actually a promontory north of the Bay of Naples which would no doubt seldom see snow—but so it seemed to my poet's eye.

It may be Triton heard
His echoing horn in caves
Of stone or tombs and pale abandoned
Shells, and challenged him.
But Triton's is a rounder
Horn of the howling sea:

Ai here lies Aeolus' son
Come bury him in the wood;
How use this rock for sorrow
These dried stars' arms this
Rigid face of the fish?
Axe now strike the ilex! Pitch
Trees fall quivering
Ashes cleave and the giant
Rowan trees roll from the hill!

We build his pyre with resined
Wood and the long firing
Oak that's interwove
With mourning boughs, and place
The funeral cypress. And last
Arrange on top the towering altar
His radiant arms,
That catch the glint of flames
Underneath the brazen kettles.

These limbs are cold to wash
With water from the fire. This oil
Anoints more durably than tears
This oil anoints more
Durably than tears.
Now lay him on the bier with purple
Cloths beside his coat;
And now this last melancholy
Office tops his pyre.

We turn our eyes aside to
Fix the funeral torch;
The incense burns, the gifts
And meats and chalices of olive oil.

At last the altar ashes
Fall and flames burn out; we pour
Much wine on the red embers.
And here the priest collects
The bones in a bronzed cask,

And walking round us thrice
Sprinkles us with white
Water as with dew he shook
From a branch of the lucky olive;
And says our farewell word.
We bury him, his spear his
Oar and his remembered horn
Beneath a snowy peak,
A massed a blue and airy

Tomb for Aeolus' son.

in memoriam F. C. M.
killed with his father
in a plane crash
17 December 1954

Other Latin authors I translated or (in the first case) used in translation were St. Athanasius, St. Augustine, Lucretius, and Pliny. Athanasius's *Life of St. Anthony of the Desert* was my source for my "A Short Life of the Hermit"; Augustine (mainly *Confessionum*), for "Prologue and Questions for St. Augustine" (which also uses Botticelli's portrait of him[4]); Lucretius, as I will describe in detail below, gave me the idea for "A Dialogue with La Mettrie"; and Pliny's *Naturalis Historia* for "A Pathological Case in Pliny."

I had been reading in Pliny in connection with my work as a tutor in biology (and Greek and Geometry and so-called "Great Books") at St. John's College, and I came on the amazing story of a man who had killed three hundred enemies but could not be captured himself despite many forthright attempts. When at last his enemies did succeed in capturing

---

[4] The portrait of Augustine bears the remarkable inscription (in Latin): "St. Augustine so lived that he does not know he is dead." I was fascinated by the presence in the portrait (of Augustine in ecstasy) of various scientific instruments and mathematical books in the background and puzzled in the poem about their significance.

him, they immediately threw him to the ground and opened his chest to examine his brave heart.

They found the heart covered with hair! The story engaged my feeling strongly and I translated it (again, with some help from the Loeb edition) and published it as one of the two first poems to appear in print since I had begun to take myself seriously as a poet—in *Partisan Review* for Jan.–Feb. 1953, when I had just turned thirty.

Two motifs have developed here, one, the influence of writers of other languages (classical and modern) on my work, and, another, the influence of my studies, particularly of biology, on my poetry. Let me first follow out the latter theme: That tale of Pliny's I actually used in a biology class, for we were studying Virchow's *Cellular Pathology,* and I found there a possible explanation for the astonishing phenomenon (true or legendary) reported by Pliny—the pathological growth, in the inner part of the body for which they were not intended, of cells of a certain type which do function normally in other parts. This visceral juxtaposition of substances foreign to each other is a recurring theme in my poetry. I remember being very moved in college by a passage from Mann's *Magic Mountain*[5] where, in an operation on one lung (to deflate it in connection with the treatment of tuberculosis) the meeting of the metal of the scalpel and the living flesh of the lung is described. This kind of juxtaposition I believe becomes generalized in my poetry into a feeling for a clash of textures, a kind of *collage* of things and also of types of language. An early poem where this clash or collage occurs in a specifically biological context (it describes the preparation of a frog for a laboratory) is this one, published in *Saturday Review* but not yet collected in a book:

THE PREPARATION

While the class waited
I prepared the frog:

I had to hurry the needle
Through the handy opening
Just at the back of the head;

It slipped upon the skin
As on a plastic bag
For iceboxes, as on

---

[5] This consideration is also relevant to the question of the influence of modern writers on my work.

A rind of ripe melon,
Then under urging
Entered to touch parts

Never meant for metal—
Causing one eye slightly
To drop from its accustomed

Plane, a cold nearly
Unmuscled leg to draw
Too far up the belly,

An almost imperceptible
Darkening of green
Along the back, in whose

Depression a small amount
Of blood collected, like ours
Red, and causing the mouth

White and inside moist
To stretch (but it was a rabbit
In his cage who

Screamed)
As the hour began.

I am also aware of the heavy influence of readings in biology on some other poems. I have been proud of my use of the anatomical (and musically beautiful) word "hyaline" in this passage from "Mother Cabrini Crosses the Andes"[6]:

But there is nowhere mountain air
So cold or keen or bright or
Thin as is Francesca's wrist
Humming hyaline
Along the risen limb.

Two poems which use material from *The Source Book of Animal Biology*[7] are "The Experiment that Failed" from my *Spring of the Thief*

---

[6] As a literary source for the events in Mother Cabrini's life I used two biographies, one by Theodore Maynard, and another by Lucille Borden. Both books were bad and I got my impulse to write rather from reading *between* these other lines.
[7] Edited by T. S. Hall.

(where I use a description of an early blood transfusion experiment involving Pope Innocent VIII) and "A Dialogue with La Mettrie" from *Cycle for Mother Cabrini*. (Concerning this latter poem, it made me very proud as a thirty-three-year-old poet who had just published his first book (1955) to have so eminent a critic as Stanley Kunitz remark in his review in *Poetry* that the poem should be in any anthology hoping to represent current writing.) Beyond the sharing of feeling—or perhaps *through* the sharing of feeling, my object in this poem was to take some phrases of the eighteenth-century mechanist La Mettrie and to refute his philosophical position by repeating his own words from inside the framework of a poem. The influence of classical languages and of science, especially biology, come together at this point, for in my close reading of passages of Lucretius's *De Rerum Natura* in Latin I became convinced there was a strong emotional undertone working in counterpoint against the intellectual statements of the poem, which gives an account of Empedocles's materialism. Surely it is meaningful, I thought, that one of the most horrifying accounts of death and dying in the history of Western literature is the last chapter of Lucretius, which is a description of the plague: yet Lucretius had "explained" why we need not fear death. Lucretius tells us he uses poetry to sugar-coat philosophy and make it palatable. This statement is made *in* the poem, so that it is subject to the feeling-tone of the whole work, and I would say, considering this, that in fact he uses poetry to *refute* Empedocles's atomic philosophy of materialism. If poetry is "mightier than the sword" it is also mightier than the prose statements it embodies. Poetry (and the creative expression of feeling) is a most difficult phenomenon to account for in atomic terms and, thus, Lucretius chose the least likely literary form to teach materialism. It is necessary to conclude that he was either a bad philosopher or a good poet. Reading him, one is overwhelmed by the truth of the second alternative. *The very presence of poetry is both a refutation of materialism and also a witness to some form of human transcendence.* I would never have realized this, a conclusion so important to my own stance as a poet, had I not discovered the dynamics of Lucretius's poetry: I applied it directly in my writing of the poem on La Mettrie (whose mechanism is a variant of Lucretius's, i.e., the materialism of Empedocles). My poem on La Mettrie ends thus:

> For to what do we look
> To purify his remarks, or purge
> His animal images? What

> Piece in us may be cut free
> Of the grievéd matter of La Mettrie,
> That underneath a temporal reeling
> *Took on this arch of feeling.*

The passage I wrote for the book jacket of this first book is relevant to my discussion, and (whatever else has changed) I would still repeat it. The last sentence is most to the point, but I will give the context:

> These poems are concerned with the Saints as heroes of the will and lovers, as incredibles. They treat myth, rememberings of childhood and anticipations of death as acts of spirit, good, bad, or trimming.[8] They reintroduce the superstition of ghosts and the lonely fallacy[9] of the lack of a natural place for man. These poems try to disprove materialism by coming into existence; and that is the extent of their apostolate.[10]

One can see that the influences on my early poetry came not from my contemporaries but from the living language of such long dead writers as Homer, Virgil, Augustine (and other devotional writers as St. Thomas, Athanasius, the translators of the King James Version and the Vulgate "Apocrypha," the Catholic novelist and essayist Sigrid Undset[11]), Dante and Shakespeare, who, I will acknowledge, took me out of biology into literature.[12] The recent poets who influenced me were not American but

---

[8] This word is a coinage (I believe) from Dante's use of the word "trimmer" (meaning timeserver) to describe persons made to wander in Limbo because they followed changing winds of fashion in thought and act and were not worth condemning to Hell.

[9] I.e., according to Aristotelian and Thomistic philosophy—Pico Mirandola (whom I much admire) to the contrary.

[10] I added this because I feared that, as a Catholic, I would be branded a "Catholic Poet," and thought of as using poetry to proselytize for the Church.

[11] I should note here that somewhat later the Catholic philosophers Jacques Maritain and Gabriel Marcel and the Catholic novelist George Bernanos became important.

[12] Shakespeare was the only literary course I took as an undergraduate. He worked in me, and I read further in English literature. When I graduated, deciding against medicine for financial and emotional reasons (I was afraid of the body!), I became a graduate student in zoology at Berkeley. Haunted by the new world of literature which had been opened to me, along about November (1943) I took my expensive scientific textbooks to a store on Telegraph Ave. and exchanged them for two leather bound volumes of verse—Keats and Shelley. I dropped out. In the fall of 1944 I began an M.A. in English at Iowa and read my first contemporary poetry with Austin Warren there.

European—Rilke, Rimbaud, Lorca, and Cavafy. Rilke gave me the original, strongest impulse toward writing; Rimbaud, Lorca, and Cavafy expanded irrevocably the horizons of what poetry could be and what it could say.

II

Let me go back to the story of how the poems started at St. John's College. I wrote that sonnet in 1947, the year I arrived there with my wife and my oldest son, and then shortly I began to keep a kind of journal, two entries in which were prose poems I wrote sitting on the steps of Great Hall on the campus. These pieces were based as directly as I could make them (the "biologist" writing) on observation. One was about two trees at the back of the college. Their branches intertwined, and the leaves had fallen, and I was struck with the question of how difficult it was to tell whether those entangled limbs were alive or dead. I later published it in an issue of *Beloit Poetry Journal* dedicated to Robert Frost[13] because Frost had used a similar image in a poem (which, however, I had not seen before I wrote my own). Here it is:

TWO TREES

"The tree has no leaves and may never have them again.
We must wait til some months hence in the spring to know."
Robert Frost

Two trees lose clothes of leaves
And light, uncovering their nice embrace:
Distinct trunks with one crown which moulds
Itself like a brain inside a skull
Of sky. The trees' rapture starts the breeze

And whips the talking wind. I joined the quiet,
Anxious men, who cannot comprehend
This age-long intercourse of trees
And who dread that secret spring when two
Trees' bones make the reach of limbs.

This was, so to speak, my "first" poem, because it was based on that earliest journal. But it was revised over a period of some ten years, and it was not my earliest publication of serious poetry. I have not collected

[13] Chapbook #5 (1957).

it in a book. The second prose poem I spoke of was based on an observation of the changed relationship between trees, grass, and light after rain. I rewrote this one several times and published it twenty-five years later first in a magazine[14] and then in my most recent book, *The Anonymous Lover*, under the title "Abstract Love Poem."

About 1950 (still at St. John's) I began to write poetry in earnest. So far as I can see there were four factors which came together to make this beginning possible. The first was the fact that students had learned I was interested in poetry and began to bring me their work to comment on. This intimidated me—I thought what the hell is the matter with me that I am not writing. I think particularly of the poetry of Robert Hazo (brother of the poet Samuel Hazo) who was my student and who later gave up poetry to become an associate of Mortimer Adler's Institute for Philosophical Research. Thus students have been involved with my work from the beginning, and in fact I have never felt the conflict between teaching and the writing of poetry which some speak of.

Secondly, I had begun work on a Ph.D. in philosophy,[15] taking night courses at Georgetown University, and I began to work up my German in connection with this. If one can see why I chose to pursue German by reading Rainer Maria Rilke rather than by reading Kant or Hegel, he may understand how it happened I became a poet instead of a philosopher. I chose to work at Rilke's early poems, because I could find no cribs for them. These are written in iambic pentameter, and thus I got a feel for this venerable line in English, and my own early line was written in it.[16] Rilke primed my pump to do my own work. I think (apart from the fact that translation got me actually writing lines of verse) this is because I found the translations deeply satisfying—partly because the labor was really hard for an unaccomplished student, partly because it is the nature of the German language to delay essential meaning, since the verb comes last, and partly because it is the nature of Rilke's poems to delay their own secrets because in the latter part of his poems he often changes key and expands the meaning of the whole poem beautifully.

---

[14] *Rapport*, #1 (1971), edited by Tony Petrosky and Tim Burke.
[15] I had finished an M.A. in English Literature at State University of Iowa in 1949. Although the Creative Writing Program was already in existence, I did no work with them, not yet being interested much in writing.
[16] My own early work, including the first published poems, was in this metric, but I quickly abandoned it and wrote the whole of my first book in three stress lines, rewriting some pieces in order to accomplish this. I lost most of my first big fee (from *Poetry*) because I rewrote "Mother Cabrini Crosses the Andes" after acceptance.

Thirdly, there is the fact that I became a confirmed Catholic in 1950 and was rendered more sensitive to (and more self-conscious of) religious experience which I was moved to express and share. I read deeply in the writings of the church fathers and in the lives of the saints, and although I came to see later that some of this reading (and some of that writing) was defensive in character (against anxiety), there is no question that the Sacrament of Confirmation[17] was indispensable to the beginning of my writing and, indeed, to the production of my first three books, all written at Notre Dame where I taught from 1951–1963. Here is an example of a poem on a religious theme written first at St. John's in 1950 and then revised for inclusion in a longer poem ("Epilogue, Songs of the Spouses, Complaint of Love") in my second volume *Ghosts of the Heart*[18]:

> And others cry for you
> Melancholy
> Unicorn though your bright pen
> Keep you splendid in a field
> Of color where ev'ry flower
> Bends to you. Over-
> Whelmed by violence of scent,
> Struck with color, one fails almost
>
> To see where your white
> Fur bleeds
> Lanced with a formal strength
> Strange to such a gentle one,
> Such eyes! There is another
> Hunt and another gentler
> Hunter. There is another
> Love and another holier lover.

The final factor involved in my beginning to write seriously (and, by the way, I have found no way to place these four factors in an order of

---

17 I had been baptized a Catholic in Hawaii in 1946.
18 The poem, based on a contemplation of #7 of The Unicorn Tapestries at The Cloisters in New York, was written at the same time as "A Chance Visit to Her Bones," part of *Cycle for Mother Cabrini*, for I had gone out to The Cloisters but by chance got off the A train a stop too early and found myself at Mother Cabrini High School, which houses the remains of the Saint at her shrine.

importance) was that I was encountering experiences in the summers of 1949 and 1950 that I could not handle emotionally: I was working summers in a Maryland State Hospital for insane blacks (we said "negroes" then). My work and most of my colleagues' was largely custodial and was totally inadequate to the suffering with which we were faced. I turned to poetry as a kind of incantatory prayer for these unfortunate people, feeling, as it were, unable to do anything else for them. Of the first two poems I published (with Horace Gregory's generous help) in *Partisan Review* in 1953, one was the poem of literary allusion and heroism referred to above, "A Pathological Case in Pliny" and the other was a poem of direct experience about feeding an aged, blind, insane, tubercular black. The poem was called "Contagious Ward." I wrote about eight of these hospital poems in all and published some of them in magazines but did not feel they fit in any of my books. Here is one I was fairly well satisfied with[19]:

AT SUNDOWN A SLOW PROCESSION

At sundown a slow procession
Lurches up to bed. Some grin.
Some frown and form contortions,
Child-like. The faces of most
Are blank. None talk. They slump or
Shuffle while others mince arth-
Ritic with age and inching
Painfully. One runs pell mell.

There are stragglers loathe to leave one
Vacant place for another.
Or wishing to breathe and bask
In the twilight air. One night
I saw a gnome move slowly
Through the gray half-light. He car-
Ried upon his back I thought
A lute, as the troubador

Goes sadly from beside his love.

I wanted to speak of these very early poems because it needs to be noticed that I began writing poems out of direct experience (the unicorn poem is perhaps more removed because based on a work of art), but

---

[19] I cannot remember for sure if I published this in a magazine but it may have been in Russell Kirk's *The Modern Age.*

these I excluded from my early book because I didn't think them good enough or somehow they didn't seem to fit. There is one exception: I included "A Chance Visit to Her Bones," which was based on a *religious* experience. Other than this one, which is perhaps somewhat qualified by the description "religious," I did not use contemporary, adult experience for the poems in that first book, but instead wrote about saints and heroes (who, however, were very real to me) and about childhood. I returned to writing out of adult observation part way through *Ghosts of the Heart* after making an astonishing discovery through paying attention to my own writing. The discovery was that I was drawing smaller circles around myself, that I was getting closer to home. The saints and heroes and children of my first book had given way in the final poem of the book, I realized, to a (more human?) *near* saint and martyr, who happened also to be a *poet*, namely Blessed Robert Southwell. I can tell you that when I first read about Southwell, in a brief biography by Sigrid Undset, I knew I would ultimately have to write a poem about him—which happened months later.[20]

Now, in *Ghosts of the Heart* I noticed I was not only writing about *poets* such as Byron and Shelley, but I was also unmistakably writing poems about poets who had problems with their mothers: Rimbaud, Heine, Hart Crane; and I had even written a poem about a classical hero who had a problem with his mother, namely, Achilles. (My poem ends with his moaning for his mother's aid at the edge of the sea.) How much such a self-discovery was due to the fact that I had gone into analysis a few months before (late 1955) I can't say, but I can say it was such a startling revelation it stopped me completely for a while and I wrote fiction—about fifteen stories, twelve of them published—which concerned my adult, personal experience. However, I first wrote a poem in which I faced as clearly as I was able, my adult feeling about my mother's death ("On the Death of the Artist's Mother Thirty-Three Years Later"), for I had decided, after my recognition, that one could use poetry in one of two ways: either to *avoid* encountering the truth about oneself or to *seek* encounter with it, and I had decided on the latter move. It seemed to me that otherwise poetry would finally become boring. Here is the last stanza of that poem:

She suffers there [in the grave] the natural turns;
Her nests on nests of flesh

---

[20] I was particularly suited to write about a martyr at the time for I was suffering from pleurisy and finding it difficult to breathe (live).

Are spelt to that irrational end,
The surd and faithful Change. And stays
to gain the faultless stuff reversed
From the numbers' trace at the Lasting Trump.
So here my mother lies. I do not
Resurrect again her restless
Ghost out of my grievous memory:
She waits the quiet hunt of saints.
Or the ignorance of citizens of hell.
And here is laid her ophan child with his
Imperfect poems and ardors, slim as sparklers.[21]

Then the stories intervened, and when I returned to poetry my style
was changed. It was more directly observational and used the simple
discipline of a ten-syllable line (altered from the stress writing of my
first book and of the earlier part of *Ghosts of the Heart*). Here is an example of the changed style written upon the occasion (never explained
to me) of seeing some old ladies at twilight in New York move down
East Tenth Street in a kind of parade carrying lighted lamps. The poem
is called:

NEW YORK SCENE: MAY 1958

It is just getting dark as the rain stops.
He walks slow and looks, though he's late. It's all
Muted. It's like a stage. A tender light
In the street, a freshness. He wonders, a
Funeral?: at uncertain intervals,
Up the block, the corner, small, old women
Walk home with soft lamps, holding them with love
Like children before them in the May night.
A few people move down East 10th Street. They
Do not look at these ladies with their lights
Blowing in the rain-wet airs by the stores,
Their ancient hands guarding their ancient flames.

[21] This poem was written in February 1956. I made this further discovery years later
looking back at the poem: I thought I had, so to speak, laid my mother's ghost, but
instead I found, rereading the final line, that I had buried myself beside her. The
fact that I was still to write more poems about her (and about my guilt, for she had
died a month after I was born) was confirmed by the first "Monologue of the Son
of Saul" and "Poem on his Birthday," both from *Spring of the Thief*.

Three boys race out of the YMCA
At the corner, carrying the brief god-
like gear of the runner. Two jackets hunch
Over two kids. There is high, choked laughter.
The third wears a sweater, black as his head
Lit with the wet. They sprint across the street,
And are gone into a tiny candy shop
Half underneath the walk. A dialogue
As the jackets and sweater cross leaves him
One clean phrase, "tomorrow again." He grins.
He turns, pauses by a store with small tools
Held in half spool boxes in the window,
With beads, clocks, one hand-turned coffee grinder
And way in the back, a wooden Indian.
Now he stops a girl he feels he knows. He
Asks her where he's going, gives an address.
She teaches him, lifting her arm up, rais-
ing a breast inside her poplin raincoat.
He listens carelessly. He wants to see
The long, full hair that gives form to her scarf
Of a wine and golden colored woolen,
Some turns of it loose about her forehead
Like a child, some lengths of it falling at
Her back as she walks away, having smiled.

After my discovery and my decision to use poetry to encounter and explore immediate experience, and to share this, I did not use reading and allusion and personae nearly as frequently or fully as I had before —with one, large exception, "The Monologues of the Son of Saul" from my third book, *Spring of the Thief*.[22] They were the earliest poems in the book,[23] and I will conclude this discussion of my earlier work with some notes about those sometimes difficult poems.

These poems are written in a thirteen-syllable line, which I believe I invented, and which I came to partly from a desire to experience more commitment to the line, so to speak, and partly because I wanted to break up the somewhat cliché rhythms set up by the ten-syllable line I had been using and which a longer line, say, of fifteen syllables would tend to fall back into.

[22] And of course the translations and the Melville poem from *Zigzag Walk*.
[23] Joseph Bennett writing in *The Hudson Review* thought them the best!

Except for the first one, the five "Monologues of the Son of Saul" are heavily allusive, dealing as they do both with the Saul figure of the Old Testament and that of the New (later "Paul") and with Odysseus as well, who in my treatment is identified with the latter Saul through his wanderings in the same general area. As father to Odysseus and grandfather to Bellerophon the poet, Sisyphus comes into view, and the final Monologue is conceived of as being voiced by him.

The death of King Saul and his sons together at the hands of the Philistines recalls Pyrrhus's murder of Priam and his son, which enables one to find another bridge to the Greek myths, and the fourth Monologue is virtually a retelling of the story of the death of Priam from *Aeneid* II. The starvation of Ugolino and his sons in the tower, as told by Dante in *The Inferno,* also comes to mind, and with it the ambivalent themes of the attack of the father on the son (or vice versa), which further recalls the story of David, Jonathan, and Saul ("Monologue II"). The counterpointed motif of the *salvation* of father by son or daughter brings with it the story of the young Roman girl Pero, who nursed her father when he was condemned to die of hunger, as told by Valerius Maximus and as painted by Peter Paul Rubens in his "Piété Filiale d'une Romaine." "Monologue III" deals with this and with related material taken from a modern tale of the saving of a dying father by his son and a compassionate girl: I mean the final scene of Steinbeck's *The Grapes of Wrath.* The first line of this monologue is quoted from that.

Some other examples in the Monologues of the blending of materials from several sources include the analogizing of the slaying of Goliath by David to the wounding of Polyphemus by Odysseus and the comparing of the accusation against Joseph (by the wife of Potiphar) to that against Bellerophon (by women of Greece).

The stories of Saul, David, and Jonathan, of David and the son of Jonathan, of Joseph and the Wife of Potiphar and that of Moses and Aaron of course come from the Old Testament, and I have made use also of modern commentators on these stories like Joseph Campbell. The story of Saul's conversion obviously is from the New Testament while the stories of Polyphemus, Penelope, and Odysseus are in Homer. I used Robert Graves's version of the Greek myths dealing with Odysseus, Orpheus, Bellerophon, and Sisyphus as well as Camus's commentary on the latter.

The themes probed by the Monologues as a group as well as by the companion poem in Part I of the book (*To a Young Poet Who Fled*) are the tragic ones of guilt within the family—or within a family sur-

rogate relationship as that of teacher and student—and the creative ones
of the metamorphosis or amelioration of guilt into art.

The movement from the usual contemporary voice of the speaker of
these poems (as in "Monologue I") to that of an ancient Hebrew figure
("Monologue II") or that of a Greek ("Monologue V"), or the mixing of
similar voices, seems justified by the universality of that community
which is determined in the first place by the presence of family and in
the second (perhaps consequent) place by human feeling. Without such
a community there would be no impetus to the structuring and sharing
of serious art. There would also be no need to mask or amplify one's own
feeling under the names and situations of others nor, hence, to account
for the fact in a note of this length.

Let me quote the poem following the Monologues because it is allied
to them in theme and structure (it uses the thirteen-syllable line) and
because it leaves us with an immediate, shared, adult experience, which
is the place I had hoped my poetry would take us. The occasion of the
poem was the fact that an unusually good student (his name is Tom
O'Donnell) had gone home at the end of a term, having left on my desk
a paper explaining why he was unable to write a paper on tragedy as he
was supposed to do. The piece he left was so beautifully written that I
took part of it out and published it as a prose poem in the first issue of
my magazine *Choice*. Here is the poem:

TO A YOUNG POET WHO FLED

Your cries make us afraid, but we love
your delicious music!
          Kierkegaard

So you said you'd go home to work on your father's farm.
We've talked of how it is the poet alone can touch
with words, but I would touch you with my hand, my lost son,
to say good-bye again. You left some work, and have gone.
You don't know what you mean. Oh, not to me as a son,
for I have others. Perhaps too many. I cannot
answer all the letters. If I seem to brag, I add
I know how to shatter an image of the father
(twice have tried to end the yearning of an orphan son,
but opened up in him, and in me, another wound).
No—I say this: you don't know the reason of your gift.
It's not the suffering. Others have that. The gift of tears

is the hope of saints, Monica again and Austin.
I mean the gift of the structure of a poet's jaw,
which makes the mask that's cut out of the flesh of his face
a megaphone—as with the goat clad Greeks—to amplify the light gestures of his soul toward the high stone seats.
The magic of the mouth that can melt to tears the rock
of hearts. I mean the wand of tongues that charms the exile
of listeners into a bond of brothers, breaking
down the lines of lead that separate a man from a
man, and the husbands from their wives, in these old, burned glass
panels of our lives. The poet's jaw has its tongue ripped
as Philomel, its lips split (and kissed beside the grave),
the jawbone patched and cracked with fists and then with the salve
of his fellows. If they make him bellow, like a slave
cooked inside the ancient, brass bull, still that small machine
inside its throat makes music for an emperor's guests
out of his cries. Thus his curse: the poet cannot weep
but with a public and musical grief, and he laughs
with the joys of others. Yet, when the lean blessings come,
they are sweet, and great. My son, I could not make your choice.
Let me take your hand. I am too old or young to say,
"I'd rather be a farmer in the hut, understood
by swine, than be a poet misunderstood by men."*

Buffalo, 30 October 1974

---

*When this poem appeared in *Spring of the Thief*, the word "guests" (8 lines from the end) was singular and "farmer" (2 lines from the end) was "swineherd." Mr. Logan has made these changes here. [w. h.]

WILLIAM MATTHEWS

WILLIAM MATTHEWS *(b. 1942 in Cincinnati) studied at Yale and the University of North Carolina at Chapel Hill where, with two friends, he founded Lillabulero Press. After teaching in the writing program at Cornell, he moved in 1974 to Boulder and the University of Colorado, where he is currently Associate Professor of English.*

(Photo by William Stafford)

Moving Around

In a recurring childhood dream I was separated from my family. We'd be out walking and a crack would appear in the earth, or a widening river. I imagined myself the dream's unwilling victim. It was years before I understood that the dream was as much about my urge to be separate as it was about my fear of separation.

As I grew older the other characters changed. It would be my wife and two sons together, me separate.

Though I didn't dream about them, other splits fit the pattern. I would want to be both a part of and apart from some community: a neighborhood, a team, a political movement whose complaints I shared but whose rhetoric I hated. . . .

I used to have a morning paper route, played baseball and basketball, had a dog named Spot. Troy, Ohio. When I was about twelve my father left his job with the Soil Conservation Service and went to work for a student exchange program, Children's International Summer Villages.

Geography had seemed abstract to me, some pleasant puzzle. Now the vast world grew in my mind. My father wrote letters to Finland, Japan. The family went to Europe. I began to realize I was American, envied and disliked and judged for that, and shaped by it. That fact went ahead of me somehow, the way that being black might, or living in a shack by the river and being three grades behind in school, poor Norbert.

We moved to Cincinnati, where CISV's American headquarters were. My father had been born there, so had I. We had family there. I went back to Europe three times. I went to boarding school in the Berkshire Hills, I went to college. Spot was an aging snuffle. In Europe buildings sat on the same spot for six hundred years—more, unless war broke them. They seemed more like stones than buildings I had known and the lives they passed through themselves seemed stable and claustrophobic.

I had lived in Ames, Iowa; Rosewood, Troy, and Cincinnati, Ohio; Sheffield, Massachusetts; New Haven, Connecticut. I was married and had a son. Moving meant opportunity. One left friends, but also dead ends, shames, bad times.

And landscape grew cumulative. A stream that ran through a roadside park near Rosewood flowed into a stream in the Berkshires. There were hollyhocks by the back steps in Troy, where I threw a tennis ball for hours against a strike zone I'd outlined on the shed door. When I got good at it, I'd load the bases, go 3-and-0, and then, nobody out, trying hard now, see if I could pitch my way out of the inning. One summer in New Haven I was doing odd jobs and worked for a family in Hamden. Beside the shed where they kept a huge glum goose at night, I found the hollyhocks unchanged, their dusty scent so thick it might as well not have rained for twelve years.

When I played those imaginary ball games, I sensed they wouldn't matter if I couldn't lose. But I could pitch an imaginary game in half an hour, and if I lost I'd pitch another, and another if I had to, until I'd won. I never slept with a loss. There'd be another game, I could be traded, there'd be another season, I could move.

I moved to North Carolina with my wife, then pregnant, and son. Two sons. Now my sport was basketball. I played on an otherwise all black team. Our mailman loved jazz and cognac, and so did I. I found out he had a team in a local league, and asked if I could play. It turned out to be the only integrated team in the league: blacks and whites played against but not with each other. I liked to pass; I liked to decide by where I'd pass if we'd run or set up plays; I liked to penetrate because it made the defense commit itself and the patterns shift. When we'd line up for the tip-off the guys on the other team, black or white, would say of one of my teammates, "I'll take number 6." Of me: "I'll take the white guy."

I've always loved in basketball its particular balance between pattern and improvisation. The rift is always there, but it shifts, and the play does, too, each moving the other. When I'm playing well I respond so well to this balance that I help cause it.

North Carolina was the first place I'd ever lived that I helped to cause a little how the place felt. A child is dwarfed by his parents, a student by his school. I was a graduate student in North Carolina, but I had two children, I knew as many people outside the university as in, I started a literary magazine with friends, I voted and paid taxes. We lived in an apartment complex. Toward the end I wanted to get away. I wrote a poem called "Moving" before we moved.

MOVING

When we spurt off
in the invalid Volvo
flying its pennant of blue fumes,
the neighbors group and watch.
We twist away like a released balloon.

I'd written poems in high school, most of them about the sadness of adolescent life. I wrote a few in college, a dozen maybe, of which I finished four. Through the kindness of one of my professors, two were published. He didn't intervene in my poems' behalf, I'm sure; he only suggested I send them out and told me where I could use his name as one reason for asking the editor's attention. When I saw them in print I was proud, then scared. They were only technically good. Otherwise they were false. Worse than that, I had believed in them wholly when I wrote them, when I sent them off, when I first saw them in print. I could be false to myself, to the language I wrote in, in ways so subtle it took me weeks to notice and years to understand.

Like many adolescents I had become a good liar. I lied about where I had been, about sex, about money, to my parents, teachers, friends, to myself. Such lies seem so crude, I thought I knew about them: I am saying X but the truth I am keeping to myself is Y.

The rift was in me. Such lies gave me power: I could *use* the language.

But, looking at my poems in print, I felt the force of something I didn't yet know about language: it is communal. Poets like to talk about the solitude of writing, but the language they use has passed through everyone who has ever spoken or read or written the same words, no matter how individually any poet combines those words. The lives of others are on the words, as palm oil is on coins long in circulation.

And there the poems were in print. I must have known my shame for those poems were as opaque to the few who read them as they were transparent to me. I didn't know enough about myself, about language, about the lives through which language passed on its way through me.

Teaching and writing poems brought me into a larger world. Landscape continued to be my deepest pleasure and most ambitious exploration. At Aurora, New York, the lake was four miles wide. In the spring Canada geese settled in for a month, foraging by day in the fields and flying back to the lake each dusk. In the winter the lake threw onto the shore, with its wave-smoothed rocks, gnarled chunks of ice. I could not— I who loved metaphor, transformation, change—make them into anything but themselves, and their resistance soothed me.

Aurora had 600 residents and the college 600 students. I liked the sparse population. The first full day we were there I walked with my sons to a cluster of houses down the road, where younger faculty with children lived. The kids all called it "the neighborhood." The boys looked around; everyone was indoors. "Where are the friends?" one of them asked. Soon they had friends.

I did, too. I wasn't lonely, but the rhythms of solitude and affection pulled me hard, surprised me.

The next year we moved to Ithaca and bought an old farmhouse on Krums Corners Road. Colonel Krum had run an inn, a stop on the stagecoach run north to Geneva, two hundred years ago. We had six apple trees, two pears, three cherries, blackberries, grapes, a 100-yard-long stretch of multiflora roses on one side of the yard. Lilacs in three colors of bloom, peonies, and irises—my favorites. One cherry was an ornamental, beautiful for its three days of bloom in May. My first book of poems had come out: now and then I'd be asked to give a reading somewhere. Every year when it came into bloom I was gone. I loved the place.

My wife and I began to fight, sometimes with long silences. In the midst of them I'd remember how the molecules in solid things, spoons or doors, are said to be constantly moving. Probably all our friends guessed before we did that we'd get divorced.

One day when I hadn't yet put up the screens on the second floor windows, I went out one window onto the roof over the front porch. The screens went on from the outside, so when I got them up I'd have sealed off my route back through the windows. She was to come prop the ladder against the porch so I could get down when I was done. But the phone rang, and she talked for a while. The boys were in the house, and my wife, and I was on the single side of the rift again. My terror was so pure I must have added to my childhood dream the still unconscious knowledge that I'd soon be divorced.

There were three huge sugar maples off the porch, forty or fifty feet tall. They interlaced at the top, and the boys and I played endlessly a game I invented called Rocket. I kicked a soccer ball high into the trees and as it fell it caromed off branches, trunks. Sometimes it fell four times as slowly for all its high pinball detours as it would by gravity. Sometimes it hit a thick branch on the way up and sliced back down. We tried different scoring systems: how much for a clean catch, how much for the first bounce, did two bounces count? The boys would giggle and make showboat catches, forgetting to sprawl until they had the ball snugly in. Or they would scuffle grimly, suddenly wanting to win by whatever rules we'd agreed on for the day, so intense I'd think they were holding their breaths except I could hear the rasps they breathed calming back down after flurries of effort or temper.

I wanted to climb down one of those maples, but the branches of all three fell just short of the porch roof. I was breathing like an old pump, hysterical, when my wife arrived with the ladder.

Some people like to tell about their lives, but that's not what I mean to do here. I'm interested in the biography of some images, some collisions between my emotional life and the language that binds me to others.

All that summer and the next year my dog, Underdog, killed woodchucks. He kept them out of the garden, though my neighbors' sheep drifted over one summer night, a cloud of teeth, and cropped the garden. They left the tomatoes and onions. We named Underdog after a character in a TV cartoon, a beagle with a cape who talked in couplets. Spot had been part beagle. Wally Cox was Underdog's voice. The boys watched Underdog every Saturday morning; often I watched with them.

I liked the traveling I did to give readings, or to work in poets-in-the-school programs. One spring I was working in schools in the Housatonic River Valley, where I'd been in boarding school years before. I was glad to be away from my eroding home, but I missed my wife and sons and felt guilty for being glad to be away. The lyrical gloom of adolescence came back to me as I was driving to Washington, Connecticut, along a road I remembered from bus trips made by the basketball team. In the motel where I stayed while I was working at Hotchkiss I wrote a poem with a deliberately lavish title:

DRIVING ALONGSIDE THE HOUSATONIC RIVER
ALONE ON A RAINY APRIL NIGHT

I remember asking
where does my shadow go at night?
I thought it went home,
it grew so sleek at dusk.
They said, you just don't
notice it, the way you don't tell yourself
how to walk or hear
a noise that doesn't stop.
But one wrong wobble
in the socket and inside the knee
chalk is falling, school
is over.

As if the ground were a rung
suddenly gone from a ladder,
the self, the shoulders bunched
against the road's each bump, the penis
with its stupid grin,
the whole rank slum of cells
collapses.
I feel the steering wheel
tug a little, testing.
For as long as that takes
the car is a sack of kittens
weighed down by stones.
The headlights chase a dark ripple
across some birch trunks.
I know it's there, water
hurrying over the shadow of water.

Soon my wife and I were separated, and I was separated from my sons, too. As soon as we could agree on the terms we would be divorced. We couldn't. Lawyers handled the last part.

I moved to Andover, Massachusetts, where I lived on an acre in young woods (maples, birch, about twenty years old), and taught in Boston. The boys lived an hour away. I moved to be near them while divorce details were worked out. The divorce went through. The county sheriff served the papers and congratulated me. I did a lot of readings. I'd been to Louisiana and walked over the rice plantation, now restored, where Audubon made his first bird paintings. He shot the birds first. He was a tutor to the owner's daughter and had his afternoons free. I'd been to Tucson and kept driving out to the resistant desert, as fiercely itself against my transforming imagination as the mountains were in Colorado when I'd been there.

My job in Boston was for one year only; soon I'd move again. The boys would live with me every summer, and could visit during every school vacation I could afford to transport them to wherever I would be. It began to look as if I'd be in Colorado, and I liked that prospect. I'd met a woman I wanted to live with: I revised some of the myths about solitude I'd been telling myself so long.

I hadn't been in Europe for ten years. I went to England to visit my parents, who live there now, and took the boys. I went to Canisy, in Normandy, when a plaque was put on the house where the French poet

Jean Follain was born. It would have been his seventieth birthday, but he'd been killed by a car in the Place de la Concorde. I'd spent four years working, with a friend, on translations of Follain's prose poems. His widow, a tiny, tough, and generous woman, showed us St. Lô, razed in World War II when the Allies took Normandy. I was an "American" again. From the train from Paris I was moved by orchards that reminded me of the house I'd loved and sold in Ithaca. Dairy cattle moved among the apple trees; though I've never lived with them they made me weep. I realized I'd become an American without knowing it. The boy who went to foreign movies, to Europe, who in his teens read Ionesco as fast as Grove Press published him but delayed reading James's *The American Scene* until he was thirty (Mme. Ionesco came to Canisy for the Follain ceremony)—the same boy grown older had learned from travel and love of his sons and love of the American language to be American. Perhaps I learned it from failing, as banks or businesses or marriages are said to fail. One declares bankruptcy—a kind of confession—and moves on.

I would be going to Colorado, early in the summer, and as soon as the boys were out of school in New Hampshire they'd come out.

In my early poems, like "Moving," time is like a lens opening and slicing shut. If I imagined something emblematic, in significant posture, I could get a good picture. The method was good for the bases loaded, 3-and-0, none out; the strain on the pitcher's face tells all.

But little of life organizes itself into symbolic moments. And symbolic moments may distort as much as they summarize; indeed, they may distort *by* summarizing.

There are after all the times when a pitcher has to live with having lost, as I would not allow myself to do when I was young, bending my private world as easily as water seems to bend light.

After learning to write poems like "Moving," I wanted to learn to write about different kinds of time. As in a snapshot, in "Moving" it is hard to tell what any of the people thinks about the event. This neutrality is an improvement from my early youth, when I would melodramatically fear the separation in my recurrent dream without realizing that I also wanted it.

Perhaps the adjective "released" suggests the speaker's attitude toward leaving his neighbors. I won't speak for the poem, but I remember the day I left. My wife and sons had gone ahead while I finished the heavy work of moving, cleaned our apartment out, haggled with the landlord for the return of our deposit money. It was nearly 100 degrees. I was glad to be going back north, singing, waving my free arm in time, sweating so heavily in the thick heat I might as well have been under spot lights, though under them I could never have been so giddily oblivious to how I must have looked as motorists grumbled by in the sapping sunlight.

The poem about driving alongside the river pleased me when I wrote it. The man in the poem is in one place, at one time, but he carries his childhood with him, his schooling, his adolescence; no snapshot can do that. We see him alone—daydreaming would be the word, except in the poem it is night. He is with those central images and myths about his own life that impede and enliven him. Though as I read the poem it is not a difficult choice, he chooses, when for an instant the possibility of not continuing seems sharp and not silly, to keep moving.

I am not surprised to find him in a poem called "Moving Again." I speak of him as "him" because he is not me. He clearly shares certain crucial situations with me (his sons have the same names as mine); he resembles me more than anyone else I know or imagine. But when I am done with a poem I walk away from it; he stays in it. In many of my poems he does not appear, or appears disguised as others.

Perhaps I have invented a sophisticated version of those imaginary playmates children have. My son Sebastian had one for a while. Sebastian's friend pulled off, at the end of his life, several amazing feats, and adults were getting skeptical about him; so Sebastian announced one day he was dead. "How did it happen?" "He got run over on his way to the store to get cheese for his family." Since his family had never been mentioned before, it was clear they were us, who had been laughing at this now dead hero, his last heroism a small generosity for us.

That's the way I like to see these imaginary selves go. They should be left behind, in some poem, on some imaginary street, whenever the continuing and moving self no longer needs them. Our poetry is full of them—Kees's Robinson, Berryman's Henry, almost everyone's "I." They are in postures of revealing, insupportable loss, held in house arrest by the beautiful poems they live in. The poet keeps moving; and, when I am the poet, keeps writing about it, wanting to include more.

When I got to Colorado I wrote the poem called "Moving Again." Nicky is the son of friends here who used to live in Illinois. I had a high-school girlfriend named Verna. And in some high-school anthology there was a story about people transported (though the story suggests the vehicle may have been only their yearning to be moved) to a magical planet named Verna. They gathered in a barn, sat on benches, and were taken away, or so I remember the story. There was some reason, like the impending end of this planet, why they wanted to be gone. But the story wasn't good enough to resist my imagination, to impose its truth on mine. So I don't remember the story's reason. ·

MOVING AGAIN

At night the mountains look like dim
hens. In a few geological eras
new mountains may
shatter the earth's shell
and poke up like stone wings.
Each part must serve for a whole.
I bring my sons to the base
of the foothills and we go up.
From a scruff of Ponderosa
pines we startle gaudy swerves
of magpies who settle in our rising
wake. Then there's a blooming
prickly pear. "Jesus, Dad, what's that?"
Willy asks. It's like a yellow tulip
grafted to a cactus: it's a beautiful
wound the cactus puts out
to bear fruit and be healed.
If I lived with my sons
all year I'd be less sentimental
about them. We go up
to the mesa top and look down
at our new home town. The thin air
warps in the melting light
like the aura before a migraine.
The boys are tired. A tiny magpie
fluffs into a pine far below
and further down in the valley
of child support and lights
people are opening drawers.

One of them finds a yellowing
patch of newsprint with a phone
number pencilled on it
from Illinois, from before they moved, before
Nicky was born. Memory
is our root system.
"Verna," he says to himself
because his wife's in another room,
"whose number do you suppose this is?"

JEROME MAZZARO

JEROME MAZZARO (b. 1934 in Detroit) was educated at
Wayne State University and the State Universiy of Iowa.
A translator and prolific critic as well as a poet, in 1964 he
was the recipient of a Guggenheim Fellowship. Mazzaro
currently teaches at the State University of New York at
Buffalo and edits Modern Poetry Studies.

(Photo by Layle Silbert)

Returns

One corner of our kitchen on South Green Street in Detroit was set aside for play, and as children we often used the area marked off by refrigerator and pantry door to construct our clothespin forts and to zoom wooden toys and model airplanes about. Later, as we outgrew these pastimes, we sat cross-legged reading comic books and magazines. Usually the magazines were *Life* and *Sport*, but occasionally there was a stray *Liberty* or *Reader's Digest*. One day my older brother brought home a copy of *Look* which contained, among other things, a survey of post-Expressionist painting. Among the illustrations was a rooster painting by Lorjou. I had no idea then that my reaction to the illustration would be a poem or that the final version of the poem, "Notes Toward an Elegy for Ben" (1961), would shape my emergence as a poet. Rather, the violence, vividness, and bright red background of the canvas reminded me of a ritual during the war. Saturday my father and I would go to the local poultry market and buy a hen, and on Sunday morning, my mother would get the hen ready for eating. She would not only have to kill and bleed it, but also pluck it. At times, my older sisters helped, but for the most part, my mother did everything alone. Having grown up in a farming community in Italy, she handled the job with detachment, usually while we were at Mass. The effect of the ritual was to introduce into our kitchen some of the natural violence that in massive terms was being described in war reports and movies and in conversations around the table with neighbors. Often the last of these would include factory accidents, operations, and suicides.

It took practically no time for us children to realize that the lives of our parents and relatives and neighbors were not easy. We learned quickly that if one was not destroyed, he was beaten into conformity, or became some sort of misfit. Our prime example was the old lady several doors down whom we jokingly called "Old Witch." Another was a woman called by the newspapers, "The Witch of Delray." She lived blocks from my parents on Medina Street when she committed the series of murders that sent her to prison. Every now and then *The American Weekly* would revive the details in its "Great Crimes of the Century" series, and in her way, she became every bit as familiar in our memories as a cousin who had killed herself, an uncle whose hand had been cut off in a factory accident, and a neighbor who had gone to the University of Moscow to become a Communist. There were also crises involving my

being struck by an automobile and my brother's nearly dying of a ruptured appendix. But, just as there was a cruelty, there was a generosity.
Those who failed would try to help others succeed. Self-sacrifice was as
common as competition. Yet, it was not until I was at Iowa City in
1955, trying to squeeze out new poems for a poetry workshop, that I
began to face having to deal with this heritage.

The workshop in the '50s faced different priorities. It was working its
way through Rainer Maria Rilke's *Das Buch der Bilder*, though some
members had progressed to *Sonnets to Orpheus*. Ekphrasis seemed its
major mode of expression, here and there complicated by an overlay of
classical myth. Paul Engle, who was in charge, impressed on us the need
to develop techniques that would carry us beyond casual inspiration
into careerism. He greatly valued regular production and could see no
more tastelessness in his own transforming of Rilke's *Sonnets to
Orpheus* into *American Child* (1945) than his students saw in their
trivializations of Wordsworth. I was working part-time in the library,
reshelving reference works and current periodicals and at times sitting
in at the reference desk when the librarians were meeting. The job gave
me time for research and writing that I might not otherwise have had.
My poem "Of the Japanese" (later revised into "In a Japanese Garden"),
had drawn extended praise from Engle at an early session of the workshop, but I had not been able to come up with anything so successful
afterward. The few poems I had written went against the themes of
nature-into-art or transience-into-permanence that typified most workshop poems. Engle rightly complained of my writing's being rhythmically
flat and monotonous, and I tried a new poem, "Santos" (now "Cycle for
Ste. Anne's"), to offset his complaints. The poem uses ekphrasis and
rhythms based on musical measure instead of traditional metrics to recall
boyhood experiences. I also glanced at *Look* and the Lorjou illustration
to construct a companion piece. The result was "Lorjou and My Mother"
(April 1955):

LORJOU AND MY MOTHER

Lorjou wrings roosters' necks on fields of red
And stretches them across a canvas where
Their feathers white and limp as rags rave at
The air and cannot stain the silence with
Their blood. The roosters that my mother bled
Raged just as lifeless from a broken chair,

Their necks cut open with a paring knife.
I used to ride a nearby bench and watch
As she would hold their necks and slit their throats
And catch the drops of blood inside a cup.
Lorjou has caught this violence of life
With palette knife and artist's stroke to match.

Majestic as mad Lear his roosters shy
My mother's fingermarks around their neck,
Her housewife mind would kill them with a stroke
And lay them on a sink where blood stains break
A harmony of white and dead beaks pry
The porcelain like dust. These proud cocks beak

A timeless death, awakened to the fact
That immortality is tangible
As fluff. Lorjou has taught them that. His art
Preserves the struggle. Mortal, my mother's cocks
Sleep out their death in frying pans or act
A child's supper in a gay-rimmed bowl.

The enjambment and the free play of the two middle lines of each stanza anticipate the failure of the poem's language to come together tonally, imagistically, or structurally. The action verbs were typical of the times. Somewhere I had been told that Dylan Thomas considered "rage" consummately poetic, and having been impressed by Shakespeare's use of the word in *King Lear*, I added it along with "rave" for vibrancy. The inclusion led to the mention of Lear and more gratuitous violence. Engle's reaction was to compare my effort to Keats's "Ode on a Grecian Urn," presuming wrongly that it was striving to reach the stasis of Lorjou. He also commented on the echo of Wallace Stevens in "immortality is tangible / As fluff," and he suggested that I might profit from abandoning the run-on line. In June of 1955, I finished a revision of the work. This draft was more closely rhymed and embraced more of the Lear motif with "scranny" and "common cocks." In December, the last of the drafts before "Notes" was ready. The new version ran four lines longer than the previous versions and tended to be even more disparate. It made overt, though not more relevant, the Western movie motif implicit in "riding a bench" and "biting the dust." The poem remained in this state for my master's thesis.

My few other efforts to deal with my childhood in the years before going into the Army in 1957 for a six-months' tour centered as well on violence. I had written "For Harold" (1957) in a direct response to a journalism professor's statement that journalists write for the man on Hastings Street, a notorious red-light, skidrow area of Detroit. As the street was falling to urban renewal, I remarked that one ought to write quickly because the street was likely not to last out the year. I composed a poem in rapid, sing-song couplets, confounding our childhood game of King of the Mountain with the deaths of Harold of Hastings and a neighbor killed in World War II. The last had been the only real death in the neighborhood, and we had watched the blue-star pennant in the window change to gold. Given the impetus for the poem, I was surprised by how much latent emotion surfaced:

FOR HAROLD

You were the king—at least you claimed to be—
of shoving landslides and a factured knee,
and we all bowed to you, taking your side
in this and that. We even helped you hide
when William came and told him you were dead
or gone. I don't remember which we said,
but he believed our tale and claimed your crown
and golden birds for having knocked you down.
You went away one winter. Exile, I think.
It's so confusing now. It was the brink
of Christmas and the snow (The telegram
came later, that I'm sure.) had covered tram
and trolley tracks. It was in all the books—
killed by a sniper near the river Luxe.
And all of Hastings Street sent masses out,
even gulled William, who began the rout.

By admitting its confusion, the poem was far more successful at containing run-on lines and the disparateness that wrecked "Lorjou." Rhyme and diction helped, but a sense of play seemed the crucial change. I used the device again in a small elegy called "Death Was a Trick" (1964) but with the knowledge that no large, durable body of work could be constructed on its premise. I would need other techniques if I wished to achieve that regular production that Engle fostered.

My release from the Army brought with it a return to graduate school at Wayne State University and more time to think about the problems of my verse. While stationed at Fort Riley, I had come across a copy of Aaron Copeland's *What to Listen for in Music* (1939) and it had given me some ideas on how to expand the musical nature of poetry beyond the mere musical measures of "Santos." Bob Bly, who had been a friend at the workshop, came up with other ideas. He invited me up to Ann Arbor to spend an afternoon with him and Donald Hall and our talk ranged into launching *The Fifties* and syllabics and free verse as alternatives to the decasyllabic line we had been schooled in. The fervor of Bly's positions naturally suited the somber, almost ministerial clothes he then wore. His deep concern for poetry offset the belligerence of his convictions. Much as Engle had made me attentive to the surface of poetry, Bly worked to waken me to poetry's inner life. By then, Ginsberg's *Howl* had begun its impact, and the various "Poems on a Line in Poem Z" and elegies for dead automobiles had given way to poetry that dealt more closely with human situations. The era of handling violence offstage like French tragedy or in such polite and neat ways that the blood and anguish hardly showed was coming to a close. Robert Lowell's *Life Studies* (1959) had not yet appeared, but a number of the poems from that volume had been published as had a number of Snodgrass's "Heart's Needle" poems and a few of Anne Sexton's breakdown poems. It seemed as if a poetry reflective of our own experiences was finally beginning to come into being.

I responded to the changes by briefly becoming reactionary. I spent some of the spring reworking "Santos" into "Cycle for Ste. Anne's" and writing a now-discarded sonnet sequence. Bly hectored from the calm of his Minnesota island or Grammercy Park about my paying more attention to images and my going beyond the sensibility of the tens. No more sonnets. This is good, he wrote, or he would pencil out a number of lines as excess. He insisted on specific products and brand names to convey emotions, and he was seconded by another young poet, Charles Paye, who badgered me about discursiveness. The neighborhood was no less condemning. Half of those I had graduated with from grade school were now dead and those who survived had so set their lives in terms of the ownership of things that they proved Bly's insistence on products. Most already looked ten years older than they were, bedraggled, overweight, dragging two or three children, and for all practical purposes, they were as anonymous as the factories and machines they married soon after high school. One who had been a classmate of my older brother and president of their senior class had been killed in an automobile crash shortly before my return from service. Reporting the events to my mother, a neighbor had spoken of the accident as a suicide since he and his wife were about to split. The information lay dormant until fall when a classmate of mine was killed driving the wrong way on a thruway. His death set me thinking about the influence of automobiles and auto-mobile factories and accidents on life generally. My thoughts went back to my own childhood accident, merging the two classmates into one, and clustering about them the rooster ritual and again Lorjou. I soon had a new elegy:

AUTO-WRECK

Yesterday as torches
cut Ben out of the wreck
of his Ford and scorched him
home to his family,

the cabinet called a cri-
sis, and Lorjou in France
wrung a rooster's head on
canvas, hung it scranny

headed as Ben (or Min-
ister Y at last news),
white on red, where feathers,
bright as sheets ragging a

wind, could never ruffle
housewives with their noise of
steel, bad politics, or love,
or finally even with

the redness of his blood.

Having incorporated into the new work a few lines from "Lorjou and My Mother," I was left to ponder what to do with the remainder of the poem. The experience of "Lorjou" seemed, because of Bly, to have be-come central in a way it had not been at Iowa. Richard Weisenseel, who saw the poem shortly after I completed it, compared its primitive violence to Lorca's, and we talked about Lorca's ability to moderate terror by using musical forms. It struck me that I might be able to develop the rest of "Lorjou" along similar lines, extending "Auto-Wreck" into a longer poem by equating metaphor to musical phrase and ending with a coda. My model was an imaginary piano piece whose separate themes would play against the silences of space. From the first, I saw that the major tension would be stasis and motion and that the expression of this tension must be as primitive and direct as possible. The result, I hoped, would be a work that was accurate in respect to the carelessness toward individual death at the same time that it was responsive to the warmth of the people I had known. On the surface, the poem would be cooly intellectual; underneath, the poetry would threaten to dissolve with every line.

My first task became that of isolating the metaphors that might best sustain the 192 lines of the poem's printed version (*The Literary Review* 4 [1961], 395–400). This was accomplished by trial and error. I immediately seized upon an epigraph from Ezra Pound's "Hugh Selwyn Mauberley" that jointly condensed the poem and my poetics: "The age demanded an image." I would concentrate on images that seemed to embrace and embody aspects of the day. Part Two (originally called "The First Metaphor") reshaped the rooster killing of the "Lorjou" work into an exposition of the life histories of both Ben and the poem's speaker. I experimented with a variety of stanza patterns based on two, four, six, and eight syllables and found that the more I concentrated on the mathematical and abstract qualities of the poem, the more I was able to contain naturally the irrational and emotional qualities that surfaced. The art was in keeping as detached from the subject as my mother had been from the hens she killed. Whatever emotion got in would not determine the work's direction or its final resignation. Other imagery took over the "dreams/aspirations" theme of Part Three, and I dropped the motif of motion pictures. Part Four worked directly with art, and the coda drew much from the discussion of motion in chapter four of Benjamin Farrington's *Greek Science* (1944). The book had been a legacy from my science major days at Wayne State. With the poem's completion, I felt a release. A long struggle with propriety was over and from now on I would be able to deal with violence on my own terms.

From using Ford instead of automobile in "Notes," I moved quickly to using John Deere and Woolworth's in "White Forms" (1962) and "Morgan Street" (1960). By focusing on particulars, I was able, too, to extend the ranges of my work to include social issues dating from my childhood. "The Witch of Delray" became entwined with a second neighborhood misfit, a young, dull-witted man who daily rummaged through ashcans in "Changing the Windows" (1964). The tone of the speaker, like that of the neighborhood, has become affluent, but the savagery, the web, the oppression that threatened all of us remains. Irony rather than abstraction is used to contain it.

CHANGING THE WINDOWS

When I am forced by circumstance and heat
to take the winter windows off the house
spotted like bass who will be stripped of lice,
I think of that old woman down the street
who got by the Depression renting rooms
to seven lonely bachelors in a row,
the last of whom fell from an open window
changing the screens one sunny afternoon.
Called Mother Witch by city columnists
who wrote how all the seven perished strangely,
each with an ample, paid-up policy
made out to her, she didn't snare one jurist
in all the headline months her trials ran—
though winter changed to summer as it must.
She sat reading a favorite *Evening Post*
as if no court could judge her for her sin.
Thinking, too, of her full grown idiot son
who scavenged in our ashcans after that
feeding himself with cast-off bits of fat
until a court ruled he'd too lost his reason,
somehow I think of husbanded black widows
and savage birds who sometimes eat their young,
and wonder at the web this world becomes,
then scuttle off to unhinge all the windows.

The art is again a keeping of the important issues peripheral, in putting civil rights and the Kennedy assassinations in the background of "The North Oaks" (1970) or in submerging the moral rot of "Monsignor Nonce" (1965) into physical decay.

Just as "Notes" made it possible for me to deal with violence, it also allowed me to become more directly personal. Bly's and Weisenseel's insistence that I go to Europe for models led me to contemporary Italian poetry and a style for my personal poems that is at once formal in diction and intimate in subject. The first of the poems in the new style, "Spring," was completed in 1959, but my two favorites were done later and are based on trips to Italy in 1965 and 1969. The first, "After Spring Storms" (1971), invokes the town my parents came from. Vergil mentions it by name in the *Aeneid* VII. 740 and medieval legend has him living there. I try to echo his first eclogue in my closing lines. On the eve of Palm Sunday, the children of the community go into the olive groves to fetch branches which are blessed the next morning. The farmers go into the groves, too, in a countermove. Their actions suggest a game at whose base is a concern for survival. Hence Noah, Claudius, and the poem's link to "Lorjou":

AFTER SPRING STORMS

Checking the olive groves after a storm,
seeing among the gnarled limbs
which lightning struck, which must be grafted,
and which, come Palm Sunday, must be watched
from the theft of town boys,
I begin to understand something of farming.
I think of Noah's dove,
Claudius dipping lobster at Capri,
the smooth, rich, buttery taste of the oil,
my own mortality,
and the immemorial stones imbedded in the land.

The second poem, "Flowers" (1969), details a Florentine market with its various stalls, including those of real and artificial flowers. Less overtly perhaps, it, too, conjures "Lorjou":

FLOWERS

One could almost taste the straw red onions
hanging there in the stall above
the fake straw flowers one would almost swear were real,
and which even in winter one could buy
for only a few pennies.
Or if real flowers were what one wanted
to bring spring to one corner of a room,
they were there in another stall,
more expensive,
wafting their sweet aromas for passers-by,
fooling no one with their fragrances,
not even the small, disinterested flies.

The pure joy of both poems in the face of fraud and mortality conveys some of the spirit of indestructability that keeps us all going in hard times and keeps me celebrating the struggle.

WILLIAM MEREDITH

William Meredith (*b. Jan. 9, 1919 in New York City*) *was graduated from Princeton in 1940 and served as a naval aviator during World War II. During the Korean War he was recalled to active duty in the Navy. He has taught at Princeton, the University of Hawaii, Middlebury College, Bread Loaf, and since 1955 at Connecticut College in New London. His honors include the Loines Award from the National Academy of Arts and Letters. Since 1964 Meredith has been a chancellor of the Academy of American Poets.*

The Luck of It

A poet approaches language in the spirit of a woodman who asks pardon of the dryad in a tree before he cuts it down. Words are inhabited by the accumulated experience of the tribe. The average poet adds about as much to the language as he adds to the nitrogen content of his native soil. But he can administer the force that resides in words.

It is the magic inhabiting the language that he administers, all the lived meaning that the noises have picked up in the days and nights since they were first uttered. He finds ways to revive that total meaning, or a part of it he wants to use, as he makes his verbal artifacts. His very attentive use of a word, associating it with other words used with equal attention (for no word is an island), astonishes us the way we would be astonished to hear a dryad speak pardon out of an oak tree. And as if this were not all elfin enough already, he does the job largely at a subconscious level. His intelligence stands around, half the time, like a big, friendly, stupid apprentice, handing him lopping-shears when he wants the chain saw.

In "Duns Scotus's Oxford," Hopkins demonstrates this magic of association in the tremendous energy of the opening and closing lines. "Towery city and branchy between towers;"—who would have imagined there was all that going on in those six words before they were joined in that sequence? And of Duns Scotus himself, the final line says, "Who fired France for Mary without spot." *Kinesis* is all, and the energy is in the words rather than in the thinky parts of man's mind.

Both superstition and modesty warn a poet against reducing his meager knowledge of these forces to theory. A poem I wrote a long time ago has come to seem to me an example of how much luck goes into the job. It was a breakthrough that I seemed at the time simply to stumble on as I went about my fairly methodical and fairly *safe* wording of experience. It was a poem that carried me into its own experience, demonstrating that simple mystery Frost has put: no surprise in the writer, no surprise in the reader. It's a poem called "A View of the Brooklyn Bridge," and I am still incapable of judging it as a poem, so strongly did it imprint itself as a revelation. Set down rationally, revelations sound like hallucination: this bush by the side of the road flared up and a voice spoke out of it—we very rational people feel foolish recounting it. But this is what happened: a series of associations, and the words they inhabited, came to me uninvited but because I was in a state of unselfcentered attention. This is apparently a rare state with me, because in the twenty-five years since then I have averaged about six poems a year. That is apparently as often as the muse can get my attention.

Before I introduce the document, I might say that it had perhaps one forerunner, a longer poem called "Love Letter from an Impossible Land" —a somewhat more willful performance but similar—that I'd written five years earlier, when I was twenty-three. Other than that, I think all the poems I had written before this were primarily rational attempts to word accurately something I thought I understood. This poem, and to a less conscious degree "Love Letter," were irrational acts of surrender to an experience I knew very little about but which I had a sudden sense was being offered to me.

A VIEW OF THE BROOKLYN BRIDGE

The growing need to be moving around it to see it,
To prevent its freezing, as with sculpture and metaphor,
Finds now skeins, now strokes of the sun in a dark
Crucifixion etching, until you end by caring
What the man's name was who made it,
The way old people care about names and are
Forever seeing resemblances to people now dead.

Of stone and two metals drawn out so
That at every time of day
They speak out of strong resemblances, as:
Wings whirring so that you see only where
Their strokes finish, or: spokes of dissynchronous wheels.

Whose pictures and poems could accurately be signed
With the engineer's name, whatever he meant,
And be called: *Tines inflicting a river, justly,*
Or (thinking how its cables owe each something
To the horizontal and something to the vertical):
A graph of the odds against
Any one man's producing a masterpiece.

Yet far from his, the engineer's, at sunrise
And again at sunset when,
Like the likenesses the old see,
Loveliness besets it as haphazard as genes:
Fortunate accidents take the form of cities

At either end; the cities give their poor edges
To the river, the buildings there
The fair color that things have to be.
Oh the paper reeds by a brook
Or the lakes that lie on bayous like a leopard
Are not at more seeming random, or more certain
In their sheen how to stand, than these towns are.

And of the rivering vessels so and so
Where the shadow of the bridge rakes them once,
The best you can think is that, come there,
A pilot will know what he's done
When his ship is fingered

Like that Greek boy whose name I now forget
Whose youth was one long study to cut stone;
One day his mallet slipped, some goddess willing
Who only meant to take his afternoon,
So that the marble opened on a girl
Seated at music and wonderfully fleshed
And sinewed under linen, riffling a harp;
At which he knew not that delight alone
The impatient muse intended, but, coupled with it, grief—
The harp-strings in particular were so light—
And put his chisel down for marvelling on that stone.

It *is* a poem of associations, isn't it? a gatherer as Robert Frost used
to call them. Let me gloss it a little.

I was living near the bridge that winter, and looked at it a lot. In the
house where I lived there were two artists who were good talkers and
my closest friend was an artist who was a good listener, so I was probably seeing things with freshly peeled eyes. I can't remember where the
image of skeins came from—I had to look the word up as I wrote this,
but the crucifixion etching was a Rembrandt, I think one I'd seen at the
Metropolitan where the wife of one of the painters had a job. I had been
more irritated than wondering at my southern grandmother and a
French woman I knew who *cared about names and were forever seeing
resemblances to people now dead.* But in the openness of the poem I
find no irritation (although I suppose the word *forever* is gently irritable), rather an affection for the old, for the associative-recollective process that is characteristic of age and of this poem. It seems to have been

a kind of grace I was experiencing—an arrogant person in my late twenties—as I followed whither the poem led.

The image of *spokes of dissynchronous wheels* came into my head from aviation. I was still flying occasionally as a reserve pilot in the Navy, and when you fly propeller planes in formation you adjust the speed of your engine (by adjusting the pitch of your propeller) by looking through the blades of your own propeller at that of the lead plane until the blades appear to be standing still. I wonder what that image conveys, if anything, to a reader who hasn't observed the spokes of dissynchronous wheels or propellers.

When the poem first appeared in a book, I glossed the line about the engineer's name, as follows: "The Brooklyn Bridge was designed by J. A. Roebling who began the work in 1869 which his son W. A. Roebling completed in 1883"—an impulse of propitiation, perhaps? as if the engineer might be helping me with my job?

With one of the three painters in particular, the now well-known Canadian Jack Shadbolt, I used to have very rangy talk. *The odds against any one man's producing a masterpiece* had been the theme of last night's talk.

The paper reeds by a brook is borrowed I think from *Psalms*, but I know it came to me from a beautiful setting by Randall Thompson, a colleague at Princeton the year before. *The lakes that lie on bayous like a leopard*—am I boring you, reader, with all these finger-nail clippings? —I had ferried a plane to the west coast that winter by way of Louisiana.

I made up the Greek sculptor and his anecdote, but *made up* is too willful a verb: the Greek boy and his muse came to me, and the story— his wanting to do something difficult with his mallet, and having it done instead without his effort or even consent—came to me as a story that I did not then understand, a story parallel to something that was happening to me in the fashioning, if I did fashion it, of the poem.

A final gloss, comprehensive of the whole 47 lines: the things I hadn't read! Whitman, Hart Crane, none of the poem's ancestors.

The opening up of form that occurred in the poem is something that had happened with me before, but more often from clumsiness or laziness than at the direction of the poem. To this day I feel surer that I'm communicating with the poem if a prosodic pattern declares itself. I have sacred texts about this.

Most of my poetry is metrical, though I have written some free verse, syllabics, etc. One reason I write metrically is very simple:

I do this better than I do in the more open forms. But I think
I have a more deliberate choice behind it: from first to last most of
my poems have dealt with violent or extreme or *non-verbal*
[italics mine] experience. Fitting such experience through a fairly
fixed form helps me to more firmly re-create it, and so to come
to terms with it, possibly even to partially understand it.
The openness of the experience is brought into relation with the
structures of the mind.

(Thom Gunn, in a letter, 1970)

This is a fragment from a dialogue between Borges and a writing student at Columbia University (from *Borges on Writing*, edited by Norman Thomas di Giovanni, Daniel Halpern, and Frank MacShane):

Question: One can read the poets of the past and interpret
what is learned into free verse.
Borges: What I fail to understand is why you should *begin* by
attempting something that is so difficult, such as free verse.
Question: But I don't find it difficult.
Borges: Well, I don't know your writing, so I can't really say.
It might be that it is easy to write and difficult to read.

Auden ("He thanks God daily/that he was born and bred/ a British Pharisee," he says of himself elsewhere) talks about the problem as if the devices of prosody were our servants:

The poet who writes "free" verse is like Robinson Crusoe on his
desert island: he must do all his cooking, laundry and darning for
himself. In a few exceptional cases, this manly independence
produces something original and impressive, but more often the
result is squalor—dirty sheets on the unmade bed and empty
bottles on the unswept floor.

(*The Dyer's Hand*)

But the fourth of these texts is the one I need most, and states the other half of what has to be a dialectic. Randall Jarrell, in his extraordinary appreciation called "Some Lines from Whitman," says:

The enormous and apparent advantages of form, of omission
and selection, of the highest degree of organization, are

accompanied by important disadvantages. . . . If we compare
Whitman with that very beautiful poet Alfred Tennyson, the
most skillful of all Whitman's contemporaries, we are at once
aware of how limiting Tennyson's forms have been, of how much
Tennyson has had to leave out. . . . Whitman's poems *represent*
his world and himself much more satisfactorily than Tennyson's
do his. In the past a few poets have both formed and represented,
each in the highest degree; but in modern times what controlling,
organizing, selecting poet has created a world with as much in it
as Whitman's, a world that so plainly *is* the world?

(Poetry and the Age)

And in the luck of the poem there is one other element: will the poem
work as well for the reader as it works for the muse and her scribe? Can
you step back from the poem and see what is *there,* having been present when all its bright ambience burned and taken down what the unearthly voice said?

In the magazine where some of my favorite poems have appeared, for
more than twenty years, a poem that I thought well enough of to place
at the front of my selected poems was read this way:

William Meredith's volume is prefaced by an elegantly thoughtful
foreword in which he tells us that although he may not have kept
the most promising poems, he has kept the ones "that try to say
things I am still trying to find ways to say, poems that engage
mysteries I still pluck at the hems of. . . ." As the patriotic sailor
was heard to say, staring out at the mid-Atlantic, it makes you feel
kinda humble and kinda proud. Meredith's poetry has all the
virtues: decency, reverence, gravity, quiet curiosity, and there is
something very depressing about it, as of poetry soft at the center.

The reviewer then quoted only the middle stanza of the opening poem.

WINTER VERSE FOR HIS SISTER

Moonlight washes the west side of the house
As clean as bone, it carpets like a lawn
The stubbled field tilting eastward
Where there is no sign yet of dawn.

The moon is an angel with a bright light sent
To surprise me once before I die
With the real aspect of things.
It holds the light steady and makes no comment.

Practicing for death I have lately gone
To that other house
Where our parents did most of their dying,
Embracing and not embracing their conditions.
Our father built bookcases and little by little stopped reading,
Our mother cooked proud meals for common mouths.
Kindly, they raised two children. We raked their leaves
And cut their grass, we ate and drank with them.
Reconciliation was our long work, not all of it joyful.

Now outside my own house at a cold hour
I watch the noncommittal angel lower
The steady lantern that's worn these clapboards thin
In a wash of moonlight, while men slept within,
Accepting and not accepting their conditions,
And the fingers of trees plied a deep carpet of decay
On the gravel web underneath the field,
And the field tilting always toward day.

His comment went on, and I have to confess that I think it's witty, though to this day I have been unable to find a revision of the poem— without betraying what I feel is its discovered language—that will make the metaphors of that second stanza less vulnerable to misfeeling:

What kind of a meal are you cooking? Oh, I think a proud meal tonight. How do you raise your children? Kindly, thank you. It's all too beautiful and shaming to be true, establishing the poet as such a splendid understander, knower and forgiver that a slightly self-congratulatory atmosphere hangs over this poem and the whole volume.

In general, a poet tries to make mis-reading and mistaking of feeling impossible, by the same attention that he pays to exact rendering of the experience he is being initiated into. Clearly he is not always lucky in both phases of his intuitive work, and there is always somebody waiting at the third stage who can say with critical detachment, Meredith is no Whitman or Tennyson. But what an ordinary poet congratulates himself on is, I suppose, being a good scribe, taking the things down as the tongue declares them. And, of course, the luck of being chosen by the tongue in the first place.

JOYCE CAROL OATES

JOYCE CAROL OATES *(b. 1938 in Lockport, New York) was educated at the Universities of Syracuse and Wisconsin. A distinguished critic and novelist as well as poet, her honors include the National Book Award for fiction for* THEM *(1969). She is currently Professor of English at the University of Windsor, Ontario.*

(Photo by Thomas Victor)

Many Are Called...

Two wills contend in us. And it is necessary that they contend, otherwise we would ascend too readily into the Void: we would surrender time and disappear into eternity: we would devalue the world and find a premature peace in another will, inhuman and perfect, "thereof one must be silent." (As Wittgenstein concludes the *Treatise*, revealing it to be—like everything!—a work of poetry: *Whereof one cannot speak, thereof one must be silent.*)

Of course I am a divided being. At times one will gains dominance over the other, and I am content to spend my time in utter peace, perfection, knowing that the hundreds—the thousands—of faces, birds, trees, flowers, and nameless forms I draw, and have drawn most of my conscious life, are "perfect" even as they are brought into the daylight world: complete, perfect, needing no judgment. A whimsical calculation of this activity of mine gives me what should be an astounding figure: to this date I have drawn more than 200,000 faces. And thrown them all away, though each is drawn with painstaking care, lovingly, the eyes especially toiled over; then discarded.

As Whitman says, "It is time to explain myself—let us stand up."

How much I value the idea of an anthology, almost as much as an anthology of poetry itself—anything that demonstrates, without verbal argument, how we are communal, joined together in space and time, if not by flesh. For though other poets in this book may believe themselves to be quite distant from me, totally "different" from their image of me, I cannot believe with much force that the differences between us are ultimately as powerful as our similarities. . . . And yet, how much I value the idea of the spaces between us. What we cannot speak of, thereof we must be silent: yet our silences are very articulate. There are many kinds of silence, many impasses. When exterior connections are broken between us, interior connections spring to life. It is not only in music and in the visual arts that "silence"—so-called negative space—blocks of "nothing"—is articulate. Poetry deals with silences as well and, like all forms of human magic, alludes to that absolute silence of which we cannot speak: by verbal indirections hinting at a primary directionless reality.

So when the other will overcomes me, the will to communicate in a temporal medium, the will to make my temporal self *defined*, I work with words, with language, and see what my conscious ego can make of the stream of images and the blocks of ineffable sensation we call "ideas": this other, more aggressive, more *conscious* activity seems to have resulted in my being known as a writer, an artist, a poet.

Yet the exterior work is only half of me, as I suspect it is but half of everyone. Isn't it time to explain ourselves?—to stand up? In our outer forms we compete, toil, scramble over one another and over former, outworn aspects of our own being; and it is quite pleasurable, this turning of the wheel. We are at the center, spinning the wheel; its circumference carries us around and around, through the seasons, the years, through the exciting melodramatic phases of our life. At times we know very well how absurdly we are divided; for the interior life, the stillness of the self, is wise beyond any possibility of the exterior life knowing; out there is history, out there is a constant assessment and re-assessment of a galaxy of facts and experiences. But our lives are lived at that circumference, as truly as they are lived in the center.

Usually, we meet on the outside: it is always the exterior forms of us that meet, that engage in conversation, that touch. How limiting it comes to seem, ultimately! And the emotions as well—so familiar—denying the absolute perfection of Chaos, mistaking a philosophical concept for a reality. The advantage of art, especially the exquisite lyric arts, is that one can forget about the exterior selves, the historical selves, and experience the essence of personality: the place at which we are not quite one, because that is impossible, but we join one another in sympathy, undifferentiated in pure being.

When the fascination with the exterior world of forms, change, names, "personalities" fades—then one sinks into the interior world, and there is no more art. There is no more individual existence. We call this "death," a way of pointing toward behavior that ceases to behave in the old way, slithering from us, resisting definition. Death, however, is only a word; a way of allusion; it is not antithetical to something called "life" —as people tell us—but undifferentiated from that other impulse, that other gravitational pull, that is called *life*. Someone appears. Someone else disappears. Are we to scream over this, are we to maul one another in our haste to climb up on stage?—in our futile yearning to hold the stage forever, and to keep "rivals" from climbing on?

THE IMPASSE

In the ditches, in the dark crevices,
shrunken glaciers keep their chill.
You cannot step across.

The cold radiates upward, even against the sun,
and you cannot step across—
a few feet, a few inches—
you fear the tremor of ice
and what is not human

Over there—an ordinary furrowed field.

You cannot step across
yet you cannot go back.
You cannot move at all.
The long meandering fingers of ice will thicken,
winter upon winter.

Later you may say *How cowardly I was!*
Now you think *Even this is my strength.*

Something about the challenge of writing about my poetry "from the inside," in this particular anthology, allows me to say things I would not say in another context; nor would I have said them, years ago. I am not that cautious person of years ago, however, but one who has approached the Abyss, the Nietzschean abyss that begins to stare back into us as we stare into it; in any case, prudence and circumspection are not qualities I much admire. . . . "The Impasse" was written as an attempt to explain to myself, and to anyone who is interested, the peculiar psychological condition of being both *in* time and *out* of it: the spiritual condition of being both one's personal, time-determined *ego* and that mysterious, seductive, infinitely wise *Other* we carry inside us. Of course it is the *Other* that carries us, but in the exterior world it is best to affirm, again and again, the independent and robust effort of the ego. Eternity will take care of itself, after all!—it is time, and current history, that needs a little help. So it is well for us, that we experience this impasse. It is only a few inches: in fact, it is no distance at all. We are always our temporal selves, and we are always, simultaneously, our eternal selves. If the exterior form eventually disappears that must be, after all, only an accident of perception.

After we survive moments of psychological turmoil, especially what is called "despair," we often judge ourselves harshly. We are too wise for those old, toiling selves, we are too superior altogether!—and this is certainly wrong. We have no right to judge anyone harshly, not even a former aspect of our own being. Therefore, it is necessary to remember that though we halfway think ourselves to have been "cowardly" during this difficult time, we know very well—and this is the only important thing—that at the present moment, living our lives to the fullest, we did embody strength of a kind.

I hope that all poets know what the novelist certainly knows and cannot help knowing: that all phases of existence are equal, all personalities equal, no moment better than another and no fictional "character" really better than another. Lyric poetry disturbs me, at times. I read it with appreciation and respect and yet wonder, occasionally: *Does this person know that other people inhabit the universe?—or does he imagine himself its only inhabitant?* The novelist struggles to express what Pascal said so succinctly: the divine is a living presence the center of which is everywhere, the circumference nowhere. And there is no motion, for we are already where we must be.

Yet of course there is motion, and anxiety. And the constant pull of time, of history, the imagined sufferings of others, which we cannot help but know are altogether real. Nature is unmindful of our crises; creatures who have not our special ego-consciousness strike us as happy, fulfilled, at least not trapped in a struggle to redefine *what is* in terms of *what ought to be.* But we are, after all, human. Our special destiny must be to pursue, even against our own happiness and pleasure, the adventure of consciousness: resisting the Edenic bliss of nature, giving ourselves up occasionally to the despair of time and history.

But have we any choice?

FLIGHT

Christmas morning. Glowing-white sands.
High clouds speeding toward noon,
like our car.
We leap into focus only
when fear subsides.

Above unreadable swamps hover wide-winged hawks
and below are crook-necked white birds,
nameless.
Here are original things.
Flaming in the perpetual sun are flamingos:
they glide like sleepwalkers, on pencil-thin legs,

then squawk themselves awake.
We awake, and drive away.

BOMBING RAIDS RESUMED—
a glimpsed unpaid-for headline,
a Miami newspaper.
We drive away in a greater hurry now
to noon at Alapha Key, from there
to Naples, on the Gulf, from there to
macaws bright as painted birds, trained
by prison inmates to perform:
to paint, play poker, to ride bird-sized bicycles,
to keep to their cross-staved perches, unchained.
They shriek melodramatically,
but without rage.

In the roadside restaurants are waitresses with stiff stacked hair
and patient, creased faces, working on Christmas Day.
Our mothers' ages, they hurry from tables to kitchen to tables
smiling endlessly, without focus,
as we drive away into a glowering sky.
It is all right, it will transform itself in the end.
But the gasoline is high-octane and propels us away—
CASUALTIES SOAR ON BOTH SIDES—
to the edge of the hard-packed sand
where droves of sandpipers flit, in fluid darts,
in one direction and then suddenly in another,
reversing themselves in communal magic.
Our heads are thunderous with surf
and nowhere left to go.

While a certain kind of art calls us to account for large-scale events, emphasizing our collective guilt, another kind of art works to deflate the ego; it suggests that no individual is important enough to be responsible for very much more than his own life. You would transform the world? —very well, then, begin with yourself. Poets write one kind of poem, and then they write the other. We swing back and forth from a sense of irrefutable kinship with our era to a sense of our relative powerlessness, our necessary isolation. People who do not understand the natural workings of the human imagination cannot see that such ostensible contradictions within a writer's work are the very stuff of nature, of sanity. All poets are familiar with the absurdity of even the most well-intentioned critics' attempts to *fix* them: to define them permanently. So long as we live, we cannot be defined. And when we are no longer living, it will really be the critics' own obsessions they claim to see in us; literary criticism is largely a matter of psychic projecting.

So there is a long tradition of poetry that celebrates the limitations of man. Poetry of this type used to be—perhaps it still is—written in rime, in rigid forms. Like most other poets, I too worked in stricter forms, even in the Petrarchan sonnet, experimentally, to see what might happen. A few of these sonnets were published but I never collected them; their form was not an adequate expression of their content, but simply a way of restraining it.

Because I experience so often the powerful, seductive tug of the Unconscious, I value all the more those attributes of ordinary consciousness wrongly considered "bourgeois" by people who must be, in a sense, quite innocent. Certainly they are innocent of knowing the potentiality for destruction in the unhuman part of the psyche; they must naively believe that everything in us is human, wonderfully human. But this is not true. Sanity is an ethical value, fundamentally; it respects what lies beyond it and does not court exciting confrontations.

Art, like other forms of human communication, is an expression of this sanity. For the artist, it is a discipline that will help him immensely in his personal life; it is a meditation in his own terms, a meditation suitable to his unique personality. (Conversely, if his art seems to be hurting him in his personal life, something is gravely wrong. I do not believe that artists are to be mere cocoons or hosts for their "art"—surrendering their personal lives in order to give birth to an impersonal achievement.) The meditation of art allows us to tame the flood of the imagination, to bring it at least half-way into a communal consciousness. Those who do not understand the healthy workings of the imagination believe that art is a kind of *exorcism*, when in fact it is a fulfillment, a blossoming, an achievement in consciousness of which one can certainly be proud—for a brief while.

Poetry is difficult for most poets; it is difficult for me. Even the placing of poems in a sequence, for a book, is incredibly difficult for me—for I know that there is a natural, necessary order to the poems, an evolving "order," which I must discover; and this discovery cannot be forced, no matter how long I contemplate what lies before me. It is possible that other poets collect their poems without much concern for their positions in a book, but this organizing of material is very important to me: for now I shift into my novelist's imagination, and imagine the book as not only poetry, but the revelation of personality. (The same is true of short story collections, of course.) There are organizations within organizations within organizations . . . contexts that include and help to define other contexts. We are all relative to one another.

Limitations are difficult for a certain kind of writer, who sees in a flash how infinitely marvelous the world is—who would like to squeeze all the world into his art—yet knows, sanely, that he cannot. Many of my poems celebrate limits, the conclusion of one phase of life and the assumption of another. I doubt that they are understood, as moral correctives to the ceaseless "drama" of exterior life (certainly my fiction is misunderstood).

PROMISCUITY

Erthe upon erthe is wonderly wrought
Erthe upon erthe hath worship of nought . . .
medieval poem

*No choice.

*A slow circling parade, shuffling
   of miscellaneous feet. Imperfect anatomies
   to mock some perfect destiny.
   They keep glancing from side to side,
   in envy.

*Each time the camera advanced
   smiles appeared.

*On Fridays the Discount Foods is open 'til 9.
   Like the decks of a sickened ship
   the aisles are awash with shapes—
   crates half-unpacked,
   pyramids of cans,
   women pushing shopping carts
   balky as wire animals.
   Children run free, freely in the aisles,
   unlabeled.

*Someone's dog begins to bark.
   A mile away, another dog barks.
   Out of wild weedy ditches the wild dogs
   stammer and howl.

Ice forms between their toes.
On a distant city street another dog
lifts its muzzle to wail.
We wake at the same moment
in the same bed.

*It looked like a mountain,
it even had jagged peaks.
But by June it began to thaw.
By August, even the rivulets in our back yards
had dried.
We did not drown.
We do not miss the drama
of the jagged peaks.

When poetry works well, as a psychological experience, as a kind of spiritual meditation, it seems to lift us out of ourselves: to emphasize the transcendence that is possible if we identify with something beyond the ego. We cannot *be* that transcendence, but we can value it. We can imagine it in words. Though the future lies beyond us, mysteriously, we can summon it a little closer by attempting to imagine it. We can place ourselves in different aspects of consciousness simply by asking different questions, giving voice to different modes of perception. So the "America" that is dreamt is not only our "America," but belongs to others—others who will outlive us. Both my poetry and my fiction are attempts to get into consciousnesses foreign to my own, to see the world from other points of view. At times these points of view seem to contradict my own . . . they seem to eradicate me entirely!

DREAMING AMERICA

When the two-lane highway was widened
the animals retreated.
Skunks, racoons, rabbits—even their small corpses
disappeared from the road—transformed into rags
then into designs
then into stains
then nothing.

When the highway was linked to another
then to another
six lanes then nine then twelve rose

sweeping to the horizon
along measured white lines.
The polled Herefords were sold.
When the cornfields were bulldozed
the farmhouses at their edges turned into shanties;
the outbuildings fell.

When the fields were paved over
Frisch's Big Boy rose seventy-five feet in the air.
The *Sunoco* and *Texaco* and *Gulf* signs competed
on hundred-foot stilts
like eyeballs on stalks
white optic-nerves
miraculous.
Illuminated at night.

Where the useless stretch of trees lay
an orange sphere like a golf ball
announces the Shopping Mall, open
for Thursday evening shopping.
There, tonight, droves of teenagers hunt
one another, alert on the memorized pavement.

Where did the country go?—cry the travellers, soaring
past. *Where did the country go?*—ask the strangers.
The teenagers never ask.

Where horses grazed in a dream that had no history,
tonight a thirteen-year-old girl stands dreaming
into the window of Levitz's Record Shop.
We drive past, in a hurry. We disappear.
We return.

    The act of writing is, like any act of communication, essentially one of faith; even the despairing poet assumes that someone will understand his despair, he assumes that someone is listening. Therefore art seems to me entirely affirmative. A really negative art would be an impossibility. As we have different personalities, of course we have different tastes in art; our faces are all unique, like our fingerprints. But the multitude of voices comes to argue very much for some vast, intangible organization that is quite democratic in its texture, desiring only the development of consciousness so that it may be articulated.

MANY ARE CALLED

The great tide of noon!—and a flood
of voices, unchorused.
Thistles regain their pollen.
Junked autos heave from ditches.

Unwary in opposition
we pass too close to each other—
we are drawn together—
voiceless, we disappear
into each other.
It is August: in a creekbed, an enormous boulder
greens and richens with slime.

Our omens were always correct.
Our interpretations alone were faulty.
And our farewells?—premature.
It seems that all are chosen.

Here, in his flamboyant generosity, is the Poet's offering:

It is you talking just as much as myself, I act as the tongue of you,
Tied in your mouth, in mine it begins to be loosen'd.
                                        Whitman, *Song of Myself*

LINDA PASTAN

LINDA PASTAN (b. 1932 in New York City) graduated from Radcliffe College and did graduate work at Brandeis. After going through what in "Roots" she calls "fourteen blank years," she began to write and publish poems steadily. She spent the summer of 1974 as a Fellow at Bread Loaf, and currently lives and teaches in Maryland.

(Photo by Thomas Victor)

Roots

I witnessed the death of an oak tree recently, amazed to learn that for every foot of branch dying above ground there was a foot of root dying underneath. It seems that my entire house rests on a subterranean system of oak roots, not unlike the sewer system under the streets of the Bronx where I grew up.

I have not come such a long way after all, though at one time I certainly meant to. The Bronx is still no further than a metaphor away. When I was growing up, however, I used to ride on the Concourse Bus dreaming of complete escape—practicing my vowels and closing my ears to the Bronx speech surrounding me.

How I despised the housewives with their soap opera eyes, their elastic stockings, and their accents which lacked even the grating energy of Brooklyn speech. It is difficult for me, thirty years later, to confess to that early snobbery; certainly it troubles me now. Yet out of it grew my earliest concern with the exact sounds of language.

Do all children dream of escape from wherever childhood happens to set them down? I wanted to be Pygmalion and Galatea both at once. And yet for me, for most children, the only flight possible was along the old, underground railroad of books.

I read constantly—obsessively my parents thought, bundling me into coat and hat and sending me out into the fresh air. I dipped chilly toes into Emerson, swam with abandon in the buoyant waters of the nineteenth-century novel, almost drowned when I dove too early into Gide and Camus.

But it was Oscar Williams and his *Little Treasury Of Modern Poetry* that I remember best. From it I learned "The Hollow Men," chanting it to myself like a charm against adolescence's crueler moments. I was sure that The Old Masters would have understood *my* suffering, or at least that Auden would have. And those locket shaped pictures at the back of the book! This poem about Emily Dickinson, written years later, certainly owes a great deal to that marvellously romantic portrait and to the words of "Parting" which I learned by heart.

EMILY DICKINSON

We think of her hidden in a white dress
among the folded linens and sachets

of well kept cupboards, or just out of sight
sending jellies and notes with no address
to all the wondering Amherst neighbors.
Eccentric as New England weather
the stiff wind of her mind, stinging or gentle
blew two half imagined lovers off.
Yet legend won't explain the sheer sanity
of vision, the serious mischief
of language, the economy of pain.

Sometime during those years I started writing poems myself. It was as natural a process for me as growing breasts, it was a part of my earliest womanhood. There were poems about the moon as a thimble, the stars as thread; poems where metaphor was allowed to grow as rampantly as I was growing; there was poem after poem about early love.

Then, abruptly, when I was scarcely twenty, early love arrived in person, and I married. During the long, important years between my twenty-first and thirty-fourth birthdays I turned my back on poetry and wrote little or nothing at all.

I have come late to the woman's movement, if indeed I have really come to it. And it is the thought of all those unwritten poems, each one as perfect as an imagined but never conceived child, that makes me able to even consider militancy.

I cannot go into all the reasons I found it impossible to be both a writer and a wife, I hardly know them myself. Sometimes I blame Archibald MacLeish and the exquisite "Poem in Prose" he wrote to his wife. I too was determined to give my husband "the well swept room / . . . candles and baked bread / And a cloth spread" as my mother had given my father.

"My own life to live in, / This she has given me— / If giver could." says MacLeish of his wife; and "if giver SHOULD" I want to shout to myself down all the years.

Ironically I found time for other things. I tried sculpting, I worked in a library, I played tennis. But I must have believed that you could serve only one true God at a time. (Who would dare make Calliope and Aphrodite share one roof—or was it Hestia I was so worried about?) Perhaps with a house full of noisy children the muse was simply drowned out.

In any case, with the birth of my last child, that floodtide of energy Margaret Mead mentions in connection with other women and the birth of their final children was released in me and swept all hesitancy aside. I have been writing steadily ever since.

But if there are no poems to show for those fourteen blank years, certainly the material forced underground then has come to the surface over and over again in the years since. In this poem, for example:

NOTES FROM THE DELIVERY ROOM

Strapped down,
victim in an old comic book,
I have been here before,
this place where pain winces
off the walls
like too bright light.
Bear down a doctor says,
foreman to sweating laborer,
but this work, this forcing
of one life from another
is something that I signed for
at a moment when I would have signed anything.
Babies should grow in fields;
common as beets or turnips
they should be picked and held
root end up, soil spilling
from between their toes—
and how much easier it would be later,
returning them to earth.
Bear up . . . bear down . . . the audience
grows restive, and I'm a new magician
who can't produce the rabbit
from my swollen hat.
She's crowning, someone says,
but there is no one royal here,
just me, quite barefoot,
greeting my barefoot child.

In a series of poems centering around Penelope I try to capture some of what it means for a woman to stay quiescently at home, as I did, while her husband adventures in the world. In the first poem of the series my equation of myself with Penelope seemed almost accidental. Only later did it occur to me that Penelope was an archetype of the woman left behind.

PENELOPE

The sun is scarcely
a shadow of itself,
it bled into the sea
all last week
and now, bandaged away,
waits out with me the long, long
month of rain.

Grey fades to grey.
The horizon is
the finest seam between
water and water, sky and sky.
Only the tide still moves,
leaving the print of its ribbed bones
on the abandoned sand
as you left yours on me
when you moved imperceptibly from my embrace.

I must wring out the towels,
wring out the swim suits,
wring my eyes dry of tears,
watching at a window
on one leg, then the other,
like the almost extinct heron.

A much later Penelope poem revealed to me a way out. It is an
acknowledgment, a kind of answer, at least for the woman as artist:

YOU ARE ODYSSEUS

You are Odysseus
returning home each evening
tentative, a little angry.
And I who thought to be
one of the Sirens (cast up
on strewn sheets
at dawn)
hide my song
under my tongue—
merely Penelope after all.

> Meanwhile the old wars
> go on, their dim music
> can be heard even at night.
> You leave each morning,
> soon our son will follow.
> Only my weaving
> is real.

Not that this answer has ever been easy. The walk between the study and the kitchen is, in a sense, the longest walk I take. Guilt still lurks in one room, anger in the other—both are ghosts that I am determined to exorcise.

But poetry itself provides some of the solutions to the very problems it raises. By allowing myself to follow a poem wherever it wants to take me, I find that I often stumble upon truths about myself, my world, that I scarcely suspected I knew.

I think that this is where much of the secret force of poetry lies, what I like to call its velocity. In the following poem, for instance, by developing what I took to be a simple metaphor about weather, I learned something about my own nature, more perhaps than was altogether comfortable.

HURRICANE WATCH

> I saw once,
> through the eyepiece of a microscope,
> a blizzard of cells.
> And at times
> the hairs on my arm lift,
> as if in some incalculable wind,
> or my throat echoes
> the first hoarse forecast
> of thunder.
> Some live in the storm's eye only.
> I rise and fall
> with the barometer,
> holding on for my life.
> Here, in a storm cellar
> of flesh,
> pale as the roots I live on,

I read my palm
as though it were a weather map
and keep a hurricane watch
all year.

In "Geneticist," written about my husband's world of science, I came
to terms not only with some troubling aspects of fatherhood but with
some difficult principles of science itself. In the working out of the metaphors of the poem I was able for the first time to understand the genetics
that my husband had been trying for so long to explain to me.

The writing of this poem became for me a kind of bridge between my
world and his—between what C. P. Snow calls the two cultures.

GENETICIST

I thought you were your father
someone said,
seeing for the first time
the blaze of curls around your neck
passed down by primogeniture,
though learned
from your own sons.
You spoke of how you used to hide
in a dim sanctuary
of women's shoes
against that father's drunken rage;
you sipped your scotch.

Now you learn the alphabet
of genes, study their silences,
the intricate switch
that turns them on and off
like lightbulbs on a hotel telephone
signalling: Someone has left a message.
And the message itself intact
for generations—a letter
that has waited in some dusty cubbyhole
delivered at last. Open it.
Its news may be
tender or brutal as fatherhood.

A novelist once told me that in a successful novel the characters take on a life of their own; as with his adolescent children he is no longer fully in charge of what they do or say. So in a poem like "Geneticist" I may sit down at my desk with something quite specific in mind to say, but I may end up writing something quite different. You must follow a poem where it leads you, Bill Stafford taught me that.

During an earlier time when I sat down with my hands on the typewriter I had felt like a medium with his hands on a tabletop. I was little more than an instrument in the making of the poem, or so I supposed. But to *follow* a poem—that idea freed me somehow, made me feel both more responsible and responsive to language itself. It is a little like following the thread through the labyrinth, trying at all costs to avoid the minotaur:

ARTIFICER

Blindfold
I follow the thread
of a poem
wherever it leads,
remembering the labyrinth,
remembering Daedalus
for whom I named
my first son:
Stephen.
I follow the thread
inward,
through hives of cells,
each storing its one
perfect image.
They call the self
a dark woods.
When I uncover
my face
I am in a clearing
painfully small,
surrounded
by the barbed wire
of my own
alphabet.

Back in the Bronx so many years ago there was a small park at the intersection of Fordham Road and The Grand Concourse. On one side of that park stood Alexander's Department Store where those house- wives I so despised searched for bargains. On the other side was Sutter's Bakery, its windows filled with sugar cookies of every form and content.

"Where is Grandpa?" I would often ask my grandmother.

"He's on the benches," she would reply. And that is all that park was, a few square feet of dull grass and row upon row of benches. But the sun was there, and the pretzel man, and the boys let out of Hebrew school, playing stick ball on the rough cement.

In the middle of that park was a tiny white house: Poe Cottage. It was a doll's house of a place and scarcely seemed big enough for real people to have lived in. There Poe brought his child bride. Think of it! Edgar Allen Poe in the middle of the Bronx, a miniature piece of American literature side by side with my grandfather's benches. The place I had been trying to escape from and the place I had finally escaped to were almost the same place.

Did I escape? Did I ever genuinely want to? Lately my poems have dealt more and more with my earliest years, this poem about my grand- father himself, for instance.

A REAL STORY

Sucking on hard candy
to sweeten the taste
of old age,
grandpa told us stories
about chickens,
city chickens sold
for sabbath soup
but rescued at the end
by some chicken loving
providence.

Now at ninety-five
sucked down
to nothing himself,
he says he feels
a coldness;

perhaps the coldness David felt
even with Abishag
in his bed
to warm
his chicken-thin bones.

But when we say
you'll soon get well
grandpa pulls the sheet
over his face,
raising it between us
the way he used to raise
the yiddish paper
when we said
enough chickens,
tell us a real story.

Clearly the road to self discovery, to any real story, loops backwards. "Man is a knot of roots," said Emerson, and my roots are all tangled up at the intersection of Fordham Road and The Grand Concourse.

Perhaps that explains how as a young woman, in the full heat of passion for literature, I named my first child after a character in a James Joyce novel. Years later I gave my last an older name, one my grandfather might have chosen.

RACHEL (rā'chəl) a ewe

We named you
for the sake
of the syllables
and for the small boat
that followed the Pequod
gathering lost children
of the sea.

We named you
for the dark-eyed girl
who waited at the well
while her lover
worked seven years
and again
seven.

We named you
for the small daughters
of the holocaust
who followed their six pointed stars
to death
and were all of them
known as
Rachel.

RAYMOND R. PATTERSON

RAYMOND R. PATTERSON *(b. Dec. 14, 1929 in New York City) was educated at Lincoln University in Pennsylvania and at New York University. Since 1968 he has been Lecturer in English at City College of the City University of New York. His poems have appeared widely in anthologies, and in 1970 he was awarded a fellowship from the National Endowment for the Arts. He lives in Merrick, New York, with his wife and daughter.*

(Photo by Thomas Victor)

Statement

On top of those few possessions we call personal, and all that baggage and camping equipment known as The Literary Tradition, the black poet carries his load of American History—a private and public property so overloaded with negatives as to encourage a stance angled perpetually to one side: the muscles bunched and straining where the murderous weight rests, the black poet sometimes appearing to thrust at invisible burdens with stylized ferocity.

With nowhere in life to lay that historical burden down, you search among possessions to find a fashionable cause for all the strain: Father, Mother (who bore their own weights as best they could), God (who is indeed heavy and at once weightless), or Chance/Fate (which rhymes with dance and wait—weight). But always the mean ton savages the back: American History—you know where it hurts.

Perhaps you split the self in two, hoping to divide the weight in half, with the results Dr. Dubois describes in *Souls of Black Folk:* "One ever feels his two-ness, —an American, a Negro: two souls, two thoughts, two unreconciled strivings; two warring ideals in one dark body, whose dogged strength alone keeps it from being torn asunder."

Nor is the remedy the enslavement of one "ideal" by the other—the constant plotting of escape or rebellion, the violence necessary to maintain control. But if one could take on more weight! —get some balance to the burden! Then perhaps it might become bearable. See this nation and its institutions through black eyes. ". . . pull the democratic and idealistic clothes off American utterance, and see what you can of the dusky body of IT underneath," as Lawrence has said. Go on to try a larger continent for size: Africa. The weight! How it improves the stance, the muscle tone, the stride! Soon you have it all on your back, balanced—*your* history. Now you can really suffer!

Yet in 1948 how innocent I was—how weightless!—it seems to me, standing in line before the bursar's office at Lincoln University, Pennsylvania, in that ritual of late tuition payments I practiced, when Robert Abrams approached to say he felt a poem I had published in the campus newspaper was promising, and had I thought much about what I was trying to do. Robert Abrams was an upperclassman and the first person I had ever met who admitted talking to trees. A brilliant student, in his senior year he would conclude that he was being miseducated and decide to pursue his studies in his room, attending classes only to take examinations, invariably passing them with an "A," but losing academic credit for the year because of "overcutting," and leaving college without graduating, thereafter earning several degrees from other institutions. Abrams started me brooding about the poems I had been thoughtlessly writing since high school. In an early note to me he had written:

I have suggested that not only you, but all of us in the group,
study the nature of our own emotionality, with each of us it is
doubtlessly different; I have suggested that we should, in every way
possible, sharpen our senses, cultivate our abilities and limitations
so that every expression of a personal intuition when put on
paper in an art form, sparkles and reveals as much as it is possible
of its own *complete* order. A study of the traditional tools of the
art of poetry will assist one in the achieving of such an end,
I believe. I do not suggest it as a substitute for *real* experience
which is, I feel, in the final analysis the basis for art.

Robert Abrams drew me into my first conversations about poetry, as did VOC—Vincent O. Carter—whose room was the attic of Cresson Hall (built 1870), its ceiling and walls cut into abrupt angular planes by a gabled roof. Drifting toward exile even then, VOC was a kind of campus mystic who preferred candlelight, his large eyes burning with intensity as mine smarted from incense fumes washing his curiously muralled walls. "Put it into some form!" he said to me one autumn afternoon. I had showed him a poem—some loose lines describing a setting sun. The poem became "Sun and I":

SUN AND I

There was anger in the sky,
In the redness of the eye,
In the grayness of the lid,
In the place the eyeball hid.

There was anguish in the eye
For it quivered as it slept,
And the glowing of it crept
Through the eyelid to the sky.

There was anger in the sky,
In the silent, glowing thunder
And it made me stop and wonder
What I'd done and why.

Long before that, because I was majoring in political science, I had joined the campus NAACP chapter in a campaign to desegregate a movie, restaurant, and hotel a few miles from campus, in Oxford—something it had never occurred to me to attempt back home on Long Island. After classes each day, we would drive to Oxford, divide into groups and sit-in at three locations, deploying sometimes as few as five students at each place. One Friday afternoon I and several other students entered the near-deserted restaurant accompanied by Professor David Swift, a tall, soft-spoken Quaker—an authentic winter soldier—who had taught me Religion of the Old Testament. Neatly dressed, wearing ties and jackets, we sat at various tables, each of us with a book at hand to pass the usually eventless hours after the waitress placed silverware, water, and menus before us and then disappeared. But this afternoon was different. Less than an hour after we had been seated, the restaurant manager burst from his office, clutching a pistol and shouting, struggling as if to keep the weapon under control, wildly pointing it in all directions. "You better get the hell out of here," he yelled, "before this thing goes off!"

A murmuring had begun outside and suddenly grew louder. Faces pressed against the restaurant window, eyes squinting and dilating to see into the dimly lit room. The faces glared, shifted, multiplied. We decided to get the hell out of there—six of us, easing our way past the manager, stern faced, now seemingly in control of his revolver; past the empty cashier's booth; out the tiny foyer; through the clogged front door, slowly pressing into the tense, packed mass of overalled men and boys crowding the sidewalk, the street lined with pickup trucks and old Fords and Chevvies parked diagonally to the curb. We inched our way single file, reached our car, pulled out and made a U turn to head back to campus and were stopped by a red light in the intersection opposite the restaurant, across from the firehouse where hoses had been hooked up, and waited behind the big closed doors. Citizens had come to town in overalls and Levi's that afternoon to put down our threat, buying what ammunition the town had for sale, storing shotguns and rifles in trucks and cars. But we were so few in number, our appearance so unwarlike, the crowd refused for a moment to believe who we were. Then seeing us again, about to escape unchallenged, a dozen or more rushed into the street, surrounding the car, yanking the door handles, one shouting, "Are you boys from the college?" rocking the car from side to side—a small boat in a gathering storm—pounding the car roof. But the traffic light changed, our driver pressed the accelerator, and the car parted the sea of faces like rough water. Flight and the threat of violence—an American heritage in black life: "I've Got a Home in That Rock":

I'VE GOT A HOME IN THAT ROCK

I had an uncle, once, who kept a rock in his pocket—
Always did, up to the day he died.
And as far as I know, that rock is still with him,
Holding down some dust of his thighbone.

From Mississippi he'd got that rock, he'd say—
Or, sometimes, from Tennessee: a different place each year
He told it, how he'd snatched it up when he first left home—
Running, he'd say—to remind him, when times got hard
Enough to make him homesick, what home is really like.

Langston Hughes, that generous, gifted man of letters, had attended Lincoln University, although it meant little to me as a student—nor did the glass-encased collection of African artifacts in the university library foyer, the sundial outside drawing my attention more. Lincoln, founded in 1854 "for the scientific, classical and theological education of colored youth of the male sex," had early established connections with Africa, so that one spring day I would not think it strange to meet and be introduced to Kwame Nkrumah in the company of President Bond, walking across the campus. (It was like hailing a cab many years later for Tom Mboya, outside Harlem's YMCA—the importance of these things lacked their true weight.) Young Julian Bond in short pants, playing on the lawn of the president's house; a roommate, Lovey, who quoted from Longfellow and the *Rubaiyat* before going to sleep at night; a semester visiting the Merion estate of Albert C. Barnes, contemplating for several hours each week his hoard of Renoirs, Cezannes, Matisses, Picassos, El Grecos,

Tintorettos, Titians, Chardins, Goyas, etc.; nights leaving the basement of the university library, elbows sore from leaning against those ancient, splintered carrels—to come out into the open and look across the sloping ground towards the soccer field, University Hall, and the Science Building beyond, Maple Drive on the left and off to the right, the old gym, Vets Village with its lights, and dark open fields extending to a stand of trees; the air clear and crisp, the sky a swirl of stars; wild with fatigue and wonder from the weight of things—to release that tension in a breath—a shout, high-pitched, ridiculous, anonymous, authentic, liberating. . . .

A half dozen of us—Robert Abrams, Lafayette Robinson, and others—met in the Blue Room for a time, to organize a literary club, its product a mimeographed magazine, and my contribution a poem with a stick-figure illustration of Siamese twins joined at the spine, one twin plodding determinedly along a downward curving path, a tool like a hammer in his hand, his eyes fixed before him, his brother carried on his back, face tilted up, contemplating the heavens, arms and legs flexed, a stick-figure bird perched on one outstretched palm—which was how I graduated from college, got drafted to serve in the Army during the Korean Conflict and became a good soldier.

Fort Dix, New Jersey: dumbly standing in line shivering in civilian clothes beside a row of buildings, a bare lightbulb staining the October dark, illuminating a flight of steps to the cave-like interior of the company supply room; a chorus of hacking, coughing, spitting souls—an army of postnasal drip, the trampled ground iridescent with gobs of phlegm. Fort Dix, New Jersey: the first time since Philosophy 101 that I seriously asked myself what am I doing here.

The summer before, in New York, after a meeting of our poetry workshop at Columbia, I had ridden the Broadway IRT downtown with Leonora Speyer. "I'm going into the service soon," I had said. "You must keep a notebook with you," she offered, encouragingly, "—and write! write!"

We roared along underground, standing in the crowded car. I was grateful for her concern. "Thank you," I had said, remembering a girl in workshop who had submitted the couplet: I am black and I am proud/ And when I die I'll wear a shroud," Miss Speyer reading it aloud to us and exclaiming, "How wonderful!—and doesn't the last line seem to call for '. . . white as a cloud' "?

Fort Bliss, near El Paso, Texas, across the border from Juarez, Mexico, we trained to fire anti-aircraft weapons; my first encounter with gigantic landscapes, into which we aimed our shells. Coming home on leave before going to Seattle for assignment to Korea, seven of us unable to get a flight for several days, hired a limousine to take us to New York: five in the back and two in the front, plus the driver: four days and three nights—nonstop except for food, restrooms or to rotate our seats. At a gas station fifty miles north of El Paso we met a group of GI's who had hired a limousine to get home. The chauffeur had stopped for fuel; they had gone to use the restrooms and to get something to eat, returning to find their duffle bags in a pile on the ground, the limousine and driver gone.

From that moment, we stuck to our driver, a tired, nervous-looking man with straight black hair and a moustache which seemed freshly erased. A few days on the road, somewhere in Louisiana, we stopped for food and saw the sign above the cafe entrance: White Only. It split us up: the driver was white, two soldiers were white, the rest of us were black. The driver was not hungry. The two white soldiers went in to eat, one bringing out some sandwiches when they returned, and climbed into the back seat, the other one grinning—where no one else was.

About a mile down the road, the fight broke out. The soldier who had grinned was crowding a soldier from New Jersey, named Murray. With no room to swing their fists, they struggled, grunted and cursed. The limousine shot forward along the road. Cursing, the three soldiers in the back seat wrestled the combatants into submission. It was calm for a while, then the battle flared up again. All across Louisiana and into Mississippi it was like that, but it did not stop the car. We were getting home. Beyond was Seattle and Korea. Besides, my girl friend had sent me a "Dear John" letter and I was mad to have her look me in the eyes and say it was true.

Early in Basic Training at Fort Dix I had made up my mind to learn whatever it would take to survive. Everything was measured against that resolution: friendships, desert sunsets, my M1, the food I ate, how far I could walk or run, the language I used, whom or what I would hate or love. One cold, wet November morning we sat in iron bleachers in a training field to receive instructions in handling land mines, booby traps, and other explosives. The demolition expert was a major, a black man possessing exceptional pyrotechnical virtuosity, who regaled us with sound and fury, his monologue a tough, witty spiel studded with scatological bursts of incandescent admonitions. For us he assembled, buried, and skillfully excavated murderous land mines, he contrived concealed and then wonderfully disarmed a variety of ingenious booby traps, demonstrating and classifying one by one a score of bombs, grenades, and explosives of odd sizes, shapes, colors, constructions, and potentials.

Some of our group were volunteered from the stands to bury and excavate dummy mines which when accidentally sprung, exploded with an audible "snap!" In the distance heavy charges roared in contrast to our make-believe devices. Canisters of colored smoke spread their signals; flares burst in the air above our heads. It was great fun.

By midmorning the rain had stopped, the sun pushed through the clouds; our clothes began to dry. There was a general lifting of spirits, more kibitzing and joking in the bleachers when a land mine "exploded" in the hands of a careless soldier or against the point of a probing bayonet. But all this had been foreseen by the major, who had wired an explosive beneath us in the bleachers against the moment when he triggered it, the blast launching us several inches above our seats, throwing dirt up around us, the sound a hollow thud like a gigantic hammer striking the underside of the grandstand. Faulty projectiles, we fell back stunned, jarred, momentarily deafened, but sensing a closer version of reality, the gray-white smoke of burnt powder rising sharp in our nostrils and tattering off in the wind.

I waited in Seattle for that explosion to occur, but none came. President Truman moved to further integrate the Army; I was sent to Alaska as a clerk-typist in the Headquarters Command, most of my old companions going to Korea, two I know getting wounded and sent home invalid before I could taste my first arctic winter.

Something in me waited for the explosion. Something had tensed, readied itself and refused to accept the calm that had come. It brought no relief that I talked in my sleep, that I woke others up with my nightmares shouting, "I will not fight!"

Eventually I was transferred to the classified section of the headquarters message center, took out a subscription to *Poetry*, and moved into a comfortable brick barracks, walking across the street each morning to work in a well-guarded office at the end of a long, narrow corridor, the office staffed by a commissioned officer, a sergeant, a civilian secretary and myself. We worked at four desks surrounded by three walls of combinations safes, the lieutenant sitting behind a screen where a smaller safe housed the top secret documents. It was a quiet, pleasant life. When we got overstocked with secrets, the sergeant and I would burn some of them—those that had been superseded, rescinded, declassified or otherwise declared obsolete. Slow work, it was done in a tiny stove in a well-guarded cellar, following a ritual of burning papers and then examining the ashes, burning and examining.

On one occasion we had an unusually large accumulation of documents to destroy, so the sergeant got the idea of dumping them into the furnace at the camp's power plant. Armed with a carbine we loaded our canvas bags into a jeep, sped to our destination, talked the soldier on duty into letting us carry out our plan, and began shoving papers into the flames, only to see whole pages sucked up the chimney flue and released in the air above the camp like leaflets—perhaps a dozen pages before we realized what was happening and rushed outside, canvas bags loaded back onto the jeep, to give chase to the loosed secrets. Who was the poet? Where was he hiding? What poems could have been written?— I asked myself blank evenings spent over dead pages.

One rare summer weekend we borrowed vehicles from the motor pool, food and water from the mess, and drove up into the mountains to escape our sedentary lives, hunting for gold and jade—two truckloads of us, tents, field gear, and stoves, leaving the vehicles where the road disappeared under a slide of boulders and backpacking it a mile to stake out camp and split up to begin our search.

A few of us moved off together in loose alliance, climbing rocks higher into the mountains, the land gradually giving way to a belt of pine and scrub oak, wildflowers, and rockfaces covered with thick moss, water spilling out of fissures from snows light-years back in the mountains.

Gaining the crest of a rise we discovered ourselves on a hill, a lush valley below, the true mountain range in the distance rising a dull brown, patches of black on its flank and bare places made by erosion and rockslides. Part of the way down the hill, into the valley, we saw the chimney and roof of a cabin and headed for it. Coming closer we could see that the exterior had suffered from the elements. It was deserted. The inside, divided into three or four rooms, was littered with broken furniture, clothing, toilet articles, several medicine bottles reading "Take two every hour to relieve pain," shoes, paperbacks, magazines, papers—all rainsoaked, battered, and falling into decay. Floorboards had worked themselves loose and lay mutely beside their places. Holes gaped in the walls between the rooms. A calendar for the year 1953 hung on the back of a closet door.

The cabin, which had at first given us hope of some discovery, began to pall. Bored with poking into the debris and clumping about the rooms on loose floorboards, some of our group had already gone outside into the sunlight when my foot, prodding a mass of sodden papers, exposed the envelope, its address melted away. I picked it up, opened it and read the letter inside. I called Ken from the other room—we had often shared our interests. In three months we would be back in the States for discharge from the Army, he to South Bend, Indiana, and I to New York City, before us, two decades of our lives: readjustments, work, universities, marriage, families, despair, loss, deaths, riots, conspiracies, a Third World, treasons, spacewalks, moon landings, wars, assassinations, my going to Greenwich Village to the White Horse Tavern one night to lean against the bar where Dylan Thomas had stood, to sip my beer; a brawl erupting, glass splintering around me, tables upturned, men and women yelling, falling down, struck by bottles, fists, and one of the troublemakers, a wild man, whirling about with a chair upraised in both hands, seeing me and hurling it: "—You! You black sonofabitch!"

Ken read the letter. I read it again, then dropped it on the pile and walked outside.

Written in a neat feathery hand, the letter was from a woman. "My Darling—" it began. Eager and excited she could hardly wait to see the man who had lived in the cabin. What clothes to bring? What was it like there? Places to go? Could she bring him anything when she came? X died. Y and Z had a baby girl. I love you.

Nothing in the shack suggested that she had ever come. But those decades were ahead of us, as we believe others are.

WHEN I AWOKE

When I awoke, she said:
Lie still, do not move.

They are all dead, she said.

Who?
I said.

The world,
She said.

I had better go,
I said.

Why?
She said. What good will it do?

I have to see,
I said.

JOHN PECK

JOHN PECK *(b. 1941 in Pittsburgh, Pa.) grew up in
northwestern Pennsylvania, was graduated from
Allegheny College with a B. A. in 1962 and from Stanford
with a Ph. D. (dissertation on Ezra Pound) in 1973. Since
1972 he has been a visiting lecturer in the writing program
at Princeton.*

(Photo by Tom Sherman)

Strata Satura

Simone Weil "was five years old in 1914 when the sight of wounded soldiers made her refuse to touch sugar and insist that it should be given away." The narrator impressed by this was the unsentimental George Lichtheim, who remarked to a friend that one of his earliest political memories came from his sixth year when he watched from an apartment near Berlin's Kurfuerstendamm the return of the defeated Imperial army. Between the moral passion that would become what it sees, and the cooler, latently analytic glimpse of spectacle, lies the more groping and tangled recollection, which first must conjure for itself puttees smacking saddle leather, and the agitation of brass helmet points. But this is the ordinary lot. When obscure recognitions beckon through such tangles, we have no Mayan calendar with which to plot the symmetries of their recurrence. They swerve under the mute hand, and our geometry for them must be a blind one, uncalibrated (though we are left as their templates), tenacious if only because things do wait for us to regard them as the common property they are—whether some alluvial intimation of early thirst, or a carved ring.

EARLY THIRST AND THE CARVED RING

Mica spun hints of wet through the sandpath,
I was younger than the war: glitter ahead sinking,
Mother set table and ate nothing, knowing of that death
Before word of it. Leaves smelled of uncut apples.
And her foreknowledge, did it seal me from memory
Of her brother, leavetakings, some first glare off water?

Cold leaves smoking under my clear spurt,
Their stains choked in the glaze throats of apples.
With the photo, the buttons down his tunic, I could fit
The jaw's curve to my own and ask nothing.
But with that, where the mute pact would seem
To close off, an afternoon has brimmed when I waited,

High and clear, and it is hers, hers as if
I were seeing it: playing hooky from the white
Lutheran hill school open in dry heat,

238

Her neck a stem downfield in brown barley,
Declensions carrying unbroken *lieblich liebliches*
Half an acre to where she sucked oranges.

When ripe sheen rounds back to hang with its first weight,
Original saturation, that odd pressure
That engulfs, is memory enough? And is it anyone's?
His jaw's curve fit my own, and carved on his ring
Two leapers sail through a bull's horns, their legs
Slimming over his neck's burl into sleep's ease.

So then: the machinist in his yard, the scrap hoard,
Muttering Budapest seated toward slag hills
Holding out his stub finger for me to verify:
Well it has grown maybe a little bit this week.
Toward evening hoppers shunted from the open hearths,
Pouring orange down those mounds to the pool's sizzle.

In following this old man, this uprooted figure who rests in the foreground of blurred memorial, I face the question: what is it to which I gain access in recovering something not strictly my own? The illusion is that I step onto sure ground, that I inhabit a "place." ("There is no place," saith Augustine.) That illusion invites me both to sustain it and penetrate it. The sleep guarded by der Alte might bear its own wakefulness.

RICK OF BURNING WOOD

The partisan, his wound
                    whole again
crouches in nets
                  shawled for the crossing
where stars lean up
                    through black glass
undizzied
                while the fisherman
drops rhythmically
                  on his glistening pole
scanning past
                the small rick of burning wood

forked off his bow, gleaning
                the lapse of ripples—
his punt drags
        into the riffle, holds
against its flow, and
           the form of a man
trails bent shadow
        into pines uncut
by the terse flare—
         which backs off now into
velvet exhalation,
        brands jarring loose from it
to drift in the Tornio
        breeding smoke
with a low sound, slowly
        less and less.

In 1926 Ungaretti looked back on the nineteenth century as an attempt to saturate spirit with memory, whose issue was into a collapse figured repeatedly as shipwreck. The safeguard on which he had seen his own generation fall back was "the innocence of the object." Yet the *naufragé* continues to wash up in the poems of Péret and other surrealists, beached in crystalline fixity, no longer simply the consequence of *"mémoire, le profondeur de l'homme,"* but to some extent its substitute. While Nietzsche's mentions of shipwreck retain the flavor of Odyssean brine, a homecoming to even the innocent object has defined the horizon behind us less than we might like to believe. Does not the traffic between fixity and flux in that sunlit cranium called *"Le cimitière marin"* catch light from Leopardi's *"l'Infinito"* and refract it into surrealist poetics?

The interwound sleep and waking of Cronos: as mythologized by the stranger in *The Statesman*, it accounts for that legendary race of men who were autochthonous or earth-born; and as painted into the upper left of Blake's "Sea of Time and Space" in neoplatonic outlines, it presides over the original castaway's return to his Ithaka. Shipwreck, autochthony, and nostos, the root of nostalgia: these have been our obsessions also, but too often separately rather than as parts of one mythos. "The forest flees from one's eyes," Ortega; and Sorley Maclean: "the giddy great wood, / russet, green, two plaitings."

I find myself pouring together that mixture of opinionated reflection and poems for which only the Gaels seem to find good names. And in doing so, turning toward another face of sleep and memory. For in their dispersed and denatured forms they do not wait for us to meet them; they confront us by inviting a contact which they withdraw or interrupt, thinning attention to distraction. None of us escapes this, the sleep of the polity—that somnolence which some have called bestial. But we can do without humorlessness, as without the astroturf on postcards. No, that sleep may be something more interesting and dangerous: half-wakeful but quite sealed off nonetheless, absolute of its kind, next to which the primeval sleep of Earth-shaker in the Iroquois narrative, while staying mythic and self-induced, seems pure, and the legend of silver-bearded Rip seems merely charming, the safe fable of a stillborn revolution (or what Randolph Bourne called one of history's smoothest coups d'état). The organism is busy but does not "come out of it"; it does what some translator of our language might find in one of its more capable verbs: it stirs. And the stir lacks that tension born of either memory or the desire to wake.

As a boy watching from a Pittsburgh rooftop in 1877, my grandfather saw the Union Depot and machine shops, along with the entire freight yard, go up in flames during the railway riots, centerpiece of our first general strike. He played hooky to watch John Brashear make telescope mirrors in his lens shop, the kindly old man whom H. D. remembers visiting her astronomer father during her childhood. When steelworkers at Homestead held off barges of Pinkertons with cannon and burning oil slicks, young Sayenga was a blower in one of six dozen glassworks, and soon after that a railway fireman, then engineer. His freights ran down one side of that river along which Alexander Berkman, the man who had shot Henry Clay Frick ineffectually during the Homestead strike, heard river rats at work near his place of solitary confinement. So that while Sayenga the engineer thought twice about strike votes, Berkman was reciting Nekrasov to fellow prisoners. And while confederates worked at their abortive tunnel meant to spring Berkman, burrowed improbably next to a marsh and an old gas well, the engineer may have been hauling in that mountain of cement which was used to stuff it—a care seldom lavished on the defunct mines that honeycomb the region, the most obliging of which has swallowed a bank. One of the saloons he visited may have belonged to still another branch of the family; but these taverns could not have included the Black Horse, razed by then, where the Whiskey Rebels had gathered. The drivewheels on his coal-fired consolidation have been remelted. The houseboat built by his father on the Monongahela, as only a former Dutch sea captain would build it, was of a draught and beam no one has recorded. And the stout German Bible kept by the saloon owners, with family history and snippets of homemade verse, has been lost.

REFINDING THE SEAM

Near the old walk, the same smolder
From a dead gallery venting at hill crotch
Where no man has yet built his anonymous house.

The mines of Nero and the ovens of Frick
Peter out at this boreface, but its buried
Stinkfire, unabated, leaves

Hill lines wavering in its shimmer, clearest
Through shutdowns, the strike's weird clair-obscur
When the pigeon dislodged by your footfall

Can raise dust puffs under his maroon wings
That mean Arcturus and the bear
Will not go unattended that evening in heaven.

Speaking for his own moment in *Passages*, Robert Duncan finds himself "adrift / between two contrary educations," the revolution that disowns but would remake and the reaction that pretends to reclaim. Yet his dichotomy might have seemed congenial to Henry Adams. How long have we split ourselves, now, between programs of action and nostalgias variously sentimental and panicky? Or rather between allegiances to programs of force nominally opposed, but kindred in their rejection of memory's oppressive limestone growth? The Bildads and Zophars among us have isolated a stripped action and a brittle nostalgia alike from the encumberance and incoherence of that accumulation—from the risk of dispersion into its layers and metamorphic pressures, its slippages and faultings; from that submission to other contours, and that embrace of a recovered self, which memory always has asked of action in its perpetual homecoming. From either side, these counselors have refused that embrace, repudiating the earth and its heaviness. Only those staying in the crossfire, the stewards of autochthony or rootedness or a humanism sedimented and hidden, have recognized in the mutual immanence of act and memory one description of their Ithaka. But there is no telling when they will be able to shed the heavy armor forced upon them by their antagonists, the ideologies.

When Augustine wished to argue without absurdity that there is a memory of things present, he turned to Virgil's idiom about Odysseus mustering himself to put out the eye of Cyclops: *nec oblitusve sui*, he did not forget himself. "He kept his head," one version renders it, and another, "he proved true to himself"—a spread that embraces both intention and result, in a stiffening of inner consistency. And Augustine found memory in the center of that moment of danger, bringing the mind into its own presence, "at hand to itself." He thereby lets us equip presence, and presence of mind prior to resolve, with the dimension usually reserved for things past and out of reach. His Odysseus announces the permanence of waking, in which a man's ordinary moments do not believe; for with the onset of the strange—of danger, love, vacancy—there comes a moment when we see more clearly than we do either before or after. But simple idiom preserves this, in Virgil and in English: action lives on the precondition that "one does not forget oneself."

Action lives, then, in the stressed metamorphic rock of presence (*praesens*, being before itself) and of anamnesis, which seems to be more than recollection (getting back into getting-it-there, to oversimplify). It lives also in words that emerge from a way of life. But it cannot live in that shadowy presence more familiar to us, the state of mind whose strange dimensionality, among other things, bugged Charles Olson to generate his specific hunger for some analogue of the grammatical middle voice. Whitman used no sleight-of-hand when he telescoped December and June into one glimpse, for was he not seeing something remember itself? "Watched the Twelfth-month sea-gulls, saw them high in the air floating with motionless wings, oscillating their bodies, / . . . Saw the slow wheeling circles and the gradual edging toward the south, / Saw the reflection of the summer sky in the water. . . ."

LET US CALL THIS THE HILL OF SOTATSU

There is, finally, the cleanliness
Of profusion. Basho and spring roads,
Profusion, fogged dawns, walks among huts
    Smoking after raids;

Purslane's invasion of whiter rue
Along the first hill where this trail bends—
Smoke as a dead lake up to the knees
    And griefless, small sounds.

Big drones already busy, and now
The declaration stands one week clear,
Rue anemone takes hold where large trees
    Stand off the younger

And some fugitive has plunged from that
Drift of whites, his sleep's curve still pressed in—
Otium tense in *negotium,*
    The meditation

Contained already in the action.
And when *il Signore* Chancellor
Orders cavalry to rebillet
    Away from farms where

They press olives, he writes of choked barns
But also of "young women who would be
Made uneasy by your soldiers. Yours,
    Machiavelli."

Profusion and spring roads, emergent
Delicacy still formulaic,
And beneath it all some great stone head
    Overgrown, Olmec

Victim relenting, crannying into
Flower and asking no dreams of us
(I found my name for this local hill
    Thus, sitting in place)

Nor intent on tasting some root blend
Of moss, honey of the great mastoids,

And the narcotic pulse of rain, sun,
    Rain: the cleanliness

Of blank regard jaguar-helmeted,
Light once each day through chinks light has bored,
Mineral distillates foreknown in
    Taste not yet savored . . .

General Braddock's four-mile column, like leviathan, chewed roads
through transmontane forests and log-paved them for cannons and
wagons: a parade of engineering followed in the British and colonial
press by brigadiers and investors. The most industrious of these investors, B. Franklin, dryly noted the commander's contempt for Indian am-
bushes. Humming that same contempt two-hundred-ten years later,
Huey Hog helicopter gunships twittered through our pseudo-latinate
press releases. Six years before Braddock there were Céloron's reiterative
lead plates at the mouths of tributaries along the OYO AVTREMENT BELLE
RIVIERE POVR MONVMENT DV RENOVVELLEMENT DE POSSESSION QVE NOVS
AVONS PRIS DE LE DITTE RIVIERE OYO, one of which may have been nailed to
the lily-tipped cross carved into a stone found at Peters Creek. A compact between leviathanic evil and telluric evil was forged by 1830 in "the
smoke of the chimies." As for the bark baskets found under a dry rock
overhang at nearby Avella, they were manufactured when sundiscs were
being chipped into rocks of the Camonica Valley; and the stone blades at
Avella were fashioned under the breath of the last retreating ice sheets.
Far upstream, where Handsome Lake's tribe did its spearfishing at Kinzua
Creek, waters impounded by the Corps of Engineers preserve their own
silts.

Over against the busy sleep, the sleep-walking stir, stands some kind
of mental presence, but it too may have roots in a subaqueous world, no
blinding light; and I need only look beyond those things to which that
presence might be "applied" to see it emerge from Warren County river
valleys as they drift under bridges or mark the boundaries of a climb. Or
I can find myself, earlier and not far from steelworks, sweeping toward
those portals I called "the green city" when my eyes still came up to a
car window: with each descent off bridge ramps onto Duquesne bluffs,
a cut into sheer rockface past green guardrails blurring through moiré
patterns toward a short tunnel. The city that lay beyond it was never,
of course, the city that seemed imminent with each approach, and that

difference kept alive the innocent name it had called from me, and also must have triggered stony monumental dreams (later I'd think of El Amarna, or the backdrops of Bibiena and Mazzi; but echoes fade into echoes). The place behind that cut, intriguingly other than the promise— neither simply short of it nor unredeemed—must have kept everything else distinct: the yielding glide toward a place always virtual, and then the rock itself. The child sank into his fabulous journey, but he also tested with that plunge the resistance of rock layers, and found his world. For to enter such cuts and drift along their faces is to squeeze a terrain like Bellini's, with its sliced upthrusts and foreshortened glimpse of labor, toward blunt will and irresistible choice; it is to meet arbitrary power, the antonym of action. While this unsettling effect works its way in, the material itself insinuates its own layered deposit or melded mass. Which explains nothing. But then the Clavis Apocalypticus, which sets out to explain everything, would telescope presence into an igneous block that somehow retains its formative heats.

LUCIEN

Were those flares new to you
Their pulse downriver
Still would prompt accurate
Guesses: something is being poured,
Something fused beyond trace
Of any former shape
Or life, puddling to magma.
Only the face itself
Of yearning would seem strange,
Though spores of it now gutter
Down afternoon, powdering
Over the obdurate
Skin of what is, warehouse
Mill rail steeple, grit spurring you
Irrelevantly to turn
The pronoun's lash against
Yourself, *you* and then *you*

Until in the street's eyes
It is your own that jell, the maze
Familiar,

The bridge alone letting you
Watch the late summer front .
Shred toward storm, and there is no damping
The quiver underfoot
At midspan (or the flash
Of a fin tucking under),
Cables muttering
Their chill life to the hand,
And colder if you hold
In the same gust that floats
The pigeon every lunge
Of the ranked spans
And their lights threading homeward—

Lucien, your fury still
Veins with the muskellunge
Nudging at locks; and while
Your own breath blown from you
Augurs the focus, some projection's
Pure point out there at last
Churning to rise,
The channel scrawls its white
Flawed cursives. Evening waits,
And the swimmer toward the moored barge
Rolls his stroke without haste,
From his lean arm the veil
Splits evenly across
His flowing face.

Peripheral
To screen walls glassing their own
Lines of force—rigid
Telemetries—the flicker
That endures whirls dirt over tracks
And settles. You refine your grasp
And it all spins without
Touching: gunships that once
Slid through your fists, a child's
Gripping this rail until
They hung bloodless (you hid
Your delirium), shipbuilders' flags

In that thin amber of fever,
And now the hiss of small prows
Stirring the hoard of ash
Among towers, a rust
Drum that flames bannering
An abuttment with soot, two boys
Chucking in rubber—

And the space cleared in you
Glazes, that some fissure might sheer
Up through strata, insinuate
The full torque of its ice,
And cloud seem less far
Where it luffs tugging the glared
Half-coiling river, and the hid
Spindle rides, hub of your gaze;
That your forearm, Lucien, might twist
Beneath silt where the fires
Burn colder and the lost
Turn more urgently, to grab
That column at its base
In murk, rotate the profile
One notch, another world
Shine through—
                    But the front masses

Elsewhere, . . . and if spasm
Clicks into place behind
Your eyes, it is because
You turn too quickly, you pivot
Into the trick: the car
That nearly hits and then
Shuts you into its speed,
The night driver whose mirror
Stripes his eyes, his cheek molten
Where its core would break through
The slow char: he has yet
To come, that messenger
Whom you wish, obscurely, to touch,
Indifference that survives
The crossing, the change of suns
And a cope of stars altered.

Stumbling into the propane heat of farm kitchens from a young blizzard, to peddle tickets for an inept class play to Mrs. Noah rocking by the stove and nursing whiskey; ducking back out from that stifling linoleum, from pappy's mountainous gums, his joke a hot cherry lost in the wool of his red check shirt—back into snow, awake.

Perhaps because we know few among us who, as Czeslaw Milosz describes them, "do not disdain continuity as it is written in the slope of a roof, the curve of a plow handle, in gestures or proverbs," we misconstrue the stratigraphy of such vision, presuming it to be rigid. But isn't it the other kind of mind that grows rigid, shelving beneath its collective head the stone pillow of an order thought to be blessedly inflexible, all the while inducing cave-in synclines in its own holdings, as do the hill-splitting miners in Pliny, *spectant victores ruinam naturae?* Or regarding the crust of Gothic spiredoodles icing the office block of Pittsburgh's Union Trust, a banker's bland appropriation of Flemish accolade, as a purchase on the past and one definition of "charm"? The negative strength of vision, its opposable thumb or alternate biceps, is its resistance to lies. "Biggest damn keep-off-the-grass sign I have ever seen," snorted Wright at the Cathedral of Learning's pillar Gothic sheath (his own call-to-order was the Mayan temple, during the same years in which Tatlin's tower spiraled up from a revived golden section). Over the river from Union Trust lies the antidote for it, one of H. H. Richardson's last designs, a tiny 1885 Romanesque church in brick with bake-oven entry arches. Antidote, but of course it could hardly stem the drift, tidal within a decade, toward self-congratulatory Romanitas, that shift sensed by Adams as he stood before the plaster façades of the 1893 Chicago Exposition, "the first expression of American thought as a unity" —imperial pastiche laid over George Westinghouse's dynamo, the centralized capital mechanism finally chosen after a century of hesitation.

A toothless half-deaf bachelor who drawled to us as kids, through 180-proof blasts, that he had dug up a mastodon's jaw while excavating part of the Riverside golf course, used to confide in us, too, that the only reports from which you could get any satisfaction, if they came from outside the county, arrived as did the closer intelligence about his own cronies: as gossip. "OTHERwise," boomed old Rex, "it has the het of MAK-ings all over it; it's an e-VENT." Later I recognized in this counsel echoes of more than the Appalachian plateau. As for event, memoryless and therefore beautiful in the manner of skinned muscle, presence hollowed out and flattened to surface, each man can name his own example.

Walking into a dwarf-pine forest off the main road, looking for tar lichens that grow there, I meet a rise and find myself stopped by two roaring glints raking the flats ahead, stooping from high trajectories into their dry runs and looping back. A shirtless fat man groping belly-up under his derelict Nash is intent on grease. His shack and gutted outbuilding counterweight, along the frail crest, the bombing range's block-letter sign and crater of half-buried duds, nipples rusted. Stringy puffs lean overhead through the backlighting of late afternoon, fleecing apart at free angles; the receding dirt slash, across a seafloor unsubmerged during the last influx, erupts and plumes free of a firetruck scuttling toward the next rise. The pink mouth lolling under the chassis dilates in a prolonged act of attention. Those twin knives turn screaming through cedarish air of the barrens, darken and diminish, and swoop in again, closer this time, wearing squat heads inside shiny blisters. The lichens wait everywhere.

STANLEY PLUMLY

STANLEY PLUMLY *(b. May 23, 1939 in the southeastern hills of Ohio) grew up in Virginia and Ohio, and was educated at Wilmington College and Ohio University. He has taught at both of these schools and also at Louisiana State University and at the State University of Iowa Writers Workshop. He has been the recipient of a Guggenheim Fellowship for poetry, and in 1974 received the Delmore Schwartz Memorial Award for* In the Outer Dark.

(Photo by William Stafford)

The One Thing

*One must not come to feel that
   he has a thousand threads
   in his hands,
He must somehow see the one thing;
This is the level of art
There are other levels
But there is no other level of art*
                    George Oppen

I

Aside from the Friday school movies, which consisted almost exclusively of dark continent documentaries (lots of bare breasts and big lips) embellished by the overvoice of a Lowell Thomas, the thing I remember most about the sixth grade was the semester field-trip. So there were two that year. The first was to the slaughter-house, where we were treated to the entire process, from hammer to knife. The second, in late spring I think, 1951, was to the local hospital to see, to watch the iron lung.

By age ten I had already, in my mind, become a great moviegoer. I went two or three times a week, often, out of necessity, to the same film, as there were only two moviehouses in the town. Or I would sit through two or three runs of the same double-feature, a near catatonic feat. The era of the '40s and '50s was the best for the short-subject, the sandwich film, ranging from Pete Smith shorts to things like *The March of Dimes*. The March was particularly impressive, as its intent was so singular. Collection cans would be passed among the audience: the dimes were all marching for an end to *infantile paralysis*, poliomyelitis. Polio. The film's narration was like the dream-voice of Jehovah, an auditory sweep that made you feel guilty as hell for not being afflicted. No single edition ever lasted more than a few minutes, but the stark-raving sight of some bodiless, pubescent girl, prone and smiling heroically into her rear-view mirror—except for her head, totally encapsulated—had all the subconscious possibilities of permanent memory. She was a head and a lung, and little else. Just under the narrator's big voice, you could hear the machine's bigger breath. I sat through endless such moments, with my fingers crossed and my dime in my pocket.

Then there were the dog days, the grim auguries of August. For my parents the period of the polio scare must have had something of the repressive quality of the Depression—the threat, psychic or physical, lay largely in its ambiguity. It seemed only forces like purity and good works could countervail. All across America, in the peak month of August, swimming pools and playgrounds, movie theaters and fairs would become shy of anyone under, say, fourteen. Heat, as I remember, was the great fear. There seemed to be some intimate connection between high body temperature, sudden chill, and the potential for paralysis. Crowds, by their very claustrophobic and germ-generating natures, were therefore suspect. And crowded activity. Playing it safe and playing it cool, that's the best our parents could do for us. I spent a lot of warm hours behind open windows those late summer afternoons. No one knew what caused polio, but you knew it was as easily come by as catching cold.

It turned out our parents were right—the source of the affliction was practically spiritual. It would be called a virus, as indiscriminate as air. That spring morning, gathered in full circle around the iron lung, within the perfect four-square walls of that hospital room, we twenty or so sixth-graders witnessed an event incandescent in our imaginations. Again, it was a girl's head, face, a thing apart, looking into the mirror. I remember being embarrassed for her, and for myself, for being there. Somehow, in the most terrible and inevitable way, this was her business only. And we were clumsily presuming on that privacy. Perhaps she enjoyed the company. I don't know. I think she talked, rather garbled, as into a glass of water. The nurse had tried to make her face look pretty, but it was the beauty of the mortuary. Still, she smiled at herself. Her body was turning to stone, and she smiled. I think I thought I was looking into the mirror too. The lung itself, which resembled a great hot-water tank on its side, huffed and puffed like an asthmatic.

THE IRON LUNG

So this is the dust that passes through porcelain,
so this is the unwashed glass left over from supper,
so this is the air in the attic, in August,
and this the down on the breath of the sleeper . . .

If we could fold our arms, but we can't.
If we could cross our legs, but we can't.
If we could put the mind to rest . . .
But our fathers have set this task before us.

My face moons in the mirror, weightless,
without air, my head propped like a penny.

I'm dressed in a shoe, ready to walk out
of here. I'm wearing my father's body.

I remember my mother standing in the doorway
trying to tell me something. The day is thick
with the heat rising from the road. I am
too far away. She looks like my sister.

And I am dreaming of my mother in a doorway
telling my father to die or go away.
It is the front door, and my drunken father falls
to the porch on his knees like one of his children.

It is precisely at this moment I realize
I have polio and will never walk again.
And I am in the road on my knees, like my father,
but as if I were growing into the ground

I can neither move nor rise.
The neighborhood is gathering, and now
my father is lifting me into the ambulance
among the faces of my family. His face is

a blur or a bruise and he holds me
as if I had just been born. When I wake
I am breathing out of all proportion to myself.
My whole body is a lung; I am floating

above a doorway or a grave. And I know
I am in this breathing room as one
who understands how breath is passed
from father to son and passed back again.

At night, when my father comes to talk,
I tell him we have shared this body long enough.
He nods, like the speaker in a dream.
He knows that I know we're only talking.

Once there was a machine for breathing.
It would embrace the body and make a kind of love.
And when it was finished it would rise
like nothing at all above the earth

to drift through the daylight silence.
But at dark, in deep summer, if you thought you heard
something like your mother's voice calling you home,
you could lie down where you were and listen to the dead.

II

I believe in a poetry of protagonist-antagonist relationship, in which
the energy, the tension, of the poem is the result of what happens between the two. *What* in fact happens is that third thing, the between
thing, content. Even if the speaker of the poem is opposed by objects or
events, I sense, certainly in my own work, the presence of another person behind them. An antagonist could be, of course, a projected version
of the speaker himself. Whatever the case, the poems, anyone's, that hold
power for me are those that generate such oppositions, polarities, poems
that work out such problems on the page.

Which means that for me a poem is a problem of the trinity, father-
son-ghost. Often the father is replaced by a woman, but the tension
remains the same. Now when I say tension I of course refer to an
aesthetic balancing of the poem's primary forces. Chekhov says that all
stories come down to a single center of gravity: he and she. In my poems,
he and he. The ghost, the third, the created thing, that which was un-
provided, becomes the content. That is why even the darkest or angriest
poems can speak past such limitations, can celebrate. The despair is never
in the content; it is in the actor or actors who are working out the
conflict.

I loved and hated my father, deeply. For the first five or six years of
my making poems I could not get past the hate. They were all bad
poems. Because art first of all is a moral act, and morality without love
is a contradiction in terms. Then at twenty-five, I wrote a poem called
"Now That My Father Lies Down Beside Me."

NOW THAT MY FATHER LIES DOWN BESIDE ME

We lie in that other darkness, ourselves.
There is less than the width of my left hand
between us. I can barely breathe,
but the light breathes easily,
wind on water across our two still bodies.

I cannot even turn to see him.
I would not touch him. Nor would I lift
my arm into the crescent of a moon.
(There is no star in the sky of this room,
only the light fashioning fish along the walls.
They swim and swallow one another.)

I dream we lie under water,
caught in our own sure drift.
A window, white shadow, trembles over us.
Light breaks into a moving circle.
He would not speak and I would not touch him.

It is an ocean under here.
Whatever two we were, we become
one falling body, one breath. Night lies down
at the sleeping center—no fish, no shadow,
no single, turning light. And I would not touch him
who lies deeper in the drifting dark than life.

Surely, this is a sexual poem, but mostly it falls in love. Since that time
I have been about my father's work.

His work: from lumberjack to machinist—an odyssey of dwindling
resources and lower and lower hopes. He was a man built for the outdoors but one who got trapped inside his own small view of himself. But
he did farm a little, raise cattle in a hobby, half-assed way. Evening
work, he called it. And almost every evening he would come back from
the barn as if he had been in conference. I suppose he had. As he was
drunk most of the time, the cattle must have understood his mumbling
soliloquies as a kind of music. They were peaceable masters; they listened. Every spring when he slaughtered them, he wept. Then he would
stomp around the house raising hell, threatening lives, shouting the walls
down, "I'm a dead tree in this room!" And after a while, worn out,
sobered, he would pick up his violin.

OUT-OF-THE-BODY TRAVEL

1
And then he would lift this finest
of furniture to his big left shoulder
and tuck it in and draw the bow
so carefully as to make the music

almost visible on the air. And play
and play until a whole roomful of the sad
relatives mourned. They knew this was
drawing of blood, threading and rethreading

the needle. They saw even in my father's
face how well he understood the pain
he put them to—his raw, red cheek
pressed against the cheek of the wood . . .

2
And in one stroke he brings the hammer
down, like mercy, so that the young bull's
legs suddenly fly out from under it . . .
While in the dream he is the good angel

in Chagall, the great ghost of his body
like light over the town. The violin
sustains him. It is pain remembered.
Either way, I know if I wake up cold,

and go out into the clear spring night,
still dark and precise with stars,
I will feel the wind coming down hard
like his hand, in fever, on my forehead.

III

"The human body is universal, but that does not make it a planet of
flesh." So says Gil Elliot, in his book *Twentieth Century Book of the
Dead*. I wonder. Alive, my father walked around in my life like something wounded. Dead: I sometimes think I walk around in his. He died
of a massive coronary, drinking of course. He was as big as a bull. So
I imagine him ramming the walls, breaking down in large pieces of himself, his body flying apart. Actually, as I was told, he was on his knees
and simply, suddenly ran out of breath.

I was in Scotland, out of touch.

Over the past several years one of my recurring dreams is to be lying
in bed, as if held down, while a grand, bell-shaped, bird-cage of a thing
swings, sort of tolls, over me. There is a large, bone-thin, bone-white
horse standing in this cage, the apparatus barely big enough for the
length of its body. Its face, therefore, is squeezed against the bars. From

somewhere, as in a movie, I hear a man's voice explaining, as if to an audience, how marvelous his horse is: it has never been off its feet. Some time seems to pass; people are talking. And then the horse's big face comes down to mine and I wake up in front of it.

Once, when I was nine or ten, my father and I were walking in a neighbor's pasture. He was going to show me something or other. (He was always instructing me and I was always a slow learner.) There was a small bay mare grazing off to one side, lifting its head occasionally to look at us. It was a good horse, used to people. Suddenly my father decided that one of us was going to ride; both of us, in fact, bareback. That was to be the lesson: riding bareback. He approached the horse all wrong—from the front and too fast. It ran off, naturally, but not too far. Same approach, same result. This went on for about ten minutes, with me tagging along, more afraid than the horse. Finally, my father got close enough to grab its mane; the horse rose, knocking him down. Again he got a piece of the animal, and this time, hurling himself, he hit it in the face. The horse rose full up and could have stomped us, but instead ran for the barn. By now the neighbor was closing in. We headed home.

A heart specialist once said to me that he was tired of people confusing acute indigestion with a heart attack. He said the difference was clear: a heart attack was like being kicked by a horse.

Bringing the disparate into immediate and intimate relation. That is the hope I have for my poems. My father in the ground is a unifying principle.

HORSE IN THE CAGE

Its face, as long as an arm, looks down & down.

Then the iron gate sound of the cage swings shut
above the bed, a bell as big as the room: quarter-
moon of the head, its nose, its whole lean body
pressed against its cell . . .

I watched my father hit a horse in the face once.

It had come down to feed across the fence.
My father, this stranger, wanted to ride.
Perhaps he wanted only to talk. Anyway,
he hit the ground and something broke.

As a child I never understood how an animal
could sleep standing. In my dream the horse
rocks in a cage too small, so the cage swings.

I still wake up dreaming, in front of a long face.
That day I hugged the ground hard.

Who knows if my heartbroken father was meant
to last longer than his last good drunk.
They say it's like being kicked by a horse.

You go down, your knees hug up.
You go suddenly wide awake, and the gate shuts.

ISHMAEL REED

ISHMAEL REED *(b. 1938 in Chattanooga, Tenn.) attended the University of Buffalo, has taught in various places, and currently lives and writes in Berkeley, California. A brilliant and frequently controversial novelist and poet, he was nominated for National Book Awards in both fiction and poetry in 1973.*

(Photo by Jill Krementz)

Flight to Canada

I

Traveling north from Virginia after the third visit to Porke Plantation, John Swell, fugitive slave, stopped off for a night of ale drinking with the free community in good olde Manhattan.

The next day he was in Brockport, breaking bread with some Sympathizers of the Cause. They drank wine and talked after he had read his anti-slavery poetry.

A Jewish student was questioning him as he relaxed in his French-Canadian host's eighteenth-century American home. The Jewish student was reminding him that he was a slave and what did the other slaves left behind in slavery feel about his "deserting" them and what did he think of those slave poets who had charged him with not being slavery enough?

Nowadays they call slavery ethos, which was being hooked on values you had no hand in creating. While the Jewish student was questioning him he thought of Katz's delicatessen on Houston Street where he had bought some sour-krauted hotdogs the night before. An older Jewish gentleman was arguing with a Puerto Rican gentleman over the quality of Katz's seltzer. Over near the entrance, next to the man who was handing out the red coupons, stood a large slave, the kind of slave John Swell remembered working in the fields or studding. The slave was packing a gun and so maybe that's why the Jewish gentleman felt confident in his discussion with the Puerto Rican: "Look, I used to work in a seltzer factory and so I know the difference between seltzer and this crap you're selling; I'm never coming in here again."

"Whaddya want me to do cry now, or later," said the old Jewish gentleman.

So you see we all have our ethos as they say these days—we all have our slaveholes, John Swell thought, wondering how this young, eager, apparently brilliant student would have reacted to the old man.

Only one x-slave had showed up for his reading and the French-Canadian host complained: "They ask me to get some x-slave poets and when I bring one, the x-slaves don't show up."

John Swell didn't mind if the x-slaves hadn't shown up for his reading. It has been a long time since they were all manacled together in ratty boats and now they were free to attend whatever they wished.

The one x-slave who did show up was a runaway from Georgia. She was round-faced, black-skinned and wore bright red lipstick. She wore some beads around her neck and a sharp bandanna. She wanted John Swell to tell her about Egypt. She wanted to know everything there was to know about Egypt. He referred her to *The African Origin of Civilization, Myth or Reality* written by Cheikh Anta Diop and translated into English by Mercer Cook.

It was fortunate that the host was French-Canadian because John Swell was full of questions about Canada. Ever since he was a slave child he had heard people whisper about Canada. They talked about Canada as if it was heaven. They talked about its forests, its lakes, its snow-capped mountains. They talked about how the CBC was superior to American radio and television. How it was real cultural. They talked about how the Prime Minister was rumoured to have some native-American blood in him.

One day, John Swell would go to Canada, but first he would have to clear up a little stateside Business, not the kind people are accustomed to with its Lost Leaders, Loan Sharks, and Hi-Pressure Salesmanship; he wasn't trying to peddle a thing.

He was a wanderer and would have escaped from slavery even if it had been the paradise painted by its apologists. He was a nomad— moving about, from sky to sky, on the run.

"One must always defeat the bloodhounds of one's existence," he had told the Jewish student, wearily. When he talked like this he knew he was tired and so John Swell returned to the motel. He rose to leave when a poet, one of the guests, reminded him of a letter he had sent requesting some of John Swell's writing for a book he was working on. In his letter he had written:

> "My idea was to have each poet write about his or her own work. This still seems fine to me. Best. But it is an awful thing to ask for. Still, I hope many of you will write directly about your own work, as difficult as this may be.
> "I decided to ask poets to write about *anything*. I thought that the book as a *whole*, even if the poets did not write directly about themselves, even if I asked them to write about anything, would manifest our vital concerns, would be an eclectic collection of the feelings of American poets in '76."

John Swell was embarrassed. He couldn't say that he didn't have a staff. His mail had increased in volume after his sixth book as an x-slave poet and so he wasn't always prompt in replying to his mail.

"I don't want to bother you," the poet said, "but if you could work up something, say 3,000 words, I'd like to have you in the book."

He would work something up but it wouldn't be in essay form. Essays aroused passions. His essays had always gotten him into trouble by pointing out to his kidnappers, claimants, and enemies where he was at. Someone had called him, "A Rascal on the Plantation," because of an essay he had written.

The last time he had visited Beulahland Publishers they had trotted out an x-slave from South Carolina and dressed up like a low budget peacock to give him a verbal whipping and the negro warmed up to his role; his hair pressing against his skull and a dental-floss thin mustache spread out in delight. The Negro told him how much his books were worth and by inference how much he was worth—said he could prove it with "A-tistics"; said he knew all about "A-tistics," as the white gentleman, smoking cigars, chuckled over this good show. He was a green negro and so he didn't know about the Manhattan pat juber game where one slave is encouraged to knock another slave.

When he told his friends about this—about these x-slaves, claimants, bounty hunters, and bloodhounds on his tail they called him "paranoid."

John Swell lived in Emancipated, California. Everyone was free from the old passions like jealousy and hate—they didn't fear things anymore and had imported new words to describe their Freedom and Liberty. He would trust his old instincts until the day he died. They might call it "paranoid," but he would always be on the lookout because they weren't going to send him back to Virginia. He had heard horror stories about what happened to slaves who had been returned to Virginia. The worst thing you could do to a fugitive slave was to return him to " 'Ginny."

The next day he flew an American Airlines plane out of Brockport. Shortly, on the right side, below, he could see Niagara Falls. It looked like a bright bowl of white sherbet from the sky. Once in a poem he had compared the situation of being a slave poet to that of going over Niagara Falls in a barrel.

II

John Swell sits in the North Star cafe which caters to runaways, indians, chicanos, and whites of Abolitionist sentiments though once in a while a Confederate wanders in and like Confederates they are polite in a steely way, concealing their disdain arising from the spectacle of negro and white runaways mixing it up.

Some Confederate spies are in town, too. They drink at places with

names like *The Alabama Club* where the waiters wear greasy ducktail
hairstyles and smash the bottles after a slave has drunk from them.
Behind the bar, on the shelves, cheap coney-island liquor bottles can be
seen and the jukebox is all Country-Western. Confederate flags wave
from their pick-up trucks.

Some of the followers of John Brown who came North after the
Harper's Ferry shootout, where Federal forces were able to test some
counterinsurgency devices, roll by on motorcycles, and here and there
can be seen a survivor of the Nat Turner skirmish which put heat on
everybody and according to some postponed the emancipation of the
Virginia slaves.

Swell was sipping a Bloody Mary, the 95-cent special in which a
cucumber was dunked, reading a poetry magazine which had been published by the free community in Palo Alto. Stray Leechfield, one of
Emancipated's runaway slaves had entered a poem—well it was set up
like a poem but reading between the lines you could see that Leechfield
was paying off his debts to various carpetbaggers, scalawags and others
in San Francisco and Emancipated who had arranged 25-dollar readings
for him. Stray didn't really runaway as the others had: Contraband, 40's,
Randy Shank, and John Swell—Stray had strayed away and had only
runaway because it was the fashionable thing to do at the time and so
his heart wasn't really in emancipation and he seemed to miss slavery,
always bringing the subject of slavery up.

Here he comes now, followed by a man who could be Eddie Cantor's
double—only sinister looking. Stray's friend, an exile from Manhattan
who's always downgrading the punishment the slaves received in Virginia and promoting the atrocities of his own people over those of the
negro slaves. To hear him tell it, no one suffered as much as his people
had under the Czar. The Czar was cruel to them and no one in the world,
in all of history, with the possible exception of the hebrew people under
the Pharaohs had endured as much as his people under the Czar. He had
talked about this so much that once John Swell went to seek a book at
the Emancipated library and had found a figure of Czarist Russia with
whom he could identify:

SPUTIN

Like Venus
My spin is retrograde
A rebel in more
Ways than one

I click my heels
In seedy taverns
& pinch the barmaids
On the cheeks

Madeira drips from
My devilish beard
My eyes sparkle dart
Flicker & sear
Man, do I love to dance

Something tells me the
Tzar will summon me to
Save his imperial hide

I peeped his messenger
Speeding through the gates of
The Winter Palace

He's heading this way

Soon, my fellow peasants will
See me in the Gazette
Taking tea with the royal family

They'll say
That crazy bum?

He had found only that every people believes their suffering and the atrocities inflicted upon their people to be the most famous and the cruelest and that there was a kind of nationalism involved in suffering, a boasting. Stray and the Eddie Cantor face: heavy eyebrows, pop eyes wandered over to where John Swell was sitting in something that looked like a winged Chippendale chair, reading a poetry magazine, minding his own business, sipping his tomato juice and vodka.

"Hey man, remember the time we was in slavery and you got flogged. The master called the whole plantation up to watch you get flogged." It was '63 but I'll never forget it. Stray squinted. He was dressed in his field-nigger overalls, and he wore his corkscrew hairdo. He was very dark.

"Look Stray, if you don't mind," Swell said, "I'd like to talk about something other than slavery. Everytime I see you you bring up slavery. Why can't you talk about emancipation sometimes?"

Stray smiles with a sneer in his eyes as he and his friend, a Whitmanite whom we will call E.C. head out into the garden of the North Star cafe which is endowed with furniture from different periods of American history, and old pictures in odd frames on the walls, a cigar store indian or two and posters: "If I were a man I'd join the navy," a 40's girl in a navy suit saying this.

E.C., Stray's friend, was a dedicated Whitmanite. John Swell had read with Whitman recently in Washington, D.C. and Whitman had read a poem called, "Repondez," recommending all manner of excesses: lunatics running the asylums, prisoners supervising the jails,—in short, a society in which everybody ran around naked, out of their minds, screaming wildly. An extreme group of Whitmanites were under the control of a former computer employee and part of their initiation rites involved carrying on fellatio with dogs, eating pig excrement.

The Washington Post carried two pictures of Whitman and none of Swell even though he had shared the program. In *The Washington Evening Star* a fair-skinned free woman in Africanesque garb could only think to mention John Swell's paunch. You could tell what people thought of him by how they saw him. His enemies could see his paunch, they see him by what he weighs not by what he does. Actually he's not fat he's swell and he's earned that swell the hard way. I mean he's swell but he's trying to do his Work. He puffs up before a book and then he goes down again. They're thin and don't do much but make spiteful, critical remarks about others—he makes spiteful critical remarks about others too and some of these have gone into his poetry.

Randy Shank enters the North Star.

Randy Shank is dressed up like an old African Dahomeyan king with bright colors, baubles, buckles, a fancy brim—all he needs is an umbrella. He is smoking a cigar. He ignores John Swell because he's sometimey or it could be because there are so many attractive women sitting about, chatting. They are dressed in clothes from different periods just as the furniture is drawn from different periods and their hairstyles are from the '20s '30s '40s and '50s. The other x-slaves ridicule Randy Shank but Shank laughs all the way to the Freedom & Trust. When he ran away from the plantation he had taken the Master for all he was worth: Mama's jewels, stocks, bonds, cash—everything. He took his Master's whole Bank-of-America. He spends this money on beautiful women, big cars, and closets full of clothes. Why, every time Randy Shank went for a drive in his custom-made Freemobile, the Emancipated police would stop him. You see, Emancipated was a liberal, progressive freedom-loving town but don't get too smart nigger: the Abolitionists liked their slaves humble not flamboyant. The posters they prepared for their anti-slavery rallies always noted: "Please help them because they cannot help themselves." Speaking of the slaves: Contraband, 40's, Randy Shank, Stray Leechfield and the others, who had escaped from 'Ginny and come to Emancipated, all had their notions of what it meant to be a fugitive slave. John Swell's poetry spoke for him. His poetry was against spiritual binding, psychological shackling. The poems about himself were "readings" for him from his inner self which knew more about his future than he did.

While others had their tarot cards, their Ouija boards, their I-Ching, and their cowrie shells he had his "writings."

John Swell was so much against slavery that he was beginning to include poetry and prose in the same book so they wouldn't be apart, a practice that his ancestor slave writers, William Wells Brown, Henry Bibb, and others had begun. He wanted to be the head of a marriage service for poetry and prose.

He preferred Canada to slavery whether Canada was exile, death, art, liberation or even a woman.

There was much avian imagery in the poetry of slaves—poetry about dreams and flight: they wanted to cross that Black Rock ferry to freedom even though they had different notions about what this freedom was. They had often disagreed about this.

Stray Leechfield, a tattle tale and someone who wanted the worst to happen to his competitors, and who maybe didn't even mean to be this way but was, had come to him and told him one day that the other slave poets were calling him a "reactionary." A word that had been making the rounds in Emancipated, California; a town which welcomes catchy words and doesn't know when the words are worn out. He had written a poem about the incident:

THE REACTIONARY POET

If you are a revolutionary
Then I must be a reactionary
For if you stand for the future
I have no choice but to
Be with the past

Bring back suspenders!
Bring back Mom!

Homemade ice cream
Picnics in the park
Flagpole sitting
Straw hats
Rent parties
Corn liquor
The banjo
Georgia quilts
Krazy Kat
Restock
The syncopation of
Fletcher Henderson
The Kiplingesque lines
of James Weldon Johnson
Black Eagle
Mickey Mouse
The Bach Family
Sunday School
Even Mayor LaGuardia
Who read the comics
Is more appealing than
Your version of
What Lies Ahead

In your world of
Tomorrow Humor
Will be locked up and
The key thrown away
The public address system
Will pound out headaches
All day
Everybody will wear the same
Funny caps
And the same funny jackets

Enchantment will be found
Expendable, charm, a
Luxury
Love and kisses
A crime against the state
Duke Ellington will be

> Ordered to write more marches
> "For the people," naturally
>
> If you are what's coming
> I must be what's going
>
> Make it by steamboat
> I likes to take it real slow

Some of his poems were indeed bitter but some were sweet, too. Emancipated poets said they wrote about love; John Swell wrote about Love and Hate. He wanted to be natural and well-rounded. It's hard to be well-rounded in Emancipated, a town with one philosophy and one style. Nothing to do but write and read the newspapers. Read about the Prime Minister of Canada and how he had just won 141 seats in the House of Commons. There was a picture in *Time* of the Prime Minister standing next to his wife, she, holding his hand, he, looking down as if his sharp indian nose would beak her forehead. There was a big sign over the archway where they stood written in Halloween letters: Congratulations. His wife said of him: "He's a beautiful guy, a very loving human being who has taught me a lot about loving."

The question for John Swell was: would his bondage be completely behind him when he reached Canada? He was still not completely free though it had been a long time since he ranaway, the first time from the Porke Plantation in Virginia. It seemed like a hundred years ago since he first took off.

FLIGHT TO CANADA

> Dear Massa:
> What it was?
> I have done my Liza Leap
> & am safe in the arms
> of Canada, so
> Ain't no use your Slave
> Catchers waitin on me
> At Trailways
> I won't be there
>
> I flew in non-stop
> Jumbo jet this a.m. Had
> Champagne & somethin called
> *Yao Goh Gee Ding*

Compliments of the Cap'n
Who announced that a
Runaway negro was on the
Plane. Passengers came up
And shook my hand
& within 10 min. I had
Signed up for 3 anti-slavery
Lectures   Remind me to get an
Agent

   Traveling in style
Beats craning your neck after
The North Star and hiding in
Bushes anytime, Massa
Besides, your negro dogs
Of Hays & Allen stock can't
Fly

   By now I s'pose that
Yellow Judas Cato done tole
You that I have snuck back to
The plantation 3 maybe 4 times
Since I left the first time

   Last visit I slept in
Your bed and sampled your
Cellar. Had your favorite
Mulattress give me some
She-Bear. Mellow

   You was away at a
Slave auction at Ryan's Mart
In Charleston & so I knowed
You wouldn't mind
Did you have a nice trip, Massa?

I borrowed your cotton money
To pay for my ticket & to get
Me started in this place called
Saskatchewan   Brrrrrrrrrr!
It's cold up here but least
Nobody is collaring hobbling gagging
Handcuffing yoking chaining & thumbscrewing
You like you is they hobby horse

The Mistress Ms. Lady
Gived me the combination
To your safe, don't blame
The feeble old soul, Cap'n
I tole her you needed some
More money to shop with &
you sent me from Charleston
To get it. Don't worry
Your employees won't miss
It & I accept it as a
Down payment on my back
Wages

   I must clos now
Massa, by the time you gets
This letter old Sam will have
Probably took you to the
Deep six

That was rat poison I left
In your Old Crow
               Your boy
               John

   Suddenly there was a commotion outside. Wailing sirens. Cars and trucks were screeching honking tooting and blaring. People had gathered in little patches, talking excitedly, some staring at the fireworks in the Emancipated skies. Customers began to empty the North Star cafe. Stray Leechfield and E.C. ran out their denimed bodies passing by Swell's table. Even the imperturbable Randy Shank looked up from his date. John Swell paid his bill and left a 10 percent tip. He walked out into Democracy Street to see what was going on. Had San Francisco had an earthquake? No, the Confederates had fired on Fort Sumter. The pro- and anti-slavery forces had met head-on. The Civil War had begun.

ADRIENNE RICH

Adrienne Rich (b. May 16, 1929 in Baltimore) was
graduated from Radcliffe in 1951. In "When We Dead
Awaken: Writing as Re-Vision" she describes twenty years'
conflict in her life as woman, as wife and mother,
and as a poet. She has taught in many colleges and
universities and has read her poems widely. Since 1966
she has lived with her three sons in New York City.

(Photo by Thomas Victor)

When We Dead Awaken: Writing as Re-Vision

Ibsen's *When We Dead Awaken* is a play about the use that the male artist and thinker—in the process of creating culture as we know it—has made of women, in his life and in his work; and about a woman's slow struggling awakening to the use to which her life has been put. Bernard Shaw wrote in 1900 of this play:

> [Ibsen] shows us that no degradation ever devized or permitted is as disastrous as this degradation; that through it women can die into luxuries for men and yet can kill them; that men and women are becoming conscious of this; and that what remains to be seen as perhaps the most interesting of all imminent social developments is what will happen "when we dead awaken".[1]

It's exhilarating to be alive in a time of awakening consciousness; it can also be confusing, disorienting, and painful. This awakening of dead or sleeping consciousness has already affected the lives of millions of women, even those who don't know it yet. It is also affecting the lives of men, even those who deny its claims upon them. The argument will go on whether an oppressive economic class system is responsible for the oppressive nature of male/female relations, or whether, in fact, patriarchy—the domination of males—is the original model on which all the others are based. But in the last few years the women's movement has drawn inescapable and illuminating connections between our sexual lives and our political institutions. The sleepwalkers are coming awake, and for the first time this awakening has a collective reality; it is no longer such a lonely thing to open one's eyes.

Re-vision—the act of looking back, of seeing with fresh eyes, of entering an old text from a new critical direction—is for women more than a chapter in cultural history: it is an act of survival. Until we can understand the assumptions in which we are drenched we cannot know ourselves. And this drive to self-knowledge, for women, is more than a search for identity: it is part of our refusal of the self-destructiveness of

An earlier version of this paper was written for the MLA Commission on the Status of Women in the Profession, read at the MLA meetings in December 1971, and appeared in *College English* (October 1972).

[1] G. B. Shaw, *The Quintessence of Ibsenism* (New York, 1922), p. 139.

male-dominated society. A radical critique of literature, feminist in its impulse, would take the work first of all as a clue to how we live, how we have been living, how we have been led to imagine ourselves, how our language has trapped as well as liberated us, how the very act of naming has been till now a male prerogative, and how we can begin to see and name—and therefore live—afresh. A change in the concept of sexual identity is essential if we are not going to see the old political order re-assert itself in every new revolution. We need to know the writing of the past, and know it differently than we have ever known it; not to pass on a tradition but to break its hold over us.

For writers, and at this moment for women writers in particular, there is the challenge and promise of a whole new psychic geography to be explored. But there is also a difficult and dangerous walking on the ice, as we try to find language and images for a consciousness we are just coming into, and with little in the past to support us. I want to talk about some aspects of this difficulty and this danger.

Jane Harrison, the great classical anthropologist, wrote in 1914 in a letter to her friend Gilbert Murray:

By the by, about "Women," it has bothered me often—why do women never want to write poetry about Man as a sex—why is Woman a dream and a terror to man and not the other way around? . . . Is it mere convention and propriety, or something deeper?[2]

I think Jane Harrison's question cuts deep into the myth-making tradition, the romantic tradition; deep into what women and men have been to each other; and deep into the psyche of the woman writer. Thinking about that question, I began thinking of the work of two twentieth-century women poets, Sylvia Plath and Diane Wakoski. It strikes me that in the work of both Man appears as, if not a dream, a fascination and a terror; and that the source of the fascination and the terror is, simply, Man's power—to dominate, tyrannize, choose, or reject the woman. The charisma of Man seems to come purely from his power over her and his control of the world by force, not from anything fertile or life-giving in him. And, in the work of both these poets, it is finally the woman's sense of *herself*—embattled, possessed—that gives the poetry its dynamic charge, its rhythms of struggle, need, will, and female energy. Until recently this female anger and this furious awareness of

[2] J. G. Stewart, *Jane Ellen Harrison: A Portrait from Letters* (London, 1959), p. 140.

the Man's power over her were not available materials to the female poet, who tended to write of Love as the source of her suffering, and to view that victimization by Love as an almost inevitable fate. Or, like Marianne Moore and Elizabeth Bishop, she kept sexuality at a measured and chiselled distance in her poems.

One answer to Jane Harrison's question has to be that historically men and women have played very different parts in each others' lives. Where woman has been a luxury for man, and has served as the painter's model and the poet's muse, but also as a comforter, nurse, cook, bearer of his seed, secretarial assistant and copyist of manuscripts, man has played a quite different role for the female artist. Henry James repeats an incident which the writer Prosper Mérimée described, of how, while he was living with George Sand,

> he once opened his eyes, in the raw winter dawn, to see his companion, in a dressing-gown, on her knees before the domestic hearth, a candlestick beside her and a red *madras* round her head, making bravely, with her own hands the fire that was to enable her to sit down betimes to urgent pen and paper. The story represents him as having felt that the spectacle chilled his ardor and tried his taste; her appearance was unfortunate, her occupation an inconsequence, and her industry a reproof—the result of all which was a lively irritation and an early rupture.[3]

I am suggesting that the specter of this kind of male judgment, along with the misnaming and thwarting of her needs by a culture controlled by males, has created problems for the woman writer: problems of contact with herself, problems of language and style, problems of energy and survival.

In rereading Virginia Woolf's *A Room Of One's Own* (1929) for the first time in some years, I was astonished at the sense of effort, of pains taken, of dogged tentativeness, in the tone of that essay. And I recognized that tone. I had heard it often enough, in myself and in other women. It is the tone of a woman almost in touch with her anger, who is determined not to appear angry, who is *willing* herself to be calm, detached, and even charming in a roomful of men where things have

---

[3] Henry James, "Notes on Novelists" in *Selected Literary Criticism of Henry James*, ed. Morris Shapira (London, 1963), pp. 157–58.

been said which are attacks on her very integrity. Virginia Woolf is addressing an audience of women, but she is acutely conscious—as she always was—of being overheard by men: by Morgan and Lytton and Maynard Keynes and for that matter by her father, Leslie Stephen. She drew the language out into an exacerbated thread in her determination to have her own sensibility yet protect it from those masculine presences. Only at rare moments in that essay do you hear the passion in her voice; she was trying to sound as cool as Jane Austen, as Olympian as Shakespeare, because that is the way the men of the culture thought a writer should sound.

No male writer has written primarily or even largely for women, or with the sense of women's criticism as a consideration when he chooses his materials, his theme, his language. But to a lesser or greater extent, every woman writer has written for men even when, like Virginia Woolf, she was supposed to be addressing women. If we have come to the point when this balance might begin to change, when women can stop being haunted, not only by "convention and propriety" but by internalized fears of being and saying themselves, then it is an extraordinary moment for the woman writer—and reader.

I have hesitated to do what I am going to do now, which is to use myself as an illustration. For one thing, it's a lot easier and less dangerous to talk about other women writers. But there is something else. Like Virginia Woolf, I am aware of the women who are not with us here because they are washing the dishes and looking after the children. Nearly fifty years after she spoke, that fact remains largely unchanged. And I am thinking also of women whom she left out of the picture altogether—women who are washing other people's dishes and caring for other people's children, not to mention women who went on the streets last night in order to feed their children. We seem to be special women here, we have liked to think of ourselves as special, and we have known that men would tolerate, even romanticize us as special, as long as our words and actions didn't threaten their privilege of tolerating or rejecting us and our work according to *their* ideas of what a special woman ought to be. An important insight of the radical women's movement, for me, has been how divisive and how ultimately destructive is this myth of the special woman, who is also the token woman. Every one of us here in this room has had great luck—we are teachers, writers, academicians; our own gifts are buried or aborted. Our struggles can have meaning and our privileges—however precarious under patriarchy

—can be justified only if they can help to change the lives of women whose gifts—and whose very being—continue to be thwarted and silenced.

My own luck was being born white and middle-class into a house full of books, with a father who encouraged me to read and write. So for about twenty years I wrote for a particular man, who criticized and praised me and made me feel I was indeed "special." The obverse side of this, of course, was that I tried for a long time to please him, or rather, not to displease him. And then of course there were other men—writers, teachers—the Man, who was not a terror or a dream but a literary master and a master in other ways less easy to acknowledge. And there were all those poems about women, written by men: it seemed to be a given that men wrote poems and women frequently inhabited them. These women were almost always beautiful, but threatened with the loss of beauty, the loss of youth—the fate worse than death. Or, they were beautiful and died young, like Lucy and Lenore. Or, the woman was like Maud Gonne, cruel and disastrously mistaken, and the poem reproached her because she had refused to become a luxury for the poet.

A lot is being said today about the influence that the myths and images of women have on all of us who are products of culture. I think it has been a peculiar confusion to the girl or woman who tries to write because she is peculiarly susceptible to language. She goes to poetry or fiction looking for *her* way of being in the world, since she too has been putting words and images together; she is looking eagerly for guides, maps, possibilities; and over and over in the "words' masculine persuasive force" of literature she comes up against something that negates everything she is about: she meets the image of Woman in books written by men. She finds a terror and a dream, she finds a beautiful pale face, she finds *La Belle Dame Sans Merci*, she finds Juliet or Tess or Salomé, but precisely what she does not find is that absorbed, drudging, puzzled, sometimes inspired creature, herself, who sits at a desk trying to put words together.

So what does she do? What did I do? I read the older women poets with their peculiar keenness and ambivalence: Sappho, Christina Rosetti, Emily Dickinson, Elinor Wylie, Edna Millay, H. D. I discovered that the woman poet most admired at the time (by men) was Marianne Moore, who was maidenly, elegant, intellectual, discreet. But even in reading these women I was looking in them for the same things I had found in the poetry of men, because I wanted women poets to be the equals of men, and to be equal was still confused with sounding the same.

I know that my style was formed first by male poets: by the men I was reading as an undergraduate—Frost, Dylan Thomas, Donne, Auden, MacNiece, Stevens, Yeats. What I chiefly learned from them was craft. But poems are like dreams: in them you put what you don't know you know. Looking back at poems I wrote before I was twenty-one, I'm startled because beneath the conscious craft are glimpses of the split I even then experienced between the girl who wrote poems, who defined herself in writing poems, and the girl who was to define herself by her relationships with men. "Aunt Jennifer's Tigers" (appearing in *A Change of World* [1951]), written while I was a student, looks with deliberate detachment at this split.

AUNT JENNIFER'S TIGERS

Aunt Jennifer's tigers stride across a screen,
Bright topaz denizens of a world of green.
They do not fear the men beneath the tree;
They pace in sleek chivalric certainty.

Aunt Jennifer's fingers fluttering through her wool
Find even the ivory needle hard to pull.
The massive weight of Uncle's wedding band
Sits heavily upon Aunt Jennifer's hand.

When Aunt is dead, her terrified hands will lie
Still ringed with ordeals she was mastered by.
The tigers in the panel that she made
Will go on striding, proud and unafraid.

In writing this poem, composed and apparently cool as it is, I thought I was creating a portrait of an imaginary woman. But this woman suffers from the opposition of her imagination, worked out in tapestry, and her life-style, "ringed with ordeals she was mastered by." It was important to me that Aunt Jennifer was a person as distinct from myself as possible—distanced by the formalism of the poem, by its objective, observant tone—even by putting the woman in a different generation.

In those years formalism was part of the strategy—like asbestos gloves, it allowed me to handle materials I couldn't pick up barehanded. A later strategy was to use the persona of a man, as I did in "The Loser," which appeared in *Snapshots of a Daughter-in-Law: Poems, 1954–1962* (1963):

THE LOSER

A man thinks of the woman he once loved:
first, after her wedding, and then
nearly a decade later.

I
I kissed you, bride and lost, and went
home from that bourgeois sacrament,
your cheek still tasting cold upon
my lips that gave you benison
with all the swagger that they knew—
as losers somehow learn to do.

Your wedding made my eyes ache; soon
the world would be worse off for one
more golden apple dropped to ground
without the least protesting sound,
and you would windfall lie, and we
forget your shimmer on the tree.

Beauty is always wasted: if
not Mignon's song sung to the deaf,
at all events to the unmoved.
A face like yours cannot be loved
long or seriously enough.
Almost, we seem to hold it off.

II
Well, you are tougher than I thought.
Now when the wash with ice hangs taut
this morning of St. Valentine,
I see you strip the squeaking line,
your body weighed against the load,
and all my groans can do no good.

Because you are still beautiful,
though squared and stiffened by the pull
of what nine windy years have done.
You have three daughters, lost a son.
I see all your intelligence
flung into that unwearied stance.

My envy is of no avail.
I turn my head and wish him well
who chafed your beauty into use
and lives forever in a house
lit by the friction of your mind.
You stagger in against the wind.

(1958)

I finished college, published my first book by a fluke, as it seemed to me, and broke off a love affair. I took a job, lived alone, went on writing, fell in love. I was young, full of energy, and the book seemed to mean that others agreed I was a poet. Because I was also determined to prove that as a woman poet I could also have what was then defined as a "full" woman's life, I plunged in my early twenties into marriage and had three children before I was thirty. There was nothing overt in the environment to warn me: these were the '50s, and in reaction to the earlier wave of feminism, middle-class women were making careers of domestic perfection, working to send their husbands through professional schools, then retiring to raise large families. People were moving out to the suburbs, technology was going to be the answer to everything, even sex; the family was in its glory. Life was extremely private; women were isolated from each other by the loyalties of marriage. I have a sense that women didn't talk to each other much in the '50s—not about their secret emptinesses, their frustrations. I went on trying to write; my second book and first child appeared in the same month. But by the time that book came out I was already dissatisfied with those poems, which seemed to me mere exercises for poems I hadn't written. The book was praised, however, for its "gracefulness"; I had a marriage and a child. If there were doubts, if there were periods of null depression or active despairing, these could only mean that I was ungrateful, insatiable, perhaps a monster.

About the time my third child was born, I felt that I had either to consider myself a failed woman and a failed poet, or to try to find some synthesis by which to understand what was happening to me. What frightened me most was the sense of drift, of being pulled along on a current which called itself my destiny, but in which I seemed to be losing touch with whoever I had been, with the girl who had experienced her own will and energy almost ecstatically at times, walking around a city or riding a train at night or typing in a student room. In a poem about my grandmother I wrote (of myself): "A young girl, thought sleeping, is certified dead" ("Halfway"). I was writing very little, partly from fatigue, that female fatigue of suppressed anger and loss of contact with my own being; partly from the discontinuity of female life with its attention to small chores, errands, work that others constantly undo, small children's constant needs. What I did write was unconvincing to me; my anger and frustration were hard to acknowledge in or out of poems because in fact I cared a great deal about my husband and my children. Trying to look back and understand that time I have tried to analyze the real nature of the conflict. Most, if not all, human lives are full of fantasy—passive day-dreaming which need not be acted on. But to write poetry or fiction, or even to think well, is not to fantasize, or to put fantasies on paper. For a poem to coalesce, for a character or an action to take shape, there has to be an imaginative transformation of reality which is in no way passive. And a certain freedom of the mind is needed—freedom to press on, to enter the currents of your thought like a glider pilot, knowing that your motion can be sustained, that the buoyancy of your attention will not be suddenly snatched away. Moreover, if the imagination is to transcend and transform experience it has to question, to challenge, to conceive of alternatives, perhaps to the very life you are living at that moment. You have to be free to play around with the notion that day might be night, love might be hate; nothing can be too sacred for the imagination to turn into its opposite or to call experimentally by another name. For writing is re-naming. Now, to be maternally with small children all day in the old way, to be with a man in the old way of marriage, requires a holding-back, a putting-aside of that imaginative activity, and demands instead a kind of conservatism. I want to make it clear that I am *not* saying that in order to write well, or think well, it is necessary to become unavailable to others, or to become a devouring ego. This has been the myth of the masculine artist and thinker; and I do not accept it. But to be a female human being trying to fulfill traditional female functions in a traditional way *is* in direct conflict with the subversive function of the imagination. The word traditional is important here. There must be ways, and we will be finding out more and more about them, in which the energy of creation and the energy of relation can be united. But in those years I always felt the conflict as a failure of love in myself. I had thought I was choosing a full life: the life available to most men, in which sexuality, work, and parenthood could coexist. But I felt, at twenty-nine, guilt toward the people closest to me, and guilty toward my own being.

I wanted, then, more than anything, the one thing of which there was never enough: time to think, time to write. The '50s and early '60s were years of rapid revelations: the sit-ins and marches in the South, the Bay of Pigs, the early anti-war movement, raised large questions—questions for which the masculine world of the academy around me seemed to have expert and fluent answers. But I needed desperately to think for myself—about pacifism and dissent and violence, about poetry and society and about my own relationship to all these things. For about ten years I was reading in fierce snatches, scribbling in notebooks, writing poetry in fragments; I was looking desperately for clues, because if there were no clues then I thought I might be insane. I wrote in a notebook about this time:

Paralyzed by the sense that there exists a mesh of relationships—e.g.
between my anger at the children, my sensual life, pacifism,
sex (I mean sex in its broadest significance, not merely sexual desire)—
an interconnectedness which, if I could see it, make it valid,
would give me back myself, make it possible to function lucidly
and passionately. Yet I grope in and out among these dark webs.

I think I began at this point to feel that politics was not something "out there" but something "in here" and of the essence of my condition.

In the late '50s I was able to write, for the first time, directly about experiencing myself as a woman. The poem was jotted in fragments during children's naps, brief hours in a library, or at 3 a.m. after rising with a wakeful child. I despaired of doing any continuous work at this time. Yet I began to feel that my fragments and scraps had a common consciousness and a common theme, one which I would have been very unwilling to put on paper at an earlier time because I had been taught that poetry should be "universal," which meant, of course, non-female. Until then I had tried very much *not* to identify myself as a female poet. Over a two-year period I wrote a ten-part poem called "Snapshots of a Daughter-in-Law," in a longer looser mode than I'd ever trusted myself with before. It was an extraordinary relief to write that poem. It strikes me now as too literary, too dependent on allusion; I hadn't found the courage yet to do without authorities, or even to use the pronoun "I"— the woman in the poem is always "she." One section of it, No. 2, concerns a woman who thinks she is going mad; she is haunted by voices telling her to resist and rebel, voices which she can hear but not obey.

2

Banging the coffee-pot into the sink
she hears the angels chiding, and looks out
past the raked gardens to the sloppy sky.
Only a week since They said: *Have no patience.*

The next time it was: *Be insatiable.*
Then: *Save yourself; others you cannot save.*
Sometimes she's let the tapstream scald her arm,
a match burn to her thumbnail,

or held her hand above the kettle's snout
right in the woolly steam. They are probably angels,
since nothing hurts her anymore, except
each morning's grit blowing into her eyes.

The poem "Orion," written five years later and included in *Leaflets: Poems 1965–1968* (1969), is a poem of reconnection with a part of myself I had felt I was losing—the active principle, the energetic imagination, the "half-brother" whom I projected, as I had for many years, into the constellation Orion. It's no accident that the words "cold and egotistical" appear in this poem, and are applied to myself.

ORION

Far back when I went zig-zagging
through tamarack pastures
you were my genius, you
my cast-iron Viking, my helmed
lion-heart king in prison.
Years later now you're young

my fierce half-brother, staring
down from that simplified west
your breast open, your belt dragged down
by an oldfashioned thing, a sword
the last bravado you won't give over
though it weighs you down as you stride

and the stars in it are dim
and maybe have stopped burning.
But you burn, and I know it;

as I throw back my head to take you in
an old transfusion happens again:
divine astronomy is nothing to it.

Indoors I bruise and blunder,
break faith, leave ill enough
alone, a dead child born in the dark.
Night cracks up over the chimney,
pieces of time, frozen geodes
come showering down in the grate.

A man reaches behind my eyes
and finds them empty
a woman's head turns away
from my head in the mirror
children are dying my death
and eating crumbs of my life.

Pity is not your forte.
Calmly you ache up there
pinned aloft in your crow's nest,
my speechless pirate!
You take it all for granted
and when I look you back

it's with a starlike eye
shooting its cold and egotistical spear
where it can do least damage.
Breathe deep! No hurt, no pardon
out here in the cold with you
you with your back to the wall.

(1965)

The choice still seemed to be between "love"—womanly, maternal love, altruistic love—a love defined and ruled by the weight of an entire culture; and egotism—a force directed by men into creation, achievement, ambition, often at the expense of others, but justifiably so. For weren't they men, and wasn't that their destiny as womanly, selfless love was ours? We know now that the alternatives are false ones—that the word "love" is itself in need of re-vision.

There is a companion poem to "Orion," written three years later and included in *The Will to Change* (1971), in which at last the woman in the poem and the woman writing the poem become the same person. It is called "Planetarium," and it was written after a visit to a real planetarium, where I read an account of the work of Caroline Herschel, the astronomer, who worked with her brother William, but whose name remained obscure, as his did not.

PLANETARIUM

*(Thinking of Caroline Herschel, 1750–1848, astronomer,
sister of William; and others)*

A woman in the shape of a monster
a monster in the shape of a woman
the skies are full of them

a woman   'in the snow
among the Clocks and instruments
or measuring the ground with poles'

in her 98 years to discover
8 comets

she whom the moon ruled
like us
levitating into the night sky
riding the polished lenses

Galaxies of women, there
doing penance for impetuousness
ribs chilled
in those spaces   of the mind

An eye,
          'virile, precise and absolutely certain'
          from the mad webs of Uranusborg

                              encountering the NOVA

every impulse of light exploding
from the core
as life flies out of us

          Tycho whispering at last
          'Let me not seem to have lived in vain'

What we see, we see
and seeing is changing

the light that shrivels a mountain
and leaves a man alive

Heartbeat of the pulsar
heart sweating through my body

The radio impulse
pouring in from Taurus

    I am bombarded yet   I stand

I have been standing all my life in the
direct path of a battery of signals
the most accurately transmitted most
untranslateable language in the universe
I am a galactic cloud so deep   so invo-
luted that a light wave could take 15
years to travel through me   And has
taken   I am an instrument in the shape
of a woman trying to translate pulsations
into images   for the relief of the body
and the reconstruction of the mind.

               (1968)

In closing I want to tell you about a dream I had last summer. I dreamed I was asked to read my poetry at a mass women's meeting, but when I began to read, what came out were the lyrics of a blues song. I share this dream with you because it seemed to me to say something about the problems and the future of the woman writer, and probably of women in general. The awakening of consciousness is not like the crossing of a frontier—one step and you are in another country. Much of woman's poetry has been of the nature of the blues song: a cry of pain, of victimization, or a lyric of seduction. And today, much poetry by women—and prose for that matter—is charged with anger. I think we need to go through that anger, and we will betray our own reality if we try, as Virginia Woolf was trying, for an objectivity, a detachment, that would make us sound more like Jane Austen or Shakespeare. We know more than Jane Austen or Shakespeare knew: more than Jane Austen because our lives are more complex, more than Shakespeare because we know more about the lives of women, Jane Austen and Virginia Woolf included.

Both the victimization and the anger experienced by women are real, and have real sources, everywhere in the environment, built into society, language, the structures of thought. They will go on being tapped and explored by poets, among others. We can neither deny them, nor will we rest there. A new generation of women poets is already working out of the psychic energy released when women begin to move out towards what the feminist philosopher Mary Daly has described as the "new space" on the boundaries of patriarchy. Women are speaking to and of women in these poems, out of a newly released courage to name, to love each other, to share risk and grief and celebration.

To the eye of a feminist, the work of western male poets now writing reveals a deep, fatalistic pessimism as to the possibilities of change, whether societal or personal, along with a familiar and threadbare use of women (and nature) as redemptive on the one hand, threatening on the other; and a new tide of phallocentric sadism and overt woman-hating which matches the sexual brutality of recent films. "Political" poetry by men remains stranded amid the struggles for power among male groups; in condemning U.S. imperialism or the Chilean junta the poet can claim to speak for the oppressed while remaining, as male, part of a system of sexual oppression. The enemy is always outside the self, the struggle somewhere else. The mood of isolation, self-pity, and self-imitation that pervades "non-political" poetry suggests that a profound change in masculine consciousness will have to precede any new male poetic—or other—inspiration. The creative energy of patriarchy is fast running out; what remains is its self-generating energy for destruction. As women, we have our work cut out for us.

M. L. ROSENTHAL

M. L. ROSENTHAL (*b. March 14, 1917 in Washington, D. C.*)
took his B.A. and M.A. degrees at the University of
Chicago, and his Ph.D. from New York University in 1949,
where he has taught since 1945 and is now Professor of
English. An accomplished critic as well as poet, he is a
fellow of the American Council of Learned Societies and
has twice won Guggenheim Fellowships. He has been poetry
editor of The Nation *and is now poetry editor of*
The Humanist *and of* Present Tense.

(Photo by Thomas Victor)

We Begin These Sequences Lightly

1

Rather painfully, I have been making my way into a new sequence of poems. Something has got hold of me, something at once inside and outside myself. I recognize the impulse of energy behind these poems and yet it eludes me. The poems are casting themselves like fishermen's lines to hook the impulse and bring it back to me in a net of words.

WE BEGIN THESE THINGS LIGHTLY

We begin these affairs lightly
with an obscure smile, or an unseeing glance.

The soul, flung like rags on a greasy floor,
wavers into oneness again, tiny flames flickering.

These things, these affairs that begin so lightly—you would think the speaker was a Restoration rake. But it is only I, or some little demon speaking through me. How unexpectedly we move into deep experience. How our dispersed inner selves, fragmented by the different roles we play and by our centrifugal daily existence, flame up and startle our slumbering minds. We enter this awakening lightly, in a sort of languor, because we had no notion it was upon us. Is this perhaps a love poem, then? Oh, yes. But it has not a trace of the erotic unless read by the light, and to the rhythm, of those flickering little flames. It tells me of an order of experience in which I am caught up. The word "love" defines the order but so do a hundred other words as well that float invisibly within it.

My sequence is still in the making, and so I can say nothing certain about it. But here is another poem that has entered it out of a kindred impulse.

RIDDLE OF THE SWAN

Once, beating through the air, you amazed us.
We smiled under your shadow.

Broken-winged and raucous now, you're borne
whithersoever the torrent lists.

She and I, flung high on that arc where you made your song,
    never before saw
our joined shadows beating and riding the torrent below.

There is a dangerous joy in being seized by some noble and passionate
symbol that is at once natural and traditional: the swan in flight, or at
his song, or as a form for Zeus when he ravished Leda, or in his ice-
locked state as Mallarmé imagines him. But also, in "Riddle of the Swan,"
something else, the innocent word "flung," appears, as it did in "We
Begin These Things Lightly." In the one poem I see everything after
being flung onto the heights. In the other I am surprised into awakening
after having been flung away by self-neglect.

What brought the flying swan's shadow into my mind must have
been the irreversibility of love-awareness, once fully aroused. The greater
the arousal, the harder our wings must beat and the more intimately do
our mingled shadows join with the remembered shadows of the great
swan flights of the past. If reality touches us awake at all, it does so in
many ways. Awakening to love is awakening to anonymity, to loneliness,
to the absence of all that has been lost, to the terror of uncontrolled
vision.

The two poems have arrived kindly, to help me confront disaster from
their two opposed starting points: the one from its memory of a condition hardly noticed at the time, the other from its ecstasy so alert that it
sees everything. The images of "rags on a greasy floor" and of the
"broken-winged and raucous" swan call up all squalor, the dump-heap
we want life not to be; and they hold on to an anger turned aside by the
sheer vastness of desolation—children starving, self-righteous murder,
whatever. At this point, although no order has yet asserted itself, a poem
without a name makes room for itself in my sequence.

Suddenly at the edge, black ocean below,
and over the edge, flight without wings,
soughing of waves, stillness of star-pierced air,
tight-clenched and silent motion.

                                    Soughing of leaves
now in my memory
holds, like your smile flickering towards me,
buoyant tracers ablaze, as when you
woke lovely and drowsy and lay down beside me
and we played like dolphins, awash in the night.

I envy that anonymous, witty, sweet-voiced Elizabethan who wrote of swans and death and lost joys and silence fraught with tragedy in a spirit as flippantly uncommitted as his spelling. He flexed his muscle and showed us all suffering, then relaxed and grew playful and turned it all into satirical metaphor.

> The silver Swanne, who living had no Note,
> When deth approacht unlockt her silent throat,
> Leaning her breast against the reedie shore,
> Thus sung her first and last, and sung no more:
> Farewell all joyes, O death come close mine eyes,
> More Geese than Swannes now live, more fooles than wise.

When the tragic was but one chord in a world brimming over with melodies, it summoned to cheerful resurrections after melodramatic crucifixions. Even Shakespeare could let a mighty beginning like "Th'expense of spirit in a waste of shame" go glimmering in a waste of tedious antitheses. That old world of cornucopias is our world still—who else is there for the past or any part of it to belong to? All that has changed is the proportion of freedom and order. Overriding order prevailed in the thoughts of men from earliest times. It was taken for granted. Because order was assumed—necessary hierarchies, rituals, formal modes in the arts—the mind was freer to play at aristocratic freedom. No question that life had spiritual forms beyond death, no question there were presences all around though mere intelligence could not locate them. We do not seek out the thing we assume. But the modern age, which takes chaos and pointlessness for granted, seeks to make everything count and to create an ordered vision. Yet when the moment of glory comes we hesitate to proclaim it, fearing once again to discover what we already "know," that dissolution is more powerful than synthesis. The impulse to conceal vision in order to save it from knowledge and its corrosions is like the impulse to make our own deaths rather than simply being carried away into them.

BEQUEST

> Burn our sweet story,
> let the wind carry its smoke away.
> Hasten, hasten—

leave no shred to betray
our names, where we went, why we lingered,
whom we loved, when we wept, on what day.

Perhaps that will be the final poem of my sequence, on the desperate day I declare it completed for the time being.

2

The key to making a sequence is the key of immediacy. It is struck in the quick of language. It animates ideas and makes them organs of the poem's body. (A sequence is a larger body made of smaller units, self-sufficient for the most part.) Ideas and archetypes, symbols and motifs, attitudes and qualities of morale do not define a poem. The key of immediacy, of language rooted in the idiom of the poet's nature, makes itself felt as the energizing agent of these otherwise inert, resistant mental furnishings. No one's theism, or image of the nature of woman, or idea of what a dying nightingale may or may not mean to a lovelorn maiden, or optimism or pessimism ever made a poem, let alone made it one whit better or worse. But anyone's feeling for the language as a plastic medium, with the resources of rhythm, sound, and association available within it, will do for a beginning. The ideas, symbols, "influences" flood into a poem in a way that counts only as aspects of charged poetic movement. That movement transforms them as it does the poet's own nature and memory. They are present, a part of the realization taking place in the real world of shared sensation and emotion we all inhabit. But they are not present, intact, in the poem any more than there is a real oily rag on a real greasy floor in "We Begin These Things Lightly," or a real swan with feathers in "Riddle of the Swan."

I have never seen a broken-winged swan. I did, once, see a wild, broken-winged goose calling raucously on the water. Her reflection sailed serenely under her, past reflected trees and over stones that were visible in the clear stream. That sight—bird, water, reflections, serene drifting movement combined with the distraught cries—is all in my poem, which has nothing to do with it nevertheless.

Late in my life I had a vision stronger than any I had experienced before, in a life filled with passionate debate with myself and with imagined states of experience. The poem teaches me, better than I had hitherto realized, the simultaneity of ecstasy and dread.

The reciprocity of these opposites has many sources: in family experience, in the deaths of people we love, in the history of the world's peoples. Certainly the destiny of the Jewish people teaches it to me. It teaches me to be open to the alien and unknown and to become part of it, and also to be detached—the implicit irony of the objective mind holding steady amid minds totally given to their traditional illusions. The Jews' displacements, their separateness even in Israel from what perforce they consider their native lands, the simultaneous working in them of more than one culture—all these lead to the self-undermining of both romanticism and realism. Yet the Jews are hardly the only nation betrayed into consciousness by their history. The need to go beyond mere survival has led us all into the barren sunlight of man's general condition today.

A poet, as a man or a woman, is like other men and women. What goes on in his mind is a constant shifting—at one time a convergence of attention into the certainty of a single perception or feeling; at another time the balancing of many states of awareness and emotion in one vibrating system; at still another a frustration when all the currents and countercurrents are too much at odds for even a momentary reconciliation. Because it enables one to project these psychic shifts so readily, the poetic sequence is our form of both epic and bardic poetry. It embodies cultural tasks and it assumes prophecy. Its protean landmark is the private sensibility, against which we test everything. The touchstone of reality, now more than ever before, is intensity of experience. Moments of such intensity, high points of self-confirmation by the poem's ultimate voice, are almost essential to its genuineness and conviction.

I say "almost" essential because I can conceive of a sequence in which no one section would quite be the kind of nakedly experiential or personal poem I have in mind. In some way that tells, every part of a sequence needs its emotive dimension. It must present an *affect* that colors even an abstract thought or highly expository style and makes it a realization of a mind in the midst of life rather than the mere development of a point of argument or clarification. That kind of somewhat distanced poem still does the necessary work though its subtlety or remoteness or intellectuality may lessen its force—for there are many ways to create intensity whatever the surface character of a poem. Nevertheless, so forceful can a stripped-down, immediate, and personal lyric statement be that the absence of such a passage throws a certain pall over a sequence, while its presence seems to light up the poem as a whole and to make the less vivid movements reflect some of its vitality.

Of course, a sequence can be planned in detail, yet I doubt that a good one can be written according to any plan except the kind that simply envisions the sorts of affects and materials and themes that would necessarily be involved given certain preoccupations. The individual poems within it must ordinarily grow as any other poems do, though the pressure of closing in on the movement and patterning of a sequence will very likely speed up the process (just as preparing a book of poems does, and for the same reason—every volume of new poems all written within a limited time-span will tend to be a sequence, something a poet like Yeats was extremely conscious of in arranging his individual volumes). But a clear order will emerge, at least in the final stages, if the group of poems is anything like a true sequence generated in the heat of a strong overriding drive of feeling.

It *is* true, I think, that "we begin these affairs lightly" if we wish to be carried by more than we could possibly, at first, have understood was there. I had written sequences before "His Present Discontents," which appeared in *The View from the Peacock's Tail: Poems* (1972); and, without really formulating ideas in relation to my own practice, I had written a number of studies of sequences by various modern poets. But "His Present Discontents" began coming to me during a period, toward the end at least, already marked by the state of feeling I am still exploring in the poems from the unfinished sequence I have already quoted. At the same time, in the aftermath of the "revolutionary" 1960s, I was thinking a great deal about the connections between private intensities of all sorts and the claims of the political left, from Lenin to the Students for a Democratic Society and the Weathermen. Personal crisis and social crisis always seem to reflect one another. I took the whole range of tenderness for the willful young "into account," without quite knowing what I was doing, in the opening poem; as it happened, the experience of that poem changed my entire sense of myself and my work— *but . . .*

If I were looking at that sequence as a sympathetic reader, I would not be talking of such matters at all. I would be concerned with its structure and its varying tones that inform the structure and carry the work wherever it's going. It is made up, for instance, of poems in verse and of prose-poems, almost but not quite in regular alternation. The prose-poems vary from a relatively relaxed style to very concentrated, unmistakably poetic writing—"poetic" because of emphatic rhythmic elements and because there are so many points of evocatively sensitized phrasing. A wide range of personal notes establishes the speaker's character, anchoring the sequence in moments of extraordinary arousal that create a context of intimately inward preoccupations within the "larger" political and philosophical ones. The strongest poem, probably, comes at the beginning—such, at least, was my intention, so that the rest of the sequence would, as it were, arrange itself around it and take off from its various implied dimensions. There is a play throughout the sequence of the loving, introspective voice over the grossest and harshest, most dispiriting realities as well as over a joyous miracle or two that bemuse the delighted mind. The sequence makes its way toward the buffoonery that closes it, a juggling act typographically acted out on the page to suggest all that has been placed in the swinging balance of the sequence as a whole. The success of the poem, it seems to me, is entirely a matter of the conviction of each part, of the succession of the affects, and the placement of the sections in relation to the opening poem's closeup of one young man whose disastrous condition embodies many kinds of ambiguous and precarious predicaments. A powerful thrust forward, a number of hesitant forays thereafter, and then movements of great intensity (sometimes leavened by humor and irony) just before the circus balancing act at the end—such, at least, is the structural *aim* as finally conceived. The structure at first, when the sequence is in the making, seems impossibly arbitrary, "playing tennis without a net" in the most negative sense. But as the implicit dynamics come more and more into the foreground an order does emerge; we are improvising a game of considerable rigor in its own terms.

3

What did I forget to say just now? That "His Present Discontents" is "about" human murderousness, desire, the enterprise of beauty. I could certainly go on in this vein! But nothing matters of all I might say unless the play of feeling, the shifting tones, and the whole growing complex of elements speak for themselves.

But let me tell you something more about the new sequence (though I still know nothing about it). You have seen a few short bits of it. I think I shall call it "She," and begin it with a long first poem I have already, nearly, completed. I think my poem may have been touched off by an inadvertent but surely a real, if buried, sexual image in Wordsworth's *The Prelude*, in a passage in which one would never expect to find such a thing:

                              lustily
I dipped my oars into the silent lake,
And, as I rose upon the stroke, my boat
Went heaving through the water like a swan . . .

Swans again, too! And (in Wordsworth) what a moment in which, suddenly, ecstasy and dread become one, just a few lines further on! Let me quote the first two stanzas of the title poem of "She."

She writes of sunburnt thighs,
a terrace of stone lions,
and Naxos just barely visible from her window.

This poor vessel, I,
one-oared, rudderless, droops
or, randy, unspent, shivers
in the moist night
towards gardens blowing where she sleeps or wakes. Dawn
is breaking there. And at its eastern gate
erratic trumpets blast their notes of war.
I'll beat into the wind as best I can.

I too, as you can see, am inseparable from my vessel that is carrying me, to be sure, towards joy and disaster. But despite what I've already said, I don't mean to be all that passive in the process. Homer was clever indeed to think of the device that enabled the wily Odysseus to hear the sirens. There he showed us something I haven't really talked about, intellectual energy put to work as a shaping force. I think Homer's method probably better than Wordsworth's in one respect at least, that of the way thought is presented. Thought, even pure, abstract thought, has every bit as much a right to enter a poem as an image does. But it must not make the poetic line sag or the dynamics sputter. Interesting problem, but I won't bore you with the details—I mean, with the details of my suffering. Thinking in a poem has to come in the form of electricity or flame. My "She" is a woman who makes me think into her childhood and her humanity, something very difficult for "this poor vessel, I" at the start of the poem. He can solve the problem only by a kind of forgetting, in which thought flames up in its own right, by the same associative process that sets everything else in a poem burning.

ANNE SEXTON

ANNE SEXTON. *Fame came to this poet (b. Nov. 9, 1928 in Newton, Mass.) when she won the 1966 Pulitzer Prize for Live or Die. She describes her education and how she came to poetry in the following interview, which took place a year and a month before her suicide in October of 1974.*

(Photo by Arthur Furst)

From 1928 to Whenever:
A Conversation with Anne Sexton

One day during the summer of 1962 or 1963 I was browsing through magazines in the Ohio University library—I was in graduate school and had begun to write a little, very little and very badly, and I used to walk through the stacks of periodicals hoping that one day I would have a poem in one of those magazines—when I happened to read a review in, I believe, The Kenyon Review, of Anne Sexton's To Bedlam and Part Way Back. I didn't pay much attention to what was being said about her, but I remember that I was amazed by the lines the critic quoted. There were sharp, brilliant images like no others I'd ever seen. I'd not at this point read or even heard of Heart's Needle or Life Studies, and this woman, Sexton, was making poems out of personal materials in a way that astounded me. As I write this, I still have an impression of the vivid color and precision I felt as I read her lines; I still recall being stunned by the truth-telling power of those early cries of hers.

I never followed through, I guess, never had time to give myself to her. The following several years blurred into study and teaching. Graduate school involved immersing myself in sometimes three or four different centuries during the same semester; teaching was often a battle to get something read a week ahead of my students. In about 1970 I began using some of Sexton's poems from anthologies in classes, and during the dreary winter of 1971–72, in Germany with my family, at the same time that I was reading stories from the Penguin edition of Grimms' Fairy Tales to our children, I ordered the limited edition of her Transformations. I was happy to get Anne's book, which came boxed in mauve and with gilt edges, proper and gaudy apparel for a tour-de-force of a book by a remarkable woman.

She came to Brockport for a reading on September 10, 1973. I'd written her about writing something for this book, and the first thing she said to me was something like "You're the one who wrote me about doing an essay, but no, no, I can't, I just can't write essays." But I liked her immediately. She was warm and friendly. She had a beautiful voice, I thought, and a laugh that made me feel at ease. I nagged her into signing some books for me, and began to feel relieved about the television tape Al Poulin and I were to make with her. I knew she would be easy to talk to. I enjoyed her company. The three of us spent almost *the whole next day, the day of the reading, sipping drinks in the dark of a Brockport bar. After her fine reading that evening, I heard from students for weeks about how bowled over they had been by her poems and by her honesty and just by her presence.*

What follows is a transcription of the hour-long videotaped interview that took place the following morning. I have not tried to make this transcription any more elegant than was our conversation. It is filled with hesitancies, and in the case of Anne Sexton, particularly, her voice makes transitions in subtle ways not readily apparent in the printed words. I've used dots to indicate pauses, passing time, not ellipsis. Nothing is left out. I've tried, with commas and dashes, to catch the intention behind the staccato of her speech.

With Anne's permission and blessing, I was transcribing this interview for the beautiful little magazine Strivers' Row. *I hovered about half finished—the fate of that magazine, which has since folded, was in doubt—when news of her death reached Brockport. At her reading, talking about her abandoned idea of saving her "Furies" poems for a posthumous book, she had said: "It suddenly occurred to me, 'Well, Sexton, someday you're gonna die, and there'll be nothing, I mean, and wouldn't it be nice if there'd be a book that would come out?' " Well, there will be books, including books of her own, but she would have been happy, I know, to be here in this volume among so many of her friends.*

Well, then, here we were, Al and I, with Anne in the studio, very nervous, on September 11, 1973. Cued, she begins by speaking into a camera directly in front of her. [W.H.]

A. S. I'd like to read a poem from my second book, *All My Pretty Ones*. It was in response to a letter from a friend in Japan, who is since deceased. I introduce it by saying "For my friend, Ruth, who urges me to make an appointment for the Sacrament of Confession." The title is

WITH MERCY FOR THE GREEDY

Concerning your letter in which you ask
me to call a priest and in which you ask
me to wear The Cross that you enclose;
your own cross,
your dog-bitten cross,

no larger than a thumb,
small and wooden, no thorns, this rose—

I pray to its shadow,
that gray place
where it lies on your letter . . . deep, deep.
I detest my sins and I try to believe
in The Cross. I touch its tender hips, its dark jawed face,
its solid neck, its brown sleep.

True. There is
a beautiful Jesus.
He is frozen to his bones like a chunk of beef.
How desperately he wanted to pull his arms in!
How desperately I touch his vertical and horizontal axes!
But I can't. Need is not quite belief.

All morning long
I have worn
your cross, hung with package string around my throat.
It tapped me lightly as a child's heart might,
tapping secondhand, softly waiting to be born.
Ruth, I cherish the letter you wrote.

My friend, my friend, I was born
doing reference work in sin, and born
confessing it. This is what poems are:
with mercy
for the greedy,
they are the tongue's wrangle,
the world's pottage, the rat's star.

When Anne finishes reading the poem, there is music—our videotape theme has been Joanquin Rodrigo's stately and beautiful Concierto de Aranjuez *by Laurindo Almeida and the Modern Jazz Quartet—and the credits and taped introductions roll. The three of us sit quietly. Then the mikes open again and the camera swings to Al.*

A. P.   Anne Sexton, welcome to the Writer's Forum.
A. S.   Thank you. It's very nice to be here . . . under the heat, and the
        lights, and the early morning.
A. P.   Especially the early morning.

A. S.   Yes.

A. P.   Anne, the poem you just read always moves me a great deal—especially the lines "I was born / doing reference work in sin, and born / confessing it." Do you still feel that poetry is confession?

A. S.   Well, for a while, oh for a long while, perhaps even now, I was called a "confessional poet." And for quite a while I resented it. You know, I thought "Why am I in this bag?" And then I kind of looked around and I thought "Look, Anne, you're the *only* confessional poet around." I mean I don't see anyone else quite doing this sort of thing. And then as years go by I get into new themes, etcetera, etcetera, and really don't think about what I am. You know, it shifts, anyway.

A. P.   If it is confession, what are you confessing?

A. S.   Well, I've got to say it's not exactly, I mean it's a difficult label, "confessional," because I'll often confess to things that never happened. As I once said to someone, if I did all the things I confess to, there would be no time to write a poem. So, you know, I mean I'll often assume the first person and it's someone else's story. It's just very amenable to me to kind of climb into that persona and tell their story.

A. P.   Were the early poems in *All My Pretty Ones* and *To Bedlam*—the poems about madness—were they real poems about madness? Or were they poems about real madness?

A. S.   I don't think I was ever really mad. I mean . . . but then again, of course, perhaps I was, but it depends on the clinical evaluation, really. "Mad" is an open term. But they were about my . . . they were confession, let us put it that way. I mean they were my experiences, some of my experiences, about feelings, disorientation, mental hospitals, whatever, and I got that label very early, the "mad poet" and all that. And at one point just a short while ago I said "I shall never again write about a psychiatrist, a madhouse, or anything to do with those themes." But, you know, of course you can't really predict, you just make these little predictions.

W. H.   Someone said that *no one*, in the history of our poetry, has ever "reported" (I think that was the word) as much of the self as has Anne Sexton. And I think, when we look back, that it really is true, that there's so much of yourself coming out in *To Bedlam* and in the later books that we never did have anything quite like this in English poetry before. How did this come about? James Wright said about *To Bedlam and Part Way Back*, Al, "The book is a work of genius. It signifies a moment of major importance to American literature."

And I think it does! We've really not had that kind of poetry ever before. Where did this, how did this breakthrough come about, that you could sit down and write these sorts of poems?

A. S. I will tell you as exactly as I can. The fact is I couldn't help it. It's just natural to me. I was told over and over: "You can't write personal poems; you can't write about madness; you can't do this." Everybody I consulted said "Nix. You don't write about that, that's not a theme." Which I never understood. And I remember something I never understood, one of my first teachers, John Holmes, saying (and I'll probably get this wrong so forgive the misquote) that Richard Wilbur said poetry is a window, not a door. And apparently, I guess, I was the door, or something. . . .

W. H. Yes.

A. S. But I thought, well, I'm sorry, I can only do what I can do, and it was, you know, just natural. It was not a planned thing to come into English poetry, which I didn't even know—I was just writing, and what I was writing was what I was feeling, and that's what I needed to write.

I want to go on a little bit to say I have a new little theory. Now, it may change in a month or something, but this theory is that if you could document—I don't mean "document" because it's not altogether documentary, of course—but if you could document the imagination, experiences, everything, even some wit, whatever, of one life, one life, however long it may last, it might be of some value to someone someday just to say, well, this human being lived from 1928 to whenever, and this is what she had to say about her life. And that's really all I know. I don't know anything more cosmic, anyway, so I might as well stick with what I . . .

W. H. Would you take that a step further and not only say that maybe people will look back and say here is one life and what we can learn from it, but that here is one life that also speaks about our own lives? You see, that would be in the Whitmanian . . .

A. S. Well, that's the idea, the attempt, but it's not a very conscious attempt—rather, it's a conscious attempt, conscious thought, or rationale for what is only natural and I can't help doing anyway, so what the hell. I mean, one formulates something that has nothing really to do with the fact that one *has* to write that way.

W. H. To follow up one of Al's questions, and this is a much-asked question, too, but to what extent are you fictionalizing Anne Sexton as you write some of these poems? Can you say anything about that shaky ground?

A. S.   Well, there's enough fiction so that it's total confusion if one were to . . . I remember Ralph Mills talking about my dead brother whom I've written about. And I met Ralph and I said, "Ralph,"—this was a critical essay he'd written—"Ralph, I had no brother, but then didn't we all have brothers who died in that war?" Which was the Second World War, which is a long, a few wars ago. But didn't we all, somehow, have brothers? But I write *my* brother, and of course he believes it. I mean, why not? Why shouldn't he? But I was just telling him, incidentally, there was no brother. So, that kind of . . . I should say "Excuse me, folks, but no brother," but that would kind of ruin the poem, so . . .

A. P.   This is part of that fine line between life, or reality, and art, anyway, isn't it, all the time? The discussion about writing about your own experiences always reminds me of Stevens in "The Comedian as the Letter C" where he speaks of making "his own fate an instance of all fate," which is what you were saying.

A. S.   Only he was saying it better.

W. H.   The trouble sometimes is that the so-called confessional poet *seems* to want to draw us in and say "Here I am, and I'm baring myself and I want to tell you about myself." And then on the other hand Anne Sexton writes a poem about her brother and then we feel sort of foolish when we find out, well, this is *that* kind of brother, the archetypal brother, everyone's brother rather than the real brother. It sort of makes us nervous because we like to have our feet on the ground at the same time.

A. S.   Yes, I understand, reality is always important. I think it rather pleases me in a quizzical fashion to do this because then I don't have to really admit to anything. You know, it leaves me room to say any damned thing and say, well—not actually to lie about it, for instance, to someone, but—

W. H.   It leaves the reader with the poem, too, which is probably where he should be, and not with some biographical account.

A. P.   I'd like to go back a couple of steps. When you first started writing and when people were telling you that you couldn't write like that, who *did* tell you you *could* write that way?

A. S.   All right, I can tell you exactly. First I read it—well, I'll try to explain it more clearly. I'm writing away and I'm getting acceptances and I'm getting a book oh about three-quarters finished, and, you know, the general magazines have accepted things despite all this adverse criticism, and I read in an anthology, W. D. Snodgrass's "Heart's Needle," and I think, "That's it!" And at that moment my daughter was not living at home—she was living with my mother-in-law be-cause it was felt I was not well enough to take care of her—it was kind of a power struggle I won't go into—but I ran up and got my daughter. I said, "I must have my daughter, I've just read this poem about the loss of a daughter, etcetera." And I wrote at that time "Un-known Girl in the Maternity Ward," which is a mask—in other words, I think that's the title of it, is about having an illegitimate child and giving it away, in other words about the loss of a daughter. And as a matter of fact I had met a girl in a mental hospital who had done just this and I was projecting, I was fictionalizing, but of course, I mean, so-called confessing. At any rate, I wrote that poem, got my daughter, and what could be more beautiful than a poem to move you to action of such a type? And I thought, *this* is the thing, I like this, this is for me, boy, etcetera, and so I kind of nosed around and found out that Snodgrass would be at a writers conference—it was a five-day one or something at Antioch—and I did go out there, and he *definitely* en-couraged me, and read that poem about the loss of a daughter, that kind of fictionalized poem, and he said, "Why don't you tell the real story?" You know, he drew me out about my life. And so I spent the next seven months writing "The Double Image," which is all about many varied themes—about madness, the loss of a daughter, mother's cancer, loss of mother, regaining of daughter, and it's a long narrative piece written in very tight form.

W. H.   A lot of poets point to Snodgrass as someone who showed the way to a large extent. His poem, too, is written in very tight metrics.

A. S.   Yes, I don't think mine is quite that tight.

W. H.   You know, later on in his next book he would write poems about his daughter and he would say something like "We go about our business; / I have turned my back." So I'm a little nervous when you say it's wonderful to have a poem move us to that sort of action. Because then, speaking logically, you'd have to read his next book and then like turn your back on your daughter.

A. S.   I see. But it would only be action that is ready to be born within you, that is right there, and yet the poem lets it rise and brings you forth and out you go. I mean . . .

W. H.   Yes, I see, I see.

A. P.   Would you mind reading the unknown girl poem?

A. S.   I suppose I could read it, yeah. I don't feel it's—I'm worried that it's not too well written. It's an early, early poem, but we'll skip that and read it.

UNKNOWN GIRL IN THE MATERNITY WARD

Child, the current of your breath is six days long.
You lie, a small knuckle on my white bed;
lie, fisted like a snail, so small and strong
at my breast. Your lips are animals; you are fed
with love. At first hunger is not wrong.
The nurses nod their caps; you are shepherded
down starch halls with the other unnested throng
in wheeling baskets. You tip like a cup; your head
moving to my touch. You sense the way we belong.
But this is an institution bed.
You will not know me very long.

The doctors are enamel. They want to know
the facts. They guess about the man who left me,
some pendulum soul, going the way men go
and leave you full of child. But our case history
stays blank. All I did was let you grow.
Now we are here for all the ward to see.
They thought I was strange, although
I never spoke a word. I burst empty
of you, letting you learn how the air is so.
The doctors chart the riddle they ask of me
and I turn my head away. I do not know.

Yours is the only face I recognize.
Bone at my bone, you drink my answers in.
Six times a day I prize
your need, the animals of your lips, your skin
growing warm and plump. I see your eyes
lifting their tents. They are blue stones, they begin
to outgrow their moss. You blink in surprise
and I wonder what you can see, my funny kin,
as you trouble my silence. I am a shelter of lies.
Should I learn to speak again, or hopeless in
such sanity will I touch some face I recognize?

Down the hall the baskets start back. My arms
fit you like a sleeve, they hold
catkins of your willows, the wild bee farms
of your nerves, each muscle and fold

of your first days. Your old man's face disarms
the nurses. But the doctors return to scold
me. I speak. It is you my silence harms.
I should have known; I should have told
them something to write down. My voice alarms
my throat. "Name of father—none." I hold
you and name you bastard in my arms.

And now that's that. There is nothing more
that I can say or lose.
Others have traded life before
and could not speak. I tighten to refuse
your owling eyes, my fragile visitor.
I touch your cheeks, like flowers. You bruise
against me. We unlearn. I am a shore
rocking you off. You break from me. I choose
your only way, my small inheritor
and hand you off, trembling the selves we lose.
Go child, who is my sin and nothing more.

A. P.   That's a very moving poem. Hearing you read it, threw me. . . .
One of the things that strikes me is that the poem is very tightly
structured and many of your early poems are in rather traditional
form.

A. S.   Well, I wouldn't put it that way. Form, but usually not traditional. If I could explain: I think, or at least thought when I was writing these poems in form that it was *my* form, you know? Not that I
made it up, of course—that would be impossible. But, somehow, it
was mine, it was not a sonnet or, you know. . . . As I was just reading,
I was thinking, "Gee, you did something very strange here." If you
actually look at the end lines, I mean the first line of the stanza, or
the first two (I don't remember), it goes, anyway, "long," "bed,"
"strong," "fed," "wrong," "shepherded," "throng," "head," "belong,"
"bed," and "long," and then that follows through. . . . It's just a funny
little thing I did. I mean actually I used to . . . I found that the more
difficult the subject, then the easier it was to do in some difficult form.
And I had a theory, but I have no idea whether it's true, that I—not
in this poem, because it's not that complex—if I had something that
I felt was *impossible* to say or I didn't quite realize or, you know, I
didn't know, I'd make up some strange thing. I mean I'd write the

first, I'd begin, say, with rhyme, and then I'd count it out syllabically, maybe, and then I was stuck with it, and then I often broke it and cheated and didn't care, because I didn't want anyone to know I used such a foul trick, because what I was trying to get out was the honest, the truth, but it kind of took over, and this is my theory, you know—I would never discuss it with a psychiatrist or anything—I just call it that, and it may be totally erroneous, but it took over the superego function. In other words, there's something saying "You can't do this, so don't worry about it, it's impossible." So, that took over that problem, and then there was just, you know, and so it could come forth.

W. H.   Now the superego took over what problem?

A. S.   That I can't say this, I can't find the truth, I don't know what I'm about to reveal or say or do. . . . You're probably not following me because it's a little hazy, probably.

W. H.   I think it should be hazy, you know, I mean . . .

A. S.   Well I don't want to be *too* hazy. I like to have *some* clarity.

W. H.   You probably feel that a poem takes you where it sort of has to go, and you don't feel critically conscious, one step ahead of . . .

A. S.   Well, I never do, anyway . . .

W. H.   You once said that you considered your poems primitive, rather than intellectual.

A. S.   That's because people have told me that and I thought it sounded so nice that I'd go along with it. First of all, I'm not an intellectual of any sort that I know of. I have many friends who are intellectuals, whatever that word means exactly, but primitive, yes, because I didn't know a damn thing about poetry! Nothing! I had never gone to college, I absolutely was a flunk-out in any schooling I had, I laughed my way through exams. You know. They just kind of passed me on, but, you know, nothing came through. I don't know the multiplication table, can't spell, can't punctuate. And until I started at twenty-seven, hadn't done much reading. Oh, yes, well, of course, some, but not much, and certainly not in poetry. So I was just what one would call a primitive. . . . And, unfortunately, bad for me, I wasn't reading enough, I was writing too much. You know, I mean if I'd just told myself to put the typewriter away for a while and read up and see what's going on. . . .

A. P.   Do you struggle over poems?

A. S.   Some.

A. P.   It depends on what the poem is?

A. S.   Yes. I mean we all have, you know the term, the "given" poem. I mean that happens once in a great while and one says "Thank you, thank you, how nice of you." But, I'm afraid I'm getting, I don't know, lazy or, I don't know what it is.

W. H.   Do you mean poems seem to be fewer and further between?

A. S.   No, no, increasing at a great rate.

W. H.   Oh, I see. Yes, well someone said about Wallace Stevens that at the end of his life he found out what a Wallace Stevens poem was supposed to sound like and he sort of went ahead and wrote them out, so maybe . . .

A. S.   Well, I don't know, I don't have any feeling like that. As a matter of fact, I'm always trying to write something that doesn't, you know, that isn't, or—I don't even know what an Anne Sexton poem sounds like, unless I should read some sort of imitation I might kind of catch on—but I don't know really what I'm doing or what I sound like. I guess the only thing I really do know is that I have a great feeling for imagery. I mean it to me is the heart of the poem, and without it . . .

W. H.   These questions about—when do you write and how much do you write and how much work is it—they all sound trite but they're all very interesting to me because it seems to me that one can be very happy when he or she *manages* to write. I mean like Henry Miller wrote a book called *To Paint Is to Love Again*, so I'd like to find some way to be able to write a great deal, but I'm very crotchety myself, and Al, you go through long dry periods.

A. S.   But everyone does!

W. H.   If we could just find some way to write a lot.

A. S.   I went through a *long* dry period and since then it's just been *brmmmmmm* . . .

W. H.   We hear that William Stafford writes five poems during a lunch hour!

A. S.   Well, that's fascinating. I did do one strange thing, but it's—for a future—two books from now—but for a book which I think will be called *The Awful Rowing Toward God*. And I wrote it in two and a half weeks. . . .

A. P.   The whole book?

A. S.   Yes, but I didn't know really—this was a strange experience because I was—write a poem and then rewrite and, you know, work, and ask somebody or, you know, until I think, well, here it is, and stick it, a final copy, in a notebook. But there was no time, at this just strange moment of my life, which was of great pressure emotionally—

here were these poems coming, five, six, seven or whatever they were a day, and I happened to talk to John Brinnin, who is on the faculty at B. U. with me, and he said "Oh let them come, you can always fix them up later." Well I'm in a hell of a lot of trouble now because I've never operated that way. I don't quite know, well, what to do with these things. You know, it's like rewriting someone else's work, or something. But I haven't faced it yet. I mean this was just a rare occasion. I've *never* done anything like that before, and it's ridiculous to say you can write a book in two and a half weeks! That's a big laugh. So, the rewrite, who knows how long that will take?

A. P.   Were those poems some of them that appeared in *Salmagundi?*

A. S.   They've appeared nowhere.

A. P.   Oh, they haven't appeared.

A. S.   No, no, they are *unfinished*, I mean, let's, you know, no one has, a few people have seen them but they're not ready for any publication because, you know, they're first, there are flaws all over the place. I've done a little work on them but, preliminary work.

A. P.   What got you interested in doing the *Transformations?*

A. S.   Well, I just had a play off-Broadway, which I wasted about one year writing, and another year going through rewrites and hanging around New York, and going through that, and I don't quite remember the reviews, but they were kind. I think Walter Kerr might have pointed out that I didn't know how to write a play but that I could certainly write, or something like that, you know, it was very, it was all right, you know. And there was a *dreadful* interview in the New York *Times* theater section—I mean it came out on my birthday, my husband was away hunting, I was down anyway, and here is this *ghastly* thing. Now I, I can't say it was a lie, but I *will* say I was drunk as hell—someone was plying me very cutely—and I thought she was going to write about the play, but uh-uh, just any bit of gossip she could gather in, which I thought well of course this won't be used—that's how you learn your lessons. And it, at any rate, it soured me on the whole play, it just turned the whole thing off. And I mean people will write me who might be doing some work on me, I mean a paper or something, and say "We must get hold of *Mercy Street*." I say "You can't, because it ain't."

W. H.   It hasn't been printed?

A. S.   It will *not* be printed. . . . But one of the major reasons for that is that I've covered every theme that was covered in the play in my poetry and I think, perhaps, better. I did, as a matter of fact, send

Walter Kerr *The Death Notebooks,* which are coming out next February I guess, and *The Awful Rowing Toward God,* because I had read that he and his wife like to read poetry, aloud, and Jean Kerr herself had come to the play with Walter to see it, which is very unusual, I was told—she doesn't go to off-Broadway things. And I just thought, well, he might, you know, I don't know, but I got a *very very,* I mean *very* nice letter, etcetera, etcetera. . . . I've forgotten why I started to say this. . . .

W. H.   We were moving toward *Transformations?*

A. S.   Oh, oh, well, I don't know how I got off on that. But I guess I was saying, oh, I said to Walter Kerr, "I ain't no playwright, I'm a poet." And I did say, "Of course I don't know if you like *my* type of poetry, but I read you read poetry." And well his son and, well they all seemed to like my poetry, so they were very, you know, happy and. . . . But, then there was this huge blank period, you know, dead, dead, I mean after this thing comes out in the New York *Times.* And a friend of mine, Maxine Kumin is writing a poem about her daughter, and we talk over our poems all the time, workshop them, you know, on the phone or—she lives close to me—and I don't really remember if I led her to the theme of Snow White or she did—I don't really recall, but she said "I've forgotten," and so I call my daughter Linda to the phone and I said "Honey, will you read *Snow White* to Maxine?" And so she does, and I think "wow, wow, wow," and I had read the Grimms's stories since I could read, whatever age that was —at least I did learn to read, and type, the only things I . . . kind of type . . . the only things I got out of school at all—and I read them until I was about fifteen. At that point someone like Maxine was reading Dostoyevsky, but I'm reading the Brothers Grimm, over and over and over obsessionally, so I hear this and little sparks go and I think, "I wonder if this is something I might. . . ." I was very vague, and I'd try a little introductory poem, and then I'd another, and I still don't know what I'm doing, but. . . . Then I think—I've written about three, say—and I say "Well I don't know what I'm doing, but —if you could do *Snow White,* Anne, after Disney and all that, and make it something that's yours, and Snow White's, and the Queen's and the cast, then you've got it licked." And I think I accomplished that and so . . . but what I would do . . . my daughter would—I've forgotten her age at the time, she may have been seventeen, I don't really remember, I mean I could count back, but, I think about seventeen or sixteen—at any rate, she'd say "Why don't you try"—because she also obsessionally read these tales—not as long, but—it was her book I worked from, Modern Library edition, you know, I don't know what edition I had as a child, but. . . .

W.H.   I like those poems very much, especially the *Rumpelstiltskin* poem. . . .

A. S.   Yes.

W. H.   They're a lot of fun, and they're also scary at the same time, *The Frog Prince*, and . . .

A. S.   Well, what my real joy was was to read—sometimes my daughter would suggest "read this or that, try this one" or something, you know, or—and if I got, as I was reading it, some unconscious message that I had something to say, what I had fun with were the prefatory things, I mean that's where I got my great kicks, where I expressed whatever it evoked in me—and it had to evoke something in me or I couldn't do it. Now they all came rather quickly except for *Sleeping Beauty*, which took me three months. . . . I mean there was a break and I couldn't, I just couldn't—of course that's a very kind of serious, somber . . .

A. P.   Yes, and you went out beyond the fairy tales, also, didn't you? Because *The Little Peasant*, for example, is . . .

A.S.   *The Little Peasant* is right in there. That's a Grimms fairy tale.

A. P.   Is it? I thought it was from Chaucer.

A. S.   Well, you know, things float around. But it was in that book, if one can believe it, and of course one can't, so. . . .

A. P.   But did you embellish it?

A. S.   I've fogotten which poem we're talking about.

A. P.   *The Little Peasant.*

A. S.   *The Little Peasant.* Oh, yes, I embellished it, oh, indeed, it wasn't that way.

A. P.   It's no longer a child's story.

A. S.   None of them are children's stories.

A. P.   I suppose we should ask you to read that one, since we have talked about it.

A. S.   It takes a while, but if you'd like, I'd be glad to.

A. P.   Sure. That's a fun one, also.

A. S.   Yeah. . . . It's an unfamiliar one. Most people don't know it, but. . . . It's got a long kind of prefatory thing, and I'll tell you when I begin the story—the way I happen to retell it, which is with a few added features.

THE LITTLE PEASANT

Oh how the women
grip and stretch
fainting on the horn.

The men and women
cry to each other.
Touch me,
my pancake,
and make me young.
And thus
like many of us,
the parson
and the miller's wife
lie down in sin.

The women cry,
Come, my fox,
heal me.
I am chalk white
with middle age
so wear me threadbare,
wear me down,
wear me out.
Lick me clean,
as clean as an almond.

The men cry,
Come, my lily,
my fringy queen,
my gaudy dear,
salt me a bird
and be its noose.
Bounce me off
like a shuttlecock.
Dance me dingo-sweet
for I am your lizard,
your sly thing.

                    (Now starts the story.)

Long ago
there was a peasant
who was poor but crafty.

He was not yet a voyeur.
He had yet to find
the miller's wife
at her game.
Now he had not enough
cabbage for supper
nor clover for his one cow.
So he slaughtered the cow
and took the skin
to town.
It was worth no more
than a dead fly
but he hoped for profit.

On his way
he came upon a raven
with damaged wings.
It lay as crumpled as
a wet washcloth.
He said, Come little fellow,
you're part of my booty.

On his way
there was a fierce storm.
Hail jabbed the little peasant's cheeks
like toothpicks.
So he sought shelter at the miller's house.
The miller's wife gave him only
a hunk of stale bread
and let him lie down on some straw.
The peasant wrapped himself and the raven
up in the cowhide
and pretended to fall asleep.

When he lay
as still as a sausage
the miller's wife
let in the parson, saying,
My husband is out
so we shall have a feast.
Roast meat, salad, cakes and wine.
The parson,
his eyes as black as caviar,

said, Come, my lily,
my fringy queen.
The miller's wife,
her lips as red as pimentoes,
said, Touch me, my pancake,
and wake me up.
And thus they ate.
And thus
they dingoed-sweet.

Then the miller
was heard stomping on the doorstep
and the miller's wife
hid the food about the house
and the parson in the cupboard.

The miller asked, upon entering,
What is that dead cow doing in the corner?
The peasant spoke up.
It is mine.
I sought shelter from the storm.
You are welcome, said the miller,
but my stomach is as empty as a flour sack.
His wife told him she had no food
but bread and cheese.
So be it, the miller said,
and the three of them ate.

The miller looked once more
at the cowskin
and asked its purpose.
The peasant answered,
I hide my soothsayer in it.
He knows five things about you
but the fifth he keeps to himself.
The peasant pinched the raven's head
and it croaked, Krr. Krr.
That means, translated the peasant,
there is wine under the pillow.
And there it sat
as warm as a specimen.

Krr. Krr.
They found the roast meat under the stove.
It lay there like an old dog.
Krr. Krr.
They found the salad in the bed
and the cakes under it.
Krr. Krr.

Because of all this
the miller burned to know the fifth thing.
How much? he asked,
little caring he was being milked.
They settled on a large sum
and the soothsayer said,
The devil is in the cupboard.
And the miller unlocked it.
Krr. Krr.

There stood the parson,
rigid for a moment,
as real as a soup can
and then he took off like a fire
with the wind at its back.
I have tricked the devil,
cried the miller with delight,
and I have tweaked his chin whiskers.
I will be as famous as the king.

The miller's wife
smiled to herself.
Though never again to dingo-sweet
her secret was as safe
as a fly in an outhouse.

The sly little peasant
strode home the next morning,
a soothsayer over his shoulder
and gold pieces knocking like marbles
in his deep pants pocket.
Krr. Krr.

A. P.   We have only a limited amount of time to talk about all sorts of
things. I wanted to ask the question: It seems to me that in the

progression from your first book to your later books, including your forthcoming *Death Notebooks,* that you move increasingly away from sin and madness toward love and God. Is that a fair estimate?

A. S. Just about, but I wouldn't leave sin alone . . . because I would say one could have a great sense of sin and reach for God. I mean. . . .

W. H. This is a Pandora's box. This is on somewhat the same subject, and I hate to ask it because you've been asked it so often, I'm sure, and also because it's so difficult. . . . I've always felt that we can never, of course, dictate what a poet ought to write about. I mean, that would be absolutely foolish. At the same time—it was just a couple of weeks ago that I read Sylvia Plath's *The Bell Jar.* And now for years I've been reading Berryman's *Dream Songs,* that elegiac genius of his. And I've read Anne Sexton for a long time. An awful lot of pain and death and a preponderance of darkness in the early books—critics have complained about it again and again. James Wright, not talking about you but talking about the darkness of some of his own work said he sometimes wearies of it—"There's something also to be said for the light," he said. How do you react when critics say something like "I wish she'd look *out* further."? . . . You know, Richard Wilbur has a poem on Sylvia Plath—

A. S. I do believe I've read it . . .

W. H. Yes, and he says that she had to sound her "brilliant negative," in poems "free, and helpless, and unjust." The last word is "unjust." And he said at a reading that, well, there's a sense in which she's being somewhat unjust to the world. And, speaking honestly, some- times I read your early poems and it seems that *all* the women in the early poems have sagging breasts, and *all* the old men are unhappy, and I think of that word by Wilbur, "unjust," and I wondered, does poetry have to come out of that sense of pain, and the sense of darkness?

A. S. Actually not. It comes out of wherever you are. I mean you've got to go forward and read more recent books. . . . I mean certainly that what I just read was not the pit of darkness, or despair.

W. H. No, the *Transformations* poems are a lot of fun. And there are others in earlier books that I love—"Letter Written While Crossing Long Island Sound on a Ferry," which ends with that nice surreal image of the nuns flying away saying "Good news, good news."

A. S. Yes, yes, and then there's a whole book of love poems, and there's a bit of joy in that, I'd say. I mean, lightness.

W. H.   Yes. This is a very difficult subject, and I never would have found myself five years ago saying what I would say now . . .

A. S.   Well maybe you only can do that because I have, you know, after all one does grow, change, evolve, and you know, it . . .

W. H.   Yes. . . . Let me on somewhat this subject read one harsh statement about *Live or Die*.

A. S.   Okay.

W. H.   This was a review by a fellow in *The Southern Review* talking about *Live or Die*. He says, he gets angry and says "They are not poems. They are documents of modern psychiatry and their publication is a result of the confusion of critical standards in the general mind." He says that the poems finally are embarrassing and irritating. How do you react to something like that?

A. S.   I'd say please put my book down and don't bother with it! It's for someone else. I mean there are many . . . well, I can't do much about it, you know, so, all right, that's his critical evaluation, I respect it as such, and he's every right to think that.

W. H.   Yes, you have to go on writing what you have to write.

A. S.   Yeah.

A. P.   Another harsh statement by . . .

A. S.   Is this called harsh statement time?

A. P.   No, but it's . . .

A. S.   No, I'm kidding, come on let's get a little happy.

A. P.   Someone said, I think it was James Dickey who said that the personal poets aren't personal at all, they're very superficial, that it's only the facade of the person that's coming through. How do you respond to that?

A. S.   I think it's a goddamned lie because his poems are often personal, and I think that's one of his facades. I respect him greatly as a writer, you know, usually, you know, many of his poems I admire, and if he wishes to say that about personal poems, I don't think he knows what in hell he's talking about. As a matter of fact I think he's a very confused critic. I mean, he ought just to stick with his poetry, or movies, or novels, or . . . But that's just my opinion.

W. H.   Do you pay much attention to the reviews of your books, or criticism?

A. S.   Well, I never—I think I was telling Al this last night—I've never replied to a review. I feel that somehow it's tasteless. You know, they must give their. . . . Except once. But to go on with why I don't reply, because I can remember people saying "Well I had a review of eight books in the New York *Times* and I've heard from six of them." And —this was a former teacher saying that—I thought ferchrissakes, are you supposed to run around and say "thank you?" You know, because here's someone trying to tell the truth, the way they see it, and I don't think they deserve a "thank you" or a "to hell with you." I've never written a "to hell with you." At any rate, there *was* one review in a— I don't know if it's a big or small, but an English quarterly—which was *so* loving, like "Oh Anne, Anne"—I can't remember, but it was like a love letter or something. So I did cable—I didn't know who he was, I never met or heard of him—I cabled my publisher, you know, I cabled *him* c/o my publisher, and I just said "Will you marry me?" And I got a very nice letter back, you know, I mean he was. . . . That was, that's just the only time I've ever replied, and only in that vein. But I try not to let them get me down or up! You know, depending on which way it goes. Of course the publishers care terribly, and, you know, they need good quotes, and, you know, they're running a business, and if you've got entirely—for instance *Transformations* got absolutely the most horrible reviews in Britain, but one, which came much later, just a little while ago. I mean things like they say "like Walt" and then quote two lines "Disney, we mean, not Whitman." And then it ends, "God bless America. Ha. Ha." Etcetera. And I thought, well, I guess this didn't travel very well across the Atlantic. But it didn't get me down. It might have gotten the publishers down.

W. H.   This question fits in somewhat with what Al was asking before, and this is just a grab-bag question you might just want to throw away, because I'm sure it's too general. But it's always asked. Do you see your work as having essentially changed since you began? Is there something you can say generally about some real divisions as your books have progressed? . . . That's heavy, isn't it?

A. S.   It's heavy, but it should be able to be answered. . . . I see a progression . . . just . . . well, after *Live or Die* . . . I mean, *To Bedlam and Part Way Back*: mostly madness; *All My Pretty Ones* (*mostly*, I'm saying, because this is a great generality): death of parents, and love, and some religious poems; *Live or Die*: a mixed bag, sequentially dated as I wrote the poems, thinking, you know, live, or die; then *Love Poems*: well that's, I mean a whole book of love poems, that's certainly a step in the right direction. . . . What comes next? *Transformations*. Okay. There are two rather serious *Transformations* poems, the rest are—I didn't really mean them to be comic, I mean, I guess I did, but I mean I really didn't know what I was doing, I just did what I felt like, I was very *happy* writing those poems, I was having a good time, except for a few that gave me trouble. Then *The Book of Folly* which is really kind of a mixed bag of things. It's got a little hangover from the voice of *Transformations* with some poems called "The Jesus Papers," which are called either "blasphemous" or "devout"—it's probably blasphemous, I would say. I mean one of them my publishers forced me to take out and two friends advised me to take it out: it was "Jesus Ailing," which starts out—this is unpublished, not in the book—"There was trouble that day. / Jesus was constipated." Well they said "now look, we just can't have this," so I said "okay." But in the end of that book there's a kind of belief thing going on. One fights what one. . . . You know, it's a little war. . . .

W. H.   And now you've finished a couple of other books.

A. S.   Yes. Then comes *The Death Notebooks* which is—I'd planned, I had this crazy idea I'd publish it posthumously, you know, my friends going ha, ha, ha, as they always do—not that I was going to kill myself and bring out this book, but I thought, wouldn't it be *nice*, you know, after I was dead if there were a statement about death? But I, you know, and God, which is a predominant theme in the book. He, Being. . . . And then *The Awful Rowing Toward God*, which is about as far as I've gotten.

W. H.   We began with your poem "With Mercy for the Greedy," which talks about, I suppose it talks about your effort to come to terms with the cross, and I think it makes a statement about poetry being maybe a half-way house toward a religiousness that you can hold to. With that poem and now with—I just have the title to go by, *The Awful Rowing Toward God*—have you, have you come somewhere in regard to this religious quest, or . . . ?

A. S.   I would say I *do* in *The Awful Rowing Toward God*, and I even do to a certain degree in *The Death Notebooks*. I mean it certainly ends on, I don't know—could you say how it ends?

A. P.   Well it ends with that series of psalms, which are, praise.

A. S.   Which are praise!

A. P.   And I think even the section called "The Furies."

A. S.   Which are praise! No, well, yes, yes they are.

A. P.   And we have approximately two minutes left. I have the poem from *The Death Notebooks* that we'd like you to read as a conclusion.

A. S.   There are many fury poems. This is only one of them.

THE FURY OF COCKS

There they are
drooping over the breakfast plates,
angel-like,
folding in their sad wing,
animal sad,
and only the night before
there they were
playing the banjo.
Once more the day's light comes
with its immense sun,
its mother trucks,
its engines of amputation.
Whereas last night
the cock knew its way home,
as stiff as a hammer,
battering in with all
its awful power.
That theater.
Today it is tender,
a small bird,
as soft as a baby's hand.
She is the house.
He is the steeple.
When they fuck they are God.
When they break away they are God.
When they snore they are God.
In the morning they butter the toast.
They don't say much.
They are still God.
All the cocks of the world are God,
blooming, blooming, blooming
into the sweet blood of woman.

A. P.   Anne Sexton, Bill, thank you very much.
A. S.   Thank you.
W. H.   Thank you.

LOUIS SIMPSON

LOUIS SIMPSON *(b. March 27, 1923 in Jamaica, B.W.I.)
is Professor of English at the State University of
New York at Stony Brook. His awards for poetry include
the 1964 Pulitzer Prize for* At the End of the Open Road.
He is the only contributor to American Poets in 1976
already to have published a full-length autobiography
(North of Jamaica, *1972).*

(Photo by Layle Silbert)

Rolling Up

For some time American poets have been writing almost exclusively about their personal lives. We have become accustomed to poets' telling us what they are doing and thinking at the moment. The present moment is everything—there is no sense of the past. Nor is there any sense of a community. If poetry is the language of a tribe, it seems there is no longer a tribe, only a number of individuals who are writing a personal diary or trying to "expand their consciousness." But the stress on the individual does not seem to stimulate imagination; we have almost forgotten what it is like to read lyric or narrative poems.

It seems, however, that we are coming to an end of a period. After the life studies, the case histories. . . . We are tired of looking in mirrors. Every year there is a new style in personalities. Everyone exhibits himself, we try to draw attention to ourselves . . . and soon, what does it matter? No one is listening.

In order to feel anything at all, we exaggerate. And then we don't take pleasure in anything, because we don't believe it.

In order to break out of the prison of the self, poets have tried meditating. Some poets have used drugs. Others have studied the ways of the Indian. It is clear that meditating can make a difference. Fifty years ago in Paris the Surrealists used the technique of free association. This released images from the unconscious, or wherever images come from, and enabled them to write more freely. Meditation can have a similar effect. I suspect, however, that poets who rely on drugs for inspiration will exhaust their ability to write. Images may be released, but the desire to arrange them will be weakened. As for images and sounds without an arrangement . . . there is nothing more monotonous than the material produced by chance, if thought and feeling are not brought to bear upon it.

There is much to admire in the life and poetry of the American Indian. But it is not easy for an American of the white middle class to think like an Indian. I would go so far as to say that you can write convincingly only about things that you have been compelled to feel. It is easy to put on the costume of a nation other than your own . . . to share the emotional life of that nation is another thing entirely. Americans like to dress up and play at being what they are not. This has a good side—the social mobility of Americans, which is envied throughout the world, stems from the same impulse. But in poetry the results are not convincing. A hundred years ago Longfellow wrote about the Indian. In some ways *Hiawatha* is an impressive performance, but it remains a performance. Under the feathers and paint there is an American tourist. Ugh.

To read some American poets you would think they lived far away from roads and supermarkets, that they never had the thoughts of the people you meet, that they looked with the eyes of the crow and listened with the ears of the beaver. That their habitation was darkness and their house made of earth and stones. That they were pure in thought and deed.

But the Indian must have lived as a man. I would not be surprised if the Indian had an equivalent for television. He could not always have been thinking about animals and gods and having significant dreams.

Why is it that magical events are always happening in faraway places where we cannot see them?

The reader may think, What harm does it do? If an American poet wishes to think he is a shaman, or imagine he is a moose, what's wrong with it? Shouldn't we welcome the chance to expand our consciousness? Besides, what do we really know about the mind? Why try to set limits to it?

To the contrary, I believe that a great deal is known about the mind and that there is no shortage of consciousness. We have more consciousness than we know how to use. There is, however, a shortage of wisdom. We seem unable to live together without maiming one another. And we are running out of space; we have to learn to live with one another. This goes for people everywhere, not just in the United States. What we need is not to expand consciousness but to increase understanding. And there is no mystery about it—the tools are at hand if we wish to use them. But this would require work, while going on a trip does not. Americans like to go on trips. To the Virgin Islands, the moon, or an Indian reservation, it is all the same—an attempt to escape from necessity, the need to live an intelligent, useful life.

My objection to the pursuit of esoteric knowledge, shamanism and so on, is that it neglects the life right under your nose. While you are playing children's games you cannot think like a man. While the American poet is imitating the language of a tribe to which he does not belong, he is not learning to speak for the tribe to which he does belong. And this, like it or not, is the tribe that uses supermarkets and roads.

Here I must make a confession—but it has a point, it isn't just the expression of a personal grievance. I don't like the tribe that uses supermarkets and roads. These days I find that when I am in the company of

Americans, the people down the street, I feel as if I were living in Germany after the gas-ovens. With this difference—the Americans got away with it.

I am referring to the recent war. We still haven't paid that bill. The refusal or inability of Americans to atone for their war-crimes has brutalized American society. If we can't admit our guilt, what can we admit? It is necessary not to think seriously about anything at all. Consequently, Americans have become callous, violent, and inwardly disgraced. This is not a society that inspires you to write; these are not people who understand poetry.

I seem to have painted myself into a corner: it is necessary for the American poet to write about his tribe, the nation of roads and supermarkets. At the same time, I don't want to.

Here Confucius comes to my aid. Speaking of the philosopher, he says, "When the government is rotten, he rolls up and keeps the true process inside him."

I've been rolling up. But this isn't, as some may think, a refusal to face life. To the contrary, it is the real work that has to be done if poetry, or any feeling life, is to survive. If the nation is to survive we have to recreate a sense of the spiritual, imaginative life that we have lost. My disagreement with the cultists is that what they are talking about has no connection with the life of the nation. There is not the slightest chance that Americans will become Indians. There is not the slightest chance that Americans will cease using household appliances and, instead, attempt to sustain themselves by magic. Therefore poetry written out of these ideas has no reality.

But poets are needed to recreate the image man has of himself and in this way reconstitute the nation. There have been precedents for this. Wordsworth, for example. . . . He was for the French Revolution. Then he was frightened by the bloodshed and went back to England. Subsequently, England declared war on France, on the revolutionary ideals that Wordsworth still cherished. This was a profound shock. He tells us how, during church services when everyone was praying for the success of British arms, he hoped for their disappointment. He felt like a traitor; at any rate, he was cut off in his affections from the people around him. It is hard to imagine a more desolate situation for a poet, and it is the situation American poets have found themselves in for some time. It would be bad enough if poets alone felt so, but what poets feel many other people are feeling too. The United States contains a large number of people who no longer like it.

Wordsworth removed himself from the centers of English culture and went to live in the mountains. In effect, he left England. Then, among the mountains and lakes, he set about creating imaginary men, a race of people in his mind. He imagined men and women who were full of feeling, who communed silently with nature and loved one another. He gave them heartfelt words and high sentences. These people are not found in nature but in the imagination of a poet. Wordsworth's aim was to hold up models for human behavior. He created the nation that he could not find.

In his broodings on human character he perceived new states of feeling. He became a psychologist in poetry and enlarged our sympathies. The political revolution failed—therefore he attempted to replace it with a revolution of feeling. He wished to reveal the deep springs that join one man to another and constitute a real nation. Indeed, if this nation does not exist, there is no other.

Blake was a poet for the 'sixties—I mean, in America. He was for people who wished to blow their minds. Wordsworth is the poet of life—he shows the way to the future, a community built on human feeling and sympathy.

There was never as great a need for the poetry of feeling as there is in the United States at the present time. By this I mean poetry that addresses itself to the human condition, a poetry of truth, not dreams. The poetry I am speaking about depicts human actions and the way we live. I do not mean poetry that merely talks about the obvious, automobiles and washing-machines. Poetry must express the reality behind appearances. The poetry I mean can be subtle and mysterious, but it is related to the way we live. There is as much poetry in a suburb as by a lake, if we have a mind to see it.

As it deals with life, this poetry will frequently be in the form of a narrative. Not a mere relation of external events, but a narrative of significant actions. The poet will aim to convey states of feeling. In our time poets have stayed away from narrative because it has often been merely descriptive—there has been too much dead tissue. But this can be avoided if the poet reveals a situation with no more than a few words, and concentrates on the feeling.

In my attempts to write narrative poetry I have used the rhythms of speech. I bear in mind what it would be like to say the poem aloud to someone else. This helps me to form the lines. At the same time it eliminates confusion—I have to make my ideas clear. I eliminate words out of books, affected language, jargon of any kind.

I have tried to bring into poetry the sense of life, the gestures that Chekhov got in prose. And I have tried to bring in humor. I do not believe that this is common; there is plenty of satire, but this is not what I mean by humor. I have mixed humorous and sad thoughts in my poems, because this is the way life is. People want the sights and sounds of life; they ask for life in poetry. They ask for bread, but instead they have been given stones.

The poem "The Foggy Lane," states my ideas about poetry and its relation to life. By "the uneven, muddy surface" I mean human life. There is no end to the material—the question is what to make of it.

This kind of poetry requires a sacrifice of the individual, his peculiar fantasies. On the other hand, it is an on-going process.

THE FOGGY LANE

The houses seem to be floating
in the fog, like lights at sea.

Last summer I came here with a man
who spoke of the ancient Scottish poets—
how they would lie blindfolded
with a stone placed on the belly,
and so compose their panegyrics . . .
while we, being comfortable, find nothing to praise.

Then I came here with a radical
who said that everything is corrupt;
he wanted to live in a pure world.

And a man from an insurance company
who said that I needed 'more protection'.

Walking in the foggy lane
I try to keep my attention fixed
on the uneven, muddy surface . . .
the pools made by the rain,
and wheel-ruts, and wet leaves,
and the rustling of small animals.

DINNER AT THE SEA-VIEW INN

1
Peter said, "I'd like some air."

"That's a good idea," said Marie's father.
"Why don't you young people go for a walk?"

Marie glanced at her mother.
Something passed between them. A warning.

2
When Peter and Marie walked through the dining-room
everyone stared.

               I just think so,
he reminded himself, and said,
"Fitzgerald says that nobody thinks about us
as much as we think they do."

"Who's he?" said Marie. "Another of your favorite authors?"

3
She wanted to know where he was taking her.

"I just had to get out of there.
Wouldn't it be great to hire a taxi
and just keep going?"

                                 "Why?" said Marie.
"It's a wonderful night."

"I'd rather have my own car," said Marie.

4
"I'm getting cold," said Marie.
"How much further are we going?"

"All right," he said.
                    And they walked back.

"When I was a child," said Peter,
"I used to think that the waves were cavalry . . .
the way they come in, curling over."

She said, "Is that what you were in,
the calvary?"

He laughed. "Calvary? For Christ's sake . . . "

5
"Did you have a good walk?" said Marie's father.

Marie said something to her mother.

Shortly after, Mr. Shulman ordered the car,
and they all drove back to New York.

They let Peter out in front of his building
on West Eighty-fourth Street, saying goodnight.
All but Marie . . . She still sat stiffly,
unsmiling. She had been offended.

6

Everything was just as he'd left it . . .
the convertible couch,
the reading lamp and chair,
and the stand with the typewriter.

He undressed and went to bed,
and turned out the light.

Lying in bed, hands clasped beneath his head,
listening . . .

to the stopping and starting of traffic
in the street five floors below.
And the opening of the elevator,
and the sound of feet going down the corridor.

BARUCH

I

There is an old folk saying:
"He wishes to study the Torah
but he has a wife and family."
Baruch had a sincere love of learning
but he owned a dress-hat factory.

One night he was in his cart returning
to the village. Falling asleep . . .
All at once he uttered a cry
and snatched up the reins. He flew!
In the distance there was fire
and smoke. It was the factory,
the factory that he owned was burning.

All night it burned, and by daylight
Lev Baruch was a ruined man.

Some said that it was gypsies,
that sparks from their fire set it burning.
Others said, the workers.

But Lev never murmured. To the contrary,
he said, "It is written,
'by night in a pillar of fire.' "
He said, "Every day of my life
I had looked for a sign in that direction.
Now that I have been relieved of my property
I shall give myself to the Word."

And he did from that day on,
reading Rashi and Maimonides.
He was half way over the *Four Mountains*
when one day, in the midst of his studying,
Lev Baruch fell sick and died.
For in Israel it is also written,
"Prophecy is too great a thing for Baruch."

II
They were lovers of reading in the family.
For instance, Cousin Deborah
who, they said, had read everything . . .
The question was, which would she marry,
Tolstoy, or Lermontov, or Pushkin?

But her family married her off
to a man from Kiev, a timber merchant
who came from Kiev with a team of horses.
On her wedding day she wept,
and at night when they locked her in
she kicked and beat on the door.
She screamed. So much for the wedding!
As soon as it was daylight, Brodsky—
that was his name—drove back to Kiev
like a man pursued, with his horses.

III
We have been devoted to words.
Even here in this rich country
Scripture enters and sits down
and lives with us like a relative.

Taking the best chair in the house . . .
His eyes go everywhere, not missing anything.
Wherever his looks go, something ages
and suddenly tears or falls.
Here, a worn place in the carpet,
there, a crack in the wall.

The love of literature goes with us.

On a train approaching midnight
everyone else has climbed into his sarcophagus
except four men playing cards.
There is nothing better than poker—
not for the stakes but the companionship,
trying to outsmart one another.
Taking just one card . . .

I am sitting next to the window,
looking at the lights on the prairie
clicking by. From time to time
two or three will come together
then go wandering off again.

Then I see a face, pale and unearthly,
that is flitting along with the train,
passing over the fields and rooftops,
and I hear a voice out of the past:
"He wishes to study the Torah."

DAVE SMITH

DAVE SMITH (*b. 1942 in Portsmouth, Va.*), *received*
degrees from the University of Virginia and from
Southern Illinois University. He has taught English and
coached football at several schools and colleges,
served from 1968–72 with the U.S. Air Force, and is
currently attending Ohio University at Athens, Ohio.
(*Photo by Dee Smith*)

Sailing the Back River

After *The New Yorker* bought my poem "Cumberland Station," I received a note from an editor asking if I would like to shift its locale. Perhaps, he suggested, I was unaware that urban renewal had eliminated that venerable terminal. Having not been in Cumberland, Maryland for ten years, I was not so aware. But place has an inevitable function in my poems and I could not write otherwise.

Many of my poems root in Poquoson, Virginia, an anonymous fishing village whose name, from the Chiskiac, means "flat land." A peninsula bordered by Back River, the Poquoson River, and the Chesapeake Bay, it lies due south of Yorktown and dates settlement prior to 1631. It is neither quaint nor restored, has changed little except for urban influx in the last decade, and its strongest link with history is a hatred of the English.

William Lisle Carmines, a "Bull Islander," as the natives are called, believed American wars were a function of English cowardice. Born in September, 1900, and dying in the summer of 1967, "Peterless" or "Liss," fathered eight children. Billy, the eldest of two sons, whom I have not seen in several years, is my best friend. These men, their ancestors and kinsmen, their place, are to me as mean as shale, as infinite as the ocean. If there is a path to my swamp poems, it is through them. What follows are what trail marks I have.

Alexander Cosby Brown's book, *The Dismal Swamp Canal*, describes canal steamers in the 1870s. On the "Thomas Jefferson," there was a black mail carrier named Uncle Aleck who, napping on the rail, was startled awake and fell into the water. What he said was, "I knowed I was overboard soon's I struck de water." That is what I felt when I wrote my first poem about Poquoson. To hell with those slim-jim poems I wanted so much to imitate. A man going inland with an oar must be mythical, but he must have a name under his oar.

Why do I write about people who might kill me for some of the things I think? Why do I keep talking about old boats shoved on a marsh hump to rot? Liss told his sons, George and Billy, where his boat, known only as the "Peter Liss," was to be beached when he died. I helped them run that 36 foot hull aground. Liss said to knock a hole in her; we didn't. Two months later a northeast wind pulled her off. Now there is only keel and some ribbing. Why? Because I love to imagine the pilot-house, my face getting sticky with salt while they chew, those crusty watermen, through everything.

AMONG THE OYSTER BOATS
AT PLUM TREE COVE

I have been away growing old
at the heart of another country
where there are no boats crumbling,
or small crabs with scuttling tools.
These pines warped with early snow,
this light that slopes and breaks
as the sea slides and sloughs
against your air and earth-borne
flanks: I had loosed the dead
from memory but, coming back
confused, I find them waiting
here at the sea's rattling edge.

It is too much to speak to them, yet
to them through you I bow, politely
soiled and whiskered, wanting a drink,
to stand under the old harsh throats
sharing whiskey at Plum Tree, among
the booted ones with plaid shirts
and large loving hands. But wanting it
is not enough; you only groan or
roll and the village sleeps off
its wild hours among neat azaleas.
I stand among you tasting silence
as the wind softly licks the wave.

Mark Twain said of New England, "Every year they kill a lot of poets for writing about 'Beautiful Spring.'" So much for sentimentality. Carrie Moore taught and failed Liss in the seventh grade and he quit school for the water. He hated his cousin for life.

Hampton Institute is a black college near Poquoson, and no boat-rocker. I found an old MA thesis there which told how the Kechoughtan, a sub-tribe of the Powhatan, met our English ancestors at Old Point

Comfort. Greeting them warmly, they were enslaved, beaten, eliminated. They survive in a street name in once fashionable Hampton Rhodes, near where the Monitor fought the Merrimac, and in what is now a black ghetto. Liss disliked blacks, but like G. B. Shaw, he disliked most men equally and distrusted all women.

William Styron, from Newport News (over-town), writes of my area as if it were Connecticut. When I went to the "island," people over-town said, "Aren't you afraid those watermen will hurt you?" I was. I found violence and ugliness in those marshes. Every house had a smeared family name and a baggage of pride. My heart, however, is still there.

Howard Norman is a man I met in Michigan. He spends summers among the Canadian Cree and Ojibwa. He memorized the tribes' stories, was taught by his friend, Chief Jacob Slowstream, who died, leaving Howard the sole custodian of those legends. Isn't that a magnificent trust? Howard said that once he was sitting in a tree and listening down on Slowstream who chanted the stories when a Harvard anthropologist, much laden with gear, walked up and began to speak sign language from a book. The old man observed with sage dignity and, when the anthropologist had finished, he gave him the finger. Which sent the anthropologist off cursing in English, which Slowstream understood perfectly. The day Billy Carmines left the water for college, Liss gave him a five dollar bill. For four years!

A waterman is a man who earns his living on or near the Atlantic Ocean. He will, in season, set fike nets, clam with a rake in water to his waist, oyster with twelve-foot tongs, crab by baiting a pot made of chicken wire, a cube, setting it on the bottom and returning, when the tide turns, to retrieve what he has caught. Pots weigh maybe forty pounds and an average string will exceed eighty pots. Liss seldom "sailed" with anyone except Billy or George. At sixteen, he paid $300 for his boat. As Billy says, "She were two inch pine, low of bow, slow, stank, had a Bugeye bottom-line, always did suck-down at her stern, but were wet and able." Liss was, like most watermen, a reflection of his boat. He was banty but had shoulders and arms like vice-grip pliers. He was always a prodigious drinker. In a March storm, 1955, he was drunk and fell over. His boat circled but she was too high-sided for him to climb her. He pulled himself ashore on fike stakes, but the boat drifted in Back River. After Billy came home from college and recovered the boat, he poured out Liss's bottles and asked his father if he would at last stop drinking. Liss said no, but he was going to build some steps on that high-sided son-of-a-bitch. A waterman drinks from a bottle, whatever is in it. Liss was known to be able to find a James River oyster bed drunk or in stonewall fog; would simply sail until he stopped, anchored, and reached for tongs. He was never wrong. He actually did carry an oar inland, in the old days, when they all walked fourteen miles to their boats. That was Sunday after church; they returned on Friday night. Mostly.

HARD TIMES, BUT CARRYING ON

His eyes were once blue and pure
  as the Bay, but that too
   turned thick with grim
trails of tasteless oil and shapeless

carps of paper whose words, bleached,
  seeped away on the slow flow.
   He owns the same boat, boots,
and seine he started with forty winters

back, when running in and out alone was
  possible blind drunk, on the nose.
   He steers by a plain stick
and ropes; fancy wheels confuse him;

spits on the gilded engines that stutter
  in bad weather, lacking control
   even when all else is flush.
They ridicule the radar in his head,

the barometer in his bones, and shake
  the air with sleek waves. Even so,
   he works his hole with craft,
eats fish for lunch at noon and dots

it with a single swallow of rye, then
  drags back hard on the surging
   net, while all around the bags
crank up slack as widow's dugs in rain.

Faulkner says evil is easier to make believable in art—but the good is what it is all built on. Liss once said, about Vietnam, he wouldn't give a foot of Bull Island mud for all of Asia. He feared nothing. One day in 1934 he culled oysters from dark to dark and took them to the buy-boat. Her captain said Liss's oysters were too big and refused them. Liss was so mad that he put-a-wish on that boat to sink before it passed Newport News Point. It did. He never dropped ashes on floor or ground, carried a wooden match-box in his pocket. No man ever saw him dance with a woman, drunk or sober.

A student of mine wrote in her theme about Appalachia that she met a Mrs. Taylor who mortgaged her tin roof for enough money to "spread" her guests from the poverty agency. Two of Liss's friends, too weak to sail and with wives dead, lived all year in a doorless, windowless bait shack. They claimed they had "seen worse," playing cards in the wind.

I am thinking about the photographs by Doris Ulmann, published in 1971, with a preface by Jonathan Williams and introduction by John Jacob Niles. Good God, the stories those faces tell! They are like striated rags of rock on a gulley to a river. Williams wrote, "The art of the quiet is no less than yelling and propaganda."

Niles wrote, "Miss Ulmann's point of view about the people she photographed was quite simple. She concluded there would always be someone handy with a snapshot camera to photograph the pretty girls with frilly dresses and curled hair, with made-up eyes and lips. She was not concerned with these people, but rather with those who were downright, genuine individuals." And it was ". . . in the faces of the old men and women that she saw what attracted her most—the core and trouble of their lives, but also the ultimate serenity." A man could look in Liss's eyes and see he had fought the whore and lost, but that it was all right. He felt it was enough to fish where his fathers had fished, where Tom Buck Insley got ruptured and Si Hugget sunk, where, in the snowy March storm of 1963, his boat fared better than Jumps Firth's or Jim Snot Freeman's or Honey Evans's. He did not have to chop it out of a tree or haul it on a truck back to Back River. Billy remembers rocking with water so deep in Liss's house that it slipped into his shorts.

MARCH STORM

For three days the wind blew northeast,
reeds huddled underwater, bent back and down,

like birds with their heads bowed
in a winged darkness. The tide
held, came on slowly, not impelled
by high slopes to churn and shear
through narrows, but a wall of lapping
grey light mounting the back steps, came in
unnoised, huddled among shoes
at the corners of closets,
licked out from under sofas and rockers
to sweep the rooms free of mice.

When the sun broke the fourth day's wake
the water retreated in silence,
the boats sank, settled
in the tops of the pines,
rudders flapping gently as dogs' tongues.
As if stunned like drunks in a noon light
we walked into the fields, crowded
under the boats, in their intimate shadows,
to lift up our arms and show proof
to the scarred wounds seen at last
where we had always felt them.
All around us delicate seagrass took root,
billowed, while one by one lean figures
darted off as if to escape
the closing net of the night.

Watermen and their women cut the crap. They won't have pretense. If it doesn't strike and tell, like doctors thumping chests, they clam up. But they know when singing is going on and what it means. When Liss died, Billy couldn't sleep for many nights. He *knew* his father was haunting him for the hole in the boat; he had heart pain and he would sit up until morning, getting drunk, staring into a Bible. He let no one but me see this. I love poems which admit me to that private chapel soul of the soul where things matter, where I know what I encounter will make me pay for my life, pay in self-change. I hate adolescents in silk who cry "Suffer with me!"

Jack Matthews says that a man is defined by his work. Liss lived to work. If I take *water* from *man*, what is left? A shark under the water is one thing, a circling fin quite another. Liss married his wife Homer, a

17 year old "muddy-toe" from down the road, when he was 23. He had bought his boat and house some years before. He never worked for another man. He wanted to die working, and did. I saw George bring him to the dock. While a man breathed futilely into Liss, George rolled his waders up and down, up and down. He is a waterman too, but a failed one. Billy is a teacher, but he is always ashamed he is not a waterman. All of them know how the whore works. They do not go after sharks, but they catch them. And are caught.

THE SHARK IN THE RAFTERS

for Jim Applewhite

Under the stuttered snatch of the winch
they draw him by pulley and wheel.
Slower than the shadows of night
tracking the sun through warm furrows,
he rises into the open fishhouse
where the sea flicks its blue haze
through a hole in the slatted pier.

It is not this mechanical shriek, but another,
like that of a reed blown on in the palm,
which reaches the women and brings them
out of the darkness of pine needles
through the labyrinths of swampgrass
where ruptured boats lie half-buried.

Some come as widows and some as children,
but everyone comes as lover
to stand facing this last house at the point
where there are no windows, no doors,
only a roof and a mild iron-headed animal
who cannot swim or walk but is
at ease in air like a diving bird,

all possessed
by his long timber-shaking shadow,
whispering like women who know the quick mouths
in the sea are the reddest hearts, whispering
he is beautiful and terrible, terrible.

And this afternoon as they take
the steel bar to his unmerciful jaws,

freeing the stump of a man's leg, the fishermen
free also the old malice of soft faces
where rancid water burns and flows through a house
floor from a mouth hung in a wrenched smile,

and each of the women close at the ravelling edge
as if to reach out through water and air
one delicate finger along a forbidden hide,
blue and black a single gleam in the heat,
as he enters the space between the eyes
and the sun that is falling.

Even the children who pretend in the dead boats
they are bringing him in alone, tamed,
remember what they know of holes huge in the nets
and are still as the shadow halved
by the sun and the roof is cranked up
in the rafters where a young man waits
and fingers the promise of a knife.

Then one by one the teeth are pulled,
the eyes gouged, plopped in a paper bag,
the baby bones drawn whole and shining,
the flesh ripped away in tongue-like sheets,
the entrails and heart loosed, coiled,

until only the naked jaw remains,
the raw blush of mythical gums and chunks
of a fisherman's leg,
all debris, gobbets bloodied and sparkling
as they fall through the housefloor
and drift toward the feet of the women,
the naked, hungry children, the unburied
boats as still as mutes; and a man
begins at last to descend among them.

And this afternoon
while her children plunge and dive in the light,
a woman shall climb stairs and lie
with only a swimmer's shadow
on her breast, in the room
where a clock's familiar rasp
makes her spin and whisper

as if to a face crusted with salt,
a mouth cracked like summer clouds, bearing
the white sheer teeth of the shark
that follows her everywhere.

We get half a cent for a clam. The wholesaler sells them for seven cents
each. In Chicago, where they go now, a half-dozen costs as much as
ten dollars. The AFL-CIO has tried for years to unionize the watermen.
They all say they don't want to be told they must stay home today. The
whore won't let them stay home.

In *America A Prophecy,* Jerome Rothenberg and George Quasha talk
about "the expanded sense of poetry in our time." They quote Gary
Snyder on "the first human beings in history to have all of man's culture
available to our study." What bunk! What chauvinism to imply that Li
Po had a limited vision for lack of an information retrieval system!
Villon wrote: "I know when a sharper patters the jargon." So do I. Here
is a poem about art and poetry and life, all of which is circled up in the
eye of a fish, as William Pitt Root has put it.

THE SPINNING WHEEL IN THE ATTIC

Not for beauty's sake, or art's, this wheel
    came round in his calloused palms,
        bent willows and oak,

formed for the work of spinning whole cloth,
    gatherer of scraps fine and coarse,
        a tool, a gentle yoke.

Long nights he labored in the ways of stars,
    his back bowed at a shaft of steel,
        hewing curves and spokes

from the supple wood in his bone-yellow fist.
    No consideration of death's awl, no
        fear of time's cat

claws gouging out the wood's fine-honed finish
    deceived him in all the things he did.
        He wore a plain brown hat.

I can see his whittle marks as thick as scars,
   rough as rocks in any river bed,
      where he fretted at

the grain's refusal to have his slightest idea.
   My finger drawn in tremulous dust
      shows his sweat fall,

revealing a woody heart in several secret places,
   the way a wire buried in a limb
      buckles a man's saw

so in the dusk he curses low past a woman's ear,
   then bends with numbed fingers to work
      as winds howl and yaw.

At window, meager as old dreams, she watches him,
   thinking what she will weave, shawl,
      sweater or coverlet

for the bed blank as a grave in a dark corner, her
   eyes working the grey thread from
      the field's gold blanket

through animal mouths, shearing it, the coiled skeins
   pooled on a planked floor, even patterns
      linked as a scheme of planets.

She has no illusions in this, only a moment's delight
   in what she might make from her fear
      and the cold. The wood,

bared, glistens light and dark in smooth grooves
   where she drew together the strands
      until the stems and buds

of earth's glut silenced her humming eloquence. I
   think of him then touching the wheel,
      remembering raw wood

he had turned whole, almost alive, in her hands,
   like a metaphor of all they knew,
      spokes, singing tines,

      sparking in the moonlight as some fabric meshed,
        knowing the machine finally was useless
          as mourning chimes,

      knowing his art no more than the rain-worn heart
        of a stone, cut hollow as a cup
          on the grindstone of time.

If a man works wood he will sweat into the grain, marking it forever.
Emerson says, "They say in Architecture, 'An arch never sleeps. . . ' ."
That is what structure in poetry means to me. I think of each line as a
small arch.

As an introduction for my book *The Fisherman's Whore*, I quoted a
line from the Anglo-Saxon poem "The Seafarer." It goes: "He who goes
on the sea longs for it forever." That is a poem of hard consequence but
the speaker imagines no other life. The one he has always lived is enough.
I don't know anybody who would willingly choose such a mean, lonely,
painful life. I've seen watermen break ice from their hands to smoke. My
friend, Henry Freeman, Jr., had to clean the winch on his father's boat. It
had clipped his father into two halves. Women have taken cunners and
bateaus into the teeth of storms, and they are incredible. They have no
raised consciousness and don't know a poem from a Poe. They do know
the whore as well or better than watermen and are, to me, singularly
beautiful in their laconic strength. I often wish they were my audience as
well as my subject. What would that mean? It would mean they would
know I am celebrating their being. That I believe the world is always
speaking necessary things to the poet with a crafty hand and ear. That
the imagination is quite literally the agent of meaning. That those women
are not the clever expedients of parlor polemic.

THE WIVES AT OLD POINT COMFORT

On the last day they wake, like knives,
all knees and ribs and teeth cutting
the fishermen free of the sheets
and the flies banging on the screens
where the summer is storming.

Each one pretends her eyes are closed
as she stares at the man she must remember

at this table, before the hated bacon,
the plate of bleeding, dazzled eggs.

In her belly she feels him rise, thinks
how his sandy hair is more breathable
than water, finer than the sand
water is always stealing in the coves.
She must remember to remember his hair.

In the darkness of that night
they rise with the fishermen and bear
to the boats a terrified, womanish odor,
women who must fall back through fields

where the leaves hiss with hot winds
and children practice the curses
a father leaves like a hand on a breast.
On the last day sorrow blisters her mouth

as she remembers loving him, turning back
at the black docks, the fish scales
everywhere, tiny jewels, egg chips
like pockets of sunlight on her legs,
transparencies she must remember always.

I am much concerned with audience. Poetry is not language. It is *a* language *made*. A unique. I call it a dialect. English departments know this. They train in approved dialects, set themselves ferreting, but do not see they are equipped only to cull artifacts. Faced with a dialect, a poem, they bite it like a coin in a swamp, then discard it. One reason so many poets sound alike. Chunks of ill-digested social concern, Saroyanistic novelty, a mania for lost daddy—what are they but programs for poetry? I don't see poetry as a team sport. And, if our audience is only us, we will get what anyone gets in a hall of mirrors.

MENDING CRAB POTS

The boy had run all the way home
from school to tell the old man
about a book he'd found which put
the whole thing in a new light:
'The beautiful sea, grandfather,
in a poem you might have written,

out there always to be touched
or swum in, or worked, or just
looked at, the way you told me.'

The old man gave the wire trap
one extra twist, like a chicken's
neck, relit his dead cigar, said
he heard the slovenly bitch still
ranted around, couldn't be got
rid of, or lived with. He slit
the head from a blowfish, stuffed
it in the mouth of the pot, grinned.
'Them poets, goddam 'em, always
in school with their white hands.'

I like what Ted Hughes says of the sea: "We know it cannot get away."
And the Seafarer knows something, too, about who can get away.
Perhaps I can make something plain about Liss and many like him. He
never learned to swim.

Liss put a forty gallon gas tank on his boat's port side and kept it filled.
When a man worked with him, tonging on the starboard side, it always
appeared he wasn't working as hard as Liss. Liss had "turned the boat
over on him."

My people don't read poems. They keep my book on their coffee tables
because their names, the name of their place, is in it. If they do read, they
say the meaning escapes them. But they always offer me more whiskey.
Edwin Muir says, "Creative Love would enjoin, not sympathy, but the
will to transcend suffering."

When I read a book of poems, I look first to see if there are poems about
rivers and oceans, and to see how the poet handled them. I will always
steal here if I can. I want to know people who, in such places, have held
the hand of Death and want to shake my hand. They have, surely, got
hold of what is vital. It is this which makes me love the poems of Richard
Hugo and James Wright, especially *Two Citizens*.

I am not in sympathy with Coleridge's Mrs. Barbauld, who wanted his
poems to make morals, but I appreciate her resistance to the meaningless.

Yet, I offer no support to the Fortune Cookie School which wants to get something out of a poem.

Yeats says, "A good writer should be so simple that he has no faults, only sins." I want to be *that* simple. I have a needlepoint in my office, done by my five-year-old son, a portrait of me. There is a man, a sun, a house, two flowers, and three tufts of grass. Plain elements which intimate little. But my figure is as tall as the house, the oblong sun sits over my head like a hat, the tuft of grass grows between my legs, I am holding a flower equal to my height, and the house is crimson. Now that is marvelous. That is a vision, a right relation. I would not trade that for Yeats. What could be plainer? What more admirably decorous?

James Whitehead is a poet I would like to meet. He says of current writing, "It has no place for grace—but there is grace in the world." Damn right. Here is a poem, "Near the Docks," which I put at the front of *The Fishermen's Whore* to say grace. When I was 11 years old I spent a day with a friend in his father's workshop loft. We struck matches on old mattresses. That night the workshop and the tools by which a man lived were burned to ashes. I hung around him, guilty, for a chance to confess. He only hummed and borrowed tools to finish a house he was building, some crab pots he could sell. His wife hung clothes. Theirs was a life against the bone, but also a life in the right relation to grace.

NEAR THE DOCKS

There was a fire in the night.
Across the street I slept among the others
as the warm ashes snowed into pines.
I slept owning nothing, a child ignorant
of the blisters of light.
But the man who owned two houses
was also fortunate, losing
neither the old one whose windows bagged
with weariness, nor the one half-built
whose roofless, green timbers
were shriving themselves all summer.

I woke and he was sitting at his stool
where I had found him each morning,
half-way between the houses,

his hands weaving the wire to a trap,
making the awkward small jerks
a fish lives by. Beyond him, his wife
already had begun to stretch the skins
of her wash in first light, and a dog
lapped from the ruts of fire trucks.
I saw how little had been changed by fire,
only the tool shed limp as a black dress
in a heap which left a new, tidy hole
in the landscape. And now I remember
seeing also, as if for the first time,
the slate grey hand of the sea, where
far off the figures of boats crossed,
wove, and sank as they burned in the sun.

I am writing away from and out of my swamp poems, beginning to
evolve a sequential poem of one family's generational descent. It starts
in present time at a funeral, pushes back through "history," and settles
up in present time in Poquoson. It's my family, but I'm not confessing.
I'm taking enormous liberties with the facts and I want to make continuous truth shine through sentimentality like a knife in a mud-puddle.
Make clear the pulse of experience. But also to discover what Niles calls
the Meulungeon (the descendents of the Lost Tribe of Virginia). Here is
the title poem of this new book.

CUMBERLAND STATION

Gray brick, ash, hand-bent railings, steps so big
it takes hours to mount them, polished oak
pews holding the slim hafts of sun, and one
splash of the *Pittsburgh Post-Gazette*. The man
who left Cumberland gone, come back, no job
anywhere. I come here alone, shaken
the way I came years ago to ride down
mountains in Big Daddy's cab. He was
the first set cold in the black meadow.

Six rows of track gleam, thinned, rippling
like water on walls where famous engines steam, half
submerged in frothing crowds with something
to celebrate and plenty to eat. One engineer takes

children for a free ride, a frolic
like an earthquake. Ash cakes their hair.
I am one of those who walked uphill
through flowers of soot to zing
scared to death into the world.

Now whole families afoot cruise South Cumberland
for something to do, no jobs, no money for bars,
the old stories cracked like wallets.

This time there's no fun in coming back. The second
Death. My roundhouse uncle coughed his youth
into a gutter. His son, the third, slid on the ice,
losing his need to drink himself
stupidly dead. In this vaulted hall
I think of all the dirt poured down
from shovels and trains and empty pockets.
I stare into the huge malignant headlamps
circling the gray walls and catch a stuttered
glimpse of faces stunned like deer on a track,
children getting drunk, shiny as Depression apples.

Churning through the inner space of this godforsaken
wayside, I feel the ground try to upchuck and I dig
my fingers in my temples to bury a child
diced on a cowcatcher, a woman smelling
alkaline from washing out the soot.
Where I stood in that hopeless, hateful room
will not leave me. The scarf of smoke I saw
over a man's shoulder runs through me
like the sored Potomac River.

Grandfather, you ask why I don't visit you
now you have escaped the ticket-seller's cage
to fumble hooks and clean the Shakespeare reels.
What could we catch? I've been sitting in the pews
thinking about us a long time, long enough to see
a man can't live in jobless, friendless Cumberland
anymore. The soot owns even the fish.

I keep promising I'll come back, we'll get out,
you and me, like brothers, and I mean it.

A while ago a man with the look of a demented cousin
shuffled across this skittery floor and snatched up
the *Post-Gazette* and stuffed it in his coat
and nobody gave a damn because nobody cares
who comes or goes here or even who steals
what nobody wants: old news, photographs
of dead diesels with ashen faces
swimming into Cumberland Station.

I'm the man who stole it and I wish you were here
to beat the hell out of me for it because
what you said a long time ago welts my face
and won't go away. I admit
it isn't mine even if it's nobody else's.
Anyway, that's all I catch this trip—bad
news. I can't catch my nephew's life, my uncle's,
Big Daddy's, or yours, or the ash-haired kids
who fell down to sleep here after the war.

Outside new families pick their way along tracks
you and I have walked home on many nights.
Every face on the walls goes on smiling,
and, Grandfather, I wish I had the guts
to tell you this is a place I hope
I never have to go through again.

In 1728 William Byrd writes in his *History of the Dividing Line Betwixt Virginia and North Carolina:* "They not only maintain their stock upon it, but get boards, shingles, and other lumber out of it in great abundance." That is what I feel about his place and mine, what I hope for in my poems.

I have been a long time discovering that if I had served in the Civil War, I would have been the wretch holding Traveller's tail, lest it disturb a gentleman. Save for Warren, I cannot love the fugitive poets. On the third night of Liss's wake, five ancient and unknown blacks sang at the back door of his house. One had sailed with him in the forties. The right kind of news has its way of getting around.

Many times I have lain on the deck of a Bugeye crossing Egg Island Bar. Hanging my head over, I delight in the hull's shadow. The boat never scares crab or fish, the shadow inevitably does. We exist among so many shadows we cannot tell which to fear. Therefore, we seldom find the conviction of consequential finality in our poems. I want to say a serious *yes* and a lovely *yes*. Here is a fishing poem which means to conclude my book, *Cumberland Station*, in those ways.

NIGHT FISHING FOR BLUES

Fortress Monroe, Virginia

The big-jawed Bluefish, ravenous, sleek muscle slamming
into banked histories of rock
   pile, hair-shaggy pier legs, drives
   each year to black Bay shallows, churns,

     fin wheels, convoys, a black army, blue

stained sequins rank after rank, fluting bloodshot
gill-flowers, sucking bitter land-water, great Ocean
Blues with belly-bones ringing like gongs.

     Tonight, not far from where Jefferson Davis

hunched in a harrowing cell, gray eyes quick
as crabs' nubs, I come back over planks
deep drummed under boots, tufts of hair

floating at my ears, everything finally right
   to pitch through tideturn and mudslur
   for fish with teeth like snapped sabers.

     In blue crescents of base lights, I cast hooks

baited with Smithfield ham: they reel, zing,
plummet, coil in corrosive swirls, bump on
scum-skinned rocks. No skin divers prowl here,

     visibility an arm's length, my visions

hand-to-hand in the line's warp. A meat-
baited lure limps through limbs nippling the muck,
silhouettes, shoots forward. A cruising Blue sentry

     catches a gray glint and strikes, setting

case-hardened barbs. Suddenly, I am not alone:
   three negroes plump down in lawn chairs, shudder-
   casting into the black pod plodding under us. One

ripples with age, a grandmotherly obelisk,

her breath puffling like a coal stove. She swivels
ponderously, chewing her dark nut, spits thick juice
like a careful chum.
When I yank the first Blue
she mumbles, her eyes roll far out on the black-
blue billowing sea-screen. I hear her canting

to Africa, a cluck in her throat, a chain

song from a fisherman's house. I cannot
understand. Bluefish are pouring at me in squads.
I haul two, three at a time, torpedos, moon-shiners,
jamming my feet into the splintering floor, battling
whatever comes. I feel like I have waited
a whole life for this minute. Like purple soles

cooling on dirt cell walls, Blues walk over

our heads, ground on back-wings, grind their teeth.
They splash rings of blue and silver around us, tiaras
of lost battalions. I can smell the salt of ocean
runners as she hollers *I ain't doing so bad
for an old queen!* No time to answer. Two

car-hoods down her descendents swing sinewy arms

in Superfly shirts, exotic butterflies: I hear them
pop beer cans, the whoosh released like stale breath
through a noose no one remembers. We hang

fast flat casts, artless, no teasing fishermen,

beyond the book-bred lures of the pristine streams,
speeded-up, centrifugal, movie machines rewound
too far, belts slipped, gears gone, momentum

hauling us back, slinging lines, winging wildly

as howitzers. Incredibly it happens: I feel
the hook hammer and shake and throw my entire weight
to dragging, as if at last I have caught the goddamdest

Blue in the Atlantic. She screams: *Oh my God!*

Four of us fumbling in beamed headlight and blue
arclight cut the hook from her face. Gnats butterfly,

nag us: I put it in deep and it must be gouged out
like a cist. When it is free, I hear Blues not yet

dead flopping softly. I tell her it is a lucky
thing she can see. She mops blood blued over
gold-lined teeth and opens her arms so her dress

billows like a caftan. She wants

nothing but to fish. I hand her her pole, then cast
as far as I can. She pumps, wings a sinker and hooks
into flashing slop and reels hard. In one instant both

our lines leap rigid as daguerreotypes; we have

caught each other but we go on for the blue blood of
ghosts that thrash in the brain's empty room.
We pull at shadows until we see there is nothing, then
sit on the shaky pier like prisoners. Coil after coil
we trace the path of Bluefish-knots backward,

unlooping, feeling for holes, giving, testing,

slapping the gnats from our skins. Harried, unbound,
we leap to be fishers. But now a gray glow
shreds with the cloud curtain, an old belly-fire

guts the night. Already the tide humps around

on itself. Lights flicker like campfires in duty windows
at Ft. Monroe. She hooks up, saying, *Sons they done
let us go.* I cast once more but nothing bites. Everywhere

a circle of Blues bleaches, stiffens

in flecks of blood. We kneel, stuff styrofoam
boxes with blankets of ice, break their backs
to keep them cold and sweet, the woman gravely
showing us what to do. By dawn the stink has passed

out of our noses. We drink beer like family.

All the way home thousands of Blues fall from my head,
falling with the grey Atlantic, and a pale veiny light
fills the road with sea-shadows that drift in figure

eights, knot and snarl and draw me forward.

WILLIAM STAFFORD

WILLIAM STAFFORD (b. Jan. 17, 1914 in Hutchinson, Kansas)
received his B.A. and M.A. from the University of
Kansas, his Ph.D. from the University of Iowa. He served
four years in various camps as a conscientious
objector during World War II. Traveling Through the Dark
(1963), his second volume of poems, won the National
Book Award. He has read his poems very widely in this
country and abroad. His home is in Lake Oswego,
Oregon, where he lives with his wife Dorothy, daughter
Barbara, and any other children home from school.
He is Professor of English at nearby Lewis and
Clark College.

(Photo of William Stafford and daughter Kit Stafford by Chris Ritter)

Making a Poem / Starting a Car on Ice

A poem is anything said in such a way or put on the page in such a way as to invite from the hearer or reader a certain kind of attention. The kind of attention that is invited will appear—sort of—in what follows.

This way of identifying a poem shies away from using content or form, or any neat means. It is not meter or rhyme, or any easily seen pattern, or any selected kind of content, or any contact with gods, or a goddess, that is crucial—it is some kind of signal to the receiver that what is going on will be a performance that merits an alertness about life right at the time of living it. You can even make something not a poem become a poem by looking at it a certain way, or listening to it a certain way. Found poems are this kind of experience. They are all around us, we come to suspect; and by a certain squint or a certain way of leaning our ears, we find them. (Those whose ears don't lean may feel free to shake them sadly now.)

Once at the University of Washington a student made me aware of this oddity in a poem. She brought into the office a big scroll that when unwound said something like "Please/ consider others/ Smoking may shorten their lives/ and may deprive them/ of your living presence"— something like that. Not having a good place to display this scroll, I turned back the top of the sheet and put a book on it so that the message hung along a bookcase by my desk. The writer told me that this was her poem for the day, and that our kind of people no longer accepted orders like "No Smoking," and that poetry should function as part of the information system for society. She said her scroll was a poem. Squinting, I saw it. (I always do.) Well, after she left another student came in. He settled in a chair by the desk, got out cigarettes, and prepared to light up. Then he saw the scroll. He hastily started to put his cigarettes away, but when I said, "It's a poem," he immediately went ahead and lighted up. He examined the scroll, through the smoke he was making, and admired it. Squinting again, I thought I saw something about what a poem is.

It might be possible to elaborate on that scene to draw lessons from it, but to do so might endanger the intuition that flowered there in the office that day. It is almost as if some intuitions survive only if they are not dissected.

But it may be all right to range around for some others; and taken together they may identify each other.

For instance, try this: If you compose a poem you start without any authority. If you were a scientist, if you were an explorer who had been to the moon, if you were a knowing witness about the content being presented—you could put a draft on your hearer's or reader's belief. Whatever you said would have the force of that accumulated background of information; and any mumbles, mistakes, dithering, could be forgiven as not directly related to the authority you were offering.

But a poet—whatever you are saying, and however you are saying it, the only authority you have builds from the immediate performance, or it does not build. The moon you are describing is the one you are creating. From the very beginning of your utterance you are creating your own authority.

Surely we all know that falsity in reading a poem and judging it in terms of the author's name. We know that the writer's past—though it may deserve commendation—is not to be used to validate the current work. A poem has to stand by itself, no matter how many poems the writer has written, no matter how many prizes the writer has won. Further, we have suffered as readers when editors choose to publish by relying on the past work of an author. There is momentum and competition for names, but these understandable influences put a strain on the more important requirement that authority depends on current performance. The adventitious influences that get into the scene are always trying to corrupt the angel in us that relates to art.

This immediate-validation requirement is a constant excitement in writing. The distinction of the artist is this working in the presence of the recording angel at all times. Put so, the life of art sounds frightening, and many people find it that way. We know the turmoil and dishonesty and pride and jealousy, and breakdown, that flourish in competitive life under such conditions of constant responsibility. But without blinking that frightening connection between performance and merit, I have impulses to make art experiences that avoid strain, avoid competition. Come to think of it, though, this may be another intuition that wouldn't survive having its wings pulled off. Let me turn instead to an actual poem, one that came to me. Lean me your ears.

Once, in the morning, I took my writing position—lying on the couch by the front window—and looked out. Two of our children were away at college. The house was quiet. I saw that I should weed the lawn. And with these preliminary thoughts I began to write—this:

> When the wind ended and we came down
> it was grass all around. One of us found
> the dirt—it was rich, black and easy.
> When it rained, we began to grow, except
> two of us caught in leaves and unable to touch
> earth, which always starts things. By late June
> we sent our own off, just as we had done, floating
> that wonderful wind that promises new land. Now
> spread low and flat, on this precious part of the world,
> but my dreams—where have they found? I wish
> them well

This is the way it went, as clearly as I can decipher the scribble of that morning—the page is full of revisions and words run up the page, and some additions. But that morning it was as lined out above. Later I squinted those lines, and began to see a poem there. Skipping the intervening steps, I want to give what resulted and was published. Then I want to put pressure on the whole operation, to link with earlier assertions.

WHISPERED INTO THE GROUND

> Where the wind ended and we came down
> it was all grass. Some of us found
> a way to the dirt—easy and rich.
> When it rained, we grew, except
> those of us caught up in leaves, not touching
> earth, which always starts things.
> Often we sent off our own
> just as we'd done, floating that
> wonderful wind that promised new land.
>
> Here now spread low, flat on this
> precious part of the world, we miss
> those dreams—and the strange old places
> we left behind. We quietly wait.
> The wind keeps telling us something
> we want to pass on to the world:
> Even far things are real.

For what it is, I want to use this poem; its weaknesses can furbish into strengths, when used aright. And for its kind of utterance I want to attempt clear assertions. First—how it draws from nearby things its onward trend, becomes a found poem amid the elements that happen to be there: the lawn, the quiet house (but home), the children away at college. It makes its move to emerge as sound—ground, down, found—, but turns away from relying on such patterns and relaxes into dirt, caught, own, done, and slows into land. Its beginning is traction on the ice between writer and reader—statements that do not demand much belief, easy claims, even undeniable progressions without need of authority. No solicitation of the reader's faith: come along if you like; don't expect much. If the reader or listener enters the poem, I want the moves to come from inside the poem, the coercion to be part of the life right there.

But now it is time to take better aim, to confess biases—or to reduce the proud assertions. Let me put it this way: in the past, a poet might make big initial claims. With the mantle accorded the artist, the poet prophesies:

Avenge, O Lord, thy slaughtered saints, whose bones . . .

And even in recent times the prophetical fervor could scat-start a poem:

I saw the best minds of my generation destroyed by madness . . .

These poems to be declaimed, are proclaimed. And many fervent voices announce themselves and make clear poems, even today. But champions now are scarce. Depletion of faith is hard to overcome. Inside the voice that makes extreme requests of us, there must be accompanying, quick validation; we must have ready proof in the lines that the author is worthy company. And even then we want to make our own judgments, from the context we share with the teller. If the voice makes extreme claims but demonstrates no quality commensurate with its demands, the poem gasps at once.

But again—this analysis begins to endanger the vagueness necessary for art. There is a distinction between workaday processes and the process that brings about poems. Writers have many things to be careful not to know—and strangely one of the things not to know is how to write. Sometimes writers who have wandered into good poems have become too adept. Auden was one. Someplace he said he feared repeating himself as the years went by, and this fear shocked me, for it undercut a view I have long cherished—that a writer is not trying for a product, but accepting sequential signals and adjustments toward an always-arriving present. To slight that readiness—even in order to avoid repetition—would be to violate the process, would be to make writing into a craft that neglected its contact with the ground of its distinction. Auden's remark sufficed for wit, but wit can blur what the poet does. And Auden's own best poems stumble into each other again and again, seeking a center that belongs there.

More congenial in its attitude toward writing is something Thomas Mann said in *A Sketch of My Life* (Knopf, 1960): "The truth is that every piece of work is a realization, fragmentary but complete in itself, of our individuality; and this kind of realization is the sole and painful way we have of getting the particular experience—no wonder, then, that the process is attended by surprises." Many remarks from writers give this kind of glimpse into how they actually feel when entering the activity; frequently they say something like, "It was only recently that I was able to write this poem." The implication is that writing is something other than just an intention and the craft to carry it out. Writing is a reckless encounter with whatever comes along.

There are worthy human experiences that become possible only if you accept successive, limited human commitments, and one such is the sustained life of writing. It is far from an austere, competitive, fastidious engagement with the best, as outsiders might think. A writer must write bad poems, as they come, amongst the better—and not scorn the "bad" ones. Finicky ways can dry up the sources. And a poem may be indictable for weaknesses, without thereby yielding itself to "correction"; there may be flaws necessary for even the faltering accomplishment embodied in the poem. To avoid the flaws might lead to one big flaw—the denying of leads that carry the writer on.

And so I have entangled myself in denying the validity of what I am doing—explaining how to start and run a poem. Well, the ice is slicker than it used to be, when the heroes gunned their motors. Actually, I like it this way. It's quieter. And for too long we have been accepting moon rocks from people who live right where we live. We all have to earn any moon we present. The only real poems are found poems—found when we stumble on things around us.

When typing out "Whispered into the Ground" cited earlier here, I began to have tremors of realization—feedback from patterns deeper even than the relation between the poem and our house, and the children away. I realized that a poem written a year ago had anticipated the arguments I was even now making:

> Where the wind ended and we came down
> it was all grass. Some of us found
> a way to the dirt, easy and rich.

A wind has ended. Some of us found a way to the dirt. It is easy and rich. It always starts things. Well, almost always.

Here are some recent poems. They were lying around the desk while these prose remarks were unfolding. These poems, I found, already illustrated points I hadn't yet thought of when I wrote them.

MY MOTHER LOOKED OUT IN THE MORNING

"Announced by an ax, Daniel Boone
opened the door"—the wild ones you told,
looking out from the timid person you were!

All was hard, clear sunlight, or else
dark shadow. You never had found
the way to live either one or the other,

But you always looked out, the fence
faithful, always to extend and
mean the understanding again,

And then the inner surprises,
the result of your wonder: a miracle!—
you were you, you were you, you were you.

Reversals live now, indoors and out,
where your children carry that house
and others, and are wise. You were simple—

Your stories ran wild: "Listen, Billy—
imagine the world. Make me real. Be my child."

ONE OF THE STORIES

A square of color on Rayl's Hill
was a place where we often walked—

there under a new-killed Indian brave
pioneers buried a child.

(Once the tough grass that strangles flowers
is broken, you can't hide what's buried—
a burst of color will mark that square
for years on the open prairie.)

Out there in the sun an outlaw man
driven from his tribe killed a girl
because he couldn't stand her tears
when he frightened her there on the hill.

The settlers found and surrounded the man
and the father killed him in rage.
All around the prairie lay.
And the settlers were afraid.

Fearful, at night, the parents dug,
and beneath the Indian brave
to protect their own they hid the girl
from hate that could tear up a grave.

My father showed us that special square
with many a flower twined
for the double burial, one above one,
where death was used as a blind.

"Bandits may kill but be innocent,
and children may die but sin:
no one but God sees all the way down,"
our parents told us then.

And for years our family tended that place
with fear, with wonder, with prayers,
where God had sprung the prairie flowers
from whosesoever grave it was.

SAYING A NAME

Someone the far side of Neahkhanie Mountain
pronounces the name. Clouds come over
for the autumn visit again.

Every summer we try to look away,
to leave the mountain alone. Things
we don't say begin to belong—live
as the days move, lie on the sand. The blue
sky touches far, forgotten waves.

Then someone looks up. It always happens,
as it should, for the world, and the gray comes back,
saving the deep floating tops of the trees,
and the rocks lower down, and saving the reckless
people who glance too high for so late
a time, and forget, and pronounce a name.

RUN SHEEP RUN

Once when we hid no one ever found us.
It all changed into this kind of world—your
picture repeated wherever I turn, but
none of them you, and I can't find my way back
    into our story.

This is how it is in our town:
our house faces north, in the yard
a few relics; I stand a long time
by the gate and imagine; it is cold; it is
evening. When the stars begin, I run
away over the snow, zigzagging
as fast as I can, but wherever I turn
is the world. It is time to give up.
Wherever the others went, this is home.

KINDS OF WINTER

It was a big one. We followed it over
the snow. Even if it made no mistakes, we
would have it. That's what The World means—
there are kinds of winter that you meet.
And that big one had met us, its big winter.

But there was a hill, and when we rounded
it the tracks were gone. We had used up
the daylight. The wind had come and

emptied our trail, back of us, ahead of us.
We looked at each other. Our winter had come.

This message I write in the shelter of the overturned
sled. Later someone may find us
and mail this letter to you. Let me tell you something:
it doesn't make any difference what anyone ever said,
here at the last, under the snow.

STEREOPTICON

This can happen. They can bring the leaves back
to the cottonwood trees, those great big rooms
where our street—as long as summer—led
to the river. From a rusty nail in the alley
someone can die, but the street go on again.

Hitler and others, those pipsqueak voices,
can twitter from speakers. I can look back
from hills beyond town, and every person
and all the alleys, and even the buildings
except the church be hidden in leaves.

This can happen, my parents laughing
because they have already won. And I can
study and grow up and look back and call "Wait!"
and run after their old green car
and be lost again.

PRIMUS ST. JOHN

PRIMUS ST. JOHN *(b. 1939 in New York City), after managing the Poetry in the Schools Program in Tacoma, Washington for two years, taught at the University of Utah. He is currently a professor of English at Portland State University in Oregon. His awards include a National Endowment for the Arts Fellowship.*

(Photo by William Stafford)

The Way the World Has Entered

I

"See what you did?" Mama says. "You woke him up, and he ain't going back to sleep."

Ernest Gaines

Seeking and composing are related. How closely I don't know. They could be siblings or just family. But, they are definitely pentecostal, commemorating the descent of some ghost on our certainty . . . reminding us that we are also occupied by tentative things, by the ephemeral. The evanescent is always upon us—in fact it is our selves, that vessel we hold to our heads and drink our life. It is the way the world has entered we seek and compose. Therefore, I am going to tell you something I often think about when I write. I think when I write, I am in an interview. I find my way by the interrogative—the who and what that underlines things, that pentecostal presence that specializes in revelation. If it is holy it is because it is always there redeeming my impulse to voice. Consequently, everything I write is an interview, and I tell you this the way you show a policeman your license, because I am going to drive on in a legal way, now, to convert this essay.

What you will encounter shortly is a conversation between me and a man named Ralston. I am sitting in a room. There is a green rug, a black chair, a desk . . . black, approximately 18 books on the desk about U. S. Diplomatic History, the top book is a deep green like the carpet. There are: one, two, three, four ceiling-to-floor bookcases in this room. The bookcases are black, the walls of the room are white. Under the double windows that are both open, is a large soft sofa. I extend my feet out in front of me and slide down in the chair like a snake. It is something my grandmother called this habit. She would say "the snake is moving again." Since I am not philosophical, we will leave that lying there and say that I am under a wool blanket—plaid because it is October and I am almost cold. Fall and early spring are my nemeses but they are good women. . . . Anyway, I am almost cold and it is important to remember that though I am sitting facing Ralston who is on the sofa taking advantage of human abandon, there is only one person in this room. One person who asks and one who answers . . .

Primus: Nothing moved so I assumed I was dreaming.
Ralston: Were you intense?

Primus: Slightly, if someone had entered the room I would have heard him . . . but no one entered.

Ralston: Were you formed?

Primus: Formed?

Ralston: Yes, had inspiration entered you, filled you . . .

Primus: Wait a minute . . . It was nothing as modern or ridiculous as all that. I sat at the table looking down at a pad. I had a pencil and no ideas—it's all kind of normal. It was like any other time I tried to write . . . a note, a letter . . . It was ordinary but I was trying to write what would become my first poem.

Ralston: What was your first poem about?

Primus: My first poem was about a "Who" as well as a "What." It was about my grandfather and something we did. We walked straight down 103rd Street to Roosevelt Avenue and caught the "El." That is he walked. I was young and when you're as young as I was then, you run with your parents. You flirt with being a leader and a follower.

We took the "El" to 74th Street and transferred downstairs to the "F" to go into Manhattan. At that time in my life we had to ride in the first car of the train so I could stare out the window of the front door into the black tunnel. I wanted to see where we were going and what signs were out there for us to follow. I wanted to see. My grandfather was always a bonus on subway trips. He worked for the subway. He had driven the trains, opened the doors, and now he worked in the booth giving change. I think he liked the new job best, because he was a retiring man.

Once, at Christmas, we asked him what would he do if he was held up. We all had a secret fear for his safety. He told us not to worry about him, he could take care of himself and all of us with "no sweat." He said, "I'd say come in, help yourself, my man, what ever I've got is yours." Then he said, "You can give anything away in life without batting an eye without really missing it, but never give away your life. That's yours."

I don't remember where we got off, but I know it was on 6th Avenue. 6th and what I don't remember, but it was almost cold and we headed over to 5th Avenue to see the St. Patrick's Day Parade. Here, I walked. I was conservative. My fingers on my left hand told me they were going to get numb, but it wasn't cold enough.

Let me tell you something else about my grandfather while we walk over to, and along 5th Avenue. My grandfather always walked on the outside of the sidewalk. I used to think, quietly, that he was weird. He said his job was to protect us, and when my grandmother walked down the street with us and he wasn't there she did the same thing. I used to think, quietly, that they were both weird.

We finally found a spot we liked and stopped. We were behind a small group of people. I couldn't get a good vista without being an all-pro middle-linebacker so my grandfather said I could climb onto his shoulders. "You're the kind of guy that makes barricades barricades, son, be careful."

I think I sat up there on his shoulders for years. And it was what I should have done. This is the meaning of ancestry, and culture and human legacy.

Ralston: Was the poem that long?

Primus: No.

Ralston: Was it good?

Primus: It was a terrible poem and a wonderful revival.

Ralston: It seems like an invasion into some wilderness area. . . . A gentle but willful trek.

Primus: I call it going back to the old neighborhood without Thomas Wolfe. It's a kind of ohhh and ahhh time—without innocence and regret.

Ralston: It's like your grandfather said, you can give away anything but your life. The pain, the disappointment are superfluous to some . . . some . . . what would we call it?

Primus: I have no name for it. I just wave my hands through the air like dots on a page. I am not philosophical.

Ralston: I would like to see the poem.

Primus: No you wouldn't. Believe me it was bad. Some waste basket inherited a heavy load. But the poem, or the experience, or the process taught me, spoke to me. I discovered an invasion into myself that I would love to endure over and over again. Returning day after day the way you come home to the family. This poetry thing exposed me to a loved one that I was unaware of. One more thing here. For me it is a non-judgmental place. As wild as it is, it is non-judgmental.

Ralston: What do you mean?

Primus: It (the process of poetry and the poem) has learned the trick of quiet, of absorption, acceptance of more of one's impulses than we will entertain in other situations. It thrives on confrontation and consequently it affirms more. I used to think that my tracks melt back into the earth when the snow is gone. And they probably do. But something pentecostal keeps them warm for as long as we left them. And the poem brings them back, and the painting and the novel, maybe even the plumber and the dentist bring them back . . . let's not be effete about all this . . . at least they do so for me.

Ralston: You're not philosophical (smile).

Primus: (smile) No. I think we have a level of response that survives despite ourselves that isn't, as Bill Stafford says, wishy-washy. It can draw a bead on anything, cite down on anything, joy or pain, our worst pain and say like Ifeanyi Menkiti:

> And there was this adult pain
> Down deep in the soul
> Because of which was laughter. . . .

Like I said there is a lyrical fingering of the strings of things that invades beyond judgment to beauty. And looka here, man. I like it. That's me . . . That's me.

I don't want to suggest that all this occurred at once.

Ralston: But you do want to say it occurred on the same spot—revisited?

Primus: Yes.

Ralston: You do want to say that the process is a communion?

Primus: Yes.

II

The conversation [Logos] which the soul holds with herself in considering of anything. . . . The soul when thinking appears to me to be just talking—asking questions of herself and answering them, affirming and denying. And when she has arrived at a decision . . . this is called her opinion. I say, then, that to form an opinion is a word spoken,—I mean, to oneself and in silence, not aloud to another.

Socrates

Ralston: And soon, I got up. Looking out the window, I noticed how hard summer was burning away, and turning to him, noticed how something with wings had entered his heart. I remembered, reader, seeing a hawk circling a farm in the same place for a long time. . . . Life is what inspiration is.

Primus: Kazantzakis has a line that goes:

> I keep my head unhooked and play with all the world.
> I sit enthroned on freedom . . .   (I said, suddenly).

Looking at that broadleaf maple outside shedding its leaves, recalls that sense of dignity.

Ralston: Why does dignity concern you?

Primus: It is a fascinating impulse. I wonder if people want power or dignity.

Ralston: You like to do that . . .

Primus: What?

Ralston: Not what, why. Read "Biological Light," a minute, I want to ask you something.

Primus:

BIOLOGICAL LIGHT

We live here to eat;
Things stare at us.
Those things eat.
We call all of this hunger
The world.
Why?
Because we live here . . .

All over the world
Morning light is still happening
Like God.
It is so hard to tell
Who eats the plants first—
        Insect or Crepuscular.

The wind feels the smallest birds
It's got
If that is what we are,
It's not a lot—
Here comes the fox.

Noon: circles, logically—
Like the hawk.
God moves the rim around
Until the fox is in.

Now, the fox is the hawk
And all the small things he ate
Believe him . . .

I have come here late;
The deer look like they have gone,
But worms remind me
More is going on.

Gradually, memory sets the table back,
I have come from,
Across the water, as far back,
As I can know.
Friends there have eaten me;
Now, I stand here, that torn by hate
As I myself have eaten them.

Late:
The owl says *whoooo*
For what more will surely come.
Finally, I am older—
But not enough—
Surrounded by what I know
Is falling back toward the grass
More like luck than hope . . .

I am just lying here,
Thinking this in my sleep—
How cold it is outside.
If we were fish where it is very dark
It would all be so easy—
Light would come from the dead things that we eat.

Ralston: There is a surrender here that seems religious. Has anyone ever
asked you if you were religious in response to this poem?

Primus: (smile) Yes.

Ralston: What did you say?

Primus: I didn't want to say anything. But questions have a way of eating
away your lining. I chose the oblique direction, and responded,
"not particularly."

When I was writing the poem, it occurred to me to mention God.
You know, when I was a kid, I was very impressed by the ol' folks.
You'd hear them say, "Lord, Lord, Lord, what's going to happen
next." You remember things like that forever, and on the weary
days, you reach out for that sound inheritance. It was easy to do

here. The voice was low-keyed, feigning a weariness, leaning towards a kind of reverent brooding. I didn't have to mention God. I could have been more relevant and ridden off into some Nietzschean apocalypse. But the voice dictated or struggled forward with a perspective that asked to be heard. And I felt a responsibility to listen. And all this light happening was a benediction, a ceremony by which things are set aside to confer the advantages that are here.

I don't know if I am religious, but I sure ain't hep. I like to think of myself as an old fashioned young dude.

Besides, the process of writing is pushy and educational. You start, and suddenly you realize you've created a mood—a spirit about things. That spirit then suggests or demands. Suddenly you find an opportunity to be obliged to a perspective. Well, since I would like to be as responsible as I should be about life, I own up. I accept my outside and my inside.

If I'm lucky, I come away from the experience with a valuable contact. Even if I'm not lucky I find that I'm unexplainably rich. Is this religious?

Ralston: Yes. It's strange how surrender sometimes works. By the way, what is Biological Light?

Primus: You really should ask my wife. She understands these things. My sense of science is all hear-say.

I came to my unenlightened position at an aquarium in Tacoma, Washington. It had rained for forty days and forty nights, and when it stopped, and I saw the same old world was here, I decided to appreciate it a little bit more. So, I took the family to the zoo— the aquarium's in the zoo. Well, for me, appreciation is a combination of looking, brooding, and osmosis. No tricky stuff.

I have a way of being not too bright at intelligent places. I'm the type that wanders through museums and zoos staring at—not reading—plaques.

Joanne, on the other hand is a meaning vulture. She ascertains with a courage and conviction that's not in my gene pool. She's beautiful! Consequently, I can say she educates me and if I seem deprived—it's her fault. But I sense a good wisdom in her presence.

Well, it came to pass that we stopped before a huge plaque. I knew I'd never read it, so I picked out a word or two at some point in the middle of language to procrastinate with. I could tell when I turned to glance at "Big J's" eyes, she was reading again. I turned back to my words; they were Biological Light. I was impressed—

tortoises win sometimes. Off I went brooding. Later, I asked "Jo Annie" for the answer. She told me what it meant and that's why I said my definition is based on hear-say.

Ralston: Well, just what is your information, my man?

Primus: It's a kind of transformation process. Light shines on vegetation. The vegetation absorbs it and is eaten by fish. The fish have the light. That is—the top fish. Fish at the bottom of the ocean get it when surface plants and fish filter down. Something like that.

Ralston: Remind me to take you to the moon someday.

Primus: (smile) Well, this is what I made of it. You eat light—right. And the West has this thing for allegories in the caves of things, and light as truth. Okay, you eat truth. You devour it. It comes righteously and cannibalistically. I mean, you're in the zoo with a strong commitment to illiteracy so you have to do something. That's Biological Light.

Imagine, here we are picking the bones of our friends clean, proud of our light imagery. I picked friends because it conjures up the genteel. Western Civilization is into the genteel mode of friendship, and I wanted to acknowledge that deficiency.

Ralston: You're also into Day and Night, Sky and Underworld, too.

Primus: Yes, I'm one of those limited black writers with a conspicuously absent sense of rhythmical and imagistic sophistication in my poetry bones. But, I'm slightly cooler on the dance floor. Therefore, to realize this argument, the poem investigates some aspects of interracial consciousness. I try to be honest though, regarding some of the features of light.

The important thing for me is allowing the speaker in the poem to discover things about life and grow in respect for the world—the inner and outer world. Also, to be able to fail with a grace that encourages renewal. I think the twentieth century, and perhaps America in particular, needs a good honest dose of failure coupled with belief in life. A kind of non-either/or confirmation. Too many American poets, men and women, have a way of grabbing for their genitals or oriental philosophy the minute they confront the outskirts of pain.

Ralston: You know, there is an irony here. Good work requires good failure—not devastation—just failure.

Primus: Well, I would agree and return to our fingering with the idea of dignity. I think we need to develop the dignity to be human and not assign our fears to our disenfranchised. I believe in confronting things like our failure and our evil. Owning them, and like that broadleaf maple outside making them rich and provocative before we release them. The spirit will return, but the nature of that depends on the quality of our autumn. Have you ever seen a maple fret about its genitals. No, it's too righteous . . . too righteous.

Ralston: Maybe we are afraid of fatality.

Primus: But everything's fatal. Poems, for one, are fatal acts but they are fun too.

Ralston: Do you believe that is true for all of them?

Primus: Yes. For me.

Ralston: Even your "Violence of Pronoun" . . .

VIOLENCE OF PRONOUN

I

Loving came her way,
    vicious.
It rose up
From the earth,
And made her father's hand,
Around her throat,
A bird of prey
And carried her away—
    In mind
Like a limp patient.
He was not drunk
It is worse.
In this world,
We cannot feel . . .

II

In my sociology class—
    For understanding
Black Folks—
They tried to understand
Our homes—
    Like buckshot.
What we have done,
    To love
Is unforgivable.

They took out rakes,
And treated us like dirt
It was so perfect
They asked for grades.

III

Leaving people out of this—
I can forgive.
I married her, anyway,
And in the church,
When I unfolded her hand,
    I saw
In her palm
The way she would die . . .
Leaping out of democracy,
Through some weird window,
    white
With the wilderness of God—
1965—Memorial Day.
And I went on, crazy
    at first
And crazy even now
For being so unmilitant . . .

IV

What I told that class,
(You know) they said it hurt.
"It is our innocence
That makes us vicious."

Primus: Yes. The act of writing is fun, is joy for me. And the personae come to understand a meaning of funny. Funny, in its sense of representing an awareness of differing from the ordinary—and perhaps the expected. Funny, in its sense of suspicion, in its sense of embracing the perplexing, and in its sense of viewing with an eccentricity.

It is fun and it is funny. Yet it says no to the inappropriate. I listened to the militants in the '60s and '70s and I listened to my parents, and I chose to be alive in my human complexity the way my family suggested. If the war ends, I'll need a rich life to build a rich peace. And if the war never ends I'll need a rich life to endure with dignity. After all, this story we are living is about "the features of our face" under the stars.

Ralston: But what about the anger and the sorrow?

Primus: I was of the understanding, and I still am, that our humanity is what we are—and we are a complete people. We are everything. So I'll own my anger and my sorrow. I'll confront and engage it, and I will attempt a lyricism to transform it with the grace of that tree outside. I will affirm and transform. I would rather not be one of those Americans who cannot tell the truth. I have watched the effects of the lie enough. Our Arts and Sciences need to rediscover the honesty of substance over technique.

Ralston: And what about this fun?

Primus: I will try to be reverently joyous, and hope that our nouns will forgive our transgressions . . .

A SPLENDID THING GROWING

Chair:
It is the name of me.
The ending of my arms
And the ending of my legs
Mean nothing.
I cannot creak enough.

Dish:
It is the emptiness.
I am going to breathe
Over the edge,
And feel—
Louder.

Vase:
And water are righteousness.
So flowers are given,
So dance,
And wind
    within us.

Cup:
It is the round place.
So is intention.
So is our drinking.

Godliness:
That is knife.
Given decision.
Given harshness
      like cut.

Table:
Be with me
On this earth.
It is set with our flesh.

Come closer:
Like carpet
And trust.
Dust in us!
Everything woven.

Drapes:
They are disturbances,
And thinking.
Flapping makes no sense,
But storms.

Doom:
It is always left.
At night,
It is a splendid thing growing.
It shows us nothing.

Oh Nouns! Forgive Us.

LUCIEN STRYK

Lucien Stryk (b. April 7, 1924 in Chicago) attended
Indiana University, the Sorbonne, University of Maryland,
and the University of London. He spent 1956–58 and
1962–63 in Japan as a lecturer at Yamaguchi University
and Niigata University, and has distinguished himself not
only as a poet but as a translator of Asian texts. He is
currently Professor of English at Northern Illinois
University in DeKalb.

(Photo by Barry Stark)

Making Poems

I

"The thoughts expressed by music," wrote Mendelssohn in 1842, "are not too vague for words, but too precise." Replace "music" with "poetry" and, perhaps paradoxically, considering of what poems are made, you have a way of seeing into the difficulty of drawing conclusions about the nature of art. There are days when I feel that the main thing, all else equal, is what the poet has to say; other days, that it is his craftsmanship, not what he's trying to express, that distinguishes him. What colors my view on any given day, tipping one way or the other, may be far more interesting than the whole issue of aesthetics, which is after all the sphere of aestheticians, not artists. All theories on art strike me as collections of truisms, though some ("The poet's theme dictates structure and is at the same time modified by it," might be one) seem pretty sound. Perhaps under the circumstances, and in spite of the great difficulty, the practicing artist should be willing, when called upon, to try to explain what it is he's after and how he goes about attempting to achieve it. That accepted, in what follows I shall try to give as clear an account as possible of the steps which led to where I am now as a maker of poems.

Some, aware of my work as a translator of Zen poetry, seem to feel that my poems are much affected by that interest, in content as well as structure. I believe they are right. Anyone serious about a discipline like Zen learns soon enough that much of his life, certainly any art he may practice, is being changed by it. When as a visiting lecturer there I began translating Zen texts in Japan, I asked the Zen master Taigan Takayama whether the philosophy might be useful to an artist. As an enlightened man (he is one of the most distinguished young masters in Japan) he did not show indignation, but he was most forceful in letting me know that Zen was not something to be "used" by anyone, including the artist, and that its arts were nothing more than expressions of the Zen spirit. That was the first "reprimand" I received. There was another, at the hands of the Zen master Tenzan Yasuda, of a more serious nature. I often went to his temple, the Joeiji, for the superb rock garden laid down by Sesshu, one of Japan's greatest painters who had been a priest at the Joeiji in the fifteenth century. In interviewing the master for the volume *Zen: Poems, Prayers, Sermons, Anecdotes, Interviews*, I said some very stupid things about the rock garden. Tenzan Yasuda was patient, but finally said (I quote from the interview), "In order to appreciate his garden fully you must have almost as much insight as Sesshu himself. This, needless to say, very few possess. Ideally one should sit in Zen for a long period before looking at the garden; then one might be able to look at it, as the old saying goes, 'with the navel.' "

Even as those words were being spoken I felt acute self-disgust, and resolved to try to overcome the vanity which had led me to utter empty phrases about something which I had not even "seen," let alone understood (the Sixth Patriarch of Zen, the Chinese master Hui-neng, insisted on "pure seeing"—one must not look *at* things, but *as* things). A few nights later, while working on a conventionally structured poem set in Sesshu's rock garden, the sort of piece with which I'd already filled two "well received" but unsatisfactory books, I remembered not only Taigan Takayama's reprimand but Tenzan Yasuda's specific comments on my "view" of the garden. Suddenly I became aware, *saw* with the greatest clarity: my failing in poetry was the result in great part of a grave misunderstanding concerning the very purpose of art. The Zen masters who had written the poems I was translating did not think of themselves as "poets" at all; rather they were attempting to express in verse nothing less than the Zen spirit—and the results were astonishing. The poems, without any pretension to "art," were among the finest I had ever read, intense, compact, rich in spirit. Takayama and Yasuda were right.

Working for hours without a break, I transformed the poem I had been writing on the garden, ridding it of "filling," breaking down rigidly regular stanzas, a welter of words, to a few "image units" of around two and one-half lines, while keeping to a constant measure, the short line throughout being of the same syllabic length. In fact, though unintended, the stanzaic unit I came up with was in length and feeling very close to the haiku, and at its best as compact as the short Zen poems I was translating. Perhaps the fact that the "unit" was made up consistently of just so many lines, so controlled, was a matter of chance, the result simply of the way eye and ear, projecting my needs, meshed. I suppose anything leading to, or the result of, deep concentration might have worked as well, but fortuitous or not I was convinced that I had made, for myself, a profound discovery, and that henceforth I might work as an artist.

In the weeks following I wrote seven more pieces about Sesshu's garden, yet given the challenge and because I wanted the sequence to be the very best I could make it, it took a few years to achieve what seemed to me altogether satisfactory versions of what eventually became:

ZEN: THE ROCKS OF SESSHU

I

What do they think of
    Where they lean
Like ponderous heads, the rocks?—

In prankish spring, ducks
    Joggling here
And there, brushing tails,

Like silly thoughts shared,
    Passed from head
To head? When, gong quavering

About a ripened sky, we
    Up and go,
Do they waken from a dream of flesh?

II

In the Three Whites of
    Hokusai—
Fuji, the snow, the crane—

What startles is the black: in
    The outline
Of the mountain, the branch-tips

Piercing the snow, the quills of
    The crane's wing:
Meaning impermanence.

Here, in stainless air, the
    Artist's name
Blazes like a crow.

III

Distance between the rocks,
    Half the day
In shadow, is the distance

Between man who thinks
   And the man
Who thinks he thinks: wait.

Like a brain, the garden,
   Thinking when
It is thought. Otherwise

A stony jumble, merely that,
   Laid down there
To stud our emptiness.

IV

Who calls her butterfly
   Would elsewhere
Pardon the snake its fangs:

In the stony garden
   Where she flits
Are sides so sharp, merely

To look gives pain. Only
   The tourist,
Kodak aimed and ready for

The blast, ship pointing for the
   Getaway,
Dare raise that parasol.

V

To rid the grass of weed, to get
   The whole root,
Thick, tangled, takes a strong mind

And desire—to make clean, make pure.
   The weed, tough
As the rock it leaps against,

Unless plucked to the last
   Live fiber
Will plunge up through dark again.

The weed also has the desire
   To make clean,
Make pure, there against the rock.

VI

It is joy that lifts those pigeons to
    Stitch the clouds
With circling, light flashing from underwings.

Scorning our crumbs, tossed carefully
    To corners
Of the garden, beyond the rocks,

They rose as if summoned from
    The futile
Groveling our love subjects them to.

Clear the mind! Empty it of all that
    Fixes you,
Makes every act a pecking at the crumb.

VII

Firmness is all: that mountain beyond the
    Garden path,
Watch how against its tawny slope

The candled boughs expire. Follow
    The slope where
Spearheads shake against the clouds

And dizzy the pigeons circling on the wind.
    Then observe
Where no bigger than a cragstone

The climber pulls himself aloft
    As by the
Very guts: firmness is all.

VIII

Pierced through by birdsong, stone by stone
    The garden
Gathered light. Darkness, hauled by ropes

Of sun, entered roof and bough. Raised from
    The temple
Floor where, stiff since cockcrow,

Blown round like Buddha on the lotus,
    He began
To write. How against that shimmering,

On paper frail as dawn, make poems?
   Firm again,
He waited for the rocks to split.

There were other poems to work on, and getting rid of much, over-
hauling what remained of a bulky manuscript, I finished what I have
always considered to be my first real book *Notes for a Guidebook*
(though it was the third published and limited to a special type of poem:
it does not include, for example, "Zen: the Rocks of Sesshu," which I
saved for my next volume *The Pit and Other Poems*). That was in 1965,
the same year the first volume of Zen translations, done along with my
Japanese friend Takashi Ikemoto, was brought out. No coincidence, for
the translation of those profound and moving poems and the making of
my own new pieces went on together for a long time. And it's been
that way since: *The Pit and Other Poems* (1969) was written for the
most part while I was at work on the books *World of the Buddha* (1968)
and *After Images: Zen Poems of Shinkichi Takahashi* (1970); the most
recent collection *Awakening* was composed while I was at work on *Zen
Poems of China and Japan: The Crane's Bill*, and the books were published only months apart in 1973.

That my poems owe much to the Zen aesthetic is undeniable, yet they
owe as much surely to the many and various things which make up
the life of a Midwestern American—husband, father, teacher—in our
time, something perhaps most evident in *Awakening* (and when I deal
with the poems of others in the anthology *Heartland: Poets of the Midwest*, the second edition of which, *Heartland II*, has just been completed)
and which I have tried to explain in the interviews done with me, as in
Chicago Review, #88, 1973. It would be very disappointing to learn that
because of my interest in Asian philosophy, and the themes and settings
of some of my poems, my work was read as that of someone who had
gone "bamboo." I believe not only in the need to "hide traces," an
invisible art, but as much in the wisdom of hiding sources. "South" is a
typical poem:

SOUTH

Walking at night, I always return to
   the spot beyond
the cannery and cornfields where

a farmhouse faces south among tall trees.
   I dream a life
there for myself, everything happening

in an upper room: reading in sunlight,
    talk, over wine,
with a friend, long midnight poems swept

with stars and a moon. And nothing
    being savaged,
anywhere. Having my fill of that life,

I imagine a path leading south
    through corn and wheat,
to the Gulf of Mexico! I walk

each night in practice for that walk.

II

T. S. Eliot in an unpublished lecture on English letter writers, quoted by F. O. Matthiessen in *The Achievement of T. S. Eliot*, says something which for me virtually sums up the poet's ideal, one very close to the "less is more" aesthetic of Zen. Eliot refers to a passage in one of D. H. Lawrence's letters which runs: "The essence of poetry with us in this age of stark and unlovely actualities is a stark directness, without a shadow of a lie, or a shadow of deflection anywhere. Everything can go, but this stark, bare, rocky directness of statement, this alone makes poetry, to-day." Eliot's comment:

> This speaks to me of that at which I have long aimed, in writing poetry; to write poetry which should be essentially poetry, with nothing poetic about it, poetry standing naked in its bare bones, or poetry so transparent that we should not see the poetry, but that which we are meant to see through the poetry, poetry so transparent that in reading it we are intent on what the poem *points at*, and not on the poetry, this seems to me the thing to try for. To get *beyond poetry*, as Beethoven, in his later works, strove to get *beyond music*.

To get "beyond poetry," then, to avoid the hateful evidence of our will to impress (thereby perhaps losing that ambition), those handsprings and cartwheels, the heavy breathing down the line, so common to "early work" done at whatever age—the escape from such vulgarity—is the study of a lifetime. It can be furthered by a discipline like Zen, but everything uniquely Western leading to a like realization will of course do as well. A man's poems should reveal the full range of his life, and hide nothing except the art behind them.

As much admiration as I have for a number of English-speaking poets, I am very strongly affected by the work of—ranging both East and West —Shinkichi Takahashi and Zbigniew Herbert, precisely because their poems appear to give the totality of their lives. We may not know our neighbors, but such poets can become our intimates. The fact that some of the poets I love write in other tongues is fundamentally of little importance, for they have been translated well (though as his translator, I should not make such a claim for the poems of Shinkichi Takahashi!). Never have so many poets turned to translation, and all of us stand to gain by the collective energy and dedication, but I admit readily that there are accompanying dangers and that something very close to "translationese" is too often in evidence.

The range and swell of one of the poems of Theodore Roethke's "North American Sequence," the superb concisions of his earlier "green-house" poems, are unlikely to be matched in the translations of even the greatest modern poets. And some of the greatest, Rilke among them, have sometimes been very poorly served, with almost criminal effect. A foreign poet is, after all, only as good as his best translator. Still, to deny ourselves the profound satisfactions of the best foreign poetry, for whatever reason, to hover timorously above those deeps out of some theoretical fear, is to cut off a source of major creative growth. Often foreign poetry offers something unique: all sensitive people, for example, felt strongly about the reports of Buddhist monks burning themselves to death in Viet Nam—the ultimate protest against that insane war, a protest not condoned by Buddhism, but one powerful in its effect on the world as a whole. No response to such acts by Western writers could have been as complex, as devastatingly right as Shinkichi Takahashi's in his poem about a fellow Buddhist, "Burning Oneself to Death":

BURNING ONESELF TO DEATH

That was the best moment of the monk's life.
Firm on a pile of firewood
With nothing more to say, hear, see,
Smoke wrapped him, his folded hands blazed.

There was nothing more to do, the end
Of everything. He remembered, as a cool breeze
Streamed through him, that one is always
In the same place, and that there is no time.

Suddenly a whirling mushroom cloud rose
Before his singed eyes, and he was a mass

Of flame. Globes, one after another, rolled out,
The delighted sparrows flew round like fire balls.

In translating that poem I was put to a grave test, for the responsibility was awesome, the sort felt, I imagine, by the translator of one of Zbigniew Herbert's poems about World War II Resistance fighters in Poland. As I think back to its source, in my experience, I am certain that my work on poems like Takahashi's, my reading of Herbert and Char, among other foreign writers, lay behind the making of this poem:

LETTER TO JEAN-PAUL BAUDOT, AT CHRISTMAS

Friend, on this sunny day, snow sparkling
everywhere, I think of you once more,
how many years ago, a child Resistance

fighter trapped by Nazis in a cave
with fifteen others, left to die, you became
a cannibal. Saved by Americans,

the taste of a dead comrade's flesh foul
in your mouth, you fell onto the snow
of the Haute Savoie and gorged to purge yourself,

somehow to start again. Each winter since
you were reminded, vomiting for days.
Each winter since you told me at the Mabillon,

I see you on the first snow of the year
spreadeagled, face buried in that stench.
I write once more, Jean-Paul, though you don't

answer, because I must: today men do far worse.
Yours in hope of peace, for all of us,
before the coming of another snow.

I spoke of the responsibility felt when I was working on the Takahashi poem, but I felt an even greater when composing the piece about my friend, to the "experience" itself, one I wanted to share with (impose on?) as many as possible. I knew that in order to do so I would have to get "beyond poetry," put down without faking the truth of a young man's pain, which had nothing literary about it and was felt acutely over the years. A pain I was asked to share, and still do.

III

In response to the question (in the *Chicago Review* interview mentioned above), "Does art do anything more than manifest moments of revelation?" I say something which relates not only to poems I am always hoping to write but also to those which most move me as a reader:

It extends the imagination; more than anything else it does that. Perhaps the greatest poetry extends and directs it, but all fine poetry does extend, enlarge it. It makes us more than we have ever been. Really important poetry affects the imagination in something like a permanent way; it alters it. If we see the imaginative process (as perceivers or readers) as being constantly acted upon or acting itself, then those things which touch it have varying results. By some, the imagination is substantially affected; by others hardly at all, and of course the question is whether the latter are works of art. Once, in other words, you have read *Hamlet* as it should be read, you are no longer the same person. The possibilities of life have been altered, have been magnified. You read certain poems, they can be rather simple poems, in many ways. . . . I think a good example might be Blake's "London." It's a short poem that reveals, tremendously, a quality of life. When that happens, art takes on a kind of moral grandeur. And I choose as an example a short lyric poem because I think it would suggest what might be the hope of a poet like myself; I want, as a writer, to *reveal* in such a way, hardly with the expectation of achieving a poem like "London," but nevertheless it offers an aesthetic ideal. . . . What I'm saying, I suppose, is that after reading "London" . . . I have a feeling that my view of that time and place is crystallized by the poem. It has, thus, historical importance. Whatever London was for Blake, and many others, is given, contained in, that poem. Now, I think this is what art should do. . . . When art can do this, it takes on a dimension that we sometimes forget it is capable of having. But one should not forget. A poet should never write without the vision that such things have been done, that men have written *Hamlets* and poems like "London," because if he forgets that such things have been done, his work can become trivial. These things stand as warnings, as much as examples. Because by great works, the artist is warned: he cannot afford to use his art for unworthy purposes.

If it is true that, however full the imagination, what the poet experiences fixes the range of his art, then we should not expect him to be touching constantly the depths and the heights. He is often content to be somewhere between, unaware of the distinctions, boundaries set down about him, making some things more important than others. Poetry not being producible, it sometimes just comes, the result of miraculous convergences, the perfect meshing of eye, ear and heart. Some of my poems (the title poem of *The Pit and Other Poems* is a good example) have taken many years to complete; others—and for this I do not think less of them—have been written almost on the spot. I shall never forget wheeling around on my bike and speeding home to get "Étude" down, its music clear in my head:

ÉTUDE

I was cycling by the river, back and forth,
    Umbrella up against the
        Rain and blossoms.

It was very quiet, I thought of Woolworth
    Globes you shake up snowstorms in.
        Washed light slanted

Through the cherry trees, and in a flimsy house
    Some youngster practiced Chopin.
        I was moving

With the current, wheels squishing as the music
    Rose into the trees, then stopped,
        And from the house

Came someone wearing too much powder, raincape
    Orchid in the light. Middle-aged,
        The sort you pass

In hundreds everyday and scarcely notice,
    The Chopin she had sent
        Up to those boughs,

Petals spinning free, gave her grace no waters
    Would reflect, but I might
        Long remember.

As most poets I have been much affected by the other arts, painting and sculpture especially, and along with my involvement in Zen has come a deepening appreciation of *sumie*, the monochromic black/white scroll painting associated with it. Perhaps nothing could illustrate better my turning Eastward and what it has meant to me than the differences— technically, in attitude—between two of my poems, written years apart and dealing with art and the life of the maker. Bartolommeo Ammannati (1511–92), when he was past seventy, wrote in "To the Academy of Design in Florence": "Beware, for God's sake, as you value your salvation, lest you incur and fall into error that I have incurred in my works when I made many of my figures entirely nude." Here is, from *Notes for a Guidebook*, a poem about his most important work:

THE FOUNTAIN OF AMMANNATI

Below the pigeon-spotted seagod
The mermen pinch the mermaids,
And you shopgirls eat your food.

No sneak-vialed aphrodisiac
Can do—for me, for you—what
Mermen pinching mermaids in a whack

Of sunlit water can. And do.
These water-eaten shoulders and these thighs
Shall glisten though your gills go blue,

These bones will never clatter in the breath.
My dears, before your dust swirls either up
Or down—confess: this world is richly wet.

And consider: there is a plashless world
Outside this stream-bright square
Where girls like you lie curled

And languishing for love like mine.
And you were such as they
Until ten sputtering jets began

To run their ticklish waters down your
Spine. Munch on, my loves, you are but
Sun-bleached maidens in a world too poor

To tap the heart-wells that would flow,
And flow. You are true signorine
Of that square where none can go

> And then return. Where dusty mermen
> Parch across a strand of sails and spars,
> And dream of foamy thighs that churn.

By such works, I appear to be saying, man is made to feel his insignificance: how pitiable those shopgirls against the mermaids. Whatever its worth as poetry, "The Fountain of Ammannati" is a piece which examines one of life's profound discrepancies, measures a distance between its realities and ideals. Swirling and clashing, it makes a harsh judgment. Perhaps the most, or least, that one can say about it is that it is a young man's poem.

A growing awareness necessitates a changing language, a greater seriousness an altered structure. Just as at fifty a man has the face he has earned, the lineaments of his poems reveal the range and depth of his spiritual life. Simply by surviving I have become a middle-aged poet, and as the result of many things which have made that survival possible, this is where I am now:

> AWAKENING
> *Homage to Hakuin, Zen Master, 1685–1768*
>
> I
>
> Shoichi brushed the black
> on thick.
> His circle held a poem
> like buds
> above a flowering bowl.
>
> Since the moment of my
> pointing,
> this bowl, an "earth device,"
> holds
> nothing but the dawn.
>
> II
>
> A freeze last night, the window's
> laced ice flowers, a meadow drifting
> from the glacier's side. I think of Hakuin:
>
> "Freezing in an icefield, stretched
> thousands of miles in all directions,
> I was alone, transparent, and could not move."

Legs cramped, mind pointing
like a torch, I cannot see beyond
the frost, out nor in. And do not move.

III

I balance the round stone
    in my palm,
turn it full circle,

slowly, in the late sun,
    spring to now.
Severe compression,

like a troubled head,
    stings my hand.
It falls. A small dust rises.

IV

Beyond the sycamore
dark air moves
westward—

smoke, cloud, something
wanting a name.
Across the window,

my gathered breath,
I trace
a simple word.

V

My daughter gathers shells
where thirty years before
I'd turned them over, marveling.

I take them from her,
make, at her command,
the universe. Hands clasped,

marking the limits of
a world, we watch till sundown
planets whirling in the sand.

VI

Softness everywhere,
snow a smear,
air a gray sack.

Time. Place. Thing.
Felt between
skin and bone, flesh.

VII

I write in the dark again,
rather by dusk-light,
and what I love about

this hour is the way the trees
are taken, one by one,
into the great wash of darkness.

At this hour I am always happy,
ready to be taken myself,
fully aware.

LEWIS TURCO

LEWIS TURCO *(b. 1934 in Buffalo, N.Y.) grew up in Meriden, Connecticut and began publishing poems nationally at nineteen. He studied at the University of Connecticut and at the University of Iowa. He is currently Professor of English and Director of the Writing Arts Program at the State University of New York College at Oswego, where he has taught since 1965.*

(Photo by Clarence Premo)

Sympathetic Magic

I

Some preliminaries.

Several years back I was asked to write a comment on my work for a biographical dictionary. I said, "I regard myself as a formalist in the broadest sense of the word, not in the traditional sense, meaning perhaps an accentual-syllabic metrist; rather, in the experimental sense, meaning that the poem is the product of the whole poet, including his mind, bent on giving coherent language form to the human experience. I can only quote and echo the composer Benjamin Britten, who said, 'I try to write as Stravinsky has written and Picasso has painted. They were the men who freed music and painting from the tyranny of the purely personal. They passed from manner to manner as a bee passes from flower to flower. I try to do the same. Why should I lock myself inside a narrow personal idiom?' "

I am a rather orderly-minded person. I keep and file everything; my books are arranged alphabetically, grouped according to subject, and catalogued. However, my working surfaces are always cluttered and stacked with debris, except for brief periods when I attack the mounds and clear them away. Perhaps this is significant. At any rate, during one of these frenzies recently I disinterred from my desk this note I had written to myself, or to the shadows of the cavern: "I see the poet as a *writer*. If he's got a philosophy, that's fine. But he ain't no priest, and he ain't no prophet, and he ain't no wild old man of the woods."

When I was eighteen and serving in the Navy, I made the conscious decision to attempt to become a poet. I sent a poem to the old *American Poetry Magazine*. I received a rejection from the editor, Star Powers (!), that taught me my first great lessons. The poem, of course, was an egopoem, and Star said, "I would eliminate the 'I do not know.' Readers do not care whether you know or not—they like to decide the answer for themselves, and arrive at their own conclusions."

She said, further, "All beginners write like this at first, and poetry, like all enterprises in life, goes through stages—this is one of them. Read more modern, emulate the eccentrics for a while, and finally you will emerge with a fresh, original style of your own." She recommended some books to me—a theoretical treatise, a practical book of exercises, some anthologies, all of which I bought and worked with in my spare time at the barracks. Shortly thereafter, she accepted for publication, while I was still eighteen, the first two poems I saw in print in a little magazine.

This all sounds so very rational, and one might begin to assume that I believe learning to write poetry is some sort of computer programming system. But I am the son of a minister who attempted to find God by seeking to understand himself. I am, further, an occasional anthropological kibitzer who was, and I am still, fascinated by an article, "Man— One of Evolution's Mistakes?" that appeared in the *New York Times Magazine* on October 19, 1969. The author, Arthur Koestler, quotes Dr. Paul D. MacLean:

> "Man finds himself in the predicament that nature has endowed him essentially with three brains which, despite great differences in structure, must function together and communicate with one another. The oldest of these three brains is basically reptilian. The second has been inherited from the lower mammals, and the third is a late mammalian development [the neo-cortex], which has made man peculiarly man. Speaking allegorically of these three brains within a brain, we might imagine that when the psychiatrist bids the patient to lie on the couch, he is asking him to stretch out alongside a horse and a crocodile."

That is, to me, an amazing and an illuminating passage. The science, I take it, is accurate—but so is the allegory, and it is this metaphorical language contruction that provides the means for the flash of understanding. It is one of the essential methods of poetry. One may be *granted* insight, but one can *learn* to communicate it to others.

One of the prevalent post-Freudian tenets of certain kinds of latter-day Platonist poets is that the act of writing poetry ought to be an act of getting in touch with one's unconscious mind. Evidently these theorists believe that it is the lower brain—the crocodilian and horsey hypothalamus—that writes poetry, bypassing the specifically human "thinking cap" or neo-cortex. I have never trusted this theory. I consider that stories circulated about poetry-composing lizards and ponies are apocryphal. Koestler gave me some hope to believe that man is the only poet on earth:

> To put it crudely; evolution has left a few screws loose between
> the neocortex and the hypothalamus. [In other, less crude words,
> there is poor communication between the "human" and the "animal-

reptilian" brains. Furthermore, since the lower brain is incapable of conscious symbology, most of the "communication" seems to be upward rather than downward: It is unlikely that the thinking cap can directly get in touch with the brute.] The hypothesis that this form of schizo-physiology is built into our species could go a long way toward explaining the delusional streak in our history, the prevalence of passionately held irrational beliefs. . . .

Koestler's article is ostensibly about the physiology of the human brain, but it is in fact about poetry:

Man is a symbol-making animal; the proudest and most dangerous product of his symbol-making is language . . . its dangers are generally underestimated. In the first place, language is the main cohesive force within a given ethnic group, but, at the same time, it creates barriers and acts as a repellent force between groups.

I think I have always understood this. Therefore, I have always considered that poetry was not ultimately something private except perhaps during the process of composition. It is an act of reaching out to other human beings. Star Powers brought this home to me in her rejection letter. I have tried to keep it in mind ever since.

And I think I have always believed in the power of words that Koestler describes:

Without language there would be no poetry, but there could also be no wars.

The last pathogenic factor I shall mention is man's simultaneous discovery and rejection of death. The inevitability of death was the discovery by inductive inference, of that newly acquired thinking cap, the human cortex—but the old brain won't have any of it. Instinct and emotion passionately reject the abstract yet deadly idea of personal non-existence. This simultaneous acceptance and refusal of death reflects the deepest split in man's split mind; . . . you have to look at both sides of the medal: on one side, religious art, architecture and music in the cathedral; on the other, the paranoid delusions of eternal hellfire, the tortures of the living and the dead.

Poetry, then, for me, is a way of dealing with, and an expression of the whole of the human being. If it reflects us accurately, it will be both rational and irrational; it will be full of paradox, like ourselves; it is an exploration of the single self, but it is also a reaching out from the self to others like ourselves—there is ambiguity in this last word, for each individual has more than one self. Poetry is ambiguity made clear: the human being lying down beside the horse and the crocodile.

II

Is a poet made or born? There is so much ground to cover here that I must begin by saying that I believe I may be a freak, but I hope not: I seem to have been born a formalist. There is a good chance that most young people who work in language are born formalists also, but they are unwilling to admit it, even to themselves, perhaps for romantic or irrational (if these terms are not in fact synonymous) reasons. It is a fact that much of my juvenilia was conscious experimentation in such things as accentual-syllabics, quantitative prosodies, alliterative accentuals, and so forth; it is also a fact that I had little or no notion such states and forms existed. It was not until I was in graduate school that I felt forced to admit my formalism. At that point, I felt it made no sense to deny what I was, and I began to study with a practical eye how poets wrote poems. Contrary to lore, I have found I was not damaged by knowing what I was doing. Much of my classroom time is spent in trying to convince students they will not find the creative candle snuffed out by applying intelligence to language. They may learn English language prosodies, or they may reinvent them, as I was doing young.

My students' trauma is the ordeal of unwilling recognition. They are afraid, like many adult poets, that if they once bring to the fore what they have done "instinctively," they will lose the instinct. But Koestler shows that poetry is not instinctive—it is a product of man's thinking mind. There is a difference between instinct and "second nature"—learning something so well that it comes easily and naturally. I write very fast. I seldom revise my poems much; nearly all the revision is done either while I am composing the first draft, or while I am typing up the second (usually final) version. If I spend more than three hours on a poem, it is unusual.

My students find it hard to believe this fact when I tell them. It's true they feel they should be able to write quickly, but they usually discover that when they do it is deeply flawed, or not totally realized as a poem. They have confused instinct with second nature; they have been using the English language all their lives—they were not born knowing it. They have learned their mother tongue by rote and by repetition and practice. They therefore assume that whatever they write ought to be poetry, because the language seems to come "naturally" to them, and they fail to realize that the level of competence at which they have arrived has been achieved at the end of a long and arduous line of development. It is difficult for them to see that the poet must be many times more competent with language than the ordinary speaker, and that he must therefore continue this difficult developmental process. Understanding the elements of poetry and the capacities of the language will not damage their souls nor their talents. On the contrary, understanding will increase their capacities as the thinking cap grows more complex fold by fold. Thinking increases the ability to think, and imaginative creation is an aspect of thinking, not of primal emotions.

I do not argue that emotions have nothing to do with poetry—merely that poetry is a way of dealing with our emotions, our split minds, through language. I think I managed to say in a poem once what I believe poetry is:

A DEDICATION

On a line by Joel Sloman

> If it is true that
> "the sea worm is a decorated flute
>   that pipes in the most ancient mode"—
>   and if it is true, too, that
> the salt content of mammalian blood
>   is exactly equivalent
> to the salinity of the oceans
> at the time life emerged onto the land;
>
>   and if it is true
> that man is the only mammal with a
>   capacity for song, well, then,
>   that explains why the baroque
>   worm swims in our veins, piping, and why
>   we dance to his measure inch by
> equivocal inch. And it explains why
> this song, even as it explains nothing.

Poetry is for me, then, a product of the rational human mind attempting to deal with the reptile and the horse, the worm and the angels. Koestler's article means a great deal to me in terms of my understanding of the human condition. Something happened one summer after I read it that gave me the metaphor I needed to fix the concept of the three brains on paper where I could stare at them and watch them suck and claw: A family cat picked up a tick on its head. Our attempts to remove it were futile. Finally, my father-in-law simply broke off the tick's body and left the head imbedded in the cat's scalp. The situation kept turning over and over in my mind, until I recognized that I had taken both those minds into my own skull:

TICK

    I am a cat with a tick
buried in my head. If I could speak,
    I would tell you I can feel
the insect head nestling within my

    brain, not just against the white
bone. I can sense its mechanical
    currents buzzing in the blood,
showing the mandibles how to clench,

    the belly how to bloat, how
to make two lives one. It is not a
    matter of will for either:
It feels my claws sliding in their sheaths;

    I feel it growing stronger
on my substance.
                My master?
As he looks at us, I see our two

    minds sink into his eyes. We three
meet at the center of his thoughts. My
    claws unsheath there. The insect
bloats in dark vessels. Here is where we

    shall live together—a nest
of boxes, three separate designs,
    three steps in Becoming, a
skull within a skull within a skull.

III

Irrationality is as much a part of us as logical thinking—perhaps more so in those of us who do not consciously make an effort to control ourselves. There is no guarantee, however, that irrationality will not break out in even the most rational individual. It is even possible that our irrationality controls our rational mind, directs it to build logical constructs upon irrational bases—consider Nazism, for instance, and its pseudo-scientific rationale of the Superman, its perversion of the theory of evolution. Those people who believe that they are always in control, who deny the power of the unconscious, are perhaps in most danger of succumbing to the reptile in themselves. Perhaps there is good reason for our equating the reptile with evil. But denying evil will not eliminate it; indeed, the reptile loves to be ignored until it can rise to strike out of the darkness where it lurks.

I believe, as I have said, that poetry is a way of coping with our lower selves; I do not believe that our lower selves write the poetry. That science does little to help us cope with our essential selves is obvious—so far, at least. Poetry antedates science and the scientific system, even as it is applied to the social sciences. But science has not made poetry obsolete. It took many years before I was willing to admit this, too: Poetry is essentially religious in nature, even from its beginnings. In all likelihood, poetry was first incantation and prayer. "In the beginning was the Word, and the Word was with God."

Poetry was "invented" long before the present scientific system of knowledge became the way in which Mankind knew its world—obviously. The system that existed when poetry was new is known today as the system of "sympathetic magic," and poetry was very much at the center of man's way of knowing under this system.

We as a race have lived under various systems of knowledge at various times. Evidently, what has not been possible for us since the development of the neo-cortex is that we should exist without some sort of system. It should go without saying that our perceptions of reality have, even in the scientific age, very little to do with logic. What is "real" has to do with what we believe and experience, not necessarily with what "is" in some abstract way. The reality experienced by the madman is no less "real" than what is experienced by the scientific observer. When the psychiatrist treats the lunatic, two realities deal with one another, and six minds interact. To draw out MacLean's allegory, horse and crocodile, man subjected, stare out of a cage at horse and crocodile, man ascendant.

A system is a system, a way of ordering experience, and that way of ordering controls our perceptions of reality; hence, if we perceive for thousands of years that Earth is the center of the universe, and that the stars are mere lights in the ceiling of the world, then that is "true" as long as the system holds. If, then, this system is replaced with one that says that the Earth is the center of a much larger universe, and that the stars are the homes of gods wheeling about this world, then that too is true for thousands of years.

And if Copernicus one day comes along and throws humanity into chaos by pointing out that the earth is merely one of many bodies wheeling about the sun, and that the sun is the center of the universe; if, later on, others come to say that the sun is not the hub of creation, but merely an insignificant mote lost, with its planets, in a vast well of space. . . .

The system of sympathetic magic was based on a simple proposition: That which was once associated with something is forever associated with it, no matter what distances of time or space separate these things from one another. Thus, if one could take a lock of someone's hair and weave it into a doll—a symbol of the person—then that doll *was* the person, and one could stick pins, symbolic daggers, into the doll to kill the person.

We enlightened folk of the scientific age scoff at such nonsense. But all that is necessary is for people to believe, and the system will work— there is ample evidence that primitive societies still operate by the system of sympathetic magic.

Under this system, one of the things that everything in the world has associated with it is its Secret Name. Every object, every person, every god has its Secret Name, and if one can discover the Secret Name of a thing, he can control it. Belief in the Secret Name was at one time universal. If we think hard, we can conjure up today various societies of the Secret Name that still exist in our culture—Mankind evolves, adds to, but little is truly lost. How many lodges and fraternities and sororities are there with their totems and rituals and secret names? Jews still believe that the secret name of God must never be spoken, even if known, for that is the Word, the holiest of holies, and no mere mortal must ever believe the One God can be controlled. This is the basis for cursing. It is still taboo among those who truly believe.

It is also the basis for sorcery—conjuring of demons by pronouncing their secret names. There is magic in names, in conjure words, and this is the magic of poetry. Even if we do not believe in sympathetic magic; even if we no longer believe that the priest-poet controls the universe with the sorcery of runes, we can still believe that there is great power in words harnessed in the totally right way. If we cannot conjure gods and devils, we can, perhaps, conjure our deepest selves—our fears, hopes, beauties, uglinesses. And if the poet can do these things still, is he any different than he was in the beginning? For the system of sympathetic magic had at its core control and understanding of the way things are with Man and his realities—that much hasn't changed.

The new system of science attempts to deal with these things, too, but it is a rational method, and man is only partly a rational creature, as we have seen. That is why poetry is not necessarily a rational method: There must be some way to deal with our deeper selves, some way to handle our perceptions of reality that objective study just cannot manage. This way—these ways are religion, philosophy, and the arts.

Alexander Pope said that the proper study of mankind is Man, and literature is no less a study of man than is science. In many ways poetry can go deeper into man than any of the sciences, for its roots tap something very basic in our nature—this is true even on such a technical level as the sounds of the language.

There are theories that the rhythms of verse echo or counterpoint the beat of the human heart, and that the heart echoes the beat of the tides and waves against those primordial shores onto which our earliest ancestors climbed out of the sea-womb that gave them life. Some scientific evidence can even be conjured to support the point: "The salt content of mammalian blood is exactly equivalent to the salinity of the oceans at the time life emerged onto the land." Perhaps the heart pushes blood as waves push water; perhaps language is the will of the blood made manifest. But poetry is more than sound and ritual. It is sensation and emotion, image and thought.

On the other hand, poetry should not be construed to be more than it is. Poetry can never be the original experience, the original vision of the writer, nor the essence of anything; it can only be the simulation of an experience or of a vision. Poetry is language art. If the poet is talented and knowing in the way of words, he can communicate a simulation, never the thing itself, to an audience. The poem can enter into the experience of the reader; it can be an experience in and of itself, but the poet cannot say the secret word and conjure a real demon.

This fact was borne in upon me one night several months after the death of my father in the fall of 1968. Like many people, I was a morbid person, afraid of death and not knowing how to cope with it. My father's passing greatly aggravated the condition. My conscious mind said, "Death is nothing," but my unconscious mind—sensing a threat, if Koestler is right—radiated fear. Since the lower brain knows nothing of symbolic communication, or words, my rational assurances were to no effect.

But I believe my thinking cap invented a situation that all of my selves could experience—not in "real" life, but in a dream. When I woke, I wrote the dream down: This is what happened to me. It cannot happen to you as you read, but I can tell the story:

THE DREAM

This is the story of a dream:
the gas station in a poor location,
     shadowed, even in daylight. The cars
          on their great tires—the 'twenties
     or early 'thirties. But not many

on the road. Perhaps evening is
coming on, darkness moving in, an air
     of something waiting in the gas pumps,
          behind the cooler. It is
     summer. I am in attendance. If

the lights were on perhaps someone
might turn off the road, drive up the old tar,
     ride over the sparse grass in the cracks,
          stop there, outside the dusty
     window where I stand watching. Then with

the thought, they are there—four of them
getting out of the square sedan. As they
     come filing toward the door, heads turned,
          coming at me through the hard
     glass with their hard eyes, I know there is

no way out. They'll find no money,
though—something in me grins at the thought, and
     the thought worries it. They are staring
          at me: the first is nearly
     at the door. As our eyes lock I am

shocked by the pistol in his hand,
by the flame in the muzzle, the shattered
     glass, by my blindness as the bullet

enters the brain where I know
I am lost and reeling, blood pouring

between my fingers, bathing my
eyes, and no sensation of pain, only—

a vague regret that I will
now accomplish no more; certainty

that this is death; amazement that
I can think with a shattered brain; knowledge
that if I wake again they will
have saved me; rejection of
the possibility. But beyond

these and above them: immense joy.
It is over. It is nothing—nothing
I could have imagined. Mere joy, great
relief, release and silence.
And I awake, but cannot believe

in waking. It has not happened,
yet nothing more real has ever happened.
Stumbling out of my blood into this
walking dream, nothing is left
except these words, images of weeds,

dust, flame in a dark cylinder, and joy.

Now, this poem may or may not affect a reader, depending on a number of variables. But the dream itself would have affected anyone—perhaps as it affected me, for my unconscious mind evidently believed the
experience of its senses, that what waits at life's end is joy, not agony, for
since that night I have not been nearly as morbid as I was formerly. I still
am apprehensive about the process of dying, but I no longer lie awake
at night in the chill hollow of the hand of darkness.

Poetry has its limitations. I wish my poem could do for every morbid
person what the dream did for me. Though my poem may not be capable
of giving relief from pain, perhaps it can provide hope, if I have learned
how to write well enough in this language of ours, this set of symbols
our collective consciousnesses have invented in common—write well
enough to convince the reader of this particular reality. Language is an
imperfect substance, but the poet has chosen to try to build perfect

communications out of it. It is an impossible task, but now and then one of us comes close.

Which brings me to my final observations.

IV

The more one knows about language, the more one can do with it. Star Powers told me to read—particularly the "eccentrics," by which I assume she meant the stylists and the experimenters. One can learn to write by reinventing literature in English, or one can read to discover what has been done and to visualize what still may be done. Both ways can work, but the latter is faster, more enjoyable and revealing: These are living voices out of the past. Man has lived billions of lives. We may enter some of them if we have the imagination, and if we can read.

One day I was reading Robert Burton's *The Anatomy of Melancholy*. Burton, to drive home a point, mentioned a "silly country fellow" who "killed his ass for drinking of the moon, that he might restore the moon to the world." Two questions came to mind: Was Burton right to scoff at the bumpkin, and why did the man commit such an act of violence upon the beast that helped him? Burton provided no further information.

I remembered the system of sympathetic magic and realized that this must have been an act of ritual sacrifice, not one of irrational slaughter. I put myself imaginatively into the mind of the silly country fellow, attempted to perceive something of the system of reality in which he lived:

THE MOON OF MELANCHOLY

>   It was late when they came in
>   through the stile. He dismounted
> beside the water trough, and the donkey
>   dropped its nose into the moon to drink.
>
>   He stood fatigued underneath
>   the wind scudding high cloud. No
> light beyond reflection lit the windows
>   of the house. The barn soughed. The long grass
>
>   of the fields grew longer in
>   shadow laid over shadow.
> The journey had taken forever. For
>   as long as it takes to remember,

he forgot where he had been,
and then recalled again. He
closed his eyes, listened to the beast drinking,
and was afraid, suspended

in that quiet of the mind.
When he looked again, when wind
had become too hollow against silence,
he found his eyes were opened,

but still he could not see. His
animal had drunk the moon
out of the water. He tried to discern
clouds, moon, sky, stars, the edge of the wind,

but found there a well into
which he felt himself to be
sinking. It was a vortex no world
could withstand. In the morning he wept

over the animal that
had carried him home; he wept
in the sun that had risen with him. He
remembered the image of

bone, restored as the blade sank
homing: The moon floating in
the trough of water and blood, and the wind
not quite too hollow to bear.

Burton had been wrong to scoff. He hadn't stopped to wonder at human motives. He was writing a book about the irrational state called *melancholia* then, *depression* now, but for a moment, in haste perhaps, he failed to think about the other person. He was too interested in proving his own point.

That brings me to Star Powers's main point in the rejection letter. Though the poet must explore the self; though the act of writing is done in solitude, if he forgets that he is merely one human being among many, he is lost. If the poem the poet writes is merely private, it is nothing. It is miming in a mirror. One presumably already knows what one feels—need it be put into words? If so—if one does not know what one has to say until it is said—ought one to show the poem to others if those others are excluded from participation in the poem? Should the poet expect the reader to come to the poem simply because it has been written, or must the poet reach out and bring the reader in? Should neither care, or both?

I believe that at a minimum, the poet should care, both for his original experience, and for the reader, for what happens to one of us happens to us all:

FETCH

> To step out of a bedroom
> into a forest of darkness;
> to find oneself naked among brambles
> and shagbark, a low wind making the flesh rise.
> To turn and discover there is no door,
> only bellbloom and shadow.

> And this is waking, the path
> beaten hard beneath heaven, stars
> among limbs bare of season. And between
> the trees, glass—dark sheets parsing silence without
> image. In the wood only the mutter
> and crool of water wending.

> Pause and touch: merely surface
> smooth and cold among the boles. Search:
> only the ghost of reflection paling
> under gaze. Walk, cover the ground. Know there is
> neither graith nor tackle to take the wood.
> Move as through one more tunnel.

> Stop when you feel him near. Strain
> to see who stands in the way, who
> holds out his hand, loof and hardel. It is
> another mirror of the wood—no: likeness
> of quicksilver. Behind him, a bedroom
> lies rumpled in a gilt frame.

> It is dark, but he is known.
> He is the beast of whom they have
> spoken so often in living rooms and
> dreams. It is a familiar forest. This is
> one's own path. It is the Fetch beckoning
> welcome to the crystal glade.

JAMES WRIGHT

JAMES WRIGHT (*b. Dec. 13, 1927 in Martin's Ferry, Ohio*)
received his undergraduate degree from Kenyon College,
interrupted his studies to serve in the United States
Army in Japan during the Occupation, and later finished his
graduate degrees at the University of Washington.
He has translated Trakl, Neruda, Hesse and other poets and
prose writers. In 1972 his own Selected Poems *won*
the Pulitzer Prize. He and his wife Annie live in
New York City where he is Professor of English at
Hunter College.

(Photo by Gerard Malanga)

Letters from Europe, Two Notes from Venice, Remarks on Two Poems, and Other Occasional Prose

Letters from Europe

c/o American Express
Paris, France
Nov. 27, 1973

My dear Franz,

You'll notice that above I'm still using the Paris address, although actually at this time we're still in Rome. For the past couple of weeks Annie's sister Jane has been with us. We spent a few days in Florence, then rented a car, and wandered around Tuscany for a while. I think it would be folly for me to try to describe that place. In my lifetime I have stood on Fujiyama; I have drifted down the Seine in a boat while the summer rain turned gray; and at the *Volksoper* in Vienna I have looked down from the balcony and seen a trumpeter crouch over and hand a glass of wine to a violinist right in the middle of a performance of *Der Zigeunerbaron* by Johann Strauss; and I once spent an entire day talking to Pablo Neruda and looking at his face. But I have never anywhere and at any time seen anything so appallingly beautiful as Tuscany in late autumn. Darkness fell suddenly one evening as we descended from the fortress city of Volterra, which still broods suspiciously over the small valleys in every direction, like a paranoid dragon, or, except for the city's severe dark beauty, like Nixon keeping watch over the national security. We drove for a while, and even got lost, and found our way again at a tiny little bar-restaurant at the edge of a village, where an almost absurdly beautiful girl greeted us, gave us some coffee and grappa, spread out a huge map of Tuscany on the table, and sped us on our way. We finally found the sign pointing us to—San Gimignano. Then we drove up, and up, and around, and around, and up, and around, and up again, till we found ourselves picking our way in semi-darkness (the headlights in our rented Fiat were on the fritz) through very narrow medieval streets. At length, we emerged on a town square, not a very large one as piazzas go, and checked in at a hotel over in the corner. The town seemed pleasant enough, but we were road-weary and hungry; so, after stepping a few doors down the street to a trattoria for a small late meal, we went to bed.

The next morning Annie rose first, opened the curtained doors to bright sunlight, and went out on the balcony. I thought I heard her gasp. When she came into the room again, she looked a little pale, and said, "I don't believe it."

San Gimignano is poised hundreds of feet in the air. The city itself is comparatively small, and it is perfectly formed. We watched it glittering there in the lucid Tuscan morning, like a perfectly cut little brilliant sparkling on the pinnacle of a stalagmite. Far below us we could look almost straight down into vineyards and fields, where people—whole families, even small children—had evidently been at work for hours. In all directions below us were valleys whose villages were just beginning to appear out of the mist, a splinter of a church tower here, an olive grove there. The morning was more than beautiful. It was a life in itself. . . .

Unemployment is severe in Europe right now, and there is every indication that it, as well as inflation, will get worse. Furthermore, Europeans are not about to give a foreigner a job which could be filled by a native. I don't know much about economics, but friends in Austria, businessmen, fear a depression worldwide that will make the Great Depression of the '30s look puny. I hate to harp on these unpleasant matters, but the state of the world right now gives me no choice. Nixon's the one, without a doubt.

We'll be leaving Rome in a few days, and our next address will be in Paris. I'll try to keep in touch on the way. We think of you often and always with love.

Love,

c/o American Express
Paris, France
Dec. 17, 1973

Dear Franz,

On our last day in Italy, we were in Florence. On Saturday was the feast of the Immaculate Conception; and on Sunday, as on Saturday, nobody was allowed to drive a car. I know how hot Florence can be in the summer, caught and magically held as it is in the bowl of the Tuscan hills around the Arno; and I had been warned that it is caught there, too, in the winter, bitter and frozen.

But on that last day we spent there, all the motor traffic was gone, and some god must have taken Botticelli's Primavera seriously enough to breathe across the entire river valley. I can't remember a lovelier day in my lifetime, and I have lived through some lovely days. The great Florentines took advantage of the Feast of the Immaculate Conception and the absence of the automobiles to celebrate the coming of spring in the middle of winter. We walked over to one of the squares, and by God a parade began; we ran through back streets and met the town band of Bergamo at the Piazza Signoria, where we patriotically applauded and sang. Everywhere little Florentines were riding on their parents' shoulders and singing, conducting the musicians. The Florentines themselves seemed stunned at the incredible beauty of their city, which they could pause and contemplate without fear of being murdered in cold blood by fanatical traffic. The crowd remained, walking, strolling, singing; we walked up to the civic museum and saw David—Michelangelo's David. I will not try to describe it, or my feelings about it. I am reduced to the banality of abstraction: it is one of the precious few statements about what it means to be a human being on God's earth.

We've only been in Paris for a few days now, and we leave on January 15th. I hope you'll have time to write us here c/o American Express at least once. Today is Monday. On Saturday we took the train down to Chartres and made a reservation at a small nice hotel, where we plan to spend Christmas eve and Christmas day. After midnight mass, we return to the hotel for the *revillon*—the dinner of awakening. Although it doesn't seem likely after all these years of fraudulence and folly, Chartres is still a small town, a hick town really, and the cathedral, which took hundreds of years to build, many humorous generations and anonymous lifetimes, still broods clearly on that little hilltop. The sun was so unseasonably brilliant that day, we walked inside and, for a wonder, found the church nearly empty. When we turned to see the great rose window, we saw something we hadn't seen before, something the architects must surely have planned—seen in a vision, I should say—: one whole wall of the cathedral inside, stippled with strange lengthening color poured through the window.

There are literally hundreds of small and large sculptures all over the cathedral there, inside and out. A man named Houvet has photographed them with great care and love. I found two of his photographs which I thought you would like. In fact, they made me think of you. I believe the little sculptures are to be found way high up on the north side of the cathedral. They were done in the thirteenth century. They both made me think of you, and I am enclosing the photographs. The single figure, with his head resting on his hand, is "God creating the day and the night." The other, exquisitely beautiful in stone and, even in its conception, hair-raisingly nutty in imagination, is called "God, while creating the birds, sees Adam in his thoughts." It sounds like the title of one of your poems.

Annie will add a note. We hope you are well, and that you have a good Christmas. I love you, my fine son.

Love,

Hotel Adlerhof
Hafnersteig, 7
Wien, Oesterreich
Sept. 25, 1973

Dear Don,

I'm hoping this note will reach you while you're still in England. We just arrived in Vienna a couple of days ago, and we'll be here also till about October 8. Mails in Italy have been erratic, as I think I told you, and I'm not yet sure where to suggest that you write next. I suspect Annie will be back here at the hotel before I finish the letter, and she'll have some idea of an address.

For we do indeed want to return to Italy. This summer I found myself becoming more and more attached to the place, and of course Annie has loved it for years. Early in November we're meeting her sister Jane (that sounds nice, doesn't it?) in Rome and we'll be with her for a while, but first we want to travel back there more or less slowly, so that among other things I can return to Verona, which may or may not be the most ravishingly beautiful city in Italy but will do for me until the second coming of Christ.

I hope very much that you will be able to buy the farm. The conditions you describe remind me of the same kind of problem that Galway Kinnell faces up in New Hampshire. The last I heard, he had determined to undertake the place before the developers do, so to speak.

While you're in England I don't know if you'll get the chance to see Geoffrey Hill. But if you do, will you please give him my fondest regards? And tell him of my admiration for the Mercian Hymns. I found the book in London last summer, and by this time I must have read it at least twenty times. I wrote a good many notes on it in my notebook, and one of these days I may even try to write an essay about it. It is wonderfully original, and it also suggests further lines of development, the first polysemous book of that kind that I've seen in a good while.

It's pleasant to be back in Vienna, where I was a student so many years ago. My German is rusty but adequate. In a way, it surprises me to find that I can speak more easily in German now than I could when I was actually studying here. I was so young then, with horse manure sticking out of my ears. Still, the city is apparently thriving, and I am glad to see this, because the Viennese, like the Italians, have a strong conservative feeling for the old places in their cities and are making every effort to preserve them among necessary new construction.

Sunday was a perfect Viennese day, early September and the beginning of the peculiar gold that a bright autumn gives here. We took a bus clear up to Kahlenberg, the last little hill of the Alps before you reach the Danube plain, and walked through the beech groves all the way down to the villages of Nussdorf and Grinzing, where we found, as always, many little inns quite generous with the great Heuriger wine. But today is melancholy, heavy with a soaking rain that seems to belong especially to Vienna. All the nineteenth-century heaviness and darkness seem to emerge and become part of the weather itself, and in spite of the pathos of the fallacy, one feels a certain neurosis even in the rain, as though Dr. Freud had shrunk the buildings halfway and then the patients had run out of money. Or nerve. But I cheer myself with certain irreducible memories. One morning some twenty years ago, I was plodding light-heartedly through the sunlit snow across the huge Mariatheresianplatz, and I found a real two-schilling piece in the snow. I don't know why, but the memory still delights me. I suppose it's because in those days two schillings was, after all, two schillings.

I appreciate your mentioning the *String* and the *Moore.* And I will surely remind you about them when we get back to America next January. Annie is about to return, and I want to get this letter off to you. Look where she comes! (Enter Annie): please write to us c/o American Express in Rome. We won't be there till Nov. 1, but intermediate plans are uncertain. I'll certainly write you before then. Love to Jane.

Love,

Hotel Adlerhof
Hafnersteig, 7
Wien, Oesterreich
Sept. 30, 1973

My dearest Laura,

I have been thinking of you time and again in this beautiful city. I am sure it would belong to your heart once you visited it. Paris is of course the capital of the world, and it is an abiding pleasure to remember you there. I will always carry with me, as a secret treasure, the memory of walking with you along the Boulevard Sainte-Germaine-des-Prés.

But what makes me think of you here in Vienna is the inner life of this city, the silences, the melancholy that can become quite dark at times, on rainy days in particular, but a melancholy peculiarly responsive to the occasional and very special sunlight. It is a city whose sunlight is preserved and sustained by the faces of beautiful girls who love music. In other words, my dear Laura, Vienna is your city. Just a street away from the great University, which I attended somewhat blunderingly twenty years ago, you can find a small street where Beethoven lived; but that is not so spectacular as it sounds, considering that Beethoven, a shy, deaf, impatient man who threatened many a robust landlady with nervous breakdowns, lived (I am told) in some twenty-six houses in Vienna and its outlying areas. What is loveliest about that little street near the University is the little townhouse called the Dreimaderlhaus, where three charming girls lived and where Schubert dwelt for a time in his short and complete life, where he enjoyed their company, and where, if I'm not mistaken, he wrote his immortal Octet for Strings. The little house always makes me think of you, and of the love for Schubert you carry in your affectionate heart.

But I don't want to suggest that Vienna is a city of monuments alone, however beloved and haunted such places may be. The genius of the city is in the contemporary life of its music.

I had to interrupt this letter for some two whole days, because the weather changed. After the soaking rain, October suddenly appeared. In America we call it Indian Summer, and in Italy and Austria it is called the summer of Saint Martin. Slightly to the north of the main city of Vienna there are some several little towns (Dorfe, as you know), and three of them are Grinzing (where the great Heuriger wine flows from the vineyards below Kahlenberg to the lovely gardens of the town itself), Nussdorf, where Beethoven lived in twenty-three different houses (according to the rumor which the Viennese still tell, after more than a century—apparently he didn't get along with landlords, etc.), and the one I suppose I love best, and which I think you would love too: Heiligenstädt. As you know, I am a professor, and years ago I rummaged among the journals and letters of Beethoven. Most of them are pedantic and commonplace. But he wrote a little prose piece called "Der Heilegenstädt Testament." In it, he tried to explain to many people why he had seemed in his lifetime to be such a rude person. "The truth is," he said, "I like you very much. But, you see, I can't *hear* you. My ears hurt."

Dear, I would like to send you some message of happiness at this time. I have no special reason except the enduring one: you are my favorite niece, and one of my most delightful friends. If you would like to please me also, why don't you get a recording of Beethoven's Symphony Number 6 (the Pastoral Symphony), and listen especially to the movement called "The Brook." We found that brook! In truth, I found it alone, some twenty years ago. It runs from the unspeakably beautiful beech-grove below Kahlenberg down through the Vienna Woods into the town of Nussdorf. I first found it a long time ago, before you were born, in a soaking rain, and it made me happy, because after all, Beethoven wrote that exquisitely lovely music *after* learning that he would never be able to hear any sound again. He heard the music of that Nussdorf brook in his soul. He had something to sing to you and me, and he sang it. As Aunt Edie (my incomparable Annie) strolled down today through the long beech-grove, that natural cathedral almost as enriching as the greatest cathedral in Europe (Chartres) I thought again of you, how terrible life can be, and how much lovely people like Schubert, Beethoven, and you matter.

Love,

c/o American Express
Rome, Italy
November 9, 1973

My dear Karin,

I've owed you a letter through a long slow summer and an autumn which is hard to understand in Italy, to me, because the warmth has lasted so long. You seem to me—rather, I should say, you have seemed to me—a perfect Parisienne, and yet I have now seen so many places in Italy where you belong, that now I begin to think you would love Italy best.

Adige is the name of the river. It runs around the fairly small town of Verona. I want to tell you about the color of the water. It is a slow and milky green, like the water that comes down from the Alps. The river is called the *Adige*, and it curls around the city very like the setting of a gem.

And the gem is the city itself. I have done a good deal of wandering in my lifetime, and Verona is like nothing I have ever seen. There is no place in this city that is not ravishingly beautiful. I won't even mention the great cathedral near the river, a miracle of architecture which contains underground, beneath its towering stone interior, another whole church of nearly the same size that contains only a few perfect stone pillars to balance and sustain the entire edifice; nor the tombs of the Scala family, which are surrounded by a wrought-iron fence of such incredible delicacy that one has to change his position merely by a few inches in order to see all the forms and figures change; nor the Castelvècchio, an enormous fortified castle on the river, where one has to cross a teetering little bridge to find the smiling, delighted face on the equestrian statue of Can Grande della Scala I, the great Veronese nobleman who offered friendship and shelter to the poet Dante. These are merely the obvious glories of the city.

But what made me think of you there especially was the sweetness and loveliness of the people's faces and the gentleness of their manners.

We miss you very much.

Love,

Two Notes from Venice

Venice

August 28, 1973

This afternoon I return to these meditations—or improvisations, or notes, or whatever—after working so pleasantly, from time to time, in the small green notebook, writing in longhand. It is interesting how the rhythm of sentences changes from one part of the notebook to the other. Generally speaking, I move from one to another whenever I find myself writing too rapidly.

Venice is a deep city, yet filmy and fragile at times. I don't mean merely its physical appearance, although the outline of roofs and towers in the early morning light can be a light and spidery thing, and the shadows among the few passages and stone streets after dark can assume almost the solidity of stone. I mean that the city can change its character, its appearance and mood, at any given moment, even in broad daylight. Consequently, it is very easy to get lost here.

Yet all one needs to do is follow the sound of water, and the things and persons of the water, to find one's way home again, wherever home may be.

There are so many stairways everywhere. I learn that these were, and sometimes still are landings for small boats of many kinds; but I always imagine someone stepping slowly down the stairs, careful on the algae that is such a brilliant green in the sunlight, or another color, a moon-slime in the occasional night mist, or the color of a dead peacock I dreamed of once.

We saw a very old man appear suddenly around a corner. He entered the square very slowly, for all his quick appearance, an apparition of a kind. He carried a middle-sized wooden ladder on his shoulder, and a small curious net in one hand. A chimney-sweep, Annie said. Perhaps he was. With his coat elbows and his crushed hat scuffled enough, he could have prowled his way up and down the insides of these silvery, rotting walls.

But I am sure I noticed the green moon-slime on his shoes, and, until I hear otherwise, I will half-believe that he had just climbed up some of those odd stairs out of a nearby narrow canal. How can I know what he was doing under water? I can't. But he was doing something. This, after all, is Venice; the very streets of the city are water; and what magnificent and unseemly things must sway underneath its roads: a lost Madonna and Child frantically flung away by a harried thief last year; the perfect skeleton of a haughty cat, his bone-tail curled around his ribs and crusted with salt three centuries ago; the right hand of a disloyal artisan in spun glass, the blood long gone back to the sea; some reflection of the moon caught and kept there, snaggled between the teeth of a Turkish sailor; or the sailor himself, headless, a scimitar in one hand and a coca-cola can in the other; a snide note from Byron; an empty American Express folder; even a chimney, swept free, till this hour passes, of all the webs they weave so stoutly down there, the dark green spiders under the water who have more than all the time they need.

There he was: a chimney sweep in warm summer weather? Hardly. A sweeper of sea-stairs.

Venice
Sept. 6, 1973

The word evening has always seemed beautiful to me, and surely Venice is the city of evenings. It is renowned everywhere for its dawns, when the cathedrals and basilicas take solid shape out of the milky pearl. But their solidity is stone, even the finest of stone, the delicate sea-washed rippled marble floated here from Constantinople. It is only the evenings that give the city the shape of light; they make the darkness frail and they give substance to the light.

It is still too early for evening, and the smoke of early September is gathering on the waves of the Giudecca Canal outside my room. Steamers, motorboats, trash-scows are moving past in large numbers, and gondolas are going home. In a little while we too will meet the twilight and move through it on a vaporetto toward the Lido, the seaward island with its long beach and its immense hotel, its memories of Aschenbach and his harrowing vision of perfection, of Byron on horseback in the moonlight, and the muted shadows of old Venetians drifting as silently as possible in flight from the barbarians, drifting as far away as the island of Torcello, taking refuge as Ruskin said like the Israelites of old, a refuge from the sword in the paths of the sea. Maybe Torcello was nothing much for the princes of the sea to find, but the old Venetians discovered the true shape of evening, and now it is almost evening.

On the Occasion of a Poem

New York
June 7, 1974

Several years ago I went fishing with Richard F. Hugo, an employee of the Boeing Aircraft Company and a softball player of some distinction. We spent a pleasant afternoon drifting in a skiff all around the lake—I believe it was Lake Kapowsin, the destruction of whose congenial tavern has since been described by Hugo in one of his many beautiful books. His many friends will agree that Hugo is a fisherman of long experience and great skill. During the afternoon, he also presented an attractive appearance in his fishing togs. Standing in easy balance at the bow of our skiff, he would have served as an excellent illustration for a cover of *Field and Stream* magazine. He even carried, slung casually at his side, one of those old-fashioned wicker baskets in which serious fishermen used to carry their tackle. I myself was, of course, no fisherman at all. I enjoyed the lake, the peace, the laziness. With the understanding of a good friend who knows that he doesn't have to explain, Hugo would occasionally reach into his wicker basket and, with a certain professional flair, hand me an uncapped stubby of excellent beer.

Getting on toward dusk, we had drifted toward one end of the lake. Fifty yards or so up in the woods we saw a shack, to all appearances abandoned—unpainted, with only a few shingles left, generally ramshackle. Since the fishing for the day was more or less finished, Hugo suggested that we might walk up and explore the shack, just for the fun of it. I begged off. It's not that I was afraid of anything or anybody there. I happen to be one of those people who enjoy snakes. Since I spent a happy visit to the Sonora Desert near Tucson with my friend the poet Richard Shelton and his wife and son, I have even grown fond of tarantulas. I would far rather stroke a tarantula than attend a concert by Rod McKuen or spend an evening at dinner on the *Sequoia*. No, I just didn't want to explore the shack at the end of the lake.

It is interesting to learn, from a moving interview by Richard Hugo, recently published in *The New Salt Creek Reader*, that, even at the time of which I am writing, he was very fond of exploring abandoned houses. So it turns out that I deprived him of an innocent pleasure without knowing it. He didn't object to my reticence, though. We just returned to the shore. I think he understood that I didn't want to get out of the boat because I was too lazy or too drunk. Probably both.

Here is the poem I wrote afterwards:

ON MINDING ONE'S OWN BUSINESS

Ignorant two, we glide
On ripples near the shore.
The rainbows leap no more,
And men in boats alight
To see the day subside.

All evening fins have drowned
Back in the summer dark.
Above us, up the bank,
Obscure on lonely ground,
A shack receives the night.

I hold the lefthand oar
Out of the wash, and guide
The skiff away so wide
We wander out of sight
As soundless as before.

We will not land to bear
Our will upon that house,
Nor force on any place
Our dull offensive weight.

Somebody may be there,
Peering at us outside
Across the even lake,
Wondering why we take
Our time and stay so late.

Long may the lovers hide
In viny shacks from those
Who thrash among the trees,
Who curse, who have no peace,

Who pitch and moan all night
For fear of someone's joys,
Deploring the human face.

From prudes and muddying fools,
Kind Aphrodite, spare
All hunted criminals,
Hoboes, and whip-poor-wills,
And girls with rumpled hair,
All, all of whom might hide
Within that darkening shack.
Lovers may live, and abide.

Wherefore, I turn my back,
And trawl our boat away,
Lest someone fear to call
A girl's name till we go
Over the lake so slow
We hear the darkness fall.

Having given a brief account of a poem, I must now come to the real point of this brief essay. On another afternoon, Hugo and I went fishing again. To the best of my recollection, the Bumping River flowed near an indescribably beautiful meadow called Goose Prairie. It was surrounded by mountains whose roads were difficult to drive on even in the daylight. We and our wives rented a perfectly comfortable cabin for a reasonable price, so that we could spend the night.

Now, for some reason, serious fishermen who stay overnight always run out of beer. It's no use asking me why. I do not know. I have done it myself at least a hundred times, and many trustworthy persons have told me about their own suffering from this same curious lack of what would seem, to any reasonable person, a normal and necessary foresight. A fisherman who neglects to bring an adequate supply of beer is as unaccountably silly as a man who travels from the very northernmost tip of the Bronx to spend three days with close relatives in Far Rockaway, only to remember, as he changes trains at Times Square, that he has forgotten to bring his *petit-mal.*

Nevertheless, such things happen, and they always seem to happen to overnight fishermen.

Goose Prairie—oh, that lovely place, where we even saw some elk browse slowly across the meadow in the evening—featured only one tavern. Its proprietor and manager was a man named Ed Bedford. His wife tended bar. I do not wish to denigrate Mr. Bedford. He was not what you would call particularly intelligent or charming, in the ordinary meanings of those words. He was not handsome, but presentable. He shaved. I suspect that, as we used to remark in Ohio when I was a boy, he took a bath every March, whether he needed it or not. Generally speaking, I think it is fair to describe him as an ordinary chap, doing his best, trying to make a living, just like most other people.

But Ed Bedford possessed another quality for which I have often tried to find the appropriate word, and I am afraid that I must use the word that even approaches accuracy: Ed Bedford was a genius. In his combination of simplicity, mediocrity, and sudden, astonishing grasp of solutions which ought to be obvious to everyone else but which almost never do become obvious until it is too late to do anything but weep, I can think of only three persons in my lifetime who resemble him: Bobby Fischer, Richard M. Nixon, and the late Baldur von Schirach.

Mr. Bedford's genius consisted, first of all, in his instinctive grasp of human nature. He simply remembered what all fishermen consistently forget. Consequently, he never ran out of beer.

The second feature of Bedford's genius was geographical. He knew the severe difficulty of driving on those mountain roads even by daylight. He knew that not even Steve McQueen or Gene Hackman would have attempted to drive those roads after dark. Not even their stuntmen would have tried it. (Evel Knievel might have tried it, but I don't think he was born yet, and in any case I doubt if Ed Bedford would have hired him. He would probably have got sidetracked and tried to leap on his motorcycle from Mt. Rainier to Mt. Whitney. Worse, he might have succeeded.)

With the unapologetic aplomb of Napoleon at the battle of Austerlitz, Ed Bedford disregarded conventional tactics and disposed of the enemy (that is, the frustrated fishermen) by two classically simple strokes. He kept his beer available in unlimited supply; and he doubled the price. (Perhaps he tripled it. But the reader must remember that these events took place many years ago, and, admitting my own usual tendency to exaggerate, I am studiously attempting to write moderately.)

In spite of these difficulties, we all recognized the futility of our position. It never occurred to any of us that Bedford's practices might have been illegal. For all I know, they may have been. For that matter, for all I know, Ed Bedford may have been the game warden.

We bought his beer at his price. And we drank it.

It was obvious that I cannot hope to be a prose stylist like, say, Harold Robbins, Jacquelin Susann, Faith Baldwin, or even John Updike. But I do sincerely attempt to avoid triteness as well as I can. So I cannot, in good faith, say that Ed Bedford's beer tasted like shit. As a matter of fact, I have eaten shit, and more than once. I don't mean just bad inedible food. I mean shit. To tell the truth, it wasn't as distasteful as the prejudiced reader might assume. Nevertheless, I must make some kind of effort to suggest the quality of Bedford's beer. A direct, literal description is beyond my powers. Still, as a Professor of Literature, I do from time to time have certain belletristic aspirations. And so, as the master Henry Fielding likes to say to his friendly readers: since we are in no special hurry, I believe I shall essay a simile: The flavor of Ed Bedford's beer suggested a somewhat watery *puree* of White Castle hamburgers, half-green with decay; and this in turn offered a pungent *bouquet* of blend of at least two distinct under-arm perspirations: one from Ms. Hermione just as she was acknowledging perhaps her tenth curtain-call after the evening performance of *A Little Night Music;* and one from the late Rocky Marciano at the very moment when the referee was raising his arm in a gesture of victory after his eighth-round knockout of the gallant Archie Moore.

Recently Richard Hugo claimed that Ed Bedford is dead. Having more than once recorded in print my admiration for Hugo's splendid poetry, I think it pertinent to add here my equal admiration for his personal honesty. He is as straightforward and trustworthy a person as I have ever had the honor to know. I am not implying that he is a liar in his report of Bedford's death. What Hugo does not seem to realize is that his claim has created problems in my mind which I am not able to cope with. These problems are both physical and metaphysical. They are so abstruse, that I had better sketch them one at a time.

First, the physical. What exactly could they do with Bedford's stiff? If they tried to bury him at sea, he would poison the fishes and even the nuclear submarines. If they buried him conventionally in the ground, then, given the realities of geological time, he would eventually seep into the workings of the Anaconda Copper Mines and thereby—perhaps by interfering with the alloying process, threaten the company's profits; and I doubt if anybody, even Ed Bedford, could get away with that sort of thing. After all, even Christ was crucified. If Bedford were cremated, he would likely outlast the operators of the furnace, the way Fearless Fosdick, having scientifically determined the exact temperature which would melt his arch-enemy Anyface, courageously trapped Anyface and himself into a fiery furnace and waited as the temperature rose; when it reached the appropriate degrees, of course, it was Fosdick who melted, while Anyface escaped. I once considered the possibility, not at all unlikely, that Bedford's wife might have been persuaded to eat him. But this solution quickly turned into another problem. Bedford would certainly have been indigestible, and, in the event of his wife's death, what in God's name would the embalmers have done with her tripas?

The metaphysical problem is even worse. I thought of consulting the illustrious Dr. Abram von Elsing, who drove the silver stake through Dracula's heart in the daytime. But Bedford had no heart, and, besides, he stayed awake night and day. As for the afterlife, I don't wish the poor man in Hell. And how can he be in Heaven? I always thought that beer, like everything else in Heaven, tasted good and was free of charge.

The problem is too much for me. As far as I can figure it out, Ed Bedford is a white elephant on the hands of the Deity.

If Dick Hugo had known about the consequences of his perfectly reasonable report of news about an old acquaintance of ours, I think he would just have told me that Ed Bedford had retired, and let it go at that.

But I can conclude on a cheerful note. I have stopped drinking, and one sure sign of my improved health is the fact that I seldom think about Bedford's beer and other outlandish things.

On the Occasion of a Poem: Bill Knott

Lake Minnewaska
New Palz, New York
June 14, 1974

Although I will directly quote some verses of my own, the most important part of these reflections will deal with the poet Bill Knott, partly because of his rarity but mainly because of his value. Such persons are bound to be rare on the earth at any time, for reasons that are probably biological, although it is obvious to the reader that both my training and my knowledge in this science are more than ordinarily limited. When I speak of his value, I refer to his friendship, which I cherish, in spite of our too infrequent meetings, and most of all to his poetry, which I consider to be very fine and likely to endure long after most of our contemporary smoke has done me the unintended but nevertheless genuine personal favor of just simply drying up and blowing away.

I first read a few of Bill Knott's poems on a pleasant afternoon in Robert and Carol Bly's chicken house, which had long since been converted into a comfortable study and which also contained a perfectly lovely antique bed where, in those earlier times, so dear to me, I spent many a comfortable sleep and many pleasant dreams. I also slept there with a girl whom I loved. The previous sentence is beside the point to you, I am sure, but not to me.

There are authors in this world who work with great facility. May I offer them my respectful envy. I myself am one of those people who, granted the choice between writing the opening sentence and being hanged by the neck until I am dead, would cheerfully prefer the latter. I think I would even volunteer to slap the horse's buttocks, if my arms were as long as those of Rose Mary Woods. Since this physical condition does not obtain in my case, I have been forced to develop other devices for avoiding work, and I must confess that I pride myself in having developed over the years a good deal of adroitness in this art.

I had not reckoned with the natural and experienced intelligence of Carol Bly, however. On the afternoon in question, when I was supposed to be finishing an essay to be published in the magazine *The Sixties*, she made sure that I would finish the essay, or at least work on it, by employing the simple and effective expedient of a Napoleon at the height of his career. She locked me into the chicken house, including the door and the windows. My delicious lunch was delivered to me promptly by my incomparable goddaughter Mary Bly, who prevented my escape by simply standing at the door and watching me eat it. When I was finished, she proceeded to relock the door and leave me to my work. To this day, I remember those afternoons in the chicken house as a curious combination of a pleasant study, Yaddo, and Devil's Island. The only thing that was missing to make the comparison perfect was the butterfly tattooed for some reason that still escapes me, on Steve McQueen's chest. In those days, by the way, I was a drunk; and, no doubt with the intention of inspiring me to responsible literary labors, my realistic friends made sure that the chicken house contained no booze whatever.

During my frantic and resourceful efforts to evade the typewriter, I happened to come upon a sheaf of poems. They were unsigned. I read them.

They were short poems. I must have read them twenty times. Robert later told me they had been sent to him by a young poet named Bill Knott. They were then, and they are now, among the most beautiful poems I have ever read in any language. They were brief, gentle, totally clear in their meaning on the most casual first reading, and shocking only in the sense that they were so original: in short, they were the true thing, finally unaccountable, as even Longinus had to admit, and yet unmistakable. I remember thinking then, as I am thinking now, something that Louis Simpson said to me when he had made a similar discovery: in that sinister moment when it is so frighteningly difficult to tell the difference between the feeling of pain and feeling of gratitude, Louis observed that "sometimes, even in the weariness of literature, poetry can happen."

I did not know Bill Knott personally. We had never corresponded. We had absolutely no way of knowing that each other even existed, except for the possible fact that Yale had published a single book of mine; and, in case the reader has to be reminded of what is banally obvious, I tend to doubt that either John Updike or Jacqueline Susann need ever fear being driven into panic at the threat that my books will force one or even both of them (since, for all I can tell, they are the same person writing under two different names) into position number eleven on some best-seller list, whether it be that of the Sunday *New York Times* or the Pickwa, Ohio, *Herald-Tribune and Livestock Report*.

Some months later, I received a note from Bill Knott which I believe I can quote word-for-word. The note was quite brief. I recall that it did not even address me by name:

"I'm so lonely I can't stand it. Solitude is all right. It's not the same thing. Loneliness rots the soul." He signed the postcard and included his home address.

In case the reader hasn't noticed, we live in a strange world. The poet's desperately unhappy message arrived at a time which turned it into a happy coincidence. I received his postcard about a week before Thanksgiving. I myself had just recently recovered from an illness and been released from a hospital. My friends Alva and Edna Miriam, parents of one of my nicest students, had invited me to Thanksgiving dinner at their home in Ogden, Iowa. Moreover, they had made plans to travel to Chicago the succeeding weekend, and they kindly invited me to accompany them. I accepted their invitation, and instantly wrote to Bill Knott that, come hell or high water, I would arrive at his room in Chicago some time during the afternoon of the Saturday immediately following Thanksgiving. I also informed him that I would arrive in the company of two pretty, hilarious girls and a bunch of fresh bananas. And by God I did it. By this time the reader will be thinking that I am making up this whole story, but I don't care what the reader thinks. It is the truth. I wish I could add that the bunch of bananas was my own idea, but the fact is that one of the girls thought of it. I haven't the faintest notion how or why the thought ever occurred to her. She had never read any of Bill Knott's poetry. She had never even heard of Bill Knott. All she knew was that I had asked her if she would like to join me in a brief visit to a friend who lived in Chicago, and I had no sooner finished asking the question than she instantly suggested that we take him a bunch of bananas as a house gift. I love women.

At the time, Bill Knott was working all night at some charity hospital or other. By the time we arrived and persuaded the superintendent of the building that we were neither narcotics agents nor gangsters in disguise, Knott had had time for a morning nap. He was refreshed when he warmly greeted us. I doubt if anybody can be said to know Bill Knott really well. But he has some devoted friends—William Hunt, John Logan, Thomas Lux, and others—and I believe they would agree that Knott is nearly always reticent in manner, sometimes painfully so. But on the afternoon of the visit which I am trying to describe, he was as happily friendly and sociable as one could wish. Perhaps he was simply surprised that I had actually succeeded in fulfilling so quickly a literally nutty promise. Perhaps it was the presence of the girls, both so pretty and natural and charming. Perhaps it was the bananas. I don't really know. I do know the four of us spent a delightful half-hour or so, before the girls, having appointments with their respective families, unfortunately had to leave.

Bill Knott's room, like his clothing, was shabby and worn. He had to share a single toilet down the far end of the hall with other tenants, of whom there were many. His room contained few things: a sink, which gave only cold water; a single swaybacked bed; a shelf stuffed with books, neatly but unalphabetically arranged. Whether Bill Knott ever finished high school I do not know. I do know that he never attended college. His collection of books was what more formally and professionally academic persons like myself would call erratic. I remember in particular one volume which will serve as a typical example. It was a worn copy—thoroughly read and reread with obvious devotion and intensity of the collected works of the great Greek contemporary master Odysseus Elytis. But my most striking memory of Bill Knott's skimpy room was an object placed right in the center of his single bare wooden table. It was a full unopened quart of the finest Jack Daniels whiskey, clearly placed there as a token of welcome in the poet's anticipation of our arrival. Now, my friends, my enemies, and any number of strangers who have had the dubious experience of hearing me speak in public need hardly be reminded that I used to be what, in gentler and more civilized times, would have been known as a heavy drinker of spiritous liquors (or, for those who prefer the more euphemistic phrase, a two-bit drunk). On the afternoon of my first meeting with Bill Knott, however, the girls drank nothing at all. Knott and I drank no more than a single shot each. (Lest the reader assume, as he naturally might, that my memory on this particular is flattering me with my own virtue, I must add that I did indeed get stone-blind drunk late that evening. I awoke next morning in a room in a theological seminary. How I got there I don't remember, and, in any case, it doesn't matter. I could probably lie about it, but space is limited.)

What made Bill Knott's bottle of Jack Daniels so moving an experience to me was the fact that he could not afford to buy it. His salary at the hospital where he was working at night could not possibly have provided him with very much more than what he needed for bare subsistence. Consequently, he had clearly been saving every extra penny he could possibly spare in order to buy that bottle of whiskey as a token of greeting to his visitors. To quote a remark by Oscar Wilde which has always been dear to me: I do believe in my heart that men have gone to heaven for less.

Bill Knott was poor. I record with horror the fact that I have sometimes heard some persons, personally acquainted with Knott, describe his poverty as affectation. My personal meetings with this singular man —meetings all too infrequent—give me the authority to assert that he is poor. He is not one of those persons who, dressed in tie-dyed trousers and puce buckskin blouses, frequently suck around Lincoln Center fountain in the patient hope of procuring Alice Cooper's snake's autograph (and then, of course, selling it).

Bill Knott was poor.

Part of the vitality and difficulty of the American language is its capacity for rapid change. It may therefore be useful—to those too young to have experienced the Great Depression of the '30s—to digress briefly on the meaning of the words "poverty" and "poor."

Of course, the Depression struck the entire country. But my native place was southeastern Ohio and the West Virginia Panhandle, and I will confine my remarks to those parts of the United States which I knew best during my childhood.

The fathers of the great majority of my childhood friends were ordinary working men. For example, my father was officially employed for fifty years in Wheeling, W. Va., by the Hazel-Atlas Glass Factory, now absorbed by the Continental Can Company. Other friends' fathers worked at such places as Wheeling Steel, the Laughlin Steel Mill, Blaw-

Knox, and the usual coal-mines, which were nearly as interesting and newsworthy during the Great Depression as they are today.

Some of these working men were fired from their jobs outright. Some of them managed to support their families in unaccustomed ways. Some made a few cents a day by emptying people's garbage cans and hauling it by pushcart to the town dump. (How I remember that old town dump. It was as thrillingly unpredictable as the planet Jupiter. It contained everything from mysteriously unopened boxes of sanitary napkins to young and frolicking blacksnakes to unaccountably unemployed condoms somewhat past their prime to out-of-tune player-pianos to decaying paper flowers [sometimes even poor people love their wives and do their best to remind them of it]). Others, like my uncles Sherman and Emerson, of blessed memory, ordered boxes of something called Dr. Dade's soap (which by the way, was totally incapable of raising lather, though I personally experimented with it scores of times), drove their senile Model-T Ford into the surrounding mining towns, and occasionally succeeded in bartering their dubious product with the unsuspecting housewives of the unemployed miners in exchange for such items as undernourished live chickens. I have myself often dined on these. I would not go so far as to compare these fowl with *coq au vin* as served at Maxim's or *La Belle Epoque*. But our skinny hens had their points. Besides, you can manage to eat quite a few improbable things when you get hungry enough. Believe you me.

Other working men, like my father, were more fortunate—theoretically, at least. They were not given the kindly choice of either getting their asses the hell off the company property instantly and voluntarily or else getting those very selfsame asses kicked off, even more instantly, by the company's trained and courteous personnel (i.e., the muscular company-finks of the old days, who were for some reason constantly employed and decently paid for their services, which they were always willing and even eager, to perform with competence and dispatch). No, men like my father were never fired outright. Instead, they were frequently "laid off." This term means simply that they were told by the management to just go home and stay there, often for weeks at a time, without being paid. I have often wondered why such men's names were retained officially on the company's payroll. Perhaps the management thought of it as an "honor" of some kind. I don't know. If you should ever by chance figure out just what goes on inside the skull of a factory manager, please don't waste your time by trying to explain it to me. I just don't get it, and it is unlikely that I ever will.

These men were poor. In spite of their remarkable courage and re-sourcefulness in their determination to support their families in the face of sometimes appalling difficulties beyond ability to describe, which in fact only a great novelist could manage adequately—Nelson Algren and Dreiser got at least some of the truth on paper, and I trust the reader will excuse me when I point out that, in spite of my respect for his genius, we are not exactly dealing with Henry James country at this moment—my father and my friends' fathers were often understandably discouraged. They used to have a phrase that attempted to express their discourage-ment, and they repeated it so often that it became almost a kind of folk-saying. Hundreds of times I must have heard a man returning home after a long day's futile search for work, any work at all, and dispiritedly whispering to his anxious wife, or mumbling absent-mindedly to himself in his baffled loneliness: "I ain't got a pot to piss in or a window to throw it out of."

That is the kind of thing I meant when I said that Bill Knott was poor. For all I know, he still is, though God knows I hope that, wherever he may be at this moment, he is getting enough to eat. Let me conclude this digression by asking a favor of the reader: if you should see me and approach me with the intention of informing me that Knott's poverty is an affectation, please be kind enough to forget me and just go talk to somebody else. In my youth I used to be able to listen patiently enough to liars, cowards, and other ignorant, mentally-retarded sons of bitches. But Nature catches up with all at last, and I am unfortunately getting too old to listen. I would probably go to sleep right in your face. Or *on* your face, if I had the strength left.

Now let me return to that first meeting with Bill Knott. After the girls hurried off to keep their appointments, Knott and I chatted for a few minutes and were pleased to discover our mutual devotion to the art of shooting pool. Almost immediately we started to stroll in the direction of a local parlor.

This is where my old poem comes in.

A clear account of this odd little episode will require a few words of preliminary explanation.

Several months before I met Bill Knott, or had even heard of him, my brother Jack informed me in a letter that our uncle, William Lyons, had died. An adequate description of Uncle Willie's life and personality is hopeless. But I will do my best to offer a few suggestive details about him, because they might help the reader make a little more sense out of the poem that I will soon quote.

Willie's usual personal appearance was somewhat misleading. Though by no means a dandy, he preferred to dress in a conventional black suit, black tie, white shirt, well-polished black shoes, and, when he was outside, a conventional black hat. Seeing him standing idly on a street corner in Martins Ferry, you might naturally have taken him for one of our local morticians out for a few minutes of fresh air; or, given his somewhat puritanical dress and stance, one of our local ministers half-lost in his secret romantic fantasy of suddenly, without preliminary announcement, dropping the entire fiasco, getting decently drunk, and devoting his meager life-savings to the hope of giving Mae West a proper jump in a rumble-seat; he might even have seemed a dentist. In short, to the casual passer-by, he could have appeared to be any one of a thousand of our typical, conventional, respectable citizens. In his formal dress, he looked slight of build, perhaps even frail.

In reality, Willie was a highly skilled carpenter by trade. I have watched him for hours at work. I never once saw him fail to drive a long thin nail all the way into a two-by-four at a single flawlessly accurate stroke. Consequently, I never heard him curse. (I speak of his working occasions, of course.) With his denim sleeves rolled up, his forearms resembled those of the late Rocky Marciano. Willie's skill was such that he could have made good money at his trade, even during the Great Depression. He could have taken a job any time he chose. There was a lot of money around even then, though only a small minority of people owned it. And yet, Willie preferred to work only as long each year as he needed to achieve two goals: to earn enough to live on; and to pay the government as little income tax as was necessary to keep himself out of jail. In a word, Uncle Willie was a patriot. I am aware that the old-fashioned word "patriot" will be as unintelligible to most occupants of the United States as the punchline of an in-joke among the slaves of the Hittites. But in Uncle Willie's prime, the word had a perfectly clear and common meaning. Willie considered himself a free man. I remember his sentiments on this subject so vividly that I believe I can quote some of them with middling accuracy:

"The gummint? I don't work for the gummint. They work for me. I work good and I work hard when I choose to work. I pay them what they force me to pay them. If they don't like it, they can go hump a castrated snake."

Uncle Willie had a dour face. I can't remember ever hearing him laugh out loud. But he smiled once in a while. And when he smiled, his eyes gleamed with a wickedness of almost supernatural beauty. He wore an upper denture, which he sometimes could wiggle with his tongue into positions so improbably ugly and grotesque that these performances made my younger brother Jack nearly collapse into an epileptic faint out of sheer unqualified delight.

Willie has been dead for years. Nearly everybody alive, except a few remaining relatives like Jack and me, has forgotten him. After the few short years that remain to us, nobody will know or care that my Uncle Willie ever existed on earth. I loved him very much. I still do, even as I write these few words about him.

The afternoon Jack informed me of Willie's death, I was very busy in my office at the University of Minnesota. But the hell with busy, I thought. A few things matter in this world. I just dropped everything I was doing, whatever it was, and took a half-hour's walk all alone, to mourn Willie by myself, in my own way. While I strolled along University Avenue, deaf even to the diesel trucks that seem to roar along there one after another all day and all night, I thought about Willie. I knew he would never be an immortal historical figure, Julius 'Caesar,' Christ, Alice Cooper, or President Nixon. So I thought it might be nice to write a poem in his memory. I had to get back to work at once, so I made a mental note to try the poem whenever I managed to get a free hour or so. Then out of sheer economic necessity I forgot about the whole thing: death, Willie, poem, and all.

Bill Knott and I continued our slow walk toward the pool parlor. In his usual reticence, he didn't say a word. I didn't mind. Usually if a friend feels like talking, I'm willing to converse. If he feels like staying quiet, I'm willing to be quiet, too. (Since I've quit drinking, the reader can trust this statement.)

Abruptly Bill asked, "Do you want to hear a poem?"

I thought he meant a poem of his own, so naturally I was pleased. I answered, "I sure would."

Here is the poem, which he recited to me with flawless accuracy:

WILLY LYONS

My uncle, a craftsman of hammers and wood,
Is dead in Ohio.
And my mother cries she is angry.
Willy was buried with nothing except a jacket
Stitched on his shoulder bones.
It is nothing to mourn for.
It is the other world.

She does not know how the roan horses, there,
Dead for a century,
Plod slowly.
Maybe they believe Willy's brown coffin, tangled heavily
        in moss,
Is a horse trough drifted to shore
Along that river under the willows and grass.
Let my mother weep on, she needs to, she knows of cold winds.
The long box is empty.
The horses turn back toward the river.
Willy planes limber trees by the waters,
Fitting his boat together.
We may as well let him go.
Nothing is left of Willy on this side
But one cracked ball-peen hammer and one suit,
Including pants, his son inherited,
For a small fee, from Hesslop's funeral home;
And my mother,
Weeping with anger, afraid of winter
For her brothers' sake:
Willy, and John, whose life and art, if any,
I never knew.

I stopped stone-still on the sidewalk and glared at him, angry. "Who the hell do you think you are?"

He looked hurt and puzzled, and mumbled, "I don't know what you mean." Not that he would have minded much, but he must have really done it this time: got himself mixed up with an authentic psychotic. Such persons are not sentimentally amusing, in spite of Jerry Lewis's feeble attempts to make them seem so by imitating their hilarious pain.

I answered, "You know what I mean. I never got around to writing those verses, but they were my idea. It was my own uncle, for Christ's sake."

Knott just looked at me for a long moment. Then he asked if I would please come back to his room with him for a minute. Still furious, I went along. I had no idea what he had in mind—maybe he was going to offer me some more Jack Daniels, to calm me down.

When we got back to his place he said nothing. He just took a magazine from a shelf and opened it to a certain place. I said then, and I say still, "Well, I'll be a son of a bitch." There it was: the poem he had just recited to me, with my own name printed right under the title.

The matter explains itself.

Evidently, some time after I had spent my lonely afternoon mourning for my Uncle Willie, I actually did get a chance to write the poem. Almost immediately after I wrote it, my friend Dick Foster, then editor of *The Minnesota Review,* was caught in an uncharacteristic panic. He had a new issue all ready for the printer, and to his horror he discovered at the last minute that the number of pages hadn't come out even. He was in danger of printing an issue that contained a blank page. Usually a man of good cheer, he saw me and asked, in a hang-dog way, if I happened to have something I could give him to fill in the magazine. He was a good friend; I knew how he felt; I had just finished the poem about Uncle Willie; he printed it. This sequence of events happened so fast that I had forgotten I had written the poem and even that it had been printed.

But Bill Knott found it and liked it.

In order to write this memoir, or whatever you want to call it, I had to reread the Uncle Willie poem. It doesn't seem like much to me now. Reader, if you and I felt like puking all over each other with boredom before we both sank into terminal catatonia, I could easily name you a list of at least five hundred other persons who could have written it or something very like it. It's not a bad poem. It's not a good poem. What is it, actually? It's a conventional exercise in modish free verse or whatever the hell this week's cant word may be, which I neither know nor care to know. The real value the poem has for me is that it still reminds me of Uncle Willie. I love him, he is in the ground, he is mostly forgotten, soon I'll be forgotten, and that's the end of that. He's my precious secret.

> *Ist auf deinem Psalter,*
> *Vater der Liebe,*
> *Ein Ton seinem Ohre vernehmlich,*
> *So erquicke sein Herz!*

But when Bill Knott quoted my own commonplace poem to me, it sounded magnificent. No, he wasn't trying to imitate the great voice of Dylan Thomas. He wasn't even trying to imitate Vincent Price. He just read in his own ordinary voice: the plain midwestern twang (I have heard that he was born in Michigan, but I don't know for sure); the softness, part of his reticence no doubt, that sometimes made it hard to hear him clearly, so that you have to ask him to repeat a word or even a whole phrase. It was just Bill Knott, quoting to me my ordinary poem, and making it sound glorious. I have often wondered what the experience meant. The nearest I've ever managed to come to an explanation is that, in some way I don't hope to understand, the poem struck a live nerve somewhere in Knott and somehow became important to him. In a way, it seems to have become part of his living spirit. When that sort of thing happens to a person of great natural gifts, God alone knows what incredible beautiful thing it might move him to create. The odd thing is that the original occasion, or material, that sets a great and original artist in motion doesn't in itself have to be anything out of the ordinary. Take, as just one example of many possible examples, Beethoven's "Diabelli Variations." Diabelli, a man of good will had had a little extra money to spare, offered it to any good composer who would write a set of variations on a theme of his own invention. Did you ever happen to hear that theme itself, played in its naked original version on the piano? I don't know about you, but the original theme invented by Diabelli sounds to me neither good nor bad. But that's not quite accurate. It sounds better than a duet by Rod McKuen and Florence Foster Jenkins; but then, what in the universe doesn't? But once Beethoven got hold of it, he transformed it into one of the immortal glories of human life on earth.

This short piece began as an attempt to describe my first meeting with Bill Knott, for the purpose of further describing just how a certain set of verses came to be written and first published. It ended mainly as a discussion of Knott himself. But that's all right with me. If it's not all right with you, I can't help it.

I once heard Knott read a poem of his own. At one point, he was describing the appearance of a wretched skid-road drunk, half-starved and yet probably unable to keep any food down, literally dying for a mere sip of rot-gut, leaning on a corner of an old building that must have looked as though it had been saturation-bombed and then half-reconstructed by an architect from McDonald's. The man stood there, in Knott's phrase, "crucified in his clothes." I'm not even jealous of that phrase. What's the use? Even a hack can feel gratitude when he hears true poetry, of which we have very little in the world at any time.

I don't know where Bill Knott is at the moment. The last I heard, he had a job and enough to eat. The thought makes me happy, because we are friends, and because it means that he will be able to give us more of his indispensable poems, poems that nobody else could write.

The Infidel

Garrison, N.Y.
June 9, 1974

The strange man stepped slowly out from the sumac trees. He didn't look afraid, but I think he looked suspicious—certainly cautious. I reckon he must have been hiding for a long time back in the brush. Probably he had been waiting till we got the fire good and going and had given it enough time to burn down to nice red coals. It's also possible that the stranger had enough sense to make sure we weren't likely to be receiving a cordial social visit from a railroad dick (we had built our fire only a few yards from the B & O railroad track) who was acquainted with us and with most of our fathers. Our visitor, on the other hand, was a stranger, and a stranger is, shall we say, well advised to be discreet in his relations with a railroad dick. My friends and I, all of us between eight and ten years old, had little experience of the real world, but we did have some, and some of it was useful, and remains so even to this day.

Take the procedure of dealing with a railroad dick. If you met one walking along the railroad track, or anywhere within sight of it, you smile, say, "hello, sir," and immediately go away from there as quickly as possible. Don't run. Do not ever run. Railroad dicks during the Depression were not easily employed merely for their rugged good looks and their irresistible personal charm. They were talented men. In spite of their age, and in spite of their advanced paunches, they shared yet another quality of the elderly Jim Thorpe. They would run quite rapidly and adroitly for surprisingly long distances.

Then, if you happened to meet a railroad dick while you were actually aboard a B & O freight car, even if the car were rusted and isolated on a side track, as so many of them seemed to be in those days, you faced two possible consequences, either of which was certain. If you were lucky and the railroad dick was in a genial mood (drunk), he might just chuckle avuncularly and say, "Kid, you know you ain't allowed on these cars. Now, you git on out of this or I'll tell your old man on you." If he happened to be in a bad mood, he might do anything to you.

For the benefit of readers unfamiliar with the idiom of southeastern Ohio and the West Virginia Panhandle, I should point out that the word "anything," as commonly used, is neither an abstraction nor a vague generalization. The term has a specific meaning. I am not going to define it here. I don't like to think about it. I knew a boy who got caught by two railroad dicks and they did something to him. He didn't die. I am old enough to realize that the process of human dying is sometimes very long and painful. But it is easy to be dead.

The stranger seated with us at the fire had two black eyes. Even an eight-year-old can distinguish between bruises and dirt. The man needed a bath. He plainly hadn't washed for some time. The fact seemed odd to me. Though I myself had no passion for daily cleanliness, there were times when I felt the need. At the moment, we couldn't have been more than two hundred yards from the western channel of the Ohio. It wasn't dangerous there. There could have been no fear of drowning. On our August evening, the channel ran shallow. You could touch bottom all the way from the Ohio bank to the north tip of Wheeling Island. Of course, even in those days the river water was not quite as sanitary as a bottle of sealed *Perrier*. An open sewer from Martins Ferry poured into the river about a mile upstream; and, a little further up, such factories as Wheeling Steel, Laughlin Steel and the Blaw-Knox Company were constantly presenting their modest contributions on which the health of our American economy continue to depend. Still, the water in the river was flowing, at any rate, and the stranger could have refreshed himself briefly and got the scum off, at least. I guess he was just too tired to bother.

"You boys happen to have any mickies in that fire?"

Sure, said Junior Pugh, and speared him a nice one with a sharp little willow stick.

It was then that we understood how hungry the stranger was. To be properly roasted, a mickey has to be buried under the hot coals for a long time. The mickey Junior offered the stranger had roasted so long that its entire crust must have been charred half an inch thick. You can imagine how hot it must have been. I wouldn't have even touched that mickey till it had lain on the ground for at least five minutes, maybe even ten. But the stranger plucked it right off the end of the willow stick, broke it in half, and ate it in four or five bites.

"Thank you, son. Appreciate it."

"You happen to have any more?"

"Oh, we got plenty more. Crum's old man worked a couple days last week, unloading potatoes up at the A & P." This was a lie, of course. We had stolen that sack of potatoes. I forget where.

The stranger ate the second mickey just as he'd eaten the first.

He sat silent a while. Just to make conversation Jack asked, "Where you just come from? Hop a freight?"

"No, matter of fact I hitched a ride with a truck-driver down in Bridgeport. Nice fellow. Came right out and admitted he was a company fink. I didn't mind. Everybody's got to make a living. He let me out right down by this bridge you got at Aetnaville."

"Where you headed now?"

"Well, I got to meet a guy in Pittsburgh tomorrow, so I figured I'd catch that B & O freight they run by here at 5 in the morning."

"You better watch out for the railroad dick. They got a mean one here on the night-shift."

"Oh, don't worry. If I see him see me, I'll jump off the train. I know how to do it." He looked drowsy to me, but something told me he would make it through the night. I didn't really believe he had a friend in Pittsburgh; but, for that matter, I don't believe anybody else does either.

He sat quiet again, for a longer time than before. He was thinking. Then he said, "Boys, I'm an infidel. You know? An unbeliever?"

I didn't have the faintest idea what an infidel was, and I was pretty sure that the others didn't know either. But several of us said, "Oh, yeah, sure, we know."

He scared me a little. For all I knew, Infidel might have been one of those strange diseases like that one they used to call infantile paralysis, in the days when people were forever warning you to keep away from swimming pools and pool rooms and cheap crowded movie-theaters and other places where any rational person would be like to spend the summer vacation, except maybe church, which somehow never seemed to cause any hygienic anxiety to the Board of Health.

But we left the stranger alone. We sat there with him while he slept for about an hour. Then we went home. We never saw him again. I kind of liked him, and if he died, I hope he had a good easy death, as I hope I will some day have one, too.

I look back over the sometimes confusing years, and I remember with affection several people who were believers. I am not myself what I would call a man of much particular faith, religious or otherwise. But it always quickens my joy in the value of life to think about my friend Father George Garrelts, S. J., with whom I spent so many happy hours in Minneapolis years ago. Most of all I remember how one evening in Saint Paul my precious beloved friend, almost my brother I might call him, Ghazi Ismail Gailini, the poet from Iraq, read in Arabic and then translated into English for some students and me a little poem from his country. I forget the name of its author. But what strikes me most sharply in my recollection of Ghazi's incomparably beautiful recitation is the almost total difference between the students' response to the poem and my own response. The students were without exception highly intelligent and attentive. And yet to them the poem seemed totally obscure, impenetrable, a poem written in a tradition so exotically oriental and foreign to them that they found it hopeless. They said that they could never understand the poem in a million years.

To me, the poem was instantly perfectly accessible. Even as I write down these memories, the poem seems to me one of the clearest and most comprehensible poems I have ever heard or read anywhere. It is possible that Ghazi's poem reached out and touched, as with a kindly and understanding hand, my half-buried memory of that strange infidel, the hobo with the unwashed eyes, who stepped out of the sumac trees near the railroad track just above the Ohio River so long ago and shared with my friends and me a little of his time, a little of our time, some serious conversation we only partly understood, a few of our lies, a couple of our mickies, and the social comfort of our August fire.

Here is the poem that Ghazi translated:

> As I drifted near shore
> In the first light of morning,
> I saw my country
> Hunched over in a blackened boat,
> A fire between her knees.

Home, New York
Feb. 25, 1974

This afternoon, after I had lectured for an hour or so, a girl came up to me and exclaimed, "I feel so shaken! How can you go on and on so passionately about the poems of Robert Herrick? I think he's too—too pretty. I don't think I like him."

Ears small and delicate as the inside of a monarch butterfly's wing; her nostrils seemed strong and careful enough to catch something beyond the fragrance of the sea beside Eype, Fowey, Mousehole, the whole of ancient Cornwall. I would have liked to ask her to take her shoes off and walk across the floor of that dismal classroom. I don't know how I know, but I know that her toes would have been as sure and strong as the horns of a snail.

Anthea, Julia, Electra, why do I love Herrick?

I don't know. Lucky, I guess.

Italian Moments

1

This morning I got thrust out of a crowded train at Dezensano. Some hands were angry, but the most harried hands were kind. The next thing I knew, I was drifting over a silver olive leaf of water into the eye of all islands.

Sirmio, gone in an instant. The silver of the olive leaf turned over, the sun passed, and even when the sun returned all that was left was the dark root of this olive water.

It is almost everything, but it is not quite.

Sirmio, how I longed to visit you before.

2

Today, on the Feast of the Assumption, the Congress of the United States has required the President to order a cessation of bombing in Cambodia. Three men are standing below me on the shore of Lake Garda. They poise on the rocks, trailing their fishing lines in the clear water. Now and again a man draws in his line. Each carries a clear plastic bag perhaps one-third filled with piccolini, the little glittering silver creatures that must have been living in this water when Catullus was a boy. The year he was born, the legions of Julius Caesar attempted to invade Britain, and failed. The year he died, thirty years later, they tried again, and more or less succeeded. A Roman temple once stood in Britain. It was in Dorchester, Dorset, and now it is the site of the Church of St. Peter's and All Saints.

In front of that church this morning, far away on that northern island, sundered once from all the human race, the statue of William Barnes turns slowly greener as he looks down the West High Street towards the King's Arms Hotel in whose doorway once stood the most beautiful girl he had ever seen or was ever to see in his life. Below me on the olive-silver pebbles of the Garda shore, some small boys are scampering in search of an escaped piccolino. They are serious, hurrying before the little fish, like so much else, stops struggling back towards the water and turns to stone. I don't know what time it is in Cambodia. I wonder what the silence can be there. Where is it? It is waiting, as I want to wait. The sunlight once glinted off William Barnes's coffin, and, from the hill, so far away it seemed the other side of the earth, his friend Thomas Hardy waved goodbye.

3

When I came here to greet my brother,
I found he was already gone.

4 POETRY OF THE PRESENT MOMENT

Off the shore of Gargnano the mountains in this summer mist look
barren. But sometimes it is the conventionally homely women who have
the loveliest children. Tall and short mountains beside me as I pass by
this lake throw their own wreaths on the water that is warmer than the
oldest olive.

A few miles up the lake a town called Limone long ago lost its hope
of surviving. The lemons of Sicily, quicker and more numerous, banish
the town I will see, back to its own loveliness that lies in the Garda
water like a wreath.

Limone, wreath of the Garda mountain's shadow, the stone villa of
Catullus still lives down at the far southern end of the lake. I hope you
are still alive when his ghost comes home.

5 A SMALL GROVE

Outside our window we have a small willow, and a little beyond it a
fig tree very tempting to plundering fingers like mine. Beside a stone
shed is a small grove that includes a lemon tree, a mimosa, an oleander,
a pine, one of the tall slender cypresses that a poet here once called
candles of darkness that ought to be put out in the winter, another
willow, and a palm.

She stands among them in her flowered green clothes. Her skin is
darker gold than the olives in the morning sun. Two hours ago we got
up and bathed in the lake. It was like swimming in a vein. Everything
that can blossom is blossoming around her now. She is the eye of the
grove, the eye of mimosa and willow.

PAUL ZIMMER

PAUL ZIMMER (b. 1934 in Canton, Ohio) was an unsuc-
cessful student but dedicated poet who has developed, in
his play of personae, a unique voice. After working for
many years in various areas of the book business, he
became an editor at the University of Pittsburgh Press. A
man of many talents and hobbies, Zimmer lives in
Pittsburgh with his wife Susan and their two children.
(Photo by Paul Balaban)

The Importance of Being Zimmer

I began to be interested in poetry when I was in the Army. Before that I had swallowed, without digesting, the passages of "Snowbound," "O Captain, My Captain," and "The Charge of the Light Brigade" that were required in school, but it all was as uninteresting to me as mathematics, civics, or Latin. In the Army I was forced to cope with the incredible boredom of service life. Drinking beer in the Post Exchange and watching Elaine Stewart or Piper Laurie movies could only occupy so much time. I was actually driven in my desperation to *reading!*

So it was inevitable, I guess, that I came across an old paperback copy of an Oscar Williams anthology of modern verse. After a careful look through the portraits on the insides of the covers (Robert Graves looking like a middleweight pug, Allen Tate like an English butler, Yeats like a leprechaun, Dylan Thomas looking bilious, the lovely Elinor Wylie, Emily Dickinson as Elsa Lancaster, etc.) I began to read some of the poems. Flipping at random I read Roy Fuller's "Meditation," Delmore Schwartz's "The Heavy Bear," and Muriel Rukeyser's "Ajanta." I was puzzled, dazzled by the language and deeply intrigued. I had never encountered anything quite like it before. In my mind poets had always been dead people—solemn, white-bearded men and artsy-craftsy women pressed in books like dried flowers. But here were *living* poets writing in a vocabulary and in rhythms that I could feel. I read many more poems that day, then read and reread the book until I wore it out in the months that followed.

It was during this period that I decided that I wanted to be a poet. Haltingly I began to try to imitate what I read. I purchased a tweed coat and a pipe and told my friends that I was a poet. I got a Louis Untermeyer anthology, a paperback copy of *A Shropshire Lad*, and Modern Library editions of Whitman and Poe. I began to ply my friends with my efforts, but no one *really* believed me.

The rest of the autobiography is the old story—the years of trial and error, the rejection slips mounting, the long days of making a living in warehouses, offices, steel mills, bookstores; the short nights of scratching at the poems.

I had not been a good student when I was in school. I was too selfish to do the assignments, too self-indulgent to read anything but my own choices. In fact, I flunked out of college twice and finally left without my degree. As we measure the performance of our young people by the grades they achieve in school, I was forced to regard myself as a failure. I certainly did not regard myself as being very interesting. So my early poems were always about other people, either people I had read about and admired or people that I made up. I greatly admired Yeats and envied him his Irish mythologies. It seemed to me that all the American myths and legends had been used up by Carl Sandburg and Vachel Lindsay years before. I guess I was attempting to invent my own personal mythologies with the characters I made up.

I took a few night workshops in poetry writing but usually dropped away from the courses; mostly it was a matter of solitary hammering. It took me nine years to write a poem that was accepted by a magazine. *The Virginia Quarterly Review* published the following poem in their Summer 1963 issue:

FATHER MENDEL AT BRÜNN

Three to one inside these walls,
The sons of stilted and the long,
One tall, one short to make the talls,
Then three to one the tall ones strong.

What prince of pollen cuts these rules
And overlaps the choice of wind?
Who rubs against the grafting tools
And makes the lighter things rescind?

Three to one outside these walls
And old von Metternich is done.
Now the House of Hapsburg falls
And threes have made the Empire one.

Lord, give me touch to understand,
And I will shed my pruning glove
To feel your ever-choosing hand
Count out the strong seed's love.

Three to one inside these walls,
The sons of stilted and the long,
One tall, one short to make the talls,
Then three to one the tall ones strong.

Which is a pretty solemn, library-scented poem for a guy who had flunked out of college! There were many more similar poems on other people—Keats, Wordsworth, Joseph Conrad, Juan Belmonte, George Frederick Handel, Johnny Blood, Charlie Christian, etc. Eventually I began to make up my own people to write about, giving them names like Phineas, Alphonse, Wanda, Father Animus, Christiaan Radius, King Criswell. I arranged and rearranged these poems into a manuscript and began submitting it to publishers. In 1967, thirteen years after my discovery of the Oscar Williams anthology, my first book, *The Ribs of Death* (1967), was published by October House. One of the better poems in the book was a bright-eyed concoction of some facts, some dreaming, and a lot of whimsy. It was:

LORD FLUTING DREAMS OF AMERICA ON THE
EVE OF HIS DEPARTURE FROM LIVERPOOL

Purple Indians pas de bourrée
Around a Chippendale totem pole.
The Ute dips to the Crow,
And curtsies to the Navajo,
While the forest in its wig and stole
Claps its leaves politely.

Cotton and tobacco plants cluster
On the backland hills like
Plaster on a Spanish cloister.
The rivers and the lakes
Are filled with plumèd bass
Who browse urbanely on the watercress.

The sylvan trail to Oregon
Is thronged with gentle post chaises
Gliding toward great fortune;
For this is where the buffalo turn
Broadside to the hunting horns,
And gold is strained like sunshine
Through the heath.

This is taken from a section of the book called "Phineas, Fluting, Wanda, and Alphonse," which signaled a change in the attitude of my work. I was now headed into making clusters of poems about the characters I had made up.

In my second book, *The Republic of Many Voices* (1969), I included three groups of poems about characters named Imbellis, Mordecai,

Peregrine, and a section of individual persona poems called "Them." The extended personae sections attempted to state landscapes and collectively tell little stories about their inhabitants. For instance, Imbellis is born in his sequence as a creature of innocence who ends in rage and carnage. He goes into the landscape expecting peace, without realizing what lies latent in his being. One poem from the cluster describes his early expectations:

IMBELLIS STROLLS OUT AMONG THE TREES AND IMAGINES THE WORLD TO BE AS PEACEFUL AS THEIR SEASONS

Above me the trees do things with such simplicity.

I walk in their shadows, I feel them press up
Against the wind, hear their leaves flick rain,
And watch them take the sun completely as their due.

They are so pervasive, so abundant, so gentle.

They grow giddy with their richness in the fall,
And loosen leaves from their tiny sockets
To flash and clatter down to my feet,
Then they tighten quietly to ring another year.

Snow clings to them, curving and angling
In black and white, gathering and spilling
With its weight to tingle down on my face.

I cannot even perceive the time they enter
The gentlest of seasons.

                There are buds,
Then flowers and small leaves unclutching,
And all this so green and graceful before
My eyes I do not know it is happening.

I have seen these trees in day and night;
I have passed through their them in peace and happiness.

They have no secret periods of ferocity,
They do not surround and swallow
Each other like insidious cells in jelly.
They are strong yet meaningful through all seasons.
Surely the world I come to is like them.

The final section of *The Republic of Many Voices* is a cluster of poems about a not-so-mysterious character named Zimmer. It seemed to me that, for a fellow who had always carefully placed the names of his personae in the poems, when it came time to begin making autobiographical poems they should be called "Zimmer" poems. Besides I had grown weary of trying to manufacture my own myths and legends. I began to realize that myth-making is more than a one man operation, that myths are, indeed, not vague and fanciful little squibs, but believed and believable explanations of life on this planet. Myths are something you should be willing to give your life for, to die for, if necessary. I began to know that the only determinate myth I could attempt, albeit small and seemingly insignificant, was myself.

Thus has begun a copious outpouring of poems. It is almost as though, at long last, I have decided that I am important enough to write about, that the microcosm I can present is meaningful enough in itself. And *that* is a kind of liberating experience for a writer!

The poems seem to come in chronological groups, the first ones remembering early years, and then the subsequent ones tracing my life with memories, dreams, hopes, ending in fanciful imaginings of old age and death. No sooner do I complete such a group than another begins the cycle again. Some groups are somber and full of thumb-sucking, others complete themselves in humor. One of the earliest Zimmer poems, and the one that begins the last section of my second book is:

ZIMMER'S HEAD THUDDING AGAINST THE BLACKBOARD

At the blackboard I had missed
Five number problems in a row,
And was about to foul a sixth,
When the old, exasperated nun
Began to pound my head against
My six mistakes. When I cried,
She threw me back into my seat,
Where I hid my head and swore
That very day I'd be a poet,
And curse her yellow teeth with this.

The second to the last poem in the group is called, "Zimmer Warns Himself with Vivid Images Against Old Age," and thus this first cycle is completed.

A more recent and far more contemplative poem is "The Sweet Night

Bleeds from Zimmer," which is, essentially, a meditation on human cruelty. The poem begins with a memory of Barney, a playground bully, giving me a beating. Barney becomes a huge insect hovering over me, devouring my brains and my heart. Then the poem becomes a memory of my experiences as a witness to atomic bomb tests when I was in the Army—a recollection of what I regard as the ultimate human cruelty. Then there is a section in which I recall my own cruelty, an incident which took place once when I was fishing at night. Finally the poem returns again to Barney's cruelty to me.

THE SWEET NIGHT BLEEDS FROM ZIMMER

Barney catches me in a dark place
With no sunlight I can squirm through.
His body uncoils its frustrations
And fists plunge like the last stones
Of a landslide.
                I fall before
I feel his blows, then pain
Flies to my surfaces as though
It had always been there waiting
For Barney to challenge it out.
My skin folds back in slots and tabs
And the sweet night bleeds from my face.

Barney catches me in a dark place,
His jaws and pincers grinding.
I feel my brains sucked out of my head,
My heart clutched in his claws,
Remembering and still trying to beat.
I am ground up and spat into the weeds,
The sweet night is bleeding from my skull.

Barney catches me in a dark place
And stars descend to coil about my head,
Buzzing about my gravity, sinking
Their stingers in my lips and eyelids.
In the trees each twig and sucker
Is pointing at a separate fire.
How could I have forgotten all these stars?

Stars in the desert faded at dawn;
Then the flash and shock wave

Rammed sand in my face, uprooted cactus,
Blasted the animals, birds from the sky.
Afterwards, under the fireball
And faint stars, we wanted to kick
Dead rabbits, throw stones at each other,
Call each other sons-of-bitches.

Once on the dark still lake I dropped
My line between the stars and prayed
For fish in the midst of night.
The small pickerel swallowed my hook
And when I ripped it out the fish
Screamed like a wounded rabbit.
I rowed my boat in out of the dark,
Churning the galaxies and nebulae,
Spoiling the perfect night.

Barney catches me in a dark place,
He won't back off and let me be.
I look for a place to hide under
Mother's navel, behind father's penis.
But I can't remember who I am.
Someone wounded and breathing hard,
Trying to become the earth; sorry man
Remembering each cruelty under the stars;
Someone wagging submission forever.

I hope in the future to perhaps reconnect with that old world I tried
to make for myself some years ago. I have begun to make poems in
which I enter into the landscapes with the old personae and I feel comfortable with them. It seems possible to me now that I can create and
interact with them, maybe make poems in which we tell some old stories
together, find our way through some of the ancient earth and, perhaps,
discover some meanings together.

Selected Bibliography

This bibliography is presented in two parts. Part I lists books, chap-books, pamphlets by the contributors. I have not followed the usual practice and entered volumes of poetry in one list and "other" work—novels, editions, criticism—in another, but have preferred to let the works stand as they have appeared. A poet's development, his or her enthusiasms and ardors, will often stand out clearer for us if we look over the titles and dates of the total achievement rather than relegate work "other" than major books of poems to a separate pile for inci-dentals. In many cases I have included limited editions, small press publications that the reader of this anthology will not easily find, but I don't think anyone will have difficulty in realizing which titles are the most important books of poems and which are more ephemeral produc-tions. Again, I have sometimes indulged myself in listing small things because I believe we can more easily see where poets have been and what they have done when we are aware of even their diminutives. At the same time, I have used *some* discretion and not listed *everything* interest-ing to me as a bibliomaniac: in almost every case I have been, and am, aware of other ephemerae that could have been included. But there is usually a method to my madness: the reader will find, for example, that Robert Bly's poem, "Chrysanthemums," is included in *Jumping Out of Bed* (1973), but should he find the pamphlet *Chrysanthemums* (1967), he would see that this earlier version of the poem differs in important ways. Following the same logic, I have *not* listed a pamphlet by John Haines called *The Mirror* (Unicorn Press, 1971), because the text of its single poem is the same as that appearing in *Leaves and Ashes* (1974).

In Part II I have included, very selectively, general studies of modern and contemporary American poetry. In addition, I have listed (again, *very* selectively) essays, articles, and reviews by and about the con-tributors to *American Poets in 1976*. Within brackets that follow the final entry for each contributor, I refer the reader to other entries in this section of the bibliography dealing with this particular poet. I hope this method of pointing will prove convenient, though I hope also that the reader will browse the entire bibliography. Though the bibliography as a whole is, so far as I know, the most substantial of its kind in any anthology, I remain painfully aware of how much more material could have been included.

Part I

ROBERT BLY (b. 1926)

Twenty Poems of Georg Trakl (trans. w. James Wright). Madison, Minn.: The Sixties Press, 1961.

Silence in the Snowy Fields. Middletown: Wesleyan University Press, 1962.

The Lion's Tail and Eyes: Poems Written Out of Laziness and Silence (w. James Wright and William Duffy). Madison, Minn.: The Sixties Press, 1962.

The Story of Gosta Berling, by Selma Lagerlof (trans.). New York: Signet, 1962.

Twenty Poems of Cesar Vallejo (trans. w. John Knoepfle and James Wright). Madison, Minn.: The Sixties Press, 1962.

A Poetry Reading Against the Vietnam War (ed. w. David Ray). Madison, Minn.: The Sixties Press, 1966.

The Sea and the Honeycomb: A Book of Tiny Poems (ed.). Madison, Minn.: The Sixties Press, 1966; Boston: Beacon Press, 1971.

Chrysanthemums. Menominee, Wisc.: Ox Head Press, 1967. Ltd. 350 copies.

Hunger, by Knut Hamsun (trans.). New York: Farrar, Straus, & Giroux; 1967.

Juan Ramon Jimenez: Forty Poems (trans.). Madison, Minn.: The Sixties Press, 1967.

Late Arrival on Earth: Selected Poems of Gunnar Ekelof (trans. w. C. Paulston). London: Rapp & Whiting, 1967.

Pablo Neruda: Twenty Poems (trans. w. James Wright). Madison, Minn.: The Sixties Press, 1967; London: Rapp & Whiting, 1967.

The Light Around the Body. New York: Harper and Row, 1967; London: Rapp & Whiting, 1968.

I Do Best Alone at Night, by Gunnar Ekelof (trans.). Washington, D.C.: Charioteer Press, 1968.

The Satisfaction of Vietnam (play). In *Chelsea* 24/25 (October 1968), 32—46.

The Morning Glory (prose poems). San Francisco: Kayak, 1969; Santa Cruz: Kayak, 1970, expanded from twelve to twenty poems; New York: Harper and Row, 1975, expanded to forty-four poems.

Forty Poems Touching on Recent American History (ed.). Boston: Beacon Press, 1970.

The Teeth Mother Naked at Last. San Francisco: City Lights, 1970.

Tomas Transtromer: Twenty Poems (trans.). Madison, Minn.: The Seventies Press, 1970.

Neruda and Vallejo: Selected Poems (ed. and trans. w. John Knoepfle and James Wright). Boston: Beacon Press, 1971.

Night Vision, by Tomas Transtromer (trans.). Northwood Narrows, N.H.: Lillabulero Press, 1971.

The Fish in the Sea Is Not Thirsty: Versions of Kabir. Northwood Narrows, N.H.: Lillabulero Press, 1971.

Basho (trans.). San Francisco: Mudra Press, 1972.

Night Vision and Other Poems, by Tomas Transtromer (trans.). London: London Magazine Editions, 1972. Includes the texts of the Seventies Press and Lillabulero Press editions listed above.

Ten Sonnets to Orpheus, by Rainer Maria Rilke (trans.). San Francisco: Zephyrus Image, 1972.

Jumping Out of Bed. Barre, Mass.: Barre Publishers, 1973.

Lorca and Jiminez: Selected Poems (ed. and trans.). Boston: Beacon Press, 1973.

Sleepers Joining Hands. New York: Harper and Row, 1973.

Point Reyes Poems. Half Moon Bay, Cal.: Mudra Press, 1974.

The Hockey Poem. Duluth, Minn.: Knife River Press, 1974. Ltd. 500 copies.

Old Man Rubbing His Eyes. Greensboro, N. C.: Unicorn Press, 1975.

JOHN MALCOLM BRINNIN (b. 1916)

The Garden Is Political. New York: Macmillan, 1942.

The Lincoln Lyrics. Norfolk, Conn.: New Directions, 1942.

No Arch, No Triumph. New York: Knopf, 1945.

Modern Poetry: American and British (ed. w. Kimon Friar). New York: Appleton-Century-Crofts, 1951.

The Sorrows of Cold Stone. New York: Dodd Mead, 1951.

Dylan Thomas in America: An Intimate Journal. Boston: Little, Brown; 1955.

The Third Rose: Gertrude Stein and Her World. Boston: Little, Brown; 1959.

A Casebook on Dylan Thomas (ed.). New York: Thomas Y. Crowell, Co.; 1960.

Emily Dickinson: Selected Poems (ed.). New York: Dell, 1960.

The Modern Poets (ed. w. Bill Read). New York: McGraw-Hill, 1963. Second edition, 1970.

The Selected Poems of John Malcolm Brinnin. Boston: Little, Brown; 1963.

William Carlos Williams. Minneapolis: University of Minnesota Press, 1963.

Selected Operas and Plays of Gertrude Stein (ed.). Pittsburgh: University of Pittsburgh Press, 1970.

Skin Diving in the Virgins. New York: Delacorte Press, 1970.

The Sway of the Grand Saloon: A Social History of the North Atlantic. New York: Delacorte Press, 1971.

ROBERT CREELEY (b. 1926)

[There have been checklists of the work of several of the contributors to *American Poets in 1976*, but the only book-length work, so far as I know, has been Mary Novik's *Robert Creeley: An Inventory, 1945–1970* (Kent, Ohio: Kent State University Press, 1973). I've made no attempt to list the very thinnest and/or scarcest of the numerous Creeley items covered in her inventory, to which the reader is referred.]

Le Fou. Columbus: Golden Goose Press, 1952. Ltd. to about 500 copies.

Mayan Letters, by Charles Olsen (ed.). Palma de Mallorca: Divers Press, 1953; London: Jonathan Cape, 1968.

The Immoral Proposition. Highlands, N.C.: Jargon Press, 1953. Ltd. 200 copies.

The Kind Of Act Of. Palma de Mallorca: Divers Press, 1953. Ltd. to about 250 copies.

The Gold Diggers (stories). Palma de Mallorca: Divers Press, 1954; New York: Scribner's, 1965; London: Calder, 1965.

All That Is Lovely in Men. Ashville, N.C.: Jonathan Williams (Jargon), 1955. Ltd. 200 copies.

The Whip. Worcester, England: Migrant Books, 1957.

A Form of Women. New York: Jargon-Corinth, 1959.

For Love: Poems 1950–1960. New York: Scribner's, 1962.

The Island (novel). New York: Scribner's, 1963.

New American Story (ed. w. Donald Allen). New York: Grove Press, 1965.

Poems 1950–1965. London: Calder and Boyars, 1966.

The New Writing in the U.S.A. (ed. w. Donald Allen). Hammondsworth, Middlesex: Penguin, 1967.

Selected Writings, by Charles Olsen (ed.). New York: New Directions, 1967.

Words: Poems. New York: Scribner's, 1967.

Pieces. New York: Scribner's, 1969.

The Charm: Early and Uncollected Poems. San Francisco: Four Seasons Foundation, 1969.

A Quick Graph: Collected Notes and Essays (ed. Donald Allen). San Francisco: Four Seasons Foundation, 1970.

St. Martin's. Los Angeles: Black Sparrow Press, 1971.

A Day Book. New York: Scribner's, 1972.

Listen (play). Los Angeles: Black Sparrow Press, 1972.

Contexts of Poetry: Interviews 1961–1971 (ed. Donald Allen). San Francisco: Four Seasons Foundation, 1973.

Thirty Things. Los Angeles: Black Sparrow Press, 1974.

JOHN HAINES (b. 1924)

Winter News. Middletown: Wesleyan University Press, 1966.

Suite for the Pied Piper. Menominee, Wisc.: Ox Head Press, 1968. Pamphlet ltd. 350 copies.

The Stone Harp. Middletown: Wesleyan University Press, 1971.

Twenty Poems. Santa Barbara: Unicorn Press, 1971.
Leaves and Ashes. Santa Cruz: Kayak and West Coast Poetry Review, 1974.

JOHN HAISLIP (b. 1925)

Elegy for Jake. Portland and Corvallis: Privately printed, 1965. Ltd. 100 copies.
Not Every Year. Seattle: University of Washington Press, 1971.

WILLIAM HEYEN (b. 1940)

Depth of Field. Baton Rouge: Louisiana State University Press, 1970.
A Profile of Theodore Roethke (ed.). Columbus: Charles E. Merrill Co., 1971.
Noise in the Trees: Poems and a Memoir. New York: Vanguard, 1974.
American Poets in 1976 (ed.). Indianapolis: Bobbs-Merrill, 1976.

RICHARD HUGO (b. 1923)

A Run of Jacks. Minneapolis: University of Minnesota Press, 1961.
Death of the Kapowsin Tavern. New York: Harcourt, Brace & World, 1965.
Good Luck in Cracked Italian. New York: New American Library, 1969.
The Lady in Kicking Horse Reservoir. New York: Norton, 1973.
What Thou Lovest Well, Remains American. New York: Norton, 1975.
Rain Five Days and I Love It. Port Townsend, Wa.: Graywolf Press, 1975.

DAVID IGNATOW (b. 1914)

Poems. Prairie City, Ill.: Decker Press, 1948.
The Gentle Weight Lifter. New York: Morris Gallery, 1955.
Say Pardon. Middletown: Wesleyan University Press, 1961.
Figures of the Human. Middletown: Wesleyan University Press, 1964.
Earth Hard: Selected Poems. London: Rapp & Whiting, 1968.
Rescue the Dead. Middletown: Wesleyan University Press, 1968.
Poems: 1934–1969. Middletown: Wesleyan University Press, 1970.
The Notebooks of David Ignatow (ed. w. intro. by Ralph J. Mills, Jr.). Chicago: The Swallow Press, 1973.
Facing the Tree: New Poems. Boston: Atlantic-Little, Brown; 1975.
Selected Poems (chosen w. intro. by Robert Bly). Middletown: Wesleyan University Press, 1975.

JOHN LOGAN (b. 1923)

Cycle for Mother Cabrini. New York: Grove Press, 1955; [Berkeley]: Cloud Marauder Press, 1971.

Ghosts of the Heart. Chicago: University of Chicago Press, 1960.

Spring of the Thief. New York: Knopf, 1963.

The Zig Zag Walk: Poems 1963–1968. New York: E. P. Dutton, 1969.

The Anonymous Lover. New York: Liveright, 1973.

The House That Jack Built. Omaha, Neb.: Abbatoir editions, 1974. A prose memoir that intersperses poems.

Poem in Progress San Francisco and Washington, D.C.: Dryad Press, 1975.

WILLIAM MATTHEWS (b. 1942)

15 Poems (w. Russell Banks and Newton Smith). Chapel Hill, N.C.: Lillabulero Press, 1967. Pamphlet ltd. 500 copies.

Broken Syllables. Northwood Narrows, N.H.: Lillabulero Press, 1969. Lillabulero Poetry Pamphlet #9.

Ruining the New Road. New York: Random House, 1970.

The Cloud. Boston: Barn Dream Press, 1971. Chapbook ltd. 500 copies.

Poems for Tennessee (w. Robert Bly and William Stafford), ed. Stephen Mooney. Martin, Tenn.: Tennessee Poetry Press, 1971.

Sleek for the Long Flight. New York: Random House, 1972.

An Oar in the Old Water. Ithaca: Penyeach Press, 1973. Chapbook.

JEROME MAZZARO (b. 1934)

Six Poems. Detroit: Privately printed, 1959. Ltd. to about 50 copies.

The Achievement of Robert Lowell: 1939–1959. Detroit: University of Detroit Press, 1960. A bibliography.

Juvenal: Satires (trans.). Ann Arbor: University of Michigan Press, 1965.

The Poetic Themes of Robert Lowell. Ann Arbor: University of Michigan Press, 1965.

Changing the Windows: Poems. Athens, Ohio: Ohio University Press, 1966.

Modern American Poetry: Essays in Criticism (ed.). New York: David McKay, 1970.

Transformations in the Renaissance English Lyric. Ithaca: Cornell University Press, 1970.

A Profile of Robert Lowell (ed.). Columbus: Charles E. Merrill Co., 1971.

A Profile of William Carlos Williams (ed.). Columbus: Charles E. Merrill Co., 1971.

William Carlos Williams: The Later Poems. Ithaca: Cornell University Press, 1973.

WILLIAM MEREDITH (b. 1919)

Love Letter from an Impossible Land. New Haven: Yale University Press, 1944.

Ships and Other Figures. Princeton: Princeton University Press, 1948.

The Open Sea. New York: Knopf, 1958.

Shelley: Selected Poems (ed.). New York: Dell Publishing Co., 1962.

Alcools: Poems 1898–1913, by Guillaume Apollinaire (trans.). Garden City, N.Y.: Doubleday, 1964.

The Wreck of the Thresher. New York: Knopf, 1964.

Eighteenth-Century English Minor Poets (ed. w. Mackie L. Jarrell). New York: Dell Publishing Co., 1968.

Earth Walk: New and Selected Poems. New York: Knopf, 1970.

Hazard, the Painter. New York: Knopf, 1975.

JOYCE CAROL OATES (b. 1938)

By the North Gate (stories). New York: Vanguard, 1963.

With Shuddering Fall (novel). New York: Vanguard, 1964.

Upon the Sweeping Flood (stories). New York: Vanguard, 1966.

A Garden of Earthly Delights (novel). New York: Vanguard, 1967.

Expensive People (novel). New York: Vanguard, 1968.

Anonymous Sins and Other Poems. Baton Rouge: Louisiana State University Press, 1969.

them (novel). New York: Vanguard, 1969.

Love and Its Derangements: Poems. Baton Rouge: Louisiana State University Press, 1970.

The Wheel of Love (stories). New York: Vanguard, 1970.

Wonderland (novel). New York: Vanguard, 1971.

Marriages & Infidelities (stories). New York: Vanguard, 1972.

The Edge of Impossibility: Forms of Tragic Literature. New York: Vanguard, 1972.

Angel Fire: Poems. Baton Rouge: Louisiana State University Press, 1973.

Scenes from American Life: Contemporary Short Fiction (ed.). New York: Random House, 1973.

The Hostile Sun: The Poetry of D. H. Lawrence. Los Angeles: Black Sparrow Press, 1973.

Do With Me What You Will (novel). New York: Vanguard, 1973.

Dreaming America & Other Poems. New York: Oliphant Press, 1973. Ltd. 176 copies.

Where Are You Going, Where Have You Been (stories). New York: Fawcett, 1974.

The Hungry Ghosts (stories). Los Angeles: Black Sparrow Press, 1974.

The Goddess and Other Women (stories). New York: Vanguard Press, 1974.

New Heaven, New Earth (criticism). New York: Vanguard Press, 1974.

Miracle Play. Los Angeles: Black Sparrow Press, 1975.

The Poisoned Kiss (stories). New York: Vanguard Press, 1975.

The Seduction and Other Stories. Los Angeles: Black Sparrow Press, 1975.

* The Fawcett *Love and Its Derangements* reprints all three of the Louisiana State University Press volumes of poetry.

LINDA PASTAN (b. 1932)

A Perfect Circle of Sun. Chicago: Swallow Press, 1971.
Aspects of Eve. New York: Liveright, 1975.
On the Way to the Zoo. San Francisco and Washington, D.C.: Dryad Press, 1975.

RAYMOND R. PATTERSON (b. 1929)

Twenty-Six Ways of Looking at a Black Man. New York: Award Books, 1969.

JOHN PECK (b. 1941)

Shagbark. Indianapolis: Bobbs-Merrill, 1972.

STANLEY PLUMLY (b. 1939)

In the Outer Dark. Baton Rouge: Louisiana State University Press, 1970.
How the Plains Indians Got Horses. Crete, Nebraska: The Best Cellar Press, 1973. Chapbook.
Giraffe. Baton Rouge: Louisiana State University Press, 1973.

ISHMAEL REED (b. 1938)

The Free-Lance Pallbearers (novel). Garden City: Doubleday, 1967.
Yellow Back Radio Broke-Down (novel). Garden City: Doubleday, 1969.
19 Necromancers From Now (ed.). Garden City: Doubleday, 1970.
Mumbo Jumbo (novel). Garden City: Doubleday, 1972.
Conjure: Selected Poems, 1963–1970. Amherst: University of Massachusetts Press, 1972.
Chattanooga: Poems. New York: Random House, 1973.
The Last Days of Louisiana Red (novel). New York: Random House, 1974.

ADRIENNE RICH (b. 1929)

A Change of World. New Haven: Yale University Press, 1951.
The Diamond Cutters. New York: Harper and Row, 1955.
Snapshots of a Daughter-in-Law: Poems 1954–1962. New York: Harper and Row, 1962.
Necessities of Life: Poems 1962–1965. New York: Norton, 1966.
Selected Poems. London: Chatto and Windus, 1967.
Leaflets: Poems 1965–1968. New York: Norton, 1969.
The Will to Change: Poems 1968–1970. New York: Norton, 1971.

Diving Into the Wreck: Poems 1971–1972. New York: Norton, 1973.
Poems: Selected and New, 1950–1974. New York: Norton, 1975.

M. L. ROSENTHAL (b. 1917)

Exploring Poetry (w. A. J. M. Smith). New York: Macmillan, 1955; rev. ed., 1973.
A Primer of Ezra Pound. New York: Macmillan, 1960.
The Modern Poets: A Critical Introduction. New York: Oxford University Press, 1960.
Selected Poems and Two Plays of William Butler Yeats (ed.). New York: Macmillan, 1962.
Blue Boy on Skates: Poems. New York: Oxford University Press, 1964.
The William Carlos Williams Reader (ed.). New York: New Directions, 1966.
The New Poets: American and British Poetry Since World War II. New York: Oxford University Press, 1967.
100 Postwar Poems: British and American (ed.). New York: Macmillan, 1968.
Beyond Power: Poems. New York: Oxford University Press, 1969.
Chief Modern Poets of Britain and America (ed., w. Sanders & Nelson). Fifth edition. New York: Macmillan, 1970.
Randall Jarrell. Minneapolis: University of Minnesota Press, 1972.
The View from the Peacock's Tail: Poems. New York: Oxford University Press, 1972.
Poetry and the Common Life. New York: Oxford University Press, 1974.

ANNE SEXTON (1928–1974)

To Bedlam and Part Way Back. Boston: Houghton Mifflin, 1960.
All My Pretty Ones. Boston: Houghton Mifflin, 1962.
Selected Poems. London: Oxford University Press, 1964.
Live or Die. Boston: Houghton Mifflin, 1966.
Poems (w. Kinsella and Livingston). London: Faber and Faber, 1968.
Love Poems. Boston: Houghton Mifflin, 1969.
Transformations. Boston: Houghton Mifflin, 1971.
The Book of Folly. Boston: Houghton Mifflin, 1972.
The Death Notebooks. Boston: Houghton Mifflin, 1974.
The Awful Rowing Toward God. Boston: Houghton Mifflin, 1975.
45 Mercy Street. Boston: Houghton Mifflin, 1976.

LOUIS SIMPSON (b. 1923)

The Arrivistes: Poems 1940–1949. New York: The Fine Editions Press, 1949.
Good News of Death. In *Poets of Today II.* New York: Scribner's, 1955.

New Poets of England and America (ed. w. Donald Hall and Robert Pack). Cleveland: The World Publishing Co., 1957.

A Dream of Governors. Middletown: Wesleyan University Press, 1959.

Riverside Drive (novel). New York: Atheneum, 1962.

James Hogg: A Critical Study. New York: St. Martin's Press, 1962.

At the End of the Open Road. Middletown: Wesleyan University Press, 1963.

Selected Poems. New York: Harcourt, Brace & World; 1965.

Adventures of the Letter I. New York: Harper and Row, 1971.

Introduction to Poetry: Second Edition. New York: St. Martin's Press, 1972.

North of Jamaica (autobiography). New York: Harper and Row, 1972.

✗ *Three on a Tower: The Lives and Works of Ezra Pound, T. S. Eliot, and William Carlos Williams*. New York: Morrow, 1975.

DAVE SMITH (b. 1942)

Bull Island. Poquoson, Va.: Back Door Press, 1970.

Mean Rufus Throw Down. Fredonia, N.Y.: Basilisk Press, 1973.

The Fisherman's Whore. Athens, Ohio: Ohio University Press, 1974.

Cumberland Station. Urbana, Ill.: Illinois University Press, 1976.

WILLIAM STAFFORD (b. 1914)

Down in My Heart. Elgin, Ill.: Brethren Publishing Co., 1947. A prose memoir of Stafford's four years in camps as a conscientious objector during WWII. Reprinted in 1971.

West of Your City. Los Gatos, Cal.: Talisman Press, 1961.

Traveling Through the Dark. New York: Harper and Row, 1963.

The Rescued Year. New York: Harper and Row, 1966.

Friends to this Ground. Champaign, Ill.: N.C.T.E., 1967. Written by Stafford, this is "A Statement for Readers, Teachers, and Writers of Literature" issued by the Commission on Literature of the National Council of Teachers of English.

The Achievement of Brother Antoninus (ed. w. intro.). Glenview, Ill.: Scott, Foresman, and Co., 1967.

Eleven Untitled Poems. Mt. Horeb, Wisc.: Perishable Press, 1968. Ltd. 250 copies.

Weather. Mt. Horeb, Wisc.: Perishable Press, 1969. Ltd. 207 copies.

Temporary Facts. Athens, Ohio: Duane Schneider, 1970. Ltd. 200 copies.

Allegiances. New York: Harper and Row, 1970.

In the Clock of Reason. Victoria, B. C.: Soft Press, 1973. Ltd. 300 copies.

Someday, Maybe. New York: Harper and Row, 1973.

That Other Alone. Mt. Horeb, Wisc.: Perishable Press, 1973. Ltd. 120 copies.

Going Places. Reno, Nev.: West Coast Poetry Review Press, 1974.

PRIMUS ST. JOHN (b. 1939)

Skins on the Earth. Port Townsend, Wa.: Copper Canyon Press, 1975.
Zero Makes Me Hungry: A Collection of Poems for Today (ed. w. E. Lueders). Glenview, Ill.: Scott, Foresman, and Co., 1976.

LUCIEN STRYK (b. 1924)

Taproot. Oxford, England: Fantasy Press, 1953.
The Trespasser. Oxford, England: Fantasy Press, 1956.
Notes for a Guidebook. Chicago: Swallow Press, 1965.
Zen: Poems, Prayers, Sermons, Anecdotes, Interviews (ed. and trans. w. Takashi Ikemoto). Garden City: Doubleday, 1965.
Heartland: Poets of the Midwest (ed.). DeKalb: Northern Illinois University Press, 1967. Stryk has also edited a second edition, *Heartland II* (1975).
World of the Buddha: A Reader—from the Three Baskets to Modern Zen (ed.). Garden City: Doubleday, 1968.
The Pit and Other Poems. Chicago: Swallow Press, 1969.
Afterimages: Zen Poems of Shinkichi Takahashi (trans. w. Takashi Ikemoto). Chicago: Swallow Press, 1970.
Zen Poems of China and Japan: The Crane's Bill (trans. w. Takashi Ikemoto and Taigan Takayama). Garden City: Doubleday, 1973.
Awakening. Chicago: Swallow Press, 1973.

LEWIS TURCO (b. 1934)

First Poems. Francestown, N.H.: Golden Quill Press, 1960.
The Sketches and Livevil: A Mask. Cleveland: American Weave Press, 1962.
Awaken, Bells Falling: Poems 1959–1967. Columbia, Mo.: University of Missouri Press, 1968.
The Book of Forms: A Handbook of Poetics. New York: E. P. Dutton, 1968.
The Inhabitant. Northampton, Mass.: Despa Press, 1970.
The Literature of New York: A Selective Bibliography. New York: New York State English Council, 1970.
Pocoangelini: A Fantography. Northampton, Mass.: Despa Press, 1971.
Poetry: An Introduction Through Writing. Reston, Va.: Reston Publishing Co., 1973.
The Weed Garden. Orangeburg, S.C.: Peaceweed Press, 1973.

JAMES WRIGHT (b. 1927)

The Green Wall. New Haven: Yale University Press, 1957.
Saint Judas. Middletown: Wesleyan University Press, 1959.

Twenty Poems of Georg Trakl (trans. w. Robert Bly). Madison, Minn.: The Sixties Press, 1961.

The Lion's Tail and Eyes: Poems Written Out of Laziness and Silence (w. Robert Bly and William Duffy). Madison, Minn.: The Sixties Press, 1962.

Twenty Poems of Cesar Vallejo (trans. w. Robert Bly and John Knoepfle). Madison, Minn.: The Sixties Press, 1962.

The Branch Will Not Break. Middletown: Wesleyan University Press, 1963.

The Rider on the White Horse: Selected Short Fiction of Theodor Storm (trans.). New York: New American Library, 1964.

Pablo Neruda: Twenty Poems (trans. w. Robert Bly). Madison, Minn.: The Sixties Press, 1967; London: Rapp & Whiting, 1967.

Shall We Gather at the River. Middletown: Wesleyan University Press, 1968.

Poems by Hermann Hesse (trans.). New York: Farrar, Straus, & Giroux, 1970.

Collected Poems. Middletown: Wesleyan University Press, 1971.

Wandering, by Hermann Hesse (trans. w. Franz Paul Wright). New York: Farrar, Straus & Giroux, 1972.

Two Citizens. New York: Farrar, Straus, & Giroux, 1973.

PAUL ZIMMER (b. 1934)

The Ribs of Death. New York: October House, 1967.

The Republic of Many Voices. New York: October House, 1969.

Part II

Ackerson, Duane. Review of *Not Every Year*, by John Haislip, in *Northwest Review* XIV, 1 (1974), 126–28.

Aiken, William. " 'My Mind to Me a Mangle Is,' " *Kayak* #23 (1970), 63–67. On Robert Creeley's *Pieces*.

Aldan, Daisy. "The Words of the Tribe," *Poetry* 118, 1 (April 1971), 35–40. Review of five books, including Paul Zimmer's *Republic*.

Allen, Donald M. Ed., *The New American Poetry, 1945–1960* (New York: Grove Press, 1960). An important and influential anthology.

X ———, and Warren Tallman. Eds., *The Poetics of the New American Poetry* (New York: Grove Press, 1973).

Altieri, Charles. "The Unsure Egoist: Robert Creeley and the Theme of Nothingness," *Contemporary Literature* XIII, 2 (Spring 1972), 162–85.

———. "Poetry as Resurrection: John Logan's Structures of Metaphysical Solace," *Modern Poetry Studies* III, 5 (1973), 193–224.

André, Michael. "Two Weeks with Creeley in Texas," *Chicago Review* XXIV, 2 (1972), 81–86.

Athanor. See #4 (1973), a special issue on Robert Creeley, with an interview, essays, a chronology. Edited by Douglas Calhoun.

Banks, Russell. "The Poetry of Depression," *Tennessee Poetry Journal* II, 1 (Fall 1968), 23–5. On William Matthews.

Bell, Marvin. "Logan's Teaching," *Voyages* IV, 3–4 (Spring 1971–Spring 1972), 38–39.

Berg, Stephen, and Robert Mezey. Eds., *Naked Poetry: Recent American Poetry in Open Forms* (Indianapolis: Bobbs-Merrill, 1969). An anthology of nineteen contemporary poets, including Bly, Creeley, Stafford, and Wright.

———— Eds., *The New Naked Poetry* (Indianapolis: Bobbs-Merrill, 1976). Contemporary poets including Bly, Hugo, Ignatow, Logan, Rich, Simpson, Stafford, and Wright.

Blackmur, R. P. *Form and Value in Modern Poetry* (Garden City: Doubleday-Anchor, 1957.)

Blodgett, E. D. "Richard F. Hugo: Poet of the Third Dimension," *Modern Poetry Studies* I, 5 (1970), 268–72.

Bloom, Janet. "A Plea for Proper Boldness," *Parnassus* I, 1 (Fall–Winter 1972), 130–34. On Rosemarie Waldrop and Linda Pastan.

Bly, Robert. "Five Decades of Modern American Poetry," *The Fifties* #1 (1958), 36–39.

————. "On English and American Poetry," *The Fifties* #2 (1959), 45–47.

————. "Notes on Prose vs. Poetry," *Choice* #2 (1962), 65–80. A wide-ranging discussion of more than twenty books, including Richard Hugo's *A Run of Jacks.*

————. "A Wrong Turning in American Poetry," *Choice* #3 (1963), 33–47.

————. "The Dead World and the Live World," *The Sixties* #8 (1966), 2–7.

————. "The First Ten Issues of *Kayak*," *Kayak* #12 (1967), 45–49.

————. "The Collapse of James Dickey," *The Sixties* #9 (1967), 70–79.

————. "On Political Poetry," *The Nation* CCIV (1967), 522–24.

————. "Robert Lowell's *For the Union Dead*," in *Robert Lowell: A Portrait of the Artist in His Time,* ed. Michael London and Robert Boyers (New York: David Lewis, 1970), 73–76.

————. "Some Notes on Donald Hall," *Field* #2 (Spring 1970), 57–61.

————. "Words Emerging from Objects Again," intro. to *Everything Falling,* by William Pillin (San Francisco: Kayak, 1971), pp. 5–11.

————. "John Logan's Field of Force," *Voyages* IV, 3–4 (Spring 1971–Spring 1972), 29–36.

————. "American Poetry: On the Way to the Hermetic," *Books Abroad* 46, 1 (Winter 1972), 17–24.

————. See *The Seventies* 1 (1972). Includes several essays by Bly: "Looking for Dragon Smoke," "Spanish Leaping," "Wild Association," "Poetry of Steady Light," "Hopping," "The Three Brains," "Surrealism, Rilke, and Listening."

──────. "Living Out Dreams," *Stinktree* #2 (Nov. 1972), 18–19. On John Haines.

──────. "The War between Memory and Imagination," *American Poetry Review* II, 5 (Sept.–Oct. 1973), 49–50.

──────. "Developing the Underneath," *American Poetry Review* II, 6 (Nov.–Dec. 1973), 44–45.

──────. "Reflections on the Origins of Poetic Form," *Field* #10 (Spring 1974), 31–35.

──────. "The Network and the Community," *American Poetry Review* III, 1 (1974), 19–21. Concludes with an appreciation of David Ignatow.

[BLY: see Berg and Mezey, Haines, Hall, Heyen, Howard, Janssens, Kinnell, Libby, Malkoff, Matthews, Moran and Lensing, Oates, Ossman, Piccione, Root, Skelton, Stepanchev, *Tennessee Poetry Journal*]

Bogan, Louise. *Achievement in American Poetry* (Chicago: Henry Regnery Co., 1951).

Boyers, Robert. "Live or Die: The Achievement of Anne Sexton," *Salmagundi* II, 1 (Spring 1967), 61–71.

──────. "On Adrienne Rich," *Salmagundi* #22–23 (Spring–Summer 1973), 132–48.

──────. Ed., *Contemporary Poetry in America: Essays and Interviews* (New York: Schocken, 1975).

Brinnin, John Malcolm. "Plato, Phoebus and the Man from Hartford," *Voices* #121 (Spring 1945), 30–37. On Wallace Stevens.

──────. "The Last Minstrel," *New York Times Book Review* (August 23, 1964), 5. Review of John Berryman's *77 Dream Songs*.

──────. "Some Phases of My Work," in *Poets on Poetry*, ed. Howard Nemerov (New York: Basic Books, 1966), pp. 72–93.

──────. "The Theory and Practice of Poetry," *New York Times Book Review* (March 2, 1975), 4–5.

──────. A Review of *Hazard, the Painter*, by William Meredith, *New York Times Book Review* (Sept. 21, 1975), 35.

[BRINNIN: see Gerber, Howard]

Brooks, Cleanth. *Modern Poetry and the Tradition* (New York: Oxford University Press, 1965). First published 1939.

Cambon, Glauco. *Recent American Poetry* (Minneapolis: University of Minnesota Press, 1962). A survey whose focuses include John Logan and James Wright.

Carroll, Paul. *The Poem in Its Skin* (Chicago: Follet, 1968). Includes essays on Creeley, Logan, and Wright. Also an essay called "Faire, Foul and Full of Variations: The Generation of 1962."

Chaplin, William H. "Identity and Spirit in the Recent Poetry of John Logan," *American Poetry Review* II, 3 (May–June 1973), 19–24.

Charters, Samuel. *Some Poems/Poets: Studies in American Underground Poetry Since 1945* (Berkeley: Oyez, 1971). Discussion of ten poets, including Robert Creeley.

Ciardi, John. Ed., *Mid-Century American Poets* (New York: Twayne, 1950).

Clemons, Walter. "Joyce Carol Oates: Love and Violence," *Newsweek* (Dec. 11, 1972), 72–74, 77.

Coles, Robert. "James Wright: One of Those Messengers," *American Poetry Review* II, 4 (July–August 1973), 36–37.

Contemporary Literary Criticism. See these annual volumes of critical excerpts on recent writers from many sources. Gale Research Company, Detroit.

Contemporary Poets of the English Language. See this volume for valuable biographical and bibliographical information on most of the poets in *American Poets in 1976.* (Chicago and London: St. James Press, 1975).

Contoski, Victor. "Songs of America," *Kayak* #27 (Autumn 1971), 68–71. On David Ignatow.

Coursen, Herbert R. "A Certain Slant of Light," *Bartleby's Review* I, 1 (Fall 1972). Review of Turco's *The Inhabitant.*

Cox, C. B. "The Poetry of Louis Simpson," *Critical Quarterly* 8 (Spring 1966) 72–83.

Creeley, Robert. *A Quick Graph: Collected Notes & Essays,* ed. Donald Allen (San Francisco; Four Seasons Foundation, 1970).

[CREELEY: see Aiken, Altieri, André, Berg and Mezey, Carroll, Charters, Crunk, Howard, Levertov, Malkoff, Ossman, Rosenthal, Stepanchev].

Crunk. "The Work of Louis Simpson," *The Fifties* #1 (1958), 22–25.

————. "The Work of Robert Creeley," *The Fifties* #2 (1959), 10–21.

————. "The Work of Donald Hall," *The Fifties* #3 (1959), 32–46.

————. "The Work of W. S. Merwin," *The Sixties* #4 (1960), 32–43.

————. "The Work of John Logan," *The Sixties* #5 (1961), 77–87.

————. "The Work of Gary Snyder," *The Sixties* #6 (1962), 25–42.

————. "The Work of James Dickey," *The Sixties* #7 (1964), 41–57.

————. "The Work of James Wright," *The Sixties* #8 (1966), 52–78.

————. "The Work of Denise Levertov," *The Sixties* #9 (1967), 48–65.

————. "The Work of David Ignatow," *The Sixties* #10 (1968), 10–23.

Davie, Donald. "A Vegetable World," *Shenandoah* XXIV, 3 (1972), 92–94. On John Peck.

DeFrees, Madeline. "James Wright's Early Poems: A Study in 'Convulsive' Form," *Modern Poetry Studies* II, 6 (1972), 241–51.

Deutsch, Babette. *Poetry in Our Time* (Garden City: Doubleday-Anchor, 1963). Second edition.

Dickey, James. *Babel to Byzantium: Poets and Poetry Now* (New York: Farrar,

Straus, and Giroux; 1968). Includes essays on Ignatow, Logan, Meredith, Sexton, Simpson, Stafford, Turco.

Ditsky, John. "James Wright Collected: Alterations on the Monument," *Modern Poetry Studies* II, 6 (1972), 252–59.

Elder, Karl. Review of *Awakening*, by Lucien Stryk, in *Margins* #11 (April–May 1974), 48–50.

———. "Harnessed Energy: William Matthews," *Margins* #12 (June–July 1974), 32–34.

Engle, Paul, and Joseph Langland. Eds., *Poet's Choice* (New York: Dial Press, 1962). Includes brief prose comments by Brinnin, Meredith, Sexton, Simpson, Stafford, on their own poems.

Fields, Beverly. "The Poetry of Anne Sexton," in *Poets in Progress*, ed. Edward Hungerford (Evanston, Ill.: Northwestern University Press, 1967), pp. 251–85.

Fitz Gerald, Gregory, and Paul Ferguson. "The Frost Tradition: A Conversation with William Meredith," *Southwest Review* LVII, 2 (Spring 1972), 108–17.

Friedman, Sanford. "Torn Divinities," *Modern Poetry Studies* IV, 3 (Winter 1973), 344–49. A discussion of Richard Hugo.

Garber, Frederick. "Fat Man at the Margin: The Poetry of Richard Hugo," *The Iowa Review* III, 4 (Fall 1972), 58–69.

Garrison, Joseph. "Heart and Soul: Two Poets," *Shenandoah* XXIV, 4 (Summer 1973), 90–93. Review of David Wagoner and Linda Pastan.

Gelpi, Barbara C., and Albert Gelpi. Eds., *Adrienne Rich's Poetry* (New York: Norton, 1975). Poems, statements by Rich, reviews, critical essays.

Gerber, Philip. Ed., "A Kind of Exorcism: A Conversation with John Malcolm Brinnin," *Prairie Schooner* XLVIII, 3 (Fall 1974), 201–21.

———, and Robert Gemmett. Eds., "The Individual Voice: A Conversation with William Heyen," *Western Humanities Review* XXIII, 3 (Summer 1969), 223–33.

Goldstein, Sanford. Review of Stryk's *Zen Poems of China and Japan: The Crane's Bill*, in *Arizona Quarterly* 30, 3 (Autumn 1974), 281–85.

Gray, Johma. "The Poetry of Louis Simpson," in *Poets in Progress*, ed. Edward Hungerford (Evanston: Northwestern University Press, 1967), pp. 227–50.

Haines, John. "A Review," *Lillabulero* #6 (Fall/Winter 1968), 66–67. On H. R. Hays, *Selected Poems, 1933–67*.

———. "The Young American Poets," *Kayak* #20 (1969), 63–70.

———. "Roots," *Quarry* #1 (1971–72), 80–83.

———. "The Poet Against Life," *The Dragonfly* III, 2 (Summer 1972), 1–17. On Robert Bly and W. S. Merwin.

———. "Night Vision, Myth, and Magic," *Pebble* #8 (1972), 20–25.

———. "Excerpts from the Letters of John Haines," *Stinktree* #2 (Nov. 1972), 10–17.

———. "Further Reflections on Line and the Poetic Voice," *Field* #9 (Fall 1973), 79–82.

[HAINES: see Bly, Vernon, Witherup, Zweig]

Haislip, John. " 'Flood, Salt, Debris, Relief:' The Poetry of Dave Smith," *The Sou'wester* II, 3 (Spring–Summer 1974), 56–64.

————. "The Example of Theodore Roethke," *Northwest Review* XIV, 3 (Winter 1975), 88–95.

[HAISLIP: see Ackerson, Heyen, Kennedy, Root]

✝ Hall, Donald. Ed., *Contemporary American Poetry* (Baltimore: Penguin, 1963). Includes an important introductory essay on Bly and others.

Harrison, Jim. "Note on Shinkichi Takahashi," *American Poetry Review* III, 2 (1974), 14–15. On Stryk's *Afterimages*.

Heyen, William. "Theodore Roethke's Minimals," *The Minnesota Review* VIII (Winter 1968–69), 359–75.

————. "Three Ideas and Three Poems," *The English Record* XIX, 3 (Feb. 1969), 71–77.

————. "Inward to the World: The Poetry of Robert Bly," *The Far Point* #3 (Fall–Winter 1969), 42–50.

————. "The Distance from Our Eyes," *Prairie Schooner* XLIV, 3 (Fall 1969), 323–26. On Louise Bogan.

————. "The Divine Abyss: Theodore Roethke's Mysticism," *Texas Studies in Literature and Language* XI (Summer 1969), 1051–68.

————. "Fishing the Swamp: The Poetry of W. D. Snodgrass," in *Modern American Poetry: Essays in Criticism*, ed. Jerome Mazzaro (New York: David McKay, 1970), pp. 351–68.

————. "Sensibilities," *Poetry* 115, 6 (March 1970), 426–29. Review of four poets, including M. L. Rosenthal.

————. "The Poet's Leap into Reality," *Saturday Review* LIII (August 1, 1970), 21–24. Reprinted in *Profile of William Carlos Williams*, ed. Jerome Mazzaro (Columbus: Charles E. Merrill, 1971), pp. 25–33.

————. "William Stafford's Allegiances," *Modern Poetry Studies* I, 6 (1970), 307–18.

————. "A Note on S. S. Gardons," *Western Humanities Review* XXV, 3 (Summer 1971), 253–56. On *Remains,* by Gardons (Snodgrass).

————. "The Progress of Lewis Turco," *Modern Poetry Studies* II, 3 (1971), 115–24.

————. Review of *Sorties,* by James Dickey, and *Straw for the Fire: From the Notebooks of Theodore Roethke, 1943–1963,* ed. David Wagoner, *Saturday Review* LV, 10 (March 11, 1972), 70–71.

————. Ed., "A Conversation with James Dickey," *The Southern Review* IX, 1 (Jan. 1973), 135–56.

————. "In Consideration of Cummings," *Southern Humanities Review* VII, 2 (Spring 1973), 131–42.

————. "On Richard Wilbur," *The Southern Review* IX, 3 (Summer 1973), 617–34.

————. "Four Realities," *Poetry* 122, 4 (July 1973), 237–40. Review of four books of poems, including Ishmael Reed's *Conjure.*

————. "Being at Home," *Modern Poetry Studies* IV, 2 (Autumn 1973), 233–34. Review of John Haislip's *Not Every Year.*

————. "John Berryman: A Memoir and an Interview," *The Ohio Review* XV, 2 (Winter 1974), 46–65.

————. Ed., " 'I Would Also Like To Mention Aluminum:' A Conversation with William Stafford," *Rapport* #9 (1976).

————. "Arthur Miller's *Death of a Salesman* and the American Dream," in *Amerikanisches Drama und Theater im 20. Jahrhundert* (Gottingen: Vandenhoeck & Ruprecht, 1975), pp. 190–201.

[HEYEN: see Gerber and Gemmett, Irwin, Oberg, Piccione, Radhuber, R. Smith]

Hilberry, Conrad. "A Writer to Watch," *Mad River Review* II, 2 (Winter-Spring 1967), 81–86. On Jerome Mazzaro.

Howard, Richard. *Alone with America* (New York: Atheneum, 1969). Includes essays on forty-one poets who have come into, as Howard phrases it, "consequential identity" since the time of about the Korean War. Includes Bly, Creeley, Hugo, Logan, Meredith, Rich, Sexton, Simpson, Stafford, Wright.

————. "Cutting at the Joints," *American Poetry Review* II, 1 (Jan.–Feb. 1973), 53. Review of Peck's *Shagbark* and Matthews' *Sleek for the Long Flight.*

————. "Cutting at the Joints," *American Poetry Review* II, 5 (Sept.–Oct. 1973), 7–8. Review of Logan's *Anonymous Lover.*

————. *Preferences* (New York: Viking Press, 1974). Fifty-one American poets have chosen poems from their own work and from the past. Comments on the choices and an introduction by Howard. Includes Brinnin, Creeley, Hugo, Logan, Meredith, Rich, Sexton, Simpson, Wright.

————. "Ecstasies and Decorum," *Parnassus: Poetry in Review* II, 2 (Spring-Summer 1974), 213–20. On Thom Gunn and William Stafford.

Hugo, Richard. "The Writer's Situation," *New American Review* #11 (1971), 221–24.

————. "How Poets Make a Living," *The Iowa Review* III, 4 (Fall 1972), 69–76.

————. "Interview with Richard Hugo," *The New Salt Creek Reader* VI, 2 (Spring 1974), 84–109. Though not identified as such, this is a self-interview, Hugo asking and answering his own questions.

————. "Stray Thoughts on Roethke and Teaching," *American Poetry Review* III, 1 (1974), 50–51.

————. "Grandfather's Car," *The Ohio Review* XVI, 3 (Spring 1975), 6–27.

[HUGO: see Blodgett, Bly, Friedman, Garber, Howard, Wright]

Hungerford, Edward. Ed., *Poets in Progress* (Evanston, Ill.: Northwestern University Press, 1967).

Ignatow, David. "The Permanent Hell," *The Nation* CCII (June 20, 1966), 752–53. Review of James Dickey's *Buckdancer's Choice.*

[IGNATOW: see Bly, Contoski, Crunk, Dickey, Kazin, Malkoff, Mazzaro, Meredith, Mills, Poulin, Swados]

Irwin, John. "Four Practitioners," *Poetry* 118 (Sept. 1971), 351–53. Review of four books, including William Heyen's *Depth of Field.*

————. "The Crisis of Regular Forms," *Sewanee Review* LXXX, 1 (Winter 1973), 158–71.

Isaacs, J. *The Background of Modern Poetry* (New York: E. P. Dutton, 1952).

Isbell, Harold. "Growth and Change: John Logan's Poems," *Modern Poetry Studies* II, 5 (1971), 213–23.

Jackson, Richard. "An Interview with William Meredith," *The Poetry Miscellany* I, 2 (Spring 1972), 32–37.

Janssens, G. A. M. "The Present State of American Poetry: Robert Bly and James Wright," *English Studies* 51 (1970), 112–37.

Jarrell, Randall. *Poetry and the Age* (New York: Knopf, 1953).

Kazin, Alfred. "Oates," *Harper's* (August 1971), 78–82.

————. "The Esthetic of Humility," *American Poetry Review* III, 2 (1974), 14–15. On Ignatow's *Notebooks.*

Keane, Patrick. Ed., *William Butler Yeats* (New York: McGraw-Hill, 1972). Includes a discussion of two poems by M. L. Rosenthal.

Kennedy, X. J. "High Time," *Counter/Measures* #2 (1973), 192. Review of John Haislip's *Not Every Year.*

Kevles, Barbara. "Anne Sexton," *The Paris Review* #52 (Summer 1971), 158–91. A 1968 interview.

Kinnell, Galway. "Poetry, Personality, and Death," *Field* #4 (Spring 1971), 56–75. A wide essay turning on Bly and Logan, among others.

————. "The Poetics of the Physical World," *The Iowa Review* II, 3 (Summer 1971), 113–26.

————. "Whitman's Indicative Words," *American Poetry Review* II, 2 (March-April 1973), 9–11.

Kramer, Aaron. Review of Raymond R. Patterson's *Twenty-Six Ways of Looking at a Black Man* in *Freedomways* (1970), 279–83.

Kramer, Jane. *Allen Ginsberg in America* (New York: Vintage, 1970).

Laing, Alexander. "*The Nation* and Its Poets," *The Nation* 201 (Sept. 20, 1965), 212–18.

Lauber, John. "World's Guest—William Stafford," *The Iowa Review* V, 2 (Spring 1974), 88–100.

Leary, Paris, and Robert Kelly. Eds., *A Controversy of Poets: An Anthology of Contemporary American Poetry* (Garden City: Doubleday, 1965). Includes biographical and bibliographical information on fifty-nine poets, including Creeley, Rich, and Sexton.

Levertov, Denise. *The Poet in the World* (New York: New Directions, 1973). Includes an essay on Robert Creeley.

Libby, Anthony. "Robert Bly Alive in Darkness," *The Iowa Review* III, 3 (Summer 1972), 78–91.

Lofsness, Cynthia. "An Interview with William Stafford," *The Iowa Review* III, 3 (Summer 1972), 92–107.

Logan, John. "Dylan Thomas and the Ark of Art," *Renascence* 12 (Winter 1960), 59–66.

————. "The Poetry of Isabella Gardner," *Sewanee Review* LXX, 2 (Spring 1962), 257–60.

————. "A Note on the Poetry of David Cohen," in *Breakfast Rum*, by David Cohen (New York: 7 Poets Press, 1962), pp. 1–5.

————. "Psychological Motifs in Melville's *Pierre*," *Minnesota Review* VII, 4 (1967), 325–30.

————. "A Note on the Inarticulate as Hero," *New Mexico Quarterly* XXXVII, 4–XXXIX, 1 (Winter-Spring 1969), 148–53.

————. "The Organ-Grinder and the Cockatoo: An Introduction to E. E. Cummings," in *Modern American Poetry: Essays in Criticism*, ed. Jerome Mazzaro (New York: McKay, 1970), 249–71.

————. "New Catholic Poets," *The Critic* XIX, 2 (Oct.–Nov. 1970), 77–87.

————. "John Logan on Poets and Poetry Today," *Voyages* IV, 3–4 (Spring 1971–Spring 1972), 17–24.

————. "Foreword" to *White Buildings,* by Hart Crane (New York: Liveright, 1972), XVII–XXXIII.

————. Review of Millen Brand's *Dry Summer in Provence* and Jerome Mazzaro's *Changing the Windows, University of Windsor Review* VIII, 1 (Fall 1972), 116–18.

[LOGAN: see Altieri, Bell, Bly, Cambon, Carroll, Chaplin, Crunk, Dickey, Howard, Isbell, Kinnell, Mazzaro, Ossman, Poulin, Rust, Thompson]

Ludwig, Richard M. "The Muted Lyrics of William Meredith," *The Princeton University Library Chronicle* XXV, 1 (Autumn 1963), 73–79. This issue also contains a checklist of Meredith's writings to 1963, 79–85.

MacLeish, Archibald. *A Continuing Journey: Essays and Addresses* (Boston: Houghton Mifflin, 1967).

Malkoff, Karl. *Crowell's Handbook of Contemporary American Poetry: A Critical Handbook of American Poetry Since 1940* (New York: T. Y. Crowell Co.: 1974). Includes essays on Bly, Creeley, Ignatow, Rich, Sexton, Simpson, Stafford, Wright.

Martz, William J. Ed., *The Distinctive Voice* (Glenview, Ill.: Scott Foresman: 1966). Includes brief prose comments by Simpson, Stafford, and Wright.

Matthews, William. "Entering the World," *Shenandoah* XX, 4 (Summer 1969),

80–93. On James Wright's *Shall We Gather at the River* and A. R. Ammons's *Selected Poems*.

―――. "Thinking about Robert Bly," *Tennessee Poetry Journal* II, 2 (Winter 1969), 49–57.

―――. "Again, Entering the World," *Kayak* #22 (1970), 67–71. On Wendell Berry's *Findings* and *Openings*.

―――. "Some Thoughts on the *Book of Nightmares*," *Stone Drum* I, 2 (Fall 1972), 11–16. On Galway Kinnell.

[MATTHEWS: see Elder, Banks, Howard, Mooney, *Ohio Review*]

Mazzaro, Jerome. "The Poetry of John Logan," *Salmagundi* II, 4 (Fall 1968), 78–95.

―――. "Robert Lowell and the Circle," *New Republic* CLX (May 31, 1969), 31–33.

―――. "Robert Lowell and the Kavanaugh Collapse," *University of Windsor Review* V (Autumn 1969), 1–24.

―――. "Theodore Roethke and the Failures of Language," *Modern Poetry Studies* I, 2 (1970), 73–96. Reprinted in *Profile of Theodore Roethke*, ed. William Heyen (Columbus: Charles E. Merrill, 1971), pp. 47–64.

―――. "Feeling One's Oates," *Modern Poetry Studies* II, 3 (1971), 133–37. Discussion of Joyce Carol Oates's first two books of poetry.

―――. "Between Two Worlds: The Post-Modernism of Randall Jarrell," *Salmagundi* #17 (Fall 1971), 93–113.

―――. "The Public Intimacy of W. D. Snodgrass," *Salmagundi* #19 (Spring 1972), 96–111.

―――. "On David Ignatow," *Salmagundi* #22–23 (Spring-Summer 1973), 164–86.

―――. "A Poet of Being," *Modern Poetry Studies* IV, 2 (Autumn 1973), 228–30. On Oates's *Angel Fire*.

―――. "'Anti-Poetic from the Start,'" *The Nation* 219, #17 (Nov. 23, 1974), 538–39. Review of David Ignatow's *Notebooks*.

[MAZZARO: see Hilberry, Logan]

McClatchy, J. D. "Anne Sexton: Somehow to Endure," *The Centennial Review* XIX, 2 (Spring 1975), 1–36.

McElrath, Joseph. Ed., "'Something to Be Said for the Light:' A Conversation with James Wright," *Southern Humanities Review* VI, 2 (Spring 1972), 134–53. A 1970 interview.

―――. "Plumbing the Swamp: The Modern Mode of Self-Pity," *Southern Humanities Review* VIII, 1 (Winter 1973), 53–65. An essay that turns to Stanley Plumly.

Meredith, William. "A Steady Storm of Correspondences: Theodore Roethke's Long Journey Out of the Self," in *Theodore Roethke: Essays on the Poetry*, ed. Arnold Stein (Seattle: University of Washington Press, 1965), pp. 36–53. Reprinted from *Shenandoah* XVI (Autumn 1964), 41–54.

―――. "Henry Tasting All the Secret Bits of Life: Berryman's *Dream*

Songs," *Wisconsin Studies in Contemporary Literature* 6 (Winter-Spring 1965), 27–33.

————. "James Dickey's Poems," *Partisan Review* XXXII (Summer 1965), 456–57.

————. "A Good Time for All," *New York Times Book Review* (April 23, 1967), 4, 46. On James Dickey.

————. "The Lasting Voice," in *Randall Jarrell 1914–1965*, ed. Robert Lowell, Peter Taylor, Robert Penn Warren (New York: Farrar, Straus and Giroux; 1967), pp. 118–24.

————. "A Bright Surviving Actual Scene: Berryman's 'Sonnets,'" *The Harvard Advocate* 103, 1 (Spring 1969), 19–22. Meredith also reviewed Berryman's *Sonnets* for *New York Times Book Review* (May 7, 1967), 8.

————. Review of Robert Lowell's *Notebook 1967–68*, in *New York Times Book Review* (June 15, 1969), 1, 27.

————. Review of David Ignatow's *Poems 1934–1969*, in *New York Times Book Review* (August 2, 1970), 4, 27.

————. "Whitman to the Poet," in *Walt Whitman in Our Time*, ed. William White (Detroit: Wayne State University Press, 1970), pp. 9–11.

————. "In Loving Memory of the Late Author of *The Dream Songs*," printed as a foreword to *John Berryman: A Checklist*, ed. Richard J. Kelly (Metuchen, N.J.: Scarecrow 1972), pp. XI–XX. Reprinted in *Virginia Quarterly Review* 49, 1 (Winter 1973), 70–78.

————. "Swan Songs," *Poetry* 122, 2 (May 1973), 98–103. A review of Berryman's *Love & Fame* and *Delusions, Etc.*

————. "I Will Tell You about It Because It Is Interesting," *Parnassus: Poetry in Review* II, 1 (Fall/Winter 1973), 175–85. On A. R. Ammons's *Collected Poems 1951–1971*.

[MEREDITH: see Brinnin, Dickey, FitzGerald, Howard, Jackson, Ludwig, Reed, Robson]

Meyers, Bert. "Our Inner Life," *Kayak*, #18 (1969), 71–74. On James Wright's *Shall We Gather at the River*.

Michelson, Peter. "Poetic Convention and Lyric Force," *Chicago Review* #63 (June 1967), 117–28. On Daryl Hine and on Lucien Stryk's *Notes for a Guidebook*.

Miller, J. Hillis. *Poets of Reality* (Cambridge: Harvard University Press, 1965).

Mills, Ralph J. Jr. *Contemporary American Poetry* (New York: Random House, 1965). Essays on twelve poets, including Wright and Sexton.

————. *Cry of the Human: Essays on Contemporary American Poetry* (Urbana: University of Illinois Press, 1975). Includes an essay on David Ignatow.

Molesworth, Charles. "On James Wright," *Salmagundi*, #22–23 (Spring-Summer 1973), 222–33. Reprinted in Boyers, *Contemporary Poetry in America*.

Mood, John J. " 'A Bird Full of Bones': Anne Sexton—A Visit and a Reading," *Chicago Review* XXIII, 4–XXIV, 1 (1972), 107–23.

Mooney, Stephen. "The Very Life We're Living," *Tennessee Poetry Journal* II, 1 (Fall 1968), 26–28. On William Matthews.

Moran, Ronald. "Louis Simpson: The Absence of Criticism and the Presence of Poetry," *The Far Point* 1 (Fall-Winter 1968), 60–66.

————. *Louis Simpson* (New York: Twayne, 1972).

————, and George Lensing. "The Emotive Imagination: A New Departure in American Poetry," *The Southern Review* III, 1 (Jan. 1967), 51–67. An important essay on Stafford, Wright, Simpson and Bly.

Nathan, Leonard. "The Private 'I' in Contemporary Poetry," *Shenandoah* XXII, 4 (Summer 1971), 80–99. Ranges wide, but comes to focus on Wright's "Gambling in Stateline, Nevada."

Nemerov, Howard. Ed., *Poets on Poetry* (New York: Basic Books, 1966). Essays on their own work by nineteen poets, including John Malcolm Brinnin.

Northwest Review. See XIII, 3 (1973), a special Stafford issue. Includes photographs, memoirs, a story, essays on poetics, twenty poems, and a conversation between Stafford and Hugo on writing.

Novik, Mary. *Robert Creeley: An Inventory, 1945–1970* (Kent, Ohio: Kent State University Press, 1973).

Oates, Joyce Carol. "Evolutions," *Modern Poetry Studies* II, 4 (1971), 190–91. Review of Adrienne Rich's *The Will to Change*.

————. "A Cluster of Feelings: Wakoski and Levine," *American Poetry Review* II, 3 (May–June 1973), 55.

————. "The Death Throes of Romanticism: The Poems of Sylvia Plath," *The Southern Review* IX, 3 (Summer 1973), 501–22.

————. "A Visit with Doris Lessing," *The Southern Review* IX, 4 (Autumn 1973), 873–82.

————. "Where They All Are Sleeping," *Modern Poetry Studies* IV, 3 (Winter 1973), 341–44. A review of Bly's *Sleepers Joining Hands*.

[OATES: See Clemons, Kazin, Mazzaro, Oberg, *Ohio Review*]

Oberg, Arthur. "Deer, Doors, Dark," *The Southern Review* IX, 1 (Jan. 1973), 243–56. Includes discussion of Joyce Carol Oates and William Heyen.

Ohio Review. Interviews in this journal with Adrienne Rich, XIII, 1 (Fall 1971), 28–46; William Matthews, XIII, 3 (Spring 1972), 32–51; Louis Simpson, XIV, 3 (Spring 1973), 34–51; Joyce Carol Oates, XV, 1 (Fall 1973), 49–61.

Ossman, David. *The Sullen Art* (New York: Corinth, 1963). Interviews with fourteen poets including Bly, Creeley, Logan.

Ostroff, Anthony. Ed., *The Contemporary Poet as Artist and Critic* (Boston: Little, Brown; 1964). Contains essays by twenty-six poets, including Rich and Stafford.

Parkinson, Thomas. Ed., *A Casebook on the Beat* (New York: Crowell, 1961). Includes primary and secondary bibliographies.

[PASTAN: see Bloom, Garrison]

[PATTERSON: see Kramer, Aaron.]

Pearce, Roy Harvey. *The Continuity of American Poetry* (Princeton: Princeton University Press, 1961).

Peck, John. "Sang thair Houris," *Parnassus: Poetry in Review* I, 2 (Spring–Summer 1972), 151–62. On four poets, including Paul Zimmer.

[PECK: see Davie, Howard]

Phillips, Robert. *The Confessional Poets* (Carbondale: Southern Illinois University Press, 1973). Includes a chapter called "The Confessional Mode in Modern American Poetry" and chapters on Lowell, Snodgrass, Sexton, Berryman, Roethke, and Plath.

Piccione, Anthony. Review of *Depth of Field*, by William Heyen, *Ann Arbor Review* #12 (1970), 28–29.

—————. Review of *In the Outer Dark*, by Stanley Plumly, *Southern Humanities Review* VI, 4 (Fall 1972), 406–10.

—————. "Bly: Man, Voice and Poem," *Ann Arbor Review*, #17 (1973), 86–90.

—————. "The Poetry of Robert Bly," in *Making in All Its Forms: Contemporary American Poetics and Criticism*, ed. Al Poulin, Jr. (New York: E. P. Dutton, 1976).

Plumly, Stanley. "Robert Penn Warren's Vision," *The Southern Review* VI, 4 (Autumn 1970), 1201–1208.

—————. "From the New Poetry Handbook," *The Ohio Review* XIII, 1 (Fall 1971), 74–80. On James Tate, Jim Harrison, and Mark Strand.

—————. "The Bride as Alligator," *Sumac* III, 3 (Spring 1973), 170–73. On Donald Hall.

[PLUMLY: see McElrath, Piccione, Radhuber, Rosenthal, Ryan, Simpson]

Poulin, Al. "Unpredictable as Grace," *The Nation* (Dec. 29, 1969), 734–35. On John Logan.

—————. Ed., *Contemporary American Poetry* (Boston: Houghton Mifflin Co., 1971). Second edition, 1975. An anthology that includes selections from and brief essays on Bly, Creeley, Ignatow, Logan, Rich, Sexton, Simpson, Stafford, Wright.

✗ —————. Ed., *Making in All Its Forms: Contemporary American Poetics and Criticism* (New York: E. P. Dutton, 1976).

Radhuber, S. G. "Four First Books of Poetry," *Northwest Review* XI, 2 (Spring 1971), 84–91. Discusses Heyen and Plumly.

Ramsey, Jarold. "Shades of Regionalism: Three Northwest Poets," *The West Coast Review* IX, 2 (Oct. 1974), 48–51. Focuses on William Stafford.

Reed, John R. "Toward Benign Selfhood," *Modern Poetry Studies* I, 3 (1970), 157–60. On Meredith's *Earth Walk: New and Selected Poems*.

[REED: see Heyen, Schmitz]

Rexroth, Kenneth. *American Poetry in the Twentieth Century* (New York: Herder and Herder, 1971).

Rich, Adrienne. "On Karl Shapiro's 'The Bourgeois Poet,'" in *The Contemporary Poet as Artist and Critic*, ed. Anthony Ostroff (Boston: Little, Brown; 1964), pp. 192–94.

————. "Anne Bradstreet and Her Poetry," foreword to *The Works of Anne Bradstreet*, ed. Jeannine Hensley (Cambridge, Mass.: Harvard University Press, 1967), ix–xx.

————. "For Randall Jarrell," in *Randall Jarrell 1914–1965*, eds. Robert Lowell, Peter Taylor, and Robert Penn Warren (New York: Farrar, Straus and Giroux; 1967), pp. 182–83.

————. "Living with Henry," *The Harvard Advocate* 103, 1 (Spring 1969), 10–11. On John Berryman.

————. "Poetry, Personality and Wholeness: A Response to Galway Kinnell," *Field* #7 (Fall 1972), 11–18. A response to Kinnell's *Field* essay.

————. "Caryatid: A Column," *American Poetry Review* II, 1 (Jan.–Feb. 1973), 16–17. A tribute to Paul Goodman.

[RICH: see Boyers, Gelpi, Howard, Leary and Kelly, Malkoff, Oates, *Ohio Review*, Poulin, R. Smith, Vendler]

Robson, Jeremy. "William Meredith," in *Corgi Modern Poets in Focus: 2* (London: Transworld Publishing Co., 1971), pp. 117–21.

Root, William Pitt. "Anything But Over," *Poetry* 123, 1 (Oct. 1973), 34–56. Review of Bly, Haislip, Sexton and others.

Rosenthal, M. L. *The Modern Poets: A Critical Introduction* (New York: Oxford University Press, 1962.

————. "Dynamics of Form and Motive in Some Representative Twentieth-Century Lyric Poems," *ELH: A Journal of English Literary History* 37 (March 1970), 136–51.

————. "Olson/His Poetry," *The Massachusetts Review* XII (Feb. 1971), 45–57.

————. "The Waste Land as an Open Structure," *Mosaic* VI (Fall 1972), 181–89.

————. "Poetic Theory of Some Contemporary Poets or Notes from the Front," *Salmagundi* I, 4 (1966–1967), 69–77.

————. *The New Poets* (New York: Oxford University Press, 1967). A broad survey which deals with many of the poets in *American Poets in 1976.*

X ————. "The Pure Poetry of Horace Gregory," *Modern Poetry Studies* IV, 1 (Spring 1973), 44–55.

————. "Some Thoughts on American Poetry Today," *Salmagundi* #22–23 (Spring–Summer 1973), 57–70. Reprinted in Boyers' *Contemporary Poetry in America.*

————. "Problems of Robert Creeley," *Parnassus: Poetry in Review* II, 1 (Fall/Winter 1973), 205–14.

————. "Poetic Power—Free the Swan!" *Shenandoah* XXIV, 1 (Fall 1972), 85–91. On three poets, including Stanley Plumly.

————. "The Aroused Language of Modern American Poetry," *New York Times Magazine* (Nov. 24, 1974), 13, 40–47.

[ROSENTHAL: see Heyen, Keane, Laing]

Rothenberg, Jerome, and George Quasha. Eds. *America A Prophecy* (New York: Vintage Books, 1974). An anthology presenting "A New Reading of American Poetry from Pre-Columbian Times to the Present." Includes contributions by many of the poets in this book.

Rukeyser, Muriel. "Glitter and Wounds, Several Wildnesses," *Parnassus: Poetry in Review* II, 1 (Fall–Winter 1973), 215–21. On Anne Sexton.

Rust, Michael. "Singing for the Shadow: Elaborations on John Logan's 'Lines for Michael in the Picture,'" *Voyages* IV, 3–4 (Spring 1971–Spring 1972), 40–47.

Ryan, Michael. Ed., "A Symposium of Young Poets," *The Iowa Review* IV, 4 (Fall 1973), 52–126. Includes Stanley Plumly's discussion of a poem by Louise Glück, discussion of Plumly by Maura Stanton and Merle E. Brown, and Plumly's reaction to Stanton's reaction.

Schmitz, Neil. "The Poetry of Ishmael Reed," *Modern Poetry Studies* IV, 2 (Autumn 1973), 218–21.

————. "Down Home with Ishmael Reed: *Chattanooga*," *Modern Poetry Studies* V, 2 (Autumn 1974), 205–207.

Schwartz, Howard. "The Sound of Tearing / The Destroyer of Books," *American Poetry Review* III, 2 (1974), 50–51. On Lucien Stryk.

Seay, James. "A World Immeasurably Alive and Good: A Look at James Wright's *Collected Poems*," *The Georgia Review* XXVII, 1 (Spring 1973), 71–81.

[SEXTON: see Boyers, Dickey, Howard, Fields, Kevles, McClatchy, Malkoff, Mills, Mood, Phillips, Poulin, Root, Rukeyser]

Shapiro, Karl. *In Defense of Ignorance* (New York: Vintage, 1965).

Simpson, Louis. "On Being a Poet in America," *The Noble Savage*, #5 (New York: Meridian Periodical, 1962), pp. 24–33.

————. "Matters of Tact," *The Hudson Review* XIV, 4 (Winter 1961–1962), 614–17. Reprinted in *Robert Lowell: A Portrait of the Artist in His Time*, ed. Michael London and Robert Boyers (New York: David Lewis, 1970), pp. 109–14. A discussion of Lowell's *Phaedra* and *Imitations*.

————. "On Berryman's *Recovery*," *The Ohio Review* XV, 2 (Winter 1974), 112–14.

[SIMPSON: see Cox, Crunk, Dickey, Gray, Howard, Malkoff, Moran and Lensing, Moran, *Ohio Review*, R. Smith, Stafford, Stephanchev, Stitt]

Skelton, Robin. "Robert Bly's New Book," *Kayak*, #33 (Nov. 1973), 66–69. On *Sleepers Joining Hands*.

Smith, Dave. "That Appetite for Life so Ravenous," *Shenandoah* XXV, 4 (Summer 1974), 49–55. On the fiction of Jack Matthews and Harry Crews.

————. "Losses in Ceremonial Light," *Shenandoah* XXV, 2 (Winter 1974),

92–98. A review of four books, including Louis Simpson's *The Adventures of the Letter I*.

————. "Chopping the Distance: On James Wright," *The Back Door* #7–8 (Spring 1975), 89–95.

[SMITH: see Haislip, Young]

Smith, Raymond. "Fondness and Reverence," *Modern Poetry Studies* II, 1 (1971), 39–42. Review of Heyen's *Depth of Field*.

————. "With a Gift for Burning," *Modern Poetry Studies* V, 1 (Spring 1974), 84–87. Review of Rich's *Diving into the Wreck: Poems 1971–1972*.

Somer, John. "The Zen Aesthetic: An Interview with Lucien Stryk," *Chicago Review* XXV, 3 (1973), 62–72.

Spender, Stephen, "The Last Ditch," *New York Review of Books* #XXII, 1 (July 22, 1971), 3–4. Review of three poets, including James Wright.

Stafford, William. "Terminations, Revelations," *Poetry* 104, 2 (May 1964), 104–108. Discussion of five poets, including Louis Simpson.

————. "No Answer to This Day," in *The Contemporary Poet as Artist and Critic*, ed. Anthony Ostroff (Boston: Little, Brown; 1964), pp. 153–57. Stafford's essay is on Richard Eberhart's poem "Am I My Neighbor's Keeper?"

————. " 'There Yet Remains What Fashion Cannot Kill,' " *Poetry* 108, 3 (June 1966), 187–88. Review of *Selected Poems of Edward Arlington Robinson*.

————. "Supporting a Reputation," *Books Today* (May 14, 1967), 9. On James Dickey.

————. "Traveling through the Dark," in *Reading Modern Poetry: A Critical Anthology*, ed. Paul Engle and Warren Carrier (Glenview, Ill.: Scott, Foresman; 1968), pp. 54–56. An essay by Stafford on one of his best-known poems.

————. "Books that Look Out, Books that Look In," *Poetry* 113, 6 (March 1969), 421–25. Review of six books, including Lewis Turco's *Awaken, Bells Falling*.

————. "A Way of Writing," *Field*, #2 (Spring 1970), 10–15.

————. "The Terror in Robert Frost," *New York Times Magazine* (Aug. 18, 1974), 24–26, 31, 33, 35–36, 38.

[STAFFORD: see Berg and Mezey, Dickey, Heyen, Lauber, Lofsness, Malkoff, Moran and Lensing, *Northwest Review*, Ramsey, Stepanchev, *Tennessee Poetry Journal*]

Stepanchev, Stephen. *American Poetry Since 1945* (New York: Harper & Row, 1965). Includes discussions of Bly, Creeley, Simpson, Stafford, Wright.

Stitt, Peter. "The Poetry of James Wright," *The Minnesota Review*, NRP, #2 (Spring 1972), 13–32.

————. "James Wright and Robert Bly," *The Hawaii Review* II, 1 (Fall 1973), 89–94.

————. "North of Jamaica into the Self: Louis Simpson and Ronald Moran," *The Southern Review* X, 2 (Spring 1974), 517–24.

Stryk, Lucien. "Foreword" to *TriQuarterly*, #31 (Fall 1974), 5–11. This is a special issue on contemporary Asian literature co-edited by Stryk.

[STRYK: see Elder, Goldstein, Harrison, Michelson, Schwartz, Somer]

Swadows, Harvey. "David Ignatow: The Meshuganeh Lover," *American Poetry Review* II, 3 (May–June 1973), 35.

Tennessee Poetry Journal. See the Robert Bly issue, II, 2 (Winter 1969), for Bly's National Book Award acceptance speech, comment on Bly, an interview, and a checklist (pp. 58–60) of criticism on Bly by Samuel H. McMillan. See also II, 3 (Spring 1969), a special issue on William Stafford, also with a checklist (pp. 21–22) by McMillan; III, 2 (Winter 1970) a special Ignatow issue.

Thompson, John. "At Fours and Fives," *Parnassus: Poetry in Review* II, 2 (Spring–Summer 1974), 66–72. On Irving Feldman and John Logan.

Thorp, Willard. "Poetry, Raw or Cooked?" in *A Time of Harvest*, ed. Robert Spiller (New York: Hill and Wang, 1962), pp. 154–64.

Turco, Lewis. "The Suspect in Criticism," *Mad River Review* I (Spring 1965), 81–85. On Dickey's *The Suspect in Poetry*.

————. "Ouroboros," *Poetry* 118 (August 1971), 287–88. On Conrad Aiken's *Collected Poems*.

————. "Good Gray Poets and Bad Old Bards," *Modern Poetry Studies* III, 2 (1972), 80–91.

————. "Manoah Bodman: Poet of the Second Awakening," *Costerus: Essays in English and American Literature* VIII (1973), 219–31.

[TURCO: see Coursen, Dickey, Heyen, Stafford, Waggoner]

Vendler, Helen: " 'Ghostlier Demarcations, Keener Sounds,' " *Parnassus: Poetry in Review* II, 1 (Fall/Winter 1973), 5–33. On Adrienne Rich.

Vernon, John. Review of John Haines's *The Stone Harp* and *Twenty Poems*. *Cafe Solo* #4 (1972), 39–41.

Waggoner, Hyatt H. *American Poets from the Puritans to the Present* (Boston: Houghton Mifflin, 1968).

————. "The Formalism of Lewis Turco: Fluting and Fifing with Frosted Fingers," *Concerning Poetry* II (Fall 1969), 50–58.

Witherup, William. Review of *The Stone Harp*, by John Haines, *Kayak*, #28 (1972), 66–70.

Wright, James. "Explorations, Astonishments," *Fresco* I, 3 (Spring, 1961), 153–54. An early appreciation of Richard Hugo.

————. "Shelf of New Poets," *Poetry* (Dec. 1961), 178–83.

————. "The Delicacy of Walt Whitman," in *The Presence of Walt Whitman*, ed. R. W. B. Lewis (New York: Columbia University Press, 1962), pp. 164–88.

————. "A Foreword" to *Poems 1933–67*, by H. R. Hays (San Francisco: Kayak, 1968), pp. i–iii.

————. "Response to 'The Working Line,'" *Field*, #8 (Spring 1973), 61–64.

————. "Hugo: Secrets of the Inner Landscape," *American Poetry Review* II, 3 (May–June 1973), 13.

[WRIGHT: see Berg and Mezey, Carroll, Coles, Crunk, DeFrees, Ditsky, Howard, Janssens, McElrath, Malkoff, Matthews, Meyers, Mills, Molesworth, Moran and Lensing, Nathan, Seay, Smith, Spender, Stepanchev, Stitt, Zweig]

Young, Vernon. "Poetry Chronicle: Sappho to Smith," *Hudson Review* XXVII, 4 (Winter 1974–1975), 597–614. Focuses on Dave Smith.

[ZIMMER: see Aldan, Peck]

Zweig, Paul. "1+1+1+1+,"*Parnassus: Poetry in Review* I, 1 (Fall–Winter 1972), 171–78. Review of four poets, including John Haines.

————. "Making and Unmaking," *Partisan Review* XV, 2 (1973), 269–73. On James Wright.